THE S. MARK TAPER FOUNDATION

IMPRINT IN JEWISH STUDIES

BY THIS ENDOWMENT

THE S. MARK TAPER FOUNDATION SUPPORTS

THE APPRECIATION AND UNDERSTANDING

OF THE RICHNESS AND DIVERSITY OF

JEWISH LIFE AND CULTURE

The publisher gratefully acknowledges the generous contribution to this book provided by the Jewish Studies Endowment of the University of California Press Associates, which is supported by a major gift from the S. Mark Taper Foundation.

# Rosenzweig and Heidegger

WEIMAR AND NOW: GERMAN CULTURAL CRITICISM

*Edward Dimendberg, Martin Jay, and Anton Kaes, General Editors*

# Rosenzweig and Heidegger

*Between Judaism and German Philosophy*

Peter Eli Gordon

UNIVERSITY OF CALIFORNIA PRESS

*Berkeley   Los Angeles   London*

Publication costs for this book were offset by a
generous grant from the Koret Foundation.

The quotation from the Paul Celan poem "Sprachgitter," in the
collection *Sprachgitter,* © 1959 S. Fischer Verlag GmbH, Frankfurt am
Main, appears by permission of the publisher.

Portions of chapter 1 originally appeared in "Science, Finitude, and
Infinity: Neo-Kantianism and the Birth of Existentialism," *Jewish
Social Studies* 6, no. 1 (Spring 2000), 30–53.

Portions of chapter 5 originally appeared in "Rosenzweig and
Heidegger: Translation, Ontology, and the Anxiety of Affiliation,"
*New German Critique* 77 (Spring–Summer 1999), 113–48.

University of California Press
Berkeley and Los Angeles, California

University of California Press, Ltd.
London, England

First paperback printing 2005
© 2003 by the Regents of the University of California

Library of Congress Cataloging-in-Publication Data
Gordon, Peter Eli.
    Rosenzweig and Heidegger : between Judaism and German
philosophy / Peter Eli Gordon.
        p.    cm.—(Weimar and now ; 33)
    Includes index.
    ISBN 0-520-24636-5 (pbk : alk. paper)
    1. Judaism and philosophy.   2. Judaism — Germany —
20th century.   3. Philosophy, Jewish — Germany — 20th century.
4. Jews — Germany — 1918–1933.   5. Rosenzweig, Franz, 1886 –
1929 — Criticism and interpretation.   6. Heidegger, Martin,
1889–1976 — Criticism and interpretation.   I. Title.   II. Series.

B154.G67    2003
181'.06—dc21                                    2002012603

Manufactured in Canada

13    12    11    10    09    08    07    06    05
10   9   8   7   6   5   4   3   2   1

The paper used in this publication is both acid-free and totally
chlorine-free (TCF). It meets the minimum requirements of
ANSI/NISO z39.48-1992 (R 1997) (*Permanence of Paper*).

*To my parents, Milton and Elaine,*
*to my sister and brother, Karen and David,*
*and to the memory of my sister Nancy (ז״ל).*

*Ben Zoma says, Who is wise? He who learns from every person.*
*As it is said, "From all my teachers I grew wise."*
  —*Pirkei Avoth, IV*


*(Wär ich wie du. Wärst du wie Ich.*
*Standen wir nicht*
*unter* einem *Passat?*
*Wir sind Fremde.)*

*[Were I like you. Were you like me.*
*Did we not stand*
*beneath a* single *trade wind?*
*We are strangers.]*
—PAUL CELAN, *"Sprachgitter"*

# CONTENTS

# ABBREVIATIONS

This book employs several now-standard abbreviations for the major works that are cited frequently in the notes, as well as abbreviations of my own. When historical context has seemed relevant, however, the full citation is used in the notes as well. Most works are cited from the original German, in my own translation. Occasionally I have consulted the English texts, in which case it is so noted in the reference.

ASP       Franz Rosenzweig. "Das Älteste Systemprogramm des deutschen Idealismus: Ein handscriftlicher Fund." In KS, 230–77.

BR       Hermann Cohen. *Der Begriff der Religion im System der Philosophie.* Ed. Hermann Cohen and Paul Natorp. Gießen: Töpelmann Verlag, 1915.

*Briefe*       *Franz Rosenzweig: Briefe.* Unter Mitwirkung von Ernst Simon. Ausgewählt und herausgegeben von Edith Rosenzweig. Berlin: Schocken Verlag, 1935. Citations are followed by letter number, recipient, and, in parentheses, the dateline as it appears in the letter, followed by page number from this edition; e.g., *Briefe*, N.221, An die Mutter (15.4.1918), 299.

BT       Martin Heidegger. *Being and Time.* Trans. John Macquarrie and Edward Robinson. New York: Harper and Row, 1962. *See also* SZ.

*Büchlein*       Franz Rosenzweig. *Das Büchlein vom gesunden und kranken Menschenverstand.* Ed. Nahum Glatzer. Originally distributed privately by Rosenzweig and left unpublished in his lifetime. Published in German: Düsseldorf: Joseph Melzer

Verlag, 1964. First published in English translation: *Understanding the Sick and the Healthy.* Trans. T. Luckman. New York: Noonday Press, 1953. Citations are to the recent German reprint: Frankfurt am Main: Jüdischer Verlag, 1992.

DR      "Bericht über die II. Davoser Hochschulkurse, 17. März bis 6. April." *Davoser Revue, Zeitschrift für Literatur, Wissenschaft, Kunst und Sport.* Ed. Jules Ferdmann. 4, 7 (April 15, 1929): 181–208.

DVS      Otto Friedrich Bollnow and Joachim Ritter. "Davoser Disputation zwischen Ernst Cassirer und Martin Heidegger." Transcription, 1929. Printed as Appendix (Anhang) IV in KPM, 274–96. In English: "Davos Disputation between Ernst Cassirer and Martin Heidegger," in KPM, English, 171–85. When citations refer to both English and German, I use the form DVS, E, 174; G, 278.

EM      Martin Heidegger. *Einführung in die Metaphysik.* Tübingen: Max Niemeyer Verlag, 1953.

EM, E      Martin Heidegger. *An Introduction to Metaphysics.* Trans. Ralph Manheim. New Haven: Yale University Press, 1959.

*Ethik*      Hermann Cohen. *Ethik des reinen Willens.* Orig. pub. 1904; rev. ed. Berlin: Bruno Cassirer, 1907.

FR      *Franz Rosenzweig: Der Mensch und sein Werk. Gesammelte Schriften.* 4 vols. Dordrecht, Netherlands: Martinus Nijhoff, 1976–84. All citations from FR are followed by the appropriate volume and page numbers.

GA      Martin Heidegger. *Gesamtausgabe.* Frankfurt am Main: Vittorio Kostermann, 1978– . All citations from GA give the appropriate volume and page numbers; volume titles may also be included.

GB      Franz Rosenzweig. *Die "Gritli"-Briefe: Briefe an Margrit Rosenstock-Huessy.* Ed. Inken Rühle und Reinhold Mayer. Tübingen: Bilam Verlag, 2002. Citations give the dateline in parentheses and page number.

GM      Martin Heidegger. *Die Grundbegriffe der Metaphysik: Welt-Endlichkeit-Einsamkeit.* Lecture course of 1929–30. Frankfurt am Main: Vittorio Klostermann, 1983.

GM English      Martin Heidegger. *The Fundamental Concepts of Metaphysics.* Trans. William McNeill and Nicholas Walker. Bloomington: Indiana University Press, 1995.

HS      Franz Rosenzweig. *Hegel und der Staat.* 2 vols. Orig. pub. München and Berlin: Verlag R. Oldenbourg, 1920. Reprinted (one-volume photostat of 1920 edition) Aalen,

Germany: Scientia Verlag, 1962. Citations are to the 1962 edition.

JH         Wilhelm Dilthey. *Die Jugendgeschichte Hegels.* Vol. IV of *Gesammelte Schriften.* Leipzig: B. G. Teubner, 1921.

JS         Hermann Cohen. *Jüdische Schriften.* 3 vols. Ed. Bruno Strauß. Berlin: C. A. Schwetschke und Sohn Verlagsbuchhandlung, 1924. Articles are cited with JS and volume and page numbers.

Kassel      *Der Philosoph Franz Rosenzweig.* Internationaler Kongreß, Kassel (1986). 2 vols. Ed. Wolfdietrich Schmeid-Kowarzik. Freiburg: Verlag Karl Alber, 1986. Citations give article author and title, followed by "Kassel" and volume and page numbers.

KdrV      Immanuel Kant. *Kritik der reinen Vernunft.* Cited from the tenth edition, ed. Theodor Valentiner. Der Philosophischen Bibliothek, vol. 37. Leipzig: Felix Meiner, 1913.

KPM      Martin Heidegger. *Kant und das Problem der Metaphysik.* 5th German ed. Frankfurt am Main: Vittorio Klostermann, 1991.

KPM English      Heidegger. *Kant and the Problem of Metaphysics.* 4th ed. Trans. Richard Taft. Bloomington: Indiana University Press, 1990.

KS         Franz Rosenzweig. *Kleinere Schriften.* Berlin: Schocken Verlag, Jüdischer Buchverlag, 1937.

KTE      Hermann Cohen. *Kants Theorie der Erfahrung.* Orig. pub. Berlin: Ferd. Dümmler's Verlagsbuchhandlung, Harrwitz und Gossmann, 1871. Reprinted in Cohen, *Werke.* Ed. Hermann Cohen Archiv and Hermut Holzhey, vol. I, part 3. Hildesheim and New York: Georg Olms Verlag, 1987. Cohen himself expanded this book in subsequent editions; the fifth edition, reproducing the third edition of 1918, is found in *Werke,* vol. I, part 1. Unless noted, it is the fifth edition that is cited as KTE.

LBIY      *Leo Baeck Institute Yearbook.*

*Logik*      Hermann Cohen. *Logik der reinen Erkenntnis.* Orig. pub. Berlin: B. Cassirer, 1902, rev. 1914. Citations are to the fourth rev. ed., in Cohen, *Werke,* vol. VI.

ND        Franz Rosenzweig. "Das neue Denken: Einige nachträgliche Bermerkungen zum *Stern der Erlösung.*" *Der Morgen* 1, 4 (1925): 426–51. Reprinted in FR III: 139–61. All citations are to FR III, with the appropriate page number; e.g., ND, 140.

Nohl

Herman Nohl, ed. *Hegels Theologische Jugendschriften.* Tübingen: J. C. A. Mohr, 1907. In English: G. W. F. Hegel. *Early Theological Writings.* Trans. T. M. Knox. Philadelphia: University of Pennsylvania Press, 1971. When both versions are cited, I use the form Nohl, 209; English, 140. (Apparent inconsistencies in page numbering between the two versions result from the fact that Knox presents some of the sections in a rather different order than does Nohl.)

PFR

*The Philosophy of Franz Rosenzweig.* Ed. Paul Mendes-Flohr. Hanover, N.H.: University Press of New England / Brandeis University Press, 1988. Individual authors and essays are cited, followed by PFR and the appropriate pagination.

PJ

Julius Guttmann. *Die Philosophie des Judentums.* München: Verlag Ernst Reinhardt, 1933. In Hebrew: Y. L. Barukh, trans. Jerusalem: Mosad Byalik, 1953. For this Hebrew edition, Guttman added a final chapter on Franz Rosenzweig. In English, based on both the German original and its Hebrew companion: *Philosophies of Judaism: The History of Jewish Philosophy from Biblical Times to Franz Rosenzweig.* Trans. David Silverman. New York: Holt, Rinehart and Winston, 1964. Unless otherwise indicated, all citations are to the original German edition of 1933.

RV

Hermann Cohen. *Religion der Vernunft aus den Quellen des Judentums.* Leipzig: Fock Verlag, 1919. 2nd ed., corrected by Bruno Strauß, Frankfurt am Main: Kaufmann Verlag, 1929. Citations are to the 1978 reprint of the second edition (Wiesbaden: Fourier Verlag).

*Schrift*

*Die Schrift. Verdeutscht von Martin Buber gemeinsam mit Franz Rosenzweig.* Berlin: Lambert Schneider, 1925–29. Unless otherwise indicated all citations are to the original edition, subtitled *Die fünf Bücher der Weisung,* and refer exclusively to Buch I ("Das Buch Im Anfang") and Buch II ("Das Buch Namen"). Other occasional references (clearly indicated) are to the postwar edition, emended by Martin Buber, Heidelberg: Lambert Schneider, 1987 (orig. pub. 1954 as *Die Schrift, 2te, verbesserte Auflage,* 1954).

SE (E)

Franz Rosenzweig. *Der Stern der Erlösung.* 4th ed. Frankfurt am Main: Suhrkamp, 1993. In English: *The Star of Redemption.* Trans. William W. Hallo. Notre Dame, Ind: University of Notre Dame Press, 1985. Citations are in the form SE, 229 (E, 205), referring to page 229 of the Suhrkamp German edition and page 205 of the Hallo translation.

| | |
|---|---|
| SZ | Martin Heidegger. *Sein und Zeit.* 17th German ed. Tübingen: Max Niemeyer Verlag, 1993. *See also* BT. |
| TE | Karl Löwith, "M. Heidegger and F. Rosenzweig; or, Temporality and Eternity." *Philosophy and Phenomenological Research* 3, 1 (September 1942): 53–77. In German, with amendments: "M. Heidegger und F. Rosenzweig. Ein Nachtrag zu *Sein und Zeit,*" *Zeitschrift für philosophische Forschung* 12, 2 (1958): 161–87; reprinted in Löwith, *Heidegger—Denker in dürftiger Zeit, zur Stellung der Philosophie im 20. Jahrhundert.* In *Sämtliche Schriften.* Stuttgart: J. B. Metlersche Verlagsbuchhandlung, 1984, VIII: 72–101. |
| TYH | Georg Lukàcs. *Der junge Hegel.* Berlin: Hermann Luchterhand Verlag, 1966. Orig. pub. 1938. In English: *The Young Hegel: Studies in the Relations between Dialectics and Economics.* Trans. Rodney Livingstone. Cambridge, Mass.: MIT Press, 1976. |
| VF | Franz Rosenzweig. "Vertauschte Fronten." *Der Morgen* 6, 6 (April 1930): 85–87. Reprinted in KS and in FR III: 235–38. Citations are to the original text of 1930. |
| WM | Martin Heidegger. *Was ist Metaphysik?* 14th German ed. Frankfurt am Main: Vittorio Klostermann, 1992. Orig. pub. 1929. |
| WM English | *What Is Metaphysics?* Trans. David Farrell Krell. In *Martin Heidegger: Basic Writings.* Ed. David Farrell Krell. San Francisco: HarperCollins, 1977. |

# ACKNOWLEDGMENTS

This book represents the final fruit of my long struggle to understand the Jewish contribution to modern German thought. Franz Rosenzweig is a difficult philosopher; Martin Heidegger notoriously so. Recognizing the relationship between them was a laborious if at times exhilarating task, and without the aid of numerous scholars and friends, I could not have done it. Or perhaps I could have, but the result would have been dismal indeed.

Some of what follows first appeared in a doctoral dissertation submitted to the department of history at the University of California, Berkeley. My chief debt of gratitude is to Martin Jay, advisor, mentor, and friend. Thanks as well to David Biale, for unfailing scholarly insight and friendship, and to Hans Sluga, for his indispensable philosophical guidance and unsparing enthusiasm. Finally, I should thank Amos Funkenstein, who was tremendously supportive of my interests and whose scholarship became the chief inspiration for this book. Sadly, he did not live to see it to completion. I like to think he might have appreciated it.

I wrote the two central chapters of this book—on Rosenzweig's *The Star of Redemption*—while a fledgling member in The Society of Fellows in the Liberal Arts at Princeton University. At Princeton I should thank most of all Alexander Nehamas and Carole Rigolot, for allowing me two years' reprieve from professorial duties. The Department of German Literature also afforded me the opportunity to teach an undergraduate seminar on Heidegger during the fall semester of 1999. I must thank the many gifted students who made that seminar so pleasurable an experience. I'd like to also thank Tom Levin, Mike Jennings, Andy Rabinbach, Leora Batnitzky, and Dana Villa (also visiting) for both friendship and scholarly support.

I received invaluable criticism on portions of this book, or on related essays, from Martin Jay, David Biale, Hans Sluga, Leora Batnitzky, Robert

Gibbs, Tom Rockmore, Steven Wasserstrom, Mitchell Hart, Samuel Moyn, Patchen Markell, Sean Kelly, Nina Caputo, Eric Santner, David Myers, and Naomi Seidman. Special thanks to André Lambelet for securing a rare copy of the *Davoser Revue* from Switzerland. Zeke Reich provided much assistance on the final manuscript, and Kris Manjapra courageously prepared the index. A final, warmhearted hurrah to Sheila Levine, Julianne Brand, Jacqueline Volin, and Ellen F. Smith at the University of California Press.

Research for this work was carried out at several locations both in the United States and abroad: The Berlin Staatsbibliothek (West and East), the Humboldt Universität (Berlin), the philosophy library at the Freie Universität (Berlin), the archives of the Jüdisches Gemeindehaus (Berlin), the École des Hautes Études (Paris), the Moses Hall philosophy library and Doe Library (UC Berkeley), the Jewish Theological Seminary (New York), Butler Library (Columbia), and Widener Library (Harvard). At each institution I succeeded in locating dozens of obscure and largely forgotten documents only because of the patient aid and advice of many dedicated librarians and archivists. They are the secret geniuses of scholarship, without whom the research would have been a Borgesian nightmare.

I want also to express my deepest appreciation to some of the people who have given me much support over the past several years, especially John Schott, Naomi Seidman, Ezra-Hillel, Léonor Manent, Karen Adler, Jesse Berrett, Susan Ettlinger, Larry Glickman, Jill Frank, David Hyde, James Kwak, Sylvia Brandt, Gail Saliterman, Mindy Saliterman, Nadia Mahdi, Helen Chernikoff, Wendy Weil, Hérica Valladarés, Jonathan Ivry, Simone Schweber, Paul Rubin, Brett MacDonald, Jonathan Skolnik, Masha Belenky, Michael Goldman-Donnelly, Aaron Alexander, Bill Bloch, Andrew Jainchill, Eugene Sheppard, Samuel Moyn, David Chamberlain, Thomas Laqueur, and Carla Hesse. And special thanks to Shawnee Cuzzillo.

Finally, I would like to thank the following for their generous financial support: the Princeton Society of Fellows in the Liberal Arts; the Andrew G. Mellon Fellowship in the Humanities; the Doreen B. Townsend Center for the Humanities; the Hans Rosenberg Memorial Research Grant; the Regents-Intern Fellowship of the University of California at Berkeley; and the Deutsche Akademische Austausch Dienst. Publication costs for the book were offset through a generous grant from the Koret Foundation. And a closing acknowledgement to my new colleagues in the department of history and the committee on degrees in social studies at Harvard University.

# PREFACE

## "UNDER ONE TRADE WIND"

This book explores the relationship between two philosophers, Franz Rosenzweig and Martin Heidegger. It is devoted chiefly to making sense of Rosenzweig's philosophical corpus, though to do so it makes constant and comparative allusion to Heidegger's thought as well. More broadly, it aims to situate Rosenzweig and Heidegger within a shared philosophical horizon, so as to better indicate the profound, if troubling, resemblance between them. For understandable reasons, which I shall explore further below, previous scholarship has acknowledged their intellectual affinity only with the greatest reluctance. One purpose of this book is to urge readers to acknowledge this affinity, since to do so may help us toward a truer appreciation of Rosenzweig's place in the history of recent Continental philosophy.

Rosenzweig's work represents the culmination of what is often called the German Jewish tradition. He thought deeply about the compatibility of philosophy and theology, and he struggled to create a new species of philosophy—Rosenzweig called it "the new thinking"—that could at once recognize the philosophical merits of modernity since Nietzsche while continuing to draw nourishment from the resources of Judaism. Heidegger's intellectual achievements are more widely recognized. In his lifelong ruminations upon "the question of Being," he strove to create a new mode of philosophy that might plumb the precognitive or "existential" depths of human experience. His projected "overcoming" of the Cartesian-Platonist legacy in metaphysics remains one of the central themes of modern Continental thought. Rosenzweig and Heidegger represent two closely allied but nonetheless distinctive moments in the transformation of German philosophy in the interwar Weimar period. The intellectual bond between them warrants investigation, not only for what it tells us about philosophy, but also for what it may reveal about the difficult relationship between Germans and Jews in the twentieth century.

In the study of Rosenzweig's philosophy, the great variety of his philosophical interests—some might call it eclecticism—is often hidden from view. Especially since the Holocaust, it has become a commonplace to regard Rosenzweig as belonging most naturally and even exclusively to a Jewish canon of thought. He is often included in courses of Jewish studies and is widely considered a prophet of Jewish cultural renewal, as a partisan of dialogue, or as a founder of Jewish existentialism. More recently, he has been extolled as a proponent of a distinctively Jewish ethics, and it has been argued that his work anticipates that of the postwar French Jewish philosopher Emmanuel Levinas. While there is much to recommend these perspectives, they conceal almost as much as they reveal about Rosenzweig as an independent thinker. By dissociating Rosenzweig from his German context, one forces him into a trajectory he would not have recognized as his own. And, as I will show, the original sense of Rosenzweig's thought is best discovered by restoring him to the horizon of meaning within which his philosophy first took shape. The argument of this book is that one gains an instructive vantage on Rosenzweig's thought when it is examined alongside that of Heidegger and that, while the political ramifications of this comparison are indeed troublesome, one cannot ignore them without missing a significant share of Rosenzweig's own philosophical intentions.

At first glance, the biographical differences between Rosenzweig and Heidegger may appear so stark as to foreclose all possible comparison. Franz Rosenzweig was born in 1886 into an assimilated and financially comfortable German Jewish family in Kassel. As a young man he showed no dramatic attachment to his ancestral religion; his early letters record hopes of becoming a physician or an intellectual historian. As a student of Friedrich Meinecke, he completed a brilliant doctoral dissertation on Hegel's theory of the state just before the outbreak of the First World War, only to abandon what seemed the start of a promising university career. Upon the threshold of Christianity, Rosenzweig reasoned that he could only convert with integrity if he first passed knowingly through his Judaism. In the autumn of 1913, he attended a Yom Kippur service in Berlin, where he apparently underwent a dramatic transformation of religious perspective. He no longer regarded his Judaism as a mere preparatory step on the path to Christianity; rather, he saw as if for the first time that Judaism contained treasures all its own. He decided henceforth to remain a Jew, and so devoted the remainder of his life to a philosophical elaboration of the Jewish tradition, borrowing as he felt necessary from the German philosophical sources he knew so intimately. Rosenzweig's major work, *The Star of Redemption*, first published in 1921, was the singular fruit of those efforts. It ranges across various fields, including the comparative study of Judaism and Christianity (with passing references to Islam), the theory of knowledge, aesthetics, cosmology, ethics, and philosophical anthropology. It is a fascinating as well as baffling book, a "system of philosophy" that investigates the experiential structures of Jewish and Christian revelation and that claims for the Jewish people a uniquely metaphysical status in the advent of world redemption. Upon its completion Rosenzweig felt that his contribution to philosophy was at its end. Together with Martin Buber, he went on to translate a significant portion of the Hebrew Bible into German and helped to create Frankfurt's famous Jüdisches Lehrhaus, an institute of adult Jewish education. A near-legendary figure in the Jewish community, Rosenzweig died at a young age, succumbing to a painful and progressive paralysis (amyotrophic lateral sclerosis) in December 1929.

Heidegger's life contrasts dramatically with that of Rosenzweig. Born in 1889 into a Catholic family in the rural Swabian district of Messkirch, the young Heidegger trained as a novice for the Jesuit priesthood; he first awakened to philosophy through studies in scholasticism and Brentano, and only later adopted the revolutionary techniques of Husserlian phenomenology. At Freiburg, Heidegger attached himself to Husserl as a privileged pupil, then an assistant; finally, at Marburg, he came to rival his teacher in prestige. His seminars exerted a magical attraction upon students. (Hannah Arendt would later recall how his fame began to spread in these years like "the rumor of a hidden king.") [1] In 1927, at the urging of colleagues, Heidegger published the still-incomplete manuscript of his own philosophy under the title *Being and Time (Sein und Zeit)*. A year later, on the strength of this book, he was appointed Husserl's successor at Freiburg. Heidegger's thought was and remains controversial. A combination of phenomenological technique and Kierkegaardian passion, what Heidegger called "existential ontology" aims to seize upon the "Being of beings," the meaningful structure of the lived, temporal world. This unusual project inspired many thinkers of the time (among them Levinas, Marcuse, Löwith, Gadamer, and Arendt). But in Germany's dark years, the philosopher comported himself without greatness. Appointed rector at Freiburg in 1933, Heidegger joined the National Socialist party and affixed its jagged cross to his jacket. In letters he despaired of the so-called "Judaization" of the university; through the early 1930s he interlaced his philosophical texts with the usual slogans against Bolshevism and habitually ended his political speeches with the

---

1. Arendt, "Martin Heidegger at Eighty," in *Martin Heidegger and Modern Philosophy: Critical Essays,* ed. Michael Murray (New Haven: Yale University Press, 1978), 293; orig. pub. *New York Review of Books,* October 1971.

Hitler salute. It was a shabby record, and after the war, as new revelations of his behavior continued to surface, Heidegger offered virtually no words of contrition. His postwar philosophy, written in a style of near-Delphic opacity, abandoned the exactitude of phenomenology for a contemplative, richly poetic thinking as "gratitude." The thinker aged while his thought came to enjoy a growing and variegated influence in philosophy, social theory, literature, and the arts. Heidegger died and was buried with a Church ceremony in the graveyard of his native town, in the spring of 1976.

The obvious divergence in life paths of these two philosophers has naturally encouraged the view that they are separated by a chasm of history as well as intellectual style. A single difference appears decisive: Rosenzweig had what we might now consider the great fortune to have died young, just four years before the Nazi seizure of power. He was thereby spared the fate of millions of other European Jews; otherwise, it is quite possible he would have perished in the death camps of the very regime to which Heidegger swore allegiance.

It is unsurprising, then, that few have embraced the suggestion that Rosenzweig and Heidegger belonged to the same constellation of thought. Indeed, I am not without sympathy for those who think that it might have been best to leave the comparison unexplored. But while one should be mindful of the historical gulf that now separates the two thinkers—from each other, and from us as well—one should resist projecting this division into the past. When one writes of what Stefan Zweig called "the world of yesterday," it is difficult to avoid the elegiac mode; one forgets that our yesterday was once a today, no less real at the time than our present now is to us. Past memory becomes a mere antechamber to the present, and the present becomes, as Michael André Bernstein has called it, a realm of "foregone conclusions."[2]

The intimacy of the relationship between Germans and German Jews during the years of the Weimar Republic was arguably greater than at any time in previous experience, and few would have predicted that their shared world would be brought so viciously to an end. Celan's poem, cited in my epigraph, offers a helpful commentary on this history, as it captures three crucial moments in the historical encounter between Germans and Jews—the longing for resemblance ("Were I like you, were you like me"), the recognition of shared context ("Did we not stand beneath a single trade wind?"), and the admission of painful separation ("We are strangers"). While analytically distinct, these three moments naturally coexisted in reality. Ever since Moses Mendelssohn first entered the gates of old-regime

2. Bernstein, *Foregone Conclusions: Against Apocalyptic History* (Berkeley: University of California Press, 1994).

Berlin, Jews have longed to be included in German philosophical discussion. Throughout the nineteenth century German Jews participated passionately in the intellectual life of the age (indeed, sometimes their participation was so fierce it overwhelmed any identifiably Jewish attachment). And well into the twentieth century, they continued as productive partners in German intellectual life, right up to the very months when the Third Reich made this partnership impossible. Even afterward, here and there, Jewish participation in German thought was carried on in exile, though with a profound sense that the shared tradition had been destroyed.

One might regard the bond between Rosenzweig and Heidegger as an episode in the so-called German-Jewish dialogue. But the phrase is prone to misunderstanding. Some argue that there was never an actual dialogue between Germans and Jews, as this would have required that their differences be treated with mutual respect. Gershom Scholem famously made this point; in one essay he referred to Rosenzweig's provenance as "the desolate Jewish wasteland in Germany."[3] But there is no way conclusively to decide such matters. The debate over the reality or unreality of the German-Jewish dialogue is at core a dispute as to whether German Jews should ever have believed themselves at home in Germany. Inevitably, the argument provokes great passion on both sides. In retrospect, some have been tempted to conclude with Scholem that the idea of a shared cultural life between Germans and Jews was a fiction from the start, the respect between them superficial at best. But hindsight distorts the past even while illuminating it. Just as a lover whose heart has been broken will sometimes conclude that his love was really unrequited all along, so too those who deny the reality of the German-Jewish dialogue may be animated less by the desire for historical accuracy than by bitterness that the relationship did not endure.

Some scholars, especially those Zionists who believe in the absolute imperative of a Jewish state, are inclined to dismiss Jewish life in the Diaspora as impracticable. Some more boldly suggest that without such a state, authentic commitment to Judaism itself is impossible. Rosenzweig, however, was both a committed Jew and a strong believer in the legitimacy of exile, and his work testifies to the richness and reality of intellectual exchange between Germans and Jews. The integrity of his philosophy cannot be denied simply because "history," as some would have it, is supposed to have proven the German-Jewish dialogue a failure. Moreover, for such dialogue one needn't understand the interlocutors as engaged in actual conversation. While Rosenzweig and Heidegger remained strangers in life, much of what they wrote bespeaks an intimate commonality of ideas. As in Celan's poem,

---

3. Scholem, "Franz Rosenzweig and His Book, *The Star of Redemption*," in PFR, 20–41.

the "I" and the "Thou" express a longing for resemblance even while they sense their estrangement. They do not so much speak with each other as within a larger shared "trade wind"—"unter einem Passat."[4]

One should recall that it was Rosenzweig himself who first noted his philosophical resemblance to Heidegger. In a short, posthumously published essay entitled "Exchanged Fronts" (drafted as a commentary on the so-called Davos encounter, the famous 1929 debate between Martin Heidegger and Ernst Cassirer), Rosenzweig explicitly and apparently without reservation identified himself with Heidegger. In Heidegger's polemics against Cassirer, Rosenzweig believed he could discern something of his own struggle to break free of the Platonist-Hegelian metaphysical tradition. More surprisingly, Rosenzweig also regarded Heidegger as a thinker of religious provenance. While Heidegger's scholastic origins were well known, Rosenzweig suggested that Heidegger also owed a hidden debt to the neo-Kantian philosopher Hermann Cohen's posthumous reflections on Judaism. And since Rosenzweig considered himself Cohen's true disciple, Rosenzweig and Heidegger were thus philosophical partisans in the development of "the new thinking."[5]

In this book, I shall propose that we read this essay as Rosenzweig's intellectual epitaph. It was, in fact, one of the last pieces he ever wrote. Its genealogy is provocative, not only because it asserts an unlikely kinship between Rosenzweig and Heidegger, but also because it locates Heidegger within a hidden intellectual tradition descending from Cohen's philosophy of Judaism. However remarkable these claims, they deserve to be taken seriously, since they are Rosenzweig's own directive to future readers as to how one might best situate his work in the history of ideas.

Even today, however, the essay remains a matter of some controversy. The resemblance between Heidegger and Rosenzweig has been touched upon by many of Rosenzweig's most perspicacious critics, but in most cases they have adopted a censorious and even dismissive tone. Nearly all, with the arguable exception of Leo Strauss, have concluded that Rosenzweig was wrong to claim any real intellectual kinship with his German contemporary.[6] The only sustained comparative treatment of their philosophies is a

---

4. Paul Celan, "Sprachgitter" (Language mesh), in *Poems of Paul Celan*, trans. Michael Hamburger (New York: Persea Books, 1972), 118–19. On the theme of "I and thou" in Celan, see Hans-Georg Gadamer, *Wer bin Ich und wer bist Du? Ein Kommentar zu Paul Celans Gedichtfolge "Atemkristall"* (Frankfurt am Main: Suhrkamp Verlag, 1986), 15.

5. Rosenzweig, "Vertauschte Fronten" [VF], *Der Morgen* 6, 6 (April 1930), 85–87; reprinted in KS and in FR III: 235–38.

6. Strauss, *Spinoza's Critique of Religion*, trans. E. M. Sinclair (New York: Schocken Books, 1965), esp. 12–13; orig. pub. as *Die Religionskritik Spinozas als Grundlage seiner Bibelwissenschaft: Untersuchungen zu Spinozas Theologisch-Politischem Traktat* (Berlin: Akademie-Verlag, 1930).

1942 essay by the historian and philosopher Karl Löwith.[7] The essay remains a brilliant specimen of intellectual history, but its argument is open to serious challenge. To Löwith, it was apparent that the supposed philosophical similarities between Rosenzweig and Heidegger were negligible. Rosenzweig retained a theistic faith in "Eternity" while Heidegger had surrendered himself—philosophically as well as politically—to the vagaries of "temporality." Indeed, for Löwith one could explain Heidegger's Nazism as a consequence of this post-metaphysical surrender.

I will have occasion to comment in greater depth upon Löwith's argument in the introductory chapter. Here it is important to note that my own efforts to compare Rosenzweig and Heidegger first emerged out of a growing sense of frustration with Löwith's interpretation. For while there is no disputing his acumen, Löwith seemed to me animated first and foremost by a desire to condemn Heidegger for his political errors. This is understandable, especially if one recalls that though he was a student of Heidegger's during the 1920s, Löwith was eventually forced to leave Germany and to abandon his hopes of an academic position there because of his Jewish heritage. (It is all the more understandable for the simple reason that Heidegger's politics are eminently deserving of censure—I use the word "understandable" without condescension.) But even when it is justified, political reproach is a tricky game. As I have reflected on the various ramifications of the Rosenzweig-Heidegger comparison, Löwith's essay has become emblematic to me of how moral passion may at times obstruct more than facilitate philosophical understanding. The comparison between Rosenzweig and Heidegger has increasingly come to seem like something of a test case; it has challenged me to maintain clarity of thought despite all of the accompanying political misgivings.

One of my motives in writing this book was precisely that I wished to better understand, not succumb to, my own sense of moral discomfort. By disposition, I am suspicious of openly moralistic motivation in scholarship. (Such motivation, while always there, if left unchecked will tend to spawn scholarship in a prosecutorial spirit—in recent years a popular trend among intellectual historians.) I have tried instead to surmount my own resistance, to urge myself, even when it was most aversive, toward the recognition that there are intellectual affiliations that cut across all of the apparent divisions of political life. There is little doubt that Heidegger supported Nazism by conviction and not simply convenience. But this does not mean that one is now morally bound to read his work only for what it may tell us about his repugnant political record. One may, of course, choose to read for

7. Löwith, "M. Heidegger and F. Rosenzweig, or, Temporality and Eternity" [TE], *Philosophy and Phenomenological Research* 3, 1 (September 1942): 53–77.

this purpose as well, but it is not necessarily the most important way to read, nor is it the most instructive. Contrariwise, one may read Rosenzweig's philosophy not—as many still do—in order to affirm this or that aspect of his thought, or of Jewish identity, and so on. Rather, one may read it critically, taking cognizance of its various difficulties and even its more troublesome political ramifications. Both Rosenzweig and Heidegger deserve to be read responsibly, without undue admiration or censure.

Some readers may doubtless find this argument inadequate. They may wish to know what I think about Heidegger's politics. And they may be especially anxious to learn how this book contributes to scholarly debate concerning the possible relationship between Heidegger's politics and his philosophy. There exists much literature on this subject which I do not propose to supplement. But before launching into the substance of the book, a few words may help to alleviate possible misunderstanding. While there are indeed scholars one might justifiably call apologists for Heidegger, I do not count myself among them. But neither am I a prosecutor who wants to find the ineradicable taint of Nazism throughout his work. There is a substantial and growing number of scholars who read Heidegger's work so as to take from it what they find valuable, while disputing or even dismissing what they find cannot withstand critical scrutiny. This is of course what readers of philosophy and intellectual historians generally do when they read past philosophical works. And it is what I do as well. But for some scholars, when it comes to Heidegger, the usual habits of reading have a way of breaking down. They begin to condemn in toto, as if Heidegger alone represented a case of moral failure so egregious that it placed his work forever beyond the bounds of reasonable discussion. They forget that the intellectual tradition is replete with cases of political error and that the only reason one bothers to condemn is that something in the philosophy itself has first compelled one's attention. (Today few recall the names of the zealous but second-rate academics of the Third Reich—the Platonists, the Kantians, and so on. And fewer still would now set out to prove that this scholar's Platonism or that one's Kantianism led ineluctably to Nazism. They do not bother, largely because no one regards their work as deserving notice.) Now I think it is fair to say that, today, responsible scholars should, and indeed do, read Heidegger with a torn conscience. In their writing, one can sometimes hear them running after counterfactuals: "Would that some other man had left us these irreplaceable thoughts." "If only those politics were not so lamentably associated with this philosophy." The longing is understandable, but in vain. The burden of Heidegger's work is that it is philosophically indispensable, but for better or for worse—chiefly for worse—it was Heidegger who wrote it.

However, because the comparison between Heidegger and Rosenzweig is so troublesome, a personal word of clarification seems in order. Most of my extended family succeeded in escaping Europe before the outbreak of the Second World War. A single aunt was not so fortunate. So when Heidegger makes allusion to Nazism (sometimes ambiguously, but often with unmistakable approval), I recoil as if from a personal blow. My "identity," however, is not the most salient fact in this matter. For any reader sensitive to human dignity, Heidegger's political record and—what is perhaps equally offensive—his later refusal explicitly to apologize for his actions, cannot but arouse a sense of unease. To read Heidegger is to find oneself in a moral quandary, split between intellectual admiration and mistrust. I have not found a way to resolve this dilemma. But I am not certain any such resolution would be beneficial. I continue to believe there is little to be gained in attempting to ferret out the "real" and political sense behind Heidegger's philosophy, as if the philosophy could be finally and fully reduced to the politics. For what is truly remarkable about philosophy is that it seems always to resist this kind of reduction.

In striving to understand why Rosenzweig might have claimed philosophical kinship with Heidegger, this book also makes some steps toward reconstructing the greater climate of Weimar thought in the 1920s. A time of great cultural ferment, the Weimar era (1919–33) has long been a topic of passionate interest for historians of ideas and philosophers alike. A wealth of movements broadly associated with twentieth-century modernism were born during the brief span of years during which Germany first experimented, unsuccessfully, with democracy. I shall argue that both Rosenzweig and Heidegger are best understood within the changing context of Weimar modernism. Specifically, their work exhibits a style of thought that for convenience' sake I will occasionally refer to as *philosophical expressionism.*

By introducing this idea, I do not mean to suggest that there was in the Weimar period some unified school of philosophy that has gone previously unnoticed. Nor do I wish to argue that there was a close and conscious relationship between this philosophical style and expressionist trends in other realms such as literature and the fine arts. Culture is far too fractured, its currents too fluid and varied, to allow for any such easy correlation amongst its different regions. But there are nonetheless certain themes and modes of thought, common to both Heidegger and Rosenzweig, that seem to warrant a common title.

The origins of philosophical expressionism may be traced to the often discussed "crisis" of academic and neo-idealist philosophy at the beginning of the 1920s. The origins of this crisis first became visible toward the end of the nineteenth century, when some of the chief architects of German academic thought (neo-Kantians and neo-Hegelians) began to reconsider the troubled relationship between philosophy and religion. Some, but by no means all, of these philosophers concluded that there was an inadequacy at the heart of the older, idealist systems. Because of its emphasis on universalism and a primarily cognitive relation to the world, idealism seemed unable to capture the specificity of the human individual. Nor could idealism explain the way such an individual stakes out the meaning of religious truth in a lived, nonconceptual fashion. Confined to its arsenal of concepts, idealism seemed to miss in religion the phenomena that mattered most. It is from this confrontation between neo-idealism and theology that the new mode of philosophy first emerged.

The crisis of confidence in idealism's powers was felt most dramatically among that younger generation of thinkers who came of age just before the First World War. For many of them, German and German Jewish alike, the collapse of the older, academic style of philosophy was heralded as a great victory. The turn to religion seemed to promise a new breakthrough, a reinvigoration of the philosophical discipline. But the new attraction to theology did not spell a return to religious tradition. Paradoxically, the new philosophy articulated theological questions in a modernist, post-Nietzschean frame. The fruit of this paradox was a distinctive intellectual orientation poised between the religious nostalgia for origin and the modernist struggle to move beyond metaphysics. Like an expressionist woodcut, the new philosophy thus represented a poignant combination of archaism and modernism. The chief work of this book is to situate Rosenzweig alongside Heidegger within this unusual intellectual horizon.

A brief comment is necessary here regarding current Rosenzweig scholarship. Many of us were taken by surprise by the publication in 2002 of more than twelve hundred previously unreleased letters that Franz Rosenzweig sent to Margrit Rosenstock-Huessy in the years 1917–29. Rosenzweig and Margrit, or "Gritli" as he called her affectionately, formed two sides of a romantic triangle, for Margrit was married to Rosenzweig's good friend Eugen Rosenstock-Huessy. Out of respect for all concerned their correspondence had remained unavailable until now. Though chiefly of biographical interest, these letters also cast new light on Rosenzweig's intellectual development. Indeed, they may transform our image of Rosenzweig so profoundly as to require basic revision of earlier scholarship. I was fortunate enough to read the correspondence while it was still possible to integrate new materials into my book.

## AN OVERVIEW

In the chapters that follow, I move in chronological fashion through the chief stages of Rosenzweig's intellectual development, and I occasionally make allusion to similar themes in Heidegger's philosophy as well as in the broader context of modern German thought.

The first chapter discusses Rosenzweig's encounter with the neo-Kantian thought of Hermann Cohen, who, perhaps more than any other philosopher, became symbolic for Rosenzweig of the ambiguities of idealism and, most especially, of the troubled relation between religion and idealist thought. The second chapter explores Rosenzweig's encounter with Hegel; here I shall argue that many of Rosenzweig's mature philosophical concerns are in fact anticipated in his early (and undeservedly neglected) academic work, *Hegel and the State,* especially in its discussion of the young Hegel's theological writings.

The third and fourth chapters comprise the core of the book. Here I offer a new and systematic reading of Rosenzweig's *The Star of Redemption.* (Readers less familiar with Rosenzweig's work may wish to skip directly to this discussion and leave the contextual portions for later.) Of necessity, my interpretation leaves out much that is of interest in this controversial and endlessly challenging text. I focus chiefly upon the concept of redemption itself. And I argue that the methods and themes of *The Star* come more sharply into focus when examined in the light of Heidegger's philosophy. I further suggest that Rosenzweig's category of redemption—or, in my phrase, redemption-in-the-world—bears a surprising resemblance to what Heidegger later called authenticity.

The fifth chapter shows how many of these themes found their application in Rosenzweig's translation (with Martin Buber) of the Hebrew Bible into German. Here I explore the way that literary and philosophical concerns together left their mark on the translation, in both its style and its substance. The sixth and final chapter represents the culmination of the work; it offers a brief reconstruction of the Davos debates of 1929, showing how and why Rosenzweig perceived Heidegger as the most recent representative of the new thinking. In a sense, the book comes full circle, returning to the question of how religion and philosophy are intertwined. In a brief conclusion, I offer some more general thoughts on the political ramifications of this study and how my interpretation might inform our understanding of the relationship between German and German Jewish philosophy in the modern period.

Separately but in similar fashion, Rosenzweig and Heidegger emerged during the 1920s as two of the most original thinkers who helped to forge a new kind of philosophy, the impact of which is still felt today. In retrospect, however, it may seem difficult to believe that they were contemporaries at all. Neither read extensively in the works written by the other, and it is reasonably certain that they never met. The world they inhabited was soon to transform, disastrously, leaving us to sift among its fragments to explain how they could ever have shared a philosophical tradition in common. To recall that shared tradition is the task of this book.

# Introduction

# Germans, Jews, and the
# Transformation of Weimar Philosophy

*Traditions are lovely things—to create traditions, that is, not to live off them.*
—FRANZ MARC, *Aphorisms, 1914–15*

### THE CREATION OF A TRADITION

What Franz Marc once said of the history of art may apply to the history of ideas as well.[1] There is arguably no such objective thing as the philosophical tradition, aside from those constructions that various philosophers have fashioned from a heterogeneous manifold of ideas. Indeed, one might say that the history of philosophy consists to no small degree in philosophers' repeated attempts to imagine what came before them in such a way that this tradition will have a coherent shape. Quite often, however, philosophers create a tradition only to call its most fundamental values into question. In this way, the past they have summoned becomes a justification for their own rebellion, even while shaping the past grants their own work a certain elevated importance for the present.[2]

This may be especially true of German thinkers in the modern period. Kant believed that nearly all speculation before him was united in a common error, the belief that "all our thought must conform to objects" and not "all objects . . . to our thought." Accordingly, Kant proclaimed the critical doctrine a "Copernican revolution" in philosophy.[3] Similarly, Hegel believed that he stood in the twilight moment of world history, where all

---

1. Marc, "Aphorisms, 1914–1915," in *Briefe, Aufzeichnungen, und Aphorismen*, I: 126–32, cited in Herschel B. Chipp, *Theories of Modern Art: A Source Book by Artists and Critics* (Berkeley: University of California Press, 1968), 180.

2. On the relationship between philosophy and its history, see Richard Rorty, J. B. Schneewind, and Quentin Skinner, eds., *Philosophy in History: Essays on the Historiography of Philosophy* (Cambridge: Cambridge University Press, 1984). On the idea of philosophical rebellion, see the suggestive remarks in John McCole, *Walter Benjamin and the Antinomies of Tradition* (Ithaca, N.Y.: Cornell University Press, 1993).

3. The phrase first occurs in KdrV, "Vorrede zur zweite Auflage," 22–46.

knowledge, as if painting gray on gray, would come at last into dialectical repose with its surroundings. And Nietzsche believed that he had succeeded in overturning the entire tradition of Western philosophical speculation since Socrates, a tradition he excoriated for its supposed denial of life. But for Heidegger, Nietzsche was the last great exponent of metaphysics. Like those who came before him, Heidegger inscribed himself into the history of philosophy as both its culmination and its judge. He therefore announced the "end of philosophy" only to inaugurate "the task of thinking."[4]

The participation of Jewish thinkers in modern philosophy presents no exception to this pattern. As relative outsiders to what is sometimes called Western thought, Jewish philosophers in modern times have shown great ingenuity in imagining themselves into a tradition from which they often felt excluded. Even in the modern period, when one might have expected social emancipation to have created a greater sense of intellectual commonality, scholarly interest still seems divided between what is philosophy proper and what is Jewish philosophy. Hermann Cohen, Martin Buber, and Franz Rosenzweig, for example, are generally discussed in relative isolation from the canonical figures of the Western tradition, although each was in his own distinctive way shaped by this tradition and was deeply invested in its future course. To imagine the tradition of philosophy as including various of the outsiders it has customarily excluded seems to demand that those cast as the outsiders *re*cast the tradition in unexpected ways. Often they subscribe to a "revolution" that, like its analogue in civil society, will at last bring to an end older systems of legitimacy. This may help to explain why, in German philosophy in particular (where social emancipation was belated and incomplete), Jews from Heine to Marx often saw themselves as members of an intellectual vanguard, helping to bring an end to ossified traditions they considered intellectually as well as morally offensive.

The Jewish entry into German intellectual life helped to inaugurate a two-centuries-long tradition of great profundity between Germans and Jews. Their partnership, however, was almost always marked by ambivalence. So it is perhaps understandable if some have been tempted to read the entire tradition in the light of its end.[5] Indeed, in much scholarship

---

4. Werner Marx, *Heidegger and the Tradition,* trans. Theodore Kisiel and Murray Greene (Evanston, Ill.: Northwestern University Press, 1971).

5. See, e.g., Michel Foucault, "What is Enlightenment?" in *The Foucault Reader,* ed. Paul Rabinow (New York: Pantheon Books, 1984). Foucault perceives something "murderous" in the Enlightenment encounter between Germans and Jews, writing that "we all know to what drama that was to lead." Hence Enlightenment universalism prepares the way for the Holocaust— a provocative claim some would apply even to Kant and early proponents of Jewish emancipation. See, e.g., Berel Lang, *Act and Idea in the Nazi Genocide* (Chicago: University of Chicago

concerning the intellectual encounter between Germans and Jews retroactive judgment remains common. One regrettable consequence of Nazism was to reinvigorate the otherwise enfeebled habit of conceiving Jewish intellectuals as if they belonged to a distinctive canon, running parallel to, but nonetheless separate from, the mainstream tradition of European thought. Many of the thinkers who were in their own day considered prominent members of the philosophical tradition are now consigned to the fate that chauvinists wished for them all along. Celebrated as "Jewish" thinkers only, they are perceived as addressing topics of particularistic rather than universal concern. For this fate, a certain romanticism of the outsider may be partly to blame. Whatever the historical reasons, it remains difficult to think of modern Jewish thought as truly belonging to its European context. To set about treating Jewish philosophy as part of European philosophy means recreating the philosophical canon in a more inclusive sense, such that these distinctions, while still meaningful, no longer present a significant barrier to thought.

## THE ARGUMENT

The philosophy of Franz Rosenzweig belongs simultaneously to both the German and the Jewish traditions. The 1926 collection of his essays appeared under the title *Zweistromland*, designating Mesopotamia, but here symbolizing the two streams of thought, German and Jewish, that nourished his philosophy.[6] Such nomenclature, however, immediately invites criticism. The idea that there is a clear distinction between the German and the Jewish cannot be sustained without attributing essential and nonhistorical features to each. Clearly, intellectual traditions are too vast to sustain such claims. Still, there have been powerful, almost overwhelming forces at work that compel us to understand Rosenzweig solely as a "Jewish" thinker dissociated from the German context. Rosenzweig himself famously expressed frustration at the fact that his magnum opus had been received as a profession of Judaism. "What I have written," he objected, "is not *Jewish* philosophy, if by this one means what now customarily passes for Judaism" (ND,

---

Press, 1990); and Paul Lawrence Rose, *German Question, Jewish Question: Revolutionary Antisemitism from Kant to Wagner* (Princeton: Princeton University Press, 1990).

6. See the excellent essay by Paul Mendes-Flohr, "Franz Rosenzweig and the German Philosophical Tradition," in PFR, 1–19. Rosenzweig, *Zweistromland: Kleinere Schriften zur Religion und Philosophie* (Berlin: Philo Verlag, 1926). Rosenzweig was unhappy with the subtitle and preferred "Glauben und Denken." He avoided the term "religion" in the *Star*. On this point, see my comments in chap. 3 on the *Star,* Part I. Also see the introductory remarks by Annemarie and Reinhold Mayer, "Vorbemerkungen," in FR III: xi–xxii.

141). And elsewhere, he protested that "I am just as little a specialist in Judaica as Max Weber."[7]

Ultimately, the question concerning which philosophical tradition, German or Jewish, most explains Rosenzweig's work cannot be answered to the exclusive benefit of either. Such classificatory habits will tend to obscure what is Rosenzweig's most intriguing accomplishment, the delicate negotiation between Judaism and modern European thought. They also deny what Paul Mendes-Flohr has called the "dual identity" of the German Jews.[8] In a remarkable letter, Rosenzweig tells of an interview for a position at a Jewish school during which he was asked to take a stand on this vexed question of allegiance:

> I retorted that I would refuse to answer this question. If life were at one stage to torment me and tear me into two pieces, then I would naturally know with which of the two halves the heart—which is, after all, asymmetrically positioned—would side. I would also know that I would not be able to survive the operation.[9]

We naturally expect a surgical patient to undergo a calculated risk for what he considers a greater benefit. But in Rosenzweig's case, the surgical distinction between German and Jew would be fatal for our understanding of his work. His "heart" may have belonged to Judaism more than Germany, but his philosophical corpus belongs to both.[10]

The argument of this book is that one best understands Rosenzweig's philosophy when it is restored to its German philosophical context. One misunderstands his work when is taken as the autochthonous expression of timeless Jewish wisdom. This claim may seem uncontroversial, but it leads in several unexpected directions. Of Rosenzweig's ideas about Judaism, perhaps most characteristic is his notion that there is a peculiarly Jewish way

7. *Briefe*, N.319, An Hans Ehrenberg (September 1921), 407. But he was hardly consistent on this point. In the same letter, he clarified his relationship to Weber with the peculiar comment that "what is Jewish [*das Jüdische*] is my method, not my object of study [*mein Gegenstand*]."

8. Paul Mendes-Flohr, *German Jews: A Dual Identity* (New Haven: Yale University Press, 1999).

9. *Briefe*, N.364, An Rudolf Hallo (Ende Januar, 1923), 472–73. Also see the discussion by Karl Löwith, "On Being a German and a Jew Simultaneously," in his memoir, *My Life in Germany Before and After 1933: A Report,* trans. Elizabeth King (Urbana and Chicago: University of Illinois Press, 1994), 138–39; orig. pub. as *Mein Leben in Deutschland vor und nach 1933* (Stuttgart: J. B. Metzlersche Verlagsbuchhandlung und Carl Ernst Poeschel Verlag, 1986).

10. Similar, but less successful was the dual identity of the novelist Jacob Wassermann, who observed bitterly that the term "German Jew" holds "two concepts that to unbiased vision reveal a wealth of misunderstandings, tragedy, contradictions, strife, and suffering." *Mein Weg als Deutscher und Jude* (Berlin: S. Fischer Verlag, 1921), 1. For a variant of the surgery metaphor, see the stories collected in Jack Zipes, ed. and trans., *The Operated Jew: Two Tales of Anti-Semitism* (New York: Routledge, 1991).

of being in the world, a mode of existence that sets the Jews apart from all other peoples and, indeed, from history itself. But once Rosenzweig's philosophy is restored to its original intellectual context, we shall see that even his celebrated claim of Jewish distinctiveness is largely a philosophical effect. It is something created, not given. As I shall explain, Rosenzweig's notion of Jewish difference derives from sources beyond the orbit of Judaism, and, ironically, it bears witness to his ongoing participation in the wider philosophical developments of his time.

Specifically, I shall claim that Rosenzweig is best understood within the context of Weimar philosophical modernism, within the transformation of ideas—from idealism to existential ontology—more typically associated with the early work of Martin Heidegger. The detailed comparison between Rosenzweig and Heidegger is left to the individual chapters. My general argument is that both philosophers exhibit the characteristic tension within Weimar culture between archaism and modernism. Their works are expressive of a common longing to restore philosophy to a forgotten and "primordial" truth even while this is said to demand a revolutionary break with tradition. Both regard it as the task of the new philosophy to redeem us from an ossified tradition and from the false attachments of our surroundings, in order that we may live more authentically as who we truly are. Both therefore conceive of redemption, not as world-transcendence, but as a distinctive way of being-in-the-world. Clearly, this new philosophical perspective owes a great deal to theology. But it also stages a rebellion against the customarily metaphysical account of religious ideas. The new thinking is therefore poised, as it were, between religion and metaphysics.

### EARLY INTERPRETATIONS OF ROSENZWEIG

It is often forgotten that Rosenzweig's earliest readers regarded *The Star of Redemption* as a work of European and not exclusively Jewish thought. In her book *Die Existenzphilosophie Franz Rosenzweigs* (completed in 1933), Else-Rahel Freund presented Rosenzweig's work within the context of the Weimar-era revival of interest in Friedrich Schelling's philosophy, and she specifically drew attention to Rosenzweig's affinities with his intellectual contemporaries, especially Martin Buber and Martin Heidegger.[11] This per-

---

11. In Freund's view, the focal point for Rosenzweig's philosophy was "human existence in its finitude and temporality." Much like Heidegger, who could be understood as having oriented his thought "against the subject [*Ich*] of Idealism," Rosenzweig, too, was bent on overcoming the Cartesian split between "the reflective" and "the living" self. The leitmotif of Rosenzweig's philosophy, like that of Heidegger and Buber, was the "real existence, bound by death, of the individual, his actions and decisions in reality." *Die Existenzphilosophie Franz Rosenzweigs,* 2nd ed. (Hamburg: Felix Meiner, 1959), 1–3; orig. pub. Leipzig: Felix Meiner, 1933

spective was not uncommon. In a 1922 review, Margarete Susman also described *The Star* with little regard for its Jewish themes.[12] For both, it was clear that Rosenzweig's philosophy had emerged from the very heart of its age, not from the periphery.[13]

Perhaps the singularly most influential portrait of Rosenzweig is found in Julius Guttmann's classic study *Die Philosophie des Judentums*, first published in 1933.[14] The very rubric may seem suggestive of a separate canon, distinguished from the Western philosophical tradition by both geography and time. But in the opening lines of his survey of the philosophy of Judaism (translated into English as the more pluralistic *Philosophies of Judaism*), Guttmann denied Jewish thought any single distinguishing characteristic. "The Jewish people," he wrote, "is not driven to philosophical thought from its very own, inner power. It received philosophy from outside, *and the history of Jewish philosophy is a history of receptions of foreign intellectual goods, which were then of course adapted according to its very own, new points of view*" (PJ, 1; my emphasis).

That Guttmann admitted this habit of borrowing "from outside"—*von außen*—is significant, as it suggests the canon's permeability, not its independence. According to Guttmann, this close relationship to the ambient

---

and also printed as her dissertation under the title *Die Philosophie Franz Rosenzweigs: Ein Beitrag zur Analyse seines Werkes Der Stern der Erlösung* (Breslau: Druck von Emil und Dr. Edgar Richter, Stadtroda, 1933). In English as *Franz Rosenzweig's Philosophy of Existence*, trans. Stephen L. Weinstein and Robert Israel (The Hague: Martinus Nijhoff, 1979).

12. Susman's was one of the earliest reviews of Rosenzweig's book in the German-speaking world. As she observed, *The Star* stood "at a moment of great transformation" and was "conscious of standing there." It signaled "the dissolution of the philosophy of pure thought as it had dominated the Western world from Parmenides to Hegel." "Philosophie: *Der Stern der Erlösung*," *Der Jude* 6, 4 (1921–22): 259–64.

13. Arguably what is most characteristic of German-Jewish thought is exactly the wish not to be perceived as such. David Sorkin suggests that one of the consequences of the delay in German Jewish emancipation was an ideology of zealously asserted inclusion. *The Transformation of German Jewry, 1780–1840* (Oxford and New York: Oxford University Press, 1987). For a comment, see Anthony J. La Vopa, "Jews and Germans: Old Quarrels, New Departures," *Journal of the History of Ideas* 54, 4 (October 1993).

14. Guttmann, *Die Philosophie des Judentums* [PJ] (München: Verlag Ernst Reinhardt, 1933). The 1933 edition concludes with a chapter on Hermann Cohen's philosophy. Guttmann revised the text for its Hebrew publication and added a final chapter on Franz Rosenzweig. The English version, including the discussion of Rosenzweig, was first published as *Philosophies of Judaism: The History of Jewish Philosophy from Biblical Times to Franz Rosenzweig*, trans. David Silverman (New York: Holt, Rinehart and Winston, 1964). Eliezer Schweid observes that the change of title from the singular to the plural "lost the programmatic nature of the German title." "Religion and Philosophy: The Scholarly-Theological Debate between Julius Guttmann and Leo Strauss," in *Maimonides Studies*, ed. Arthur Hyman (New York: Yeshiva University Press, 1990), I: 163–95, quote at 163n.1.

intellectual world remained characteristic of Jewish philosophy throughout its long career.[15] Interestingly, in the original text Rosenzweig was mentioned only in an elliptical and somewhat negative concluding remark. Here Guttmann lamented that recent Jewish thought "follows the metaphysical and irrationalist tendencies that generally dominate the thinking of our day."[16] But this passage was omitted from the English translation, and since then the suggestion that Rosenzweig's work followed the "metaphysical and irrationalist" tendencies of his time has received little consideration.

## POSTWAR INTERPRETATIONS

In the wake of Nazism, the shared intellectual tradition of Germans and Jews came to seem an anomaly, a passing moment of intimacy in a larger history of mistrust. Jewish nationalist scholars such as Gershom Scholem attacked the idea of a dialogue as a myth.[17] And many refugee scholars, justifiably embittered by their recent experience, came to regard the German canon in its entirety with suspicion. In some of the most prodigious scholarship of the postwar era, great spans of German intellectual history were thus dismissed as inimical to reason and democracy. Various patterns were detected, changing according to intellectual fashion, so as to confirm that Nazism had roots deep in the German past.

15. Guttmann claimed that the Diaspora status of Jews prohibits one from speaking of a "Jewish" philosophy in the same way one might speak of Greek, Roman, or German philosophy. But he also claimed that Judaism itself possesses a single and quasi-unified philosophy, which enjoyed an "independence and special nature" in its distinctively monotheistic notion of revelation. Guttmann's thoughts about the "peculiarity" of Jewish philosophy resemble the views of his predecessor, Hermann Cohen. On Guttmann and Cohen, see Schweid, "Religion and Philosophy," esp. 170–79. Until the end of the middle ages, Jewish thought remained "closely bound to the non-Jewish sources, from which it sprang," while modern post-emancipation Jewish philosophy developed "under the influence of the contemporary philosophical development of European nations." And "even Jewish philosophy in the specific and narrow sense of the term, like its Christian counterpart, operated within the framework, the methods, and the conceptual apparatus of modern European philosophy." PJ, 4–10.

16. Compare PJ (English version, 362). On this phrase, see Leo Strauss, *Philosophie und Gesetz: Beiträge zum Verständnis Maimunis und seiner Vorläufer* (Berlin: Schocken Verlag, 1935); in English as *Philosophy and Law: Contributions to the Understanding of Maimonides and His Predecessors* (Albany: State University of New York Press, 1995), esp. 48.

17. Scholem, "Wider den Mythos vom deutsch-jüdischen 'Gespräch,'" in *Auf gespaltenem Pfad: Festschrift für Margarete Susman,* ed. Manfred Schlösser (Darmstadt: Erato-Presse, 1964). Interestingly, Scholem's famous polemic against the "myth" of German-Jewish dialogue was written for this 1964 jubilee volume honoring Susman, an important interpreter of Rosenzweig (see above). In English, see Scholem, "Against the Myth of the German-Jewish Dialogue" and also "Once More: The German-Jewish Dialogue" and "Jews and Germans," all in Scholem, *On Jews and Judaism in Crisis: Selected Essays,* ed. Werner J. Dannhauser (New York: Schocken Books, 1976), 61–92.

Such a climate obviously did very little to encourage any judicious assessment of Rosenzweig's place in the German tradition. Instead, he was ranked among that diverse coterie of intellectuals who were specifically "German-Jewish" in identity. The hyphen between the two adjectives served to indicate a special type, distinctive and separate in character. Especially for a postwar readership in North America, this struck a familiar chord. A certain kind of nostalgia now grew up around the memory of Weimar's most prominent German Jews, who became the belated representatives of a fascinating past. But while their lives were surely deserving of attention, their philosophy suffered from excessive and largely uncritical praise. The fact that Rosenzweig developed a painful and debilitating disease only added to his reputation as a "mute saint." Like Heine upon his "mattress grave," the memory of Rosenzweig lying on his deathbed could all too easily be transmogrified into a figure for Jewish suffering as such.[18]

In much of the early postwar scholarship, Rosenzweig's philosophy was exploited as a resource for Jewish inspiration.[19] The theme of Christian-Jewish dialogue held an obvious appeal. And thanks to his fascinating exchange of letters on Judaism and Christianity with Eugen Rosenstock-Huessy, Rosenzweig became known chiefly for his unapologetic affirmation of Jewish identity. The great popularity and accessibility of Martin Buber's "dialogical" philosophy helped to revive interest in Rosenzweig's thought as well.[20] Generally speaking, Rosenzweig's "new thinking" spawned a literature of appreciation sometimes lacking in philosophical depth.

More recently, however, scholars have begun to seriously explore Rosenzweig's place in the development of modern Jewish and European philosophy. Leora Batnitzky has perceptively noted his alliance with twentieth-century hermeneutics. Eric Santner has creatively suggested a link with

18. "Mute saint" from Gershom Scholem, "Franz Rosenzweig and His Book, *The Star of Redemption,*" in PFR, 20–41, quote at 40. For one recent critic, Rosenzweig's life "anticipated with a singular exemplarity the tragic destiny of the Jewish communities of Central Europe. . . . [T]he six last years of the life of Franz Rosenzweig were a lonely and long agony prefiguring individually that of all his people in an era of the most cruel and the most systematic of anti-Semitic persecutions in modern times." From opening remarks to a conference, published as *La Pensée de Franz Rosenzweig,* ed., Arno Münster, Actes du Colloque parisien organisé à l'occasion du centenaire de la naissance du philosophe (Paris: Presses Universitaires de France, 1994). On Heine's illness, see Ernst Pawel, *The Poet Dying: Heinrich Heine's Last Years in Paris* (New York: Farrar, Straus and Giroux, 1995).

19. For a more detailed account of Rosenzweig's image in North America, see Peter Eli Gordon, "Rosenzweig Redux: The Reception of German-Jewish Thought," *Jewish Social Studies* 8, 1 (fall 2001): 1–57.

20. Dialogue is a prominent theme in Wolfdietrich Schmied Kowarzik, *Existentielles Denken und gelebte Bewährung* (Munich: Verlag Karl Alber, 1991); and in Adam Zak, *Vom reinen Denken zur Sprachvernunft: Über die Grundmotive der Offenbarungsphilosophie Franz Rosenzweigs.* (Stuttgart and Berlin: Verlag W. Kohlhammer, 1987).

the "psychotheological" dimension of psychoanalysis. Various scholars have suggested (against Rosenzweig's express denial) that the new thinking bears a hidden debt to the Jewish mystical tradition.[21] One scholar has suggested that Rosenzweig (like Benjamin, Scholem, Buber, and so on) was a proponent of a specifically Central-European-Jewish brand of anarchistic utopianism. (The label is puzzling, as one finds little in Rosenzweig's oeuvre to suggest any determinate political orientation.)[22] Numerous conferences and essay collections, together with the completion in German of his collected works, have helped to rescue Rosenzweig from undeserved obscurity.[23] Overall, the new literature has helped greatly to reawaken our appreciation for the subtlety and richness of his thought.

## ROSENZWEIG AND LEVINAS

Perhaps the most significant aspect of the new critical literature is the widely shared belief that Rosenzweig was vitally concerned with ethics. This undoubtedly has much to do with the recent growth of interest in the French Jewish philosopher Emmanuel Levinas. In his book *Totality and Infinity*, Lev-

21. Batnitzky, *Idolatry and Representation: The Philosophy of Franz Rosenzweig Reconsidered* (Princeton: Princeton University Press, 2000). Santner, *On the Psychotheology of Everyday Life: Reflections on Freud and Rosenzweig* (Chicago: University of Chicago Press, 2001). And see Moshe Idel, "Rosenzweig and the Kabbalah," in PFR, 162–71, and Scholem, "Rosenzweig and His Book." Also see Yudit Kornberg Greenberg, *Better Than Wine: Love, Poetry, and Prayer in the Thought of Franz Rosenzweig*, ed. David E. Klemm, The American Academy of Religion, Reflection, and Theory in the Study of Religion, No. 7 (Atlanta: Scholars Press, 1996). Against these studies, see Nahum Glatzer, "Was Franz Rosenzweig a Mystic?," in *Studies in Jewish Religious and Intellectual History,* Presented to Alexander Altmann on his Seventieth Birthday, ed. Siegfried Stein and Raphael Loewe (Alabama: University of Alabama Press, 1979). Rosenzweig himself stated that *The Star* is "anti-mystical." See *Briefe*, N.330, An Hans Ehrenberg, (Kassel, Ende Dezember 1921), 413–14.
22. Michel Löwy, *Redemption and Utopia: Jewish Libertarian Thought in Central Europe, A Study in Elective Affinity,* trans. Hope Heaney (Stanford, Calif.: Stanford University Press, 1988). Rosenzweig's early writings on politics, published during the First World War, suggest a grandiose vision (e.g., the section "Zur Politik" in FR III: 241–368). In his letters Rosenzweig proclaimed himself a monarchist (e.g., *Briefe*, N.261, An die Mutter [19.10.1918], 351–52). But in a 1919 essay he calls capitalism "a system . . . as damned as slavery"; printed as "Hic et Ubique: Ein Wort an Leser und andre Leute," in KS, 467–76. Löwy considers this phrase an example of Rosenzweig's "romantic, anti-capitalist worldview," but it occurs as a passing remark in Rosenzweig's comments on trying to found a publishing house. For a summary of Rosenzweig and politics, see Stefan Meineke, "A Life of Contradiction: The Philosophy of Franz Rosenzweig and his Relationship to History and Politics," in LBIY, 1991, 461–89.
23. Conference collections include *Der Philosoph Franz Rosenzweig* [Kassel], Internationaler Kongreß, Kassel, 1986, ed. Wolfdietrich Schmied-Kowarzik (Freiburg: Verlag Karl Alber, 1986); *The Philosophy of Franz Rosenzweig* [PFR], ed. Paul Mendes-Flohr (1988); and Münster, ed., *La Pensée de Franz Rosenzweig* (1994). Rosenzweig's collected works are available as *Franz Rosenzweig: Der Mensch und sein Werk. Gesammelte Schriften* [FR], 4 vols. (1976–84).

inas credited Rosenzweig as one of his major sources of inspiration, suggesting that his insight was "too often present in this book to be cited." Levinas's other occasional essays on Rosenzweig only helped to strengthen the impression among recent interpreters that the philosophical speculations of Rosenzweig and Levinas should be taken together as twin manifestations of what Levinas himself called "une pensée juive moderne."[24]

But whatever their similarities, Rosenzweig and Levinas belonged to different worlds. Levinas's thought took shape during his encounter with Husserlian and Heideggerian phenomenology in the late 1920s and 1930s. Almost from the beginning, Levinas regarded Heidegger's philosophy with some mistrust, no doubt largely due to the latter's support for Nazism. Despite the considerable inspiration he derived from Heidegger's existential phenomenology, Levinas's own work bears the scars of this event. Indeed, he seems to have construed Heidegger's Nazism as symptomatic of an ethical gap in his ontology. Thus for Levinas one of the central tasks of philosophy after Auschwitz was to resist Heidegger in the name of ethics. Against the totalizing claims of ontology, he asserted an "infinite'" relation to the Other. But this relation was more than the basis of responsibility: for Levinas, it enjoyed the metaphysical primacy Heidegger had reserved for the ethically indifferent *Seinsfrage,* or "question of Being."[25]

At least two scholars, Robert Gibbs and Richard A. Cohen, have recently called attention to the philosophical affinities between Levinas and Rosenzweig. Both have proven highly instructive for our appreciation of Rosenzweig's philosophy. But one of the unintended consequences of their common approach is that Rosenzweig has become subtly dissociated from his historical setting, so that we are discouraged from admitting his various affinities with the German philosophical movements of his day.[26] Whatever

24. Levinas, *Totalité et Infini* (Dordrecht, Netherlands: Martinus Nijhoff, 1961), 14; and "Franz Rosenzweig: Une pensée juive moderne," *Les Cahiers de la Nuit Surveillée* (ed. Olivier Mongin, Jacques Rolland, and Alexandre Derczanski) 1 (Paris, 1982): 65–78. Levinas also mentions Rosenzweig in two essays: "Entre deux mondes. Biographie spirituelle de Franz Rosenzweig," in *La Conscience juive: Données et débats,* ed. Amado Levy-Valensis and Jean Halpérin (Paris: Pressses Universitaires de France, 1963), 121–49, reprinted in *Difficile Liberté,* 3rd ed. (Paris: Albin Michel, 1984), 253–81; and "Franz Rosenzweig: L'Étoile de la Rédemption," *Esprit* 6, 3 (1982): 157–65.

25. On the impact of Heidegger's Nazism on Levinas, see the early essay, "Reflections on the Philosophy of Hitlerism," trans. Séan Hand, *Critical Inquiry* 17 (autumn 1990): 63–71. A graceful summary is Samuel Moyn, "Judaism against Paganism: Emmanuel Levinas's Response to Heidegger and Nazism in the 1930s," *History and Memory* 10, 1 (spring/summer 1998): 25–58.

26. See Richard Cohen, *Elevations: The Height of the Good in Rosenzweig and Levinas* (Chicago: University of Chicago Press, 1994) and Robert Gibbs, *Correlations in Rosenzweig and Levinas* (Princeton: Princeton University Press, 1992). One problem with this line of inquiry is that it risks anachronism. To call Rosenzweig a " postmodernist," for example, seems to jeopardize

its merit, the comparison between Rosenzweig and Levinas has thus nourished the idea that there is a more or less intact tradition of "Jewish" philosophy in Europe, which endured despite differences of European nationality and across variations of time, culture, and language.[27] Each of these critics, albeit in differing fashions, has succeeded in demonstrating an intriguing bond between Rosenzweig and Levinas. (The affiliation, however, was one-sided: Levinas made creative use of Rosenzweig's thought, but whether Rosenzweig would have regarded this appropriation as legitimate is another matter.)

The new scholarship on Levinas has encouraged the view of Rosenzweig as an ethical philosopher. This view offers consolation in the wake of the Holocaust, as it supplies further evidence that German Jewry comprised what George Mosse has called Germany's "better self."[28] But to cast Rosenzweig as an ethicist is nonetheless misleading. His writing is replete with commentary upon the meaning of love, community, and the relationship between human and God. But the insomniac sense of responsibility that would later characterize Levinas's writing is quite simply absent from Rosenzweig's work. More importantly, Rosenzweig would have strongly resisted Levinas's attempt to found ethics upon a metaphysical relation to the Other. For those familiar with contemporary Rosenzweig scholarship, this claim may appear surprising. The attraction of modern Jewish thought often seems to depend upon its ethical difference from the mainstream European canon. Some may even boast that the difference of Judaism is precisely that it respects difference. "Otherness" has therefore become a much-vaunted theme of modern Jewish philosophy. And following upon the heels of recent Levinas scholarship, it is a theme frequently attached to Rosenzweig as well. (Indeed, Levinas claimed to have developed his own resistance to totalization from Rosenzweig's example.)

One purpose of this study will be to combat the misunderstanding of Rosenzweig as primarily an ethicist or theorist of alterity. I shall argue instead that Rosenzweig was a holist; that is, he was committed to the doctrine

---

the standard periodization of twentieth-century thought. More importantly, it also conflates different kinds of responses to modernity, of which "postmodernism" is only one among many. Whether Levinas himself is best characterized as a postmodernist remains open to question. See Samuel Moyn, "Selfhood and Transcendence: Emmanuel Levinas and the Origins of Intersubjective Moral Theory, 1928–1961" (Ph.D. diss., University of California, Berkeley, 2000).

27. Robert Gibbs has cautioned us to understand the relationship between Rosenzweig and Levinas as one of "adaptation," a term that suggests his sensitivity to the way that the two philosophers may have had different priorities. Richard Cohen, with greater boldness, has suggested that Rosenzweig and Levinas shared a common philosophical task, which he characterizes as that of thematizing "the Good."

28. Mosse, *German Jews Beyond Judaism* (Cincinnati: Hebrew Union College Press, 1985).

that meaning depends upon a coherent existential horizon, a bounded and self-sustaining sphere of common practices, shared language and experience.[29] I will further suggest that a morality-centered understanding of Rosenzweig has helped to deflect our attention away from some of the more unsettling aspects of his philosophy. It has proven particularly effective in allowing readers to downplay the significance of the philosophical bond between Rosenzweig and Heidegger. In light of Levinas's criticism of Heidegger, it may seem natural to infer that Rosenzweig, too, sustained the ethical values Heidegger lacked. But it is crucial to remember that Rosenzweig, unlike Levinas, was utterly ignorant of Heidegger's Nazism. When Rosenzweig died in the winter of 1929, the Weimar Republic was just beginning to crumble, so there was as yet little reason for Rosenzweig to be wary of Heidegger for "ethical" reasons alone. On the contrary, Rosenzweig, much like Heidegger himself before 1933, was chiefly preoccupied by philosophical matters that lay elsewhere than ethics. And such a preoccupation cannot in itself be considered a sign of ethical depravity or unconcern.[30]

### ROSENZWEIG AND HEIDEGGER: AN ELECTIVE AFFINITY

At first glance, the affinity between Rosenzweig and Heidegger may seem improbable. Although Rosenzweig was born into a Jewish family that seems to have lacked any robust attachment to its ancestral faith, he went on to develop a style of philosophy that was unabashedly religious in orientation, and nearly all of his mature work is expressly concerned with bridging the post-Enlightenment gulf between philosophy and theology. Heidegger, by contrast, was born into a devout Swabian-Catholic milieu, and as a young man immersed himself in the scholastic tradition. (He even considered joining the Jesuit priesthood.) But as an adult, Heidegger grew to consider religion an ancillary matter, irrelevant to, if not actually at odds with, genuinely philosophical inquiry. So although Rosenzweig and Heidegger were

29. But see Leora Batnitzky's claims against me that Rosenzweig's thought bears a greater resemblance to Gadamer, not Heidegger. Against her, I would argue that it is Heidegger who places considerable emphasis on the hermeneutics of practice. He thus theorizes a *lived and engaged* relationship to the world, which Gadamer neglects in favor of textual hermeneutics. Ironically, Heidegger's emphasis on practice gets at what Batnitzky herself considers most salient in Rosenzweig's account of Jewish *worship*. See Batnitzky, *Idolatry and Representation*.

30. A preoccupation with non-ethical questions is not itself "against" ethics. Levinas believes that to regard any ontological terrain as preceding ethics is already an ethical violation. Richard Cohen reiterates this belief in his criticism of Derrida: "from Levinas' point of view, not to decide the question of the primacy of ethics or ontology is most certainly to decide *against* ethics" and is thus a sign of "irresponsibility." *Elevations,* 319, 315.

contemporaries and lived through the common experiences of their time—
war, revolution, and the republican experiment—their intellectual lives
were seemingly worlds apart. And while Rosenzweig died in 1929, Heidegger went on just a few years later to ally himself publicly with the Nazi regime.[31] The chasm between Rosenzweig and Heidegger, both philosophical
and historical, seems formidable indeed.

But it was Rosenzweig himself who first acknowledged his intellectual
kinship with Heidegger. In a commentary entitled "Vertauschte Fronten"
(Exchanged fronts), written in 1929 shortly before his death, Rosenzweig
interpreted the recent disputation at Davos between Martin Heidegger and
Ernst Cassirer as a "representative encounter between the old and the new
thinking" (VF, 235–38). For Rosenzweig, Cassirer appeared as the advocate
of the "old" philosophical school of idealism, while Heidegger seemed to
herald the new vision of philosophy that Rosenzweig claimed to share. More
surprising, perhaps, Rosenzweig further suggested that his philosophy and
that of Heidegger derived from a single source, the posthumous religious
writings of the great neo-Kantian, Hermann Cohen.

The suggestion is curious and in some respects implausible. Heidegger
was notoriously hostile toward neo-Kantianism, and he exhibited an especially pronounced antagonism toward the so-called Marburg school of
which Cohen had been arguably the leading representative. More to the
point, Cassirer himself was considered the greatest living representative of
the Marburg tradition—Cohen had died a decade earlier. So Rosenzweig's
suggestion that Heidegger bore an unacknowledged debt to Cohen's philosophy of religion involved a dramatic reversal of popular perspectives—
Rosenzweig himself called it "an irony in the history of Spirit" (VF, 238).

A generous reader, however, should begin by taking Rosenzweig at his
word. One cannot reject his arguments simply because they run up against
the now-habitual categorization of philosophical schools. And one cannot

31. Heidegger's political engagement with National Socialism is well documented. A ju-
dicious summary is Thomas Sheehan, "Heidegger and the Nazis," *New York Review of Books,*
June 16, 1988, 38–47. Also see, inter alia, Guido Schneeberger, *Nachlese zu Heidegger* (Bern:
Buchdruckerei AG, Suhr, 1962); the controversial but still informative study by Victor Farias,
orig. *Heidegger et le nazisme* (Paris: Éditions Verdier, 1987), in English, *Heidegger and Nazism,* ed.
Joseph Margolis and Tom Rockmore (Philadelphia: Temple University Press, 1989); Gunther
Neske and Emil Kettering, eds., *Martin Heidegger and National Socialism* (New York: Paragon
House, 1990); Richard Wolin, ed., *The Heidegger Controversy: A Critical Reader* (Cambridge,
Mass.: MIT Press, 1991, 2nd ed. 1993); and Hugo Ott, *Martin Heidegger: A Political Life,* trans.
Allan Blunden. (New York: Basic Books, 1993). The broader issues raised by Heidegger's pol-
itics are discussed in Tom Rockmore, *On Heidegger's Nazism and Philosophy* (Berkeley: University
of California Press, 1992); Hans Sluga, *Heidegger's Crisis: Philosophy and Politics in Nazi Germany*
(Cambridge, Mass.: Harvard University Press, 1993); and Dominique Janicaud, *The Shadow of
That Thought,* trans. Michael Gendre (Evanston, Ill.: Northwestern University Press, 1996).

reject them solely because their political ramifications may prove disturbing. In any event it is important to hold open the possibility that affiliations of thought may at times run deeper than any apparent disagreement over matters of politics and history. Surprising as it may seem, Rosenzweig's commentary on Heidegger may provide a helpful point of departure for understanding their shared position in the history of modern thought.

However, few critics in the postwar period have considered the relationship between Rosenzweig and Heidegger as deserving closer attention. The historian Hans Liebeschütz suggested that no matter how seriously we might wish to take Rosenzweig's perspective, the suggestion of an affinity with Heidegger seems—especially for "a Jewish reader who experienced [the events of] 1933 in Germany"—"rather horrifying."[32] And the accomplished Rosenzweig scholar Stéphane Mosès writes

> The reader of today cannot fail to remain struck by the magnitude of the historical misunderstanding in whose name, in 1929, Rosenzweig identifies himself without reservation with the Heideggerian discourse whose latent violence (which struck the participants at the Davos colloquium) seems to have escaped him entirely.[33]

The reader may feel distress at Rosenzweig's "historical" misunderstanding. But it seems doubtful that Rosenzweig could have noticed a "violence" in Heidegger's thought that in 1929 remained "latent." Moreover, this is to miss the point of Rosenzweig's essay: for even if one were to blame him for not anticipating Heidegger's still hidden politics, this would still leave open the matter of whether his philosophical identification with Heidegger was in any sense correct.

### "TEMPORALITY AND ETERNITY"

The only critic to have taken up the philosophical connection between Rosenzweig and Heidegger as a matter worthy of sustained attention is Karl

---

32. Liebeschütz argues that "for Heidegger, his profession of faith to Hitler was absolutely *not* a facade, but rather the true expression of his thought concerning the task of man, that of seizing his authentic fate." He also implies that Rosenzweig's illness may have prevented his realizing the true meaning of Heidegger's philosophy. But Liebeschütz judiciously concludes: "[I]n a time, when no one yet could have had a concrete picture of what would become possible and really happen in 1933, a passionate seeker of truth might consider the continued development of philosophical directions that he himself represented as more essential than the political associations with which it could be bound at the time." *Von Georg Simmel zu Franz Rosenzweig: Studien zum Jüdischen Denken im deutschen Kulturbereich* (Tübingen: J. C. B. Mohr, Paul Siebeck, 1970), 170–71.

33. Mosès, *Système et Révélation: La Philosophie de Franz Rosenzweig* (Paris: Éditions du Seuil, 1982), 306–10.

Löwith, in a little-discussed 1942 essay, "M. Heidegger and F. Rosenzweig, or, Temporality and Eternity."[34] A fascinating specimen of comparative intellectual history, it provides the chief point of departure for any new attempt to evaluate the relationship between Rosenzweig and Heidegger.

A brief biographical sketch is helpful. Löwith was a German philosopher of Jewish descent, remembered today chiefly for his interpretation of the theological background of the philosophy of history in the modern period.[35] Trained in the phenomenological tradition, he studied with Husserl from 1919 onward at the University of Freiburg, where he became a devoted pupil of the young Heidegger (at that time Husserl's assistant). In 1933, when German antisemitism became official policy, his promising career in the German university suffered a brutal interruption. After brief stays in Rome and Japan, Löwith obtained various teaching posts in the United States, first at the Hartford Theological Seminary, and later at the New School for Social Research in New York. After the war, at the urging of former colleagues, he returned to Germany to occupy a chair in philosophy at Heidelberg, where he remained from 1953 until his death in 1973.[36]

As this itinerary suggests, Löwith's bond with Heidegger was exceedingly ambivalent. His 1953 book *Heidegger: Thinker in a Destitute Age* is a testament to both the anguish and the fascination he felt toward the man he regarded as one of the twentieth century's greatest philosophers. And his lifelong interest in the mutual entwinement of philosophical and religious categories

34. Löwith, "M. Heidegger and F. Rosenzweig, or, Temporality and Eternity" [TE], *Philosophy and Phenomenological Research* 3, 1 (September, 1942), 53–77. On the parallels between Rosenzweig's association with Rudolf Ehrenberg and Heidegger's apprenticeship under the theologian Engelbert Krebs, see Christoph von Wolzogen, "Vertauschte Fronten, Heidegger und Rosenzweig," *Zeitschrift für Religions und Geistesgeschichte* 46, 2 (1994), 109–25. And see Steven Schwarzschild, "Franz Rosenzweig and Martin Heidegger: The Turn to Ethnicism in Modern Jewish Thought," ed. Maimon Schwarzschild and Almut Schulamith Bruckstein (MS, 1999). A passionate if idiosyncratic scholar, Schwarzschild followed Hermann Cohen in seeing any departure from neo-Kantian rationalism as potentially idolatrous and inimical to Judaism. I thank Samuel Moyn for securing a copy of this still-unpublished manuscript.

35. See, e.g., Löwith, *Meaning in History* (Chicago: University of Chicago Press, 1949) and *Von Hegel zu Nietzsche: Der Revolutionäre Bruch im Denken des neunzehnten Jahrhunderts* (Zürich: Europa Verlag, 1941); in English as *From Hegel to Nietzsche: The Revolution in Nineteenth-Century Thought*, trans. David Green (New York: Holt, Rinehart and Winston, 1964).

36. In 1923, Löwith completed a doctoral thesis on Nietzsche, first published in 1935 as *Nietzsches Philosophie der ewigen Widerkunft des Gleichen;* in English as *Nietzsche's Philosophy of the Eternal Recurrence of the Same*, trans. J. Harvey Lomax (Berkeley: University of California Press, 1997). In 1924, he followed Heidegger to Marburg where he wrote a *Habilitation* in 1928 on the intersubjective constitution of the self: *Das Individuum in der Rolle des Mitmenschen*, in *Sämtliche Schriften*, vol. I: *Mensch und Menschenwelt, Beiträge zur Anthropologie*, ed. Klaus Stichweh and Marc B. de Laynay (Stuttgart: J. B. Metlersche Verlagsbuchhandlung, 1981), 9–197. Löwith's career is summarized in his *Mein Leben in Deutschland (My Life in Germany)*.

was doubtless influenced by Heidegger's example.[37] But while Löwith was a member of Heidegger's inner circle at Freiburg, his teacher's public support for Nazism ended any possibility of friendship. In 1936, when Löwith met his teacher for the last time in Rome, Heidegger did not bother to remove the party insignia from his lapel. Löwith recalls that he eventually drew Heidegger into a discussion about the political situation in Germany, and Heidegger readily confessed his belief that National Socialism was "the right course for Germany." As justification, Heidegger explained (in Löwith's words) that "his concept of 'historicity' formed the basis of his political 'engagement.'"[38]

One can only guess at the sense of betrayal Löwith must have felt at Heidegger's political alliance. In such feelings he was hardly alone. The transformation of the political landscape changed the way that many German Jews understood Heidegger's philosophy.[39] Else-Rahel Freund's monograph on Rosenzweig, first published in 1933, contained copious and apparently favorable references to Heidegger throughout. But soon thereafter, the intimate bond between Heidegger and many of his German Jewish disciples—a group which included such figures as Hannah Arendt, Werner Brock, Hans Jonas, and Herbert Marcuse as well as Löwith—began quickly to unravel. For many readers, Heidegger's political misadventure meant that any "purely philosophical" assessment of his earlier work was no longer possible. Understandably, it was often his former Jewish students most of all who could not recover their earlier, more "innocent" appreciation of his thought.[40]

37. Löwith, *Heidegger: Denker in dürftiger Zeit.*

38. Löwith, *Mein Leben,* 59, 60. Löwith harbored justifiable resentment toward intellectuals like Heidegger who publicly endorsed the Third Reich, since such endorsement conferred cultural pedigree upon a regime whose barbarity would have been otherwise transparent. Oddly, Heidegger himself expressed anger toward colleagues who didn't follow his example: "If these gentlemen had not been too refined to get involved," he explained, "then everything would be different; but instead, I am entirely alone now." *Mein Leben,* 60.

39. For a more detailed analysis of Löwith's judgment, see the introductory remarks by Richard Wolin in the recent translation, Löwith, *Martin Heidegger and European Nihilism,* ed. Richard Wolin (New York: Columbia University Press, 1995). And see, e.g., Albert Lewkowitz, "Vom Sinn des Seins: Zur Existenzphilosophie Heideggers," *Monatsschrift für Geschichte und Wissenschaft des Judentums* (Breslau) 80, 3 (May/June 1936), 184–95; and Martin Buber, "Die Verwirklichung des Menschen: Zur Anthropologie Martin Heideggers," *Philosophia* (Zürich and Leipzig: Rascher Verlag) 3, 1–4 (1938): 289–308.

40. See, e.g., Herbert Marcuse's open letter to Heidegger, reprinted as "Herbert Marcuse à Heidegger," *Les Temps Modernes* 44, 510 (January 1989): 1–4. In 1934, Marcuse announced that Heidegger's political engagement was "an act of self-abasement on the part of existentialism that is without equal in the whole of intellectual history." Quoted in Ott, *Martin Heidegger,* 166; Arendt, "What Is Existenz Philosophy?," *Partisan Review* 18, 1 (1946); reprinted in German as "Was ist Existenz-Philosophie?," in Arendt, *Sechs Essays* (Heidelberg: Schneider, 1948), and as "What is Existential Philosophy?" in Arendt, *Essays in Understanding, 1930–1954,*

Löwith's later assessment of Heidegger's philosophy is a record of dis-illusionment. Taking as a point of departure Heidegger's confession that "historicity" informed his Nazi commitments, Löwith claimed that it was Heidegger's philosophical trust in temporality as the ultimate sphere of meaning that provided the key to his political misadventure. For "no phi-losopher besides Heidegger," in Löwith's view, "has oriented philosophy so much to the coincidence of 'historical facticity.'" But this mode of think-ing "necessarily incurred its penalty as soon as the decisive 'moment' had come." "The possibility of Heidegger's political philosophy," Löwith con-cluded, was born "not as a result of a regrettable 'miscue'" but rather "from the very conception of existence that simultaneously combats and absorbs the 'spirit of the age.'"[41]

This argument provides the essential background for assessing Löwith's comparative essay on the possible resemblance between Heidegger and Rosenzweig. Originally written during Löwith's tenure at the Hartford The-ological Seminary, the essay was first published in 1942 (in English) as "M. Heidegger and F. Rosenzweig, or, Temporality and Eternity." Prompted by Rosenzweig's own reflections on Heidegger, it acknowledges that the two philosophers shared much in common.[42] But Löwith concludes by insist-ing upon a deeper and fundamental difference, summarized in the distinc-tion between *eternity* and *temporality*. Not surprisingly, Löwith argues that it was this temporality (Heidegger's radical historicism) that best explains his readiness to join up with the Nazi cause. For Heidegger's choice arose "not—as naive people thought—[as] a deviation from the main path of his philosophy," but rather as "a consequence of his concept of historical exis-tence," which "only recognizes truths that are relative to the actual and proper." Löwith calls this Heidegger's "radical temporalization of truth and existence." It meant that Heidegger could find no anchor for his political

---

ed. Jerome Kohn (New York: Harcourt, Brace and Company, 1994), 163–87. Even in her cel-ebrated essay "Martin Heidegger at Eighty," Arendt is explicit in political outrage and sees Hei-degger's politics as symptomatic of a deeper flaw in his philosophy; orig. pub. *New York Review of Books*, October 1971, reprinted in Michael Murray, ed., *Heidegger and Modern Philosophy: Crit-ical Essays* (New Haven: Yale University Press, 1978), 293–303. An excellent assessment is Dana Villa, *Arendt and Heidegger: The Fate of the Political* (Princeton: Princeton University Press, 1996). Also see Richard Wolin, *Heidegger's Children* (Princeton: Princeton University Press, 2001).

41. As Löwith later explained, in *Heidegger: Denker in dürftiger Zeit*, he aimed to "break the spell of a sterile imitation on the part of his spellbound followers, and to make them conscious of the questionability of Heidegger's existential-historical thought." *Mein Leben*, 159.

42. Löwith writes that both Rosenzweig and Heidegger begin with "the naked individual," who is characterized as "finite existence as it precedes all established civilization." Both phi-losophers wish "to go back to the primary and essential things in a genuine experience of life." The new thinking of both Rosenzweig and Heidegger "knows that it is itself like everything else at every moment, time-bound, its own past and future, whereas the old philosophy endeavored to think timelessly." TE, 57.

beliefs outside the spirit of the age, and so his philosophy confirmed Nietzsche's insight that "after the decay of Christianity and of its morality 'nothing is any longer true' but 'everything is allowed'—namely everything which
man can take upon himself and afford to do." Löwith was thus convinced
that Heidegger's denial of theology was the singularly responsible factor in
the turn to Nazism:

> Heidegger destroyed by his turning away from Christianity the old tradition so
> thoroughly that finite time becomes the inmost meaning of being and eter-
> nity an illusion, whilst up to Hegel the Greek and Christian tradition had been
> alive, according to which true being was set in the Eternal or "always pres-
> ent."(TE, 75)

On Löwith's view, then, Heidegger was thrown into a historical trajectory
where National Socialism seemed destined to triumph, and as he believed
it represented the "inner truth" of the epoch, he could do nothing else but
devote himself with all his powers to its success. Heidegger's radical acceptance of "temporality" was thus the key to explaining his political debacle.

Heidegger's temporalism, claimed Löwith, indicated a profound disagreement with Rosenzweig:

> In contradistinction to Heidegger, Rosenzweig—owing to his actual inheri-
> tance, his Judaism, . . . was in the happy position of being able to hold up
> David's star of eternal truth in the midst of time. . . . God, who as creator and
> redeemer is beginning and end of his analyses of time, is neither "dead" nor
> "alive" but "truth" and "light." God is the truth . . . even if one day everything
> by which he made known his eternity in time . . . terminated where the eter-
> nal also finds its end: in eternity. (TE, 75)

Rosenzweig's philosophy of eternity and Heidegger's philosophy of temporality were thus radically opposed. For if Heidegger's historicism led ineluctably to moral nihilism, then correlatively, a philosophy of eternity provided the sole refuge from the moral disorientation and nihilistic politics of
the twentieth century. On this view, only traditional theology (Christian and
Jewish) and its Greek counterpart (the eternal Being of Platonism) could
supply the reliable antidote to the poisonous effects of radical historicism,
for only this tradition of "Western" metaphysics gave the human being a certain fix upon atemporal truth, while he would be otherwise set adrift in time
and the world.[43] Rosenzweig was supposedly inoculated against such relativism, both historical and moral, because he confirmed a traditionally reli-

---

43. To show the absurdity of radical historicism, Löwith (TE, 76) cites an essay by one of
Heidegger's students on "existential mathematics": see O. Becker, "Mathematische Existenz,"
*Jahrbuch für Philosophie und phenomenologische Forschung* 8 (1927).

gious metaphysics by linking temporal experience to God's atemporal Being. Thus Löwith's comparison between Rosenzweig and Heidegger turns out to be a comparison between the two most fundamental positions in Western thought—the metaphysical choice between temporality and eternity (TE, 76).

This argument is open to several objections. First, although Löwith documents a number of commonalties between Rosenzweig and Heidegger, he claims these indicate merely a shared starting point. It is only their disagreement that seems truly to matter, since it is here that Löwith finds a decisive, political difference. But one must object that such a conclusion would only be justified if one believes that politics is the most urgent dimension of human experience. Rosenzweig, however, did not share this belief.[44] Moreover, it cannot be sheer coincidence that what is arguably the central distinction of all Western metaphysics turns out to be the particular point of political disagreement between Rosenzweig and Heidegger. This begs the historical question as to why so many philosophers of other, quite divergent metaphysical perspectives also turned to Nazism.[45] More importantly, it seems facile to claim that it is this one disagreement alone that happens to provide the precise key to understanding Heidegger's political errors.

These objections should alert us to the fact that Löwith has misconstrued Rosenzweig's concept of eternity. For he implies that Rosenzweig's theoretical fix on eternity inoculated him entirely against Heidegger's historicist predicament. But if this is so, then there would be no innovation in Rosenzweig's new thinking. Rosenzweig's protests against Hegel notwithstanding, the new thinking on Löwith's interpretation would be little more than a restatement of the old metaphysics (common to both Christianity and Platonism), which divides the world into a sphere of timelessness (God) and a humbler, temporal reality (human experience). We are thus forced into an interesting predicament: either eternity in the customary sense is indeed the ultimate meaning of Rosenzweig's philosophy (in which case there is nothing truly novel about his metaphysical perspective), or Löwith has misunderstood the place of eternity in Rosenzweig's thought and he is mistaken to suggest that it represents the decisive difference between Rosenzweig and Heidegger.

---

44. Freund expressly rejects this same distinction, suggesting that for both Rosenzweig and Heidegger, "Human existence in its finitude and temporality [*Endlichkeit und Zeitlichkeit*]" determines for the philosophical task "its beginning-point, its method and goal." *Existenzphilosophie*, 1.

45. As Hans Sluga shows in *Heidegger's Crisis*, a great variety of philosophers succumbed to the temptations of National Socialism, many of them surpassing Heidegger in ardor. Many were neo-Platonists, neo-Kantians, neo-Hegelians, Nietzscheans, and so on. Thus the rejection of traditional metaphysics taken alone does not signal a predisposition to National Socialism.

Political concerns notwithstanding, Löwith's philosophical contrast is overdrawn. As he notes, Heidegger, though an "atheist" in scholarship, was a "theologian by tradition."[46] So it cannot be merely the abandonment of religion itself that is the culprit. Rather, Löwith should be arguing that Heidegger's political engagement resulted from the *misapplication* of an originally religious faith to the historical world: Heidegger's faith in Christ is abandoned, as Löwith notes. But the "hidden motto" of Heidegger's work is the essentially Lutheran confession: "unus quisque robustus sit in existentia sua"—which Heidegger then "*translates . . . into German.*"[47] This translation created a hazardous, and ultimately fatal, paradox, wherein Heidegger embraced contingency itself as the new absolute.

What Löwith misses, however, is that Rosenzweig's philosophy is marked by a similar habit of translation. To characterize it as an unproblematic expression of religious faith is misleading. For Löwith, eternity in Rosenzweig's thought was the very same as eternal truth. But this returns Rosenzweig to the dogmas of Platonist idealism he wished to escape.[48] In fact, Rosenzweig's new thinking articulates a theology that has fully absorbed the lessons of post-Nietzschean modernity. Rosenzweig himself invoked the

46. Elsewhere, Löwith characterizes Heidegger's thinking as a "godless theology," and he cites a key letter from 1921 in which Heidegger calls himself a "Christian theo*logian*" (emphasis in original). The letter to Löwith can be found in *Zur philosophischen Aktualität Heideggers*, ed. Dietrich Papenfuss and Otto Pöggler, vol. II of *Im Gespräch der Zeit* (Frankfurt: Klostermann, 1990), 27–32. Löwith also calls Heidegger a "displaced preacher" and notes that on the wall of Heidegger's office in Freiburg, there hung a painting of the crucifixion in the expressionist style. See *Mein Leben*, 31. Also see Löwith, "Phänomenologische Ontologie und protestantische Theologie," *Zeitschrift für Theologie und Kirche* (Neue Folge) 11, 2 (1930): 365–99; and in the same volume, Karl Heim, "Ontologie und Theologie," 325–38; and Rudolf Bultmann, "Die Geschichtlichkeit des Daseins und der Glaube," 339–64; see also Kurt Leese, "Vom religiösen Apriori, Ein Beitrag zum Problem der Existenz," 11, 2: 81–99. On Heidegger and religion, also see Theodore Kisiel, *The Genesis of Heidegger's "Being and Time"* (Berkeley: University of California Press, 1993), esp. chap. 2, "Theo-logical Beginnings"; Richard Kroner, "Heidegger's Private Religion," *Union Seminary Quarterly Review* 11, 4 (May 1956): 23–37; Hans Jonas, "Heidegger and Theology," in his *The Phenomenon of Life: Toward a Philosophical Biology* (New York: Harper and Row, 1966); Hans-Georg Gadamer, "Anrufung des entschwundenen Gottes," *Evangelische Kommentare* 10 (1977): 204; Richard Kerney and J. S. O'Leary, *Heidegger et la Question de Dieu* (Paris: Grasset, 1980); John D. Caputo, *Heidegger and Aquinas: An Essay on Overcoming Metaphysics* (New York: Fordham University Press, 1982); and John Macquarrie, *Heidegger and Christianity* (New York: Continuum Books, 1999).

47. Löwith, *Mein Leben*, 31 (my emphasis).

48. On Rosenzweig and "faith," see Paul R. Mendes-Flohr and Jehuda Reinharz, "From Relativism to Religious Faith: The Testimony of Franz Rosenzweig's Unpublished Diaries," LBIY, 1977, 161–74. And Julius Guttmann similarly categorizes Rosenzweig and Heidegger under existentialist philosophy. "Existence and Idea: Critical Observations on the Existentialist Philosophy," in *Scripta Hierosolymitana*, vol. 6 in Studies in Philosophy, ed. S. H. Bergman (Jerusalem: The Magnes Press of the Hebrew University, 1960), 9–40.

model of translation to justify this curious partnership between theology and modern atheistic thought: "Theological problems," he wrote, "want to be translated [*übersetzt*] into the human, and the human brought forth into the theological" (ND, 153). Rosenzweig's new thinking was therefore new precisely because it aimed to wrest itself free of the traditional, theological category of eternity, even while it struggled to find theological purpose within the confines of human, temporal life.

Against Löwith, I shall argue that Rosenzweig's work represents one of the most significant modern attempts to rethink the meaning of religious experience after the collapse of metaphysics. The key challenge of this philosophy was to articulate an understanding of redemption in a new, post-metaphysical key. Admittedly, this characterization of Rosenzweig still indicates his strong disagreement with Heidegger, who in his mature thought devoted scant attention to religion. But it would be rash to conclude that Rosenzweig's philosophy was therefore capable of sustaining some normative sense of "redemption" while Heidegger's philosophy could not. A central aim of this study will be to show that there is in fact a significant overlap between Rosenzweig and Heidegger on the question of what kind of ultimacy remains available within the confines of human experience once the traditional theological model of redemption is abandoned: I shall call this new sense of ultimacy *redemption-in-the-world*.

## JUDAISM AND WEIMAR MODERNISM

Rosenzweig's philosophy of redemption, uncomfortably situated at the interstices of modern philosophy and traditional religion, is best understood within the context of Weimar modernism. This is admittedly an unfamiliar perspective, since readers have grown accustomed to imagining that Rosenzweig belonged to a specifically Jewish stream of thought. Indeed, Rosenzweig himself helped to promote the idea that there is an ahistorical Judaism untouched by time. But ironically, this notion of an authentic and distinctive Jewish tradition was itself partly an invention. And while this may seem paradoxical, it is clear that the notion of an ahistorical Jewish existence took shape within history. In fact, it is a notion that cannot be explained apart from the peculiarly troubled patterns of German culture in the early twentieth century.[49]

49. Rosenzweig was one of the most important thinkers who have helped to forge our modern definition of Jewish cultural identity. His efforts to retrieve a usable past thus illustrate what Eric Hobsbawm has called "the invention of tradition." The term is also used by Michael Brenner, *The Renaissance of Jewish Culture in Weimar Germany* (New Haven: Yale University Press, 1996), 4, n. 12, citing Hobsbawm and Terence Ranger, eds., *The Invention of Tradition* (Cambridge: Cambridge University Press, 1984).

Rosenzweig arrived in an era of German Jewish history when its various thinkers were beginning to look askance at the assimilationist ideals that had governed their thought since the Enlightenment. Whereas German Jewish philosophy from Mendelssohn to Cohen upheld the value of cultural inclusion, Rosenzweig considered Jewish cultural separateness a thing to be cherished, at times even cultivated. Like many other German Jews of his generation, Rosenzweig resisted the older, assimilationist ideal, believing that it represented a betrayal of authentic Jewish identity. Like Gershom Scholem, Rosenzweig was born into a middle-class German Jewish household in which Judaism had become largely vehicle for the expression of German bourgeois values. He might well have agreed with Scholem's famous polemic against the nineteenth-century historical movement, the Wissenschaft des Judentums, which attempted "to reduce Judaism to a purely spiritual, ideal phenomenon."[50] As Michael Brenner observes:

> Jewish culture in Weimar Germany was characterized neither by a radical break with the past nor by a return to it. Indeed, it used distinct forms of Jewish traditions, marking them as authentic, and presented them according to the demands of contemporary taste and modern cultural forms of expression. What might have appeared as authenticity was in fact a modern innovation.[51]

Thus to be an authentic Jew now required that one call upon all of one's available cultural resources. These did not need to be borrowed from Weimar culture, because German Jews were themselves lively participants within it. Peter Gay, coining a now-classic phrase, once called this remarkable moment of intellectual and artistic creation the culture of "the outsider as insider."[52] As this phrase suggests, many of the self-proclaimed outsiders of the Weimar era were not really as external to the culture as they might have wished. As a self-professed avant-garde, they consciously adopted an oppositional stance toward the German mainstream, but this could hardly hide the fact that many of them belonged to the most successful sector of the German educated middle class. Indeed, their education and considerable cultural inheritances were prerequisites for their successful rebellion.

This paradox is evident throughout Rosenzweig's writing. In his philosophy as well as his correspondence, one finds constant allusion to the idea

---

50. This reduction "represents a form of censorship of the Jewish past. . . . From the point of view of the Enlightenment-minded, purified, rational Judaism of the nineteenth century [much of this past] seemed not properly usable and hence was thrown out as un-Jewish or, at the least, half pagan." Scholem, "The Science of Judaism—Then and Now," in his *The Messianic Idea in Judaism and Other Essays on Jewish Spirituality* (New York: Schocken Books, 1971), 303–13.

51. Brenner, *Renaissance of Jewish Culture*, 5.

52. Gay, *Weimar Culture: The Outsider as Insider* (New York: Harper Torchbooks, 1968).

that Jews constitute a distinctive group that is isolated from the other nations of the world and from history itself. His early doctoral dissertation, a study of Hegel's political theory, in many respects anticipates this idea, although there the outsider status is found in Hegel's portrait of Jesus. Rosenzweig's encounter with the German philosophy of his own day, especially neo-Kantianism, bespeaks a peculiar fascination with those luminaries of the philosophical tradition whom he regarded as anticipating his own rebellion. In his assessment of Hermann Cohen's later philosophy of religion, Rosenzweig identified a moment of existential Judaism breaking free of its German Idealist framework. In his German-language translation of the Hebrew Bible (a project pursued cooperatively with Martin Buber), Rosenzweig attempted to put these ideas into practice. For while Rosenzweig and Buber claimed to have merely restored to the German text the distinctive flavor of the original, this "restoration" gave birth to a text whose substance and style reflected the modernist tendencies of the period. Here, too, we can recognize the greater paradox of German Jewish intellectuals in Weimar culture. Even when asserting their Jewish identity as a "foreign" inheritance from beyond the German sphere, they gave expression to their identity as German intellectuals as well.[53]

Quite often, this yearning for an authentic Jewish identity was expressed as a thirst for an ostensibly forgotten past. But the longing to return to "archaic" forms, though often applied to Jewish themes, was not specifically Jewish in origin. Across the spectrum of Weimar culture (and European culture more generally), one may chart a diversely structured mood of rebellion against the values of the enlightened world; many intellectuals yearned for what was more "original" than modernity. But little indicates a thinker's modernity so much as nostalgia for what is thoroughly un-modern. As Theodor Adorno observed, interwar primitivism expressed the quintessentially bourgeois desire to perform its own undoing. And while one need not agree with Adorno's judgment, he deftly exposed its moment of artifice in his phrase "the jargon of authenticity."[54]

53. In the poem "Mein Volk," Else Lasker-Schüler bemoaned that "the rock grows brittle / From which I spring. / To which my Songs-of God I sing . . . " (ellipsis in original). But the pastoral effects used to evoke the Jewish past were expressionistic devices shared with other contemporary German poets, such as Gottfried Benn. The poem ends: "I have flowed so far away / From the wine ferment / Of my blood. / And yet forever, endlessly the echo / in me, / When eastward, / awesomely, / The brittle rock of bone, / My people, / Cries out to God." Lasker-Schüler, *Hebräische Balladen* (Berlin: Paul Cassirer, 1920).

54. See, e.g., Adorno, *The Philosophy of Modern Music*, trans. Anne G. Mitchell and Wesley V. Blomster (New York: Seabury, 1973; orig. pub. in German, 1948), esp. "Stravinsky and Restoration," 135–217. For many left-intellectuals of the Weimar period, the politics of primitivism were obviously reactionary. See, e.g., *Die Expressionismusdebatte: Materialien zu einer marxistischen*

The dialectic of modernist antimodernism is notable in the Weimar era among those German Jewish intellectuals who longed for a "primordial" Jewish past. Walter Benjamin, in his famous remarks on Klee's painting *Angelus Novus* (1920), left us with a helpful allegory of this dual orientation. According to Benjamin, the angel turns his face backward in yearning for the paradise he has abandoned. But he cannot return, because his wings are caught in a storm that blows him forward in time. This may serve as a remarkably apt image for the predicament of assimilated German Jewish intellectuals in their longing for an authentic heritage. Clearly, many of them were bent on reversing the assimilationist ideals that had governed German Jewish life since the Enlightenment. The Weimar era saw an abandonment by many German Jewish intellectuals of the liberal political vision and progressive cultural stance that had typified many of their ancestors. But they could not help but become cultural innovators even while they wished to be reclaiming a lost tradition. Like Klee's angel, they looked longingly to the past, even while the surrounding storm propelled them irresistibly into the future.[55]

It is helpful to consider this context of Weimar modernism when assessing Rosenzweig's philosophy. The new thinking is torn between its celebration of theological origins and its no less passionate celebration of post-Nietzschean modernity. As I will show, its vision of redemption is itself marked by the difficult negotiation between these two poles. On the one hand, it suggested that philosophy could only succeed by returning to the "primordial" insights of religion. But, on the other hand, it demanded a violent break with prior academic thought. Moreover, this turn from philosophy to religion was itself embedded within a larger cultural transformation, as I shall explain below.

---

*Realismuskonzeption*, ed. Hans-Jürgen Schmitt (Frankfurt am Main: Suhrkamp Verlag, 1973), abridged and translated in Ernst Bloch et al., *Aesthetics and Politics*, ed. Ronald Taylor (London: New Left Books, 1977). Also see Eugene Lunn, *Marxism and Modernism* (Berkeley: University of California Press, 1982). For the reading of Heideggerian language as a "jargon," see Adorno, *Die Jargon der Eigentlichkeit: Zur deutschen Ideologie* (Frankfurt am Main: Suhrkamp Verlag, 1964); in English *The Jargon of Authenticity*, trans. Knut Tarnowski and Frederic Will (Evanston, Ill.: Northwestern University Press, 1973).

55. Benjamin, "Theses on the Philosophy of History," *Neue Rundschau* 61, 3 (1950); reprinted in Benjamin, *Illuminations*, trans. Harry Zohn (New York: Schocken Books, 1969). On the Weimar Jewish turn against Enlightenment values, see Steven Aschheim, "German Jews beyond *Bildung* and Liberalism: The Radical Jewish Revival in the Weimar Republic," in his *Culture and Catastrophe: German and Jewish Confrontations with National Socialism and Other Crises* (New York: New York University Press, 1996). Michael Brenner observes: "Much of Jewish culture in Weimar Germany was, to rephrase Goethe's Mephistopheles, . . . a part of that power which ever wants the old, yet forever creates the new." *Renaissance of Jewish Culture*, 5.

## PHILOSOPHICAL EXPRESSIONISM

On January 12, 1917, when Rosenzweig was stationed on the Macedonian front, he received from his parents a package, containing among other things a copy of Kafka's short story *The Judgment,* which had been published earlier that month. The story seems to have affected Rosenzweig deeply, no doubt in part because it concerned a conflict between father and son that struck a personal chord. He wrote his parents that he read the story "immediately," and found in it an allegory for the struggle between expressionism (embodied in the religious son) and impressionism (represented by the "natural scientist" father).[56]

Upon closer examination, it seems that Rosenzweig unburdened his own ideas onto a text that was innocent of these meanings. The alignment of each character with an aesthetic style—the father as impressionist, the son as expressionist—finds little support in Kafka's tale. Nor can we find much textual justification for Rosenzweig's claims that the father-impressionist is a natural scientist while the son-expressionist corresponds to the man of religion. The other Franz however, like Kafka himself, belonged to an age in which the struggle between fathers and sons had become a commonplace literary trope. Many of the major writers of the German expressionist movement tend to associate the father with bourgeois values of rationality and order, while the son becomes an archetype of more primal, religious, and anarchistic needs. Peter Gay has even gone so far as to suggest that the prominence of this theme in Weimar culture reflects a society-wide Oedipal conflict, culminating in Nazism's "revenge of the father."[57]

The paradigm of expressionist intergenerational conflict is Walter Hasenclever's play *The Son,* first written in 1914. One of the central conflicts of the drama has to do with radically divergent aesthetic and religious values. Early on, the son despairs of his father, "And why does he not speak to me of God?" And, according to the son, the father ignores all that is "worldly and beautiful." He thus forbids his son to read Goethe and demands that he read Kant, though the son complains that Kant "does not inspire me." Yet rebellion soon follows when the son experiences a transformative revela-

---

56. *Briefe,* N.121, An die Eltern (12.1.1917), 151. Rosenzweig's difficulties with his father are well documented; in one letter he refers explicitly to "ugly scenes." N.45, An den Vater (Freiburg, 1.7.1910), 52–53. Also see, e.g., N.214, An die Mutter (5.4.1918), 290–91; N.215, An die Mutter (7.4.1918), 291–92; and N.222, An die Mutter (16.4.1918), 299–300.

57. Gay, *Weimar Culture.* Indeed, filial rebellion is a virtual cliché of German expressionism. A useful summary is Walter Sokel, *The Writer in Extremis: Expressionism in Twentieth-Century German Literature* (Stanford, Calif.: Stanford University Press, 1959); also see Richard Sheppard, "German Expressionism," in *Modernism, 1890–1930,* ed. Malcolm Bradbury and James McFarlane (Middlesex: Penguin Books, 1976), 274–91.

tion *(Offenbarung)*. Quitting his father's home, he becomes the spokesman
for a new faith:

> O world, do take with me my evening meal!
>
> .   .   .   .   .   .   .   .   .   .   .   .   .
>
> You highest sphere of celestial faces—
> give me flight to a new being [zu einem neuen Sein]! . . .
> I must live, I must experience.[58]

As this summary may suggest, Hasenclever's expressionistic drama of
filial and theological rebellion articulates many of the ideas found in Rosenzweig's work. Rosenzweig, too, preferred Goethe to Kant, and for a time
contemplated becoming a Goethe scholar. Like the son in Hasenclever's
play, Rosenzweig's longing for religious eternity expresses a thirst for life,
not transcendence.[59] Like the son, Rosenzweig, too, was a rebel against
ossified tradition; he believed that his philosophy represented a break with
all previous thought. Indeed, one of the recurrent themes of Rosenzweig's
new thinking is that the past conventions of philosophy are without life, like
the father whose corpse is abandoned at the play's end. Now if Rosenzweig
associated the son in Kafka's story with both religion and expressionism,
one may draw a line between Rosenzweig's philosophy and the wider field
of expressionist culture. I would therefore propose that we apply the term
*philosophical expressionism* to Rosenzweig's new thinking. I shall further
suggest that this term may be fruitfully applied to Heidegger's philosophy
as well.[60]

---

58. Hasenclever, *Der Sohn: Ein Drama in fünf Akten* (Leipzig: Kurt Wolff Verlag, 1914). Citations are from Hasenclever, *Sämtliche Werke,* vol. II, part 1, "Stücke bis 1924" (233–322), ed.
Dieter Breuer and Bernd Witte (Mainz: v. Hase und Koehler Verlag, 1992), Act I, scene i, my
translations; ellipsis after "being!" in original. The son finds that "I believe that everything in
the world exists in profound community." And in contrast to his father's stuffy and respectable
exterior, he is given to bouts of ecstasy: "Birth and Existence," he exclaims, "O happiness! I will
be eternal, eternal . . . "; Act II, scene i (ellipsis in original).

59. The son longs not to transcend the world, but to inhabit it more thoroughly and with
greater immediacy. Similarly, the *Star of Redemption* ends with an exhortation to enter "life"; see
SE, 472 (E, 424). For Rosenzweig, the death of his father meant that he could at last assume
the mantle of a new and more "vital" Jewish identity no longer defined through family-ties:
"Unto this point I was only connected to the old earth of my people through my father. Now
[since the father's death] *I myself stood immediately within,* was myself the living member in the
long chain of generations, and *Abraham, Isaac and Jacob were immediately my fathers.*" GB
(5.4.1918), 67; my emphasis.

60. Expressionism primarily names a style in Central Europe's visual arts from circa 1905
(the founding of *Die Brücke* in Dresden) to the mid-1920s (when it clashed, sometimes fruitfully, with the *neue Sachlichkeit*). One of the earliest uses of the term applied it to an exhibition
of the Berlin Secession in 1911. By 1914 it was identified as a rebellion against the older
French school of impressionism. See Wolf-Dieter Lube, *Expressionism* (New York: Oxford University Press, 1972), esp. 18. In literature and poetry, expressionism was defined by Kasimir

To be sure, expressionism has been used designate many different things and so may fail to designate any one of them with precision.[61] While German expressionism in particular seems fraught with contradictory impulses, the themes of finitude and isolation are pervasive.[62] Franz Herwig believed that the expressionists were motivated by social longings they could not achieve: "What I sense in them is the impassioned cry for the ethical, the yearning for it which they themselves will never fulfill, but which some other human being will fulfill who matures far away from the group." Ludwig Marcuse suggests that expressionism was an essentially apolitical movement, "a lamentation and a gospel of salvation." And Walter Sokel has very convincingly pointed out the overwhelming theme of isolation that runs through much of expressionist literature.[63]

---

Edschmid in the 1919 essay "Über den dichterischen Expressionismus," which noted that while the message of expressionism was timeless, it had only now seized "an entire generation." In *Über den Expressionismus in der Literatur und die neue Dichtung* (Berlin: Erich Reiß Verlag, 1919), 71. As applied to German culture more generally, see Eckart von Sydow, *Die deutsche expressionistische Kultur und Malerei* (Berlin: Furche Verlag, 1920). On Heidegger's expressionism, and the "expressionist crucifixion scene" in his office, see Löwith, *Mein Leben*, 28–30. See also Fritz Heinemann, *Neue Wege der Philosophie: Geist, Leben, Existenz. Eine Einführung in die Philosophie der Gegenwart* (Leipzig: Quelle und Meyer, 1929), esp. xviii. A frequent contributor to the German Jewish intellectual journal *Der Morgen* and an advocate of Heidegger's work throughout the late 1920s and early 1930s, Heinemann authored this survey of German thought, which pairs Rosenzweig and Heidegger under the rubric of *Existenzphilosophie*, (a term Heinemann himself apparently devised). At Davos, Heidegger expressed his dislike of this label to Heinemann. Their meeting is recorded in Heinemann, *Existenzphilosophie: Lebendig oder Tot?* (Stuttgart: Kohlhammer, 1954), 11–13.

61. Thus the publisher Kurt Wolff's complaint that "[p]eople are still (and even more than ever nowadays) trying, through the concept 'Expressionism,' to give a group of writers who were getting into print between 1910 and 1925 the stamp of collectivity the never possessed." "Vom Verlegen im allgemeinen und von der Frage: Wie kommen Verleger und Autoren zusammen," in *Expressionismus: Aufzeichnungen und Erinnerungen der Zeitgenossen,* ed. Paul Raabe and Karl Ludwig Schneider (Freiburg: Walter Verlag, 1965), 282-294, quote at 292.

62. For example, while most often it seemed to celebrate isolation, at times it could also embrace the social world. As Oskar Kokoschka (quoted by Peter Selz) noted, "Expressionism does not live in an ivory tower, it calls upon a fellow being whom it awakens." Selz further observed that "The expressionist artist is not satisfied with formal construction or *belle peinture.* He seeks rather the I-Thou relationship of a Martin Buber, and hopes to establish a similar dialogue between himself and the observer." *German Expressionist Painting* (Berkeley: University of California Press, 1957), v–vii.

63. Herwig, 1916, cited in Richard Sheppard, "German Expressionist Poetry," in his *Modernism*, 390. L. Marcuse, "Ein bißchen Sintflut," in *Expressionismus: Aufzeichnungen und Erinnerungen der Zeitgenossen,* ed. Paul Raabe (Olten und Freiburg im Breisgau: Walter Verlag, 1965), 300–305, quote at 301. Marcuse further states that expressionism announced a "belief in the ahistorical, atemporal rebellion of the timeless." It desired a "revolution," but one that "aimed not like that of the Young Germans at bringing about changes in institutions in society, but at a new view of the world." It was "essentially alien to politics" (301). Sokel, *The Writer in Extremis,* chap. 3, "Poeta Dolorosus," 55-82. Similarly, Rosenzweig's estrangement from his

Because of its various manifestations, it may seem that introducing a philosophical kind of expressionism would only compound the confusion. But as many past critics have often observed, German expressionism as an aesthetic movement bears close comparison with existential philosophy, so there may therefore be some justification for a new category indicating their connection.[64] But *existentialism* (a term once attached to Rosenzweig and Heidegger) is inaccurate, especially given its association with Sartre, Camus, and Beckett. In noting the specifically German features of Rosenzweig's philosophy, a label that carries exclusively German valences is preferable. And *Existenz-philosophie* (a term used by contemporaries to describe both Rosenzweig and Heidegger) while once acceptable to some, does little to designate any precise conceptual issues.[65]

The salient feature of philosophical expressionism is a theologically inflected pathos of isolation. This is combined with a rebellious attitude toward prior intellectual traditions and a resentful sense that such traditions have missed what is most fulfilling in life. Obviously this is a vague sketch, and I would caution readers that since this "cultural" context cannot be defined with precision, it possesses little explanatory force. But while I shall rarely address the matter of philosophical expressionism outright, it may at times prove helpful to recall that the intellectual concerns discussed here were themselves part of a larger shift in cultural temperament.

### PHILOSOPHY, SCIENCE, AND CRITIQUE

"In Berlin ist die Philosophie mit Stumpf und Riehl ausgerottet worden." In his memoir of friendship with Walter Benjamin, Gershom Scholem relates how, during the winter semester of 1916–17, his friend offered this bit of humor in order to dissuade Scholem from enrolling in a Kant seminar, which was to be taught by the once-illustrious professor of philosophy Alois

---

father was an expression of his *distance* from civic life: he experienced his father as radically different in temperament, so much that he imagined that they were less like father and son than like "two quite distinct brothers, about whom *one would not wonder if they were really distinct in every way.*" Unlike Franz, the father "spoke so purely the language of *the outside, of the market, the street, the courthouse.*" GB (29.4.1918), 86–87; my emphasis.

64. Because *expressionism* embraces diverse regions of German culture, the term may help us to understand how the philosophy of the time is associated with its poetry, its drama, and its painting. This is particularly appropriate since both Rosenzweig and Heidegger possessed unusual sensitivity to language, to poetry, to painting, and even music. Cf. Selz, *German Expressionist Painting,* vii.

65. Heidegger considered both terms inappropriate. On his quarrel with Sartre over the meaning of existentialism, see "Letter on Humanism," in Heidegger, *Pathmarks,* ed. William McNeill (Cambridge: Cambridge University Press, 1998), 239–76. On *Existenzphilosophie,* see note 60 above.

Riehl.[66] Though the joke was once clear among Berlin philosophy students, shifting intellectual fashions have obscured its meaning: Riehl was an advocate of the so-called critical philosophy, a derivative stream in the neo-Kantian current that still dominated the German philosophical community in the first decades of the twentieth century. Carl Stumpf was considered one of Berlin's important representatives of the new discipline of "scientific" phenomenology. With the substitution of these names ("Stumpf und Riehl") for the German words for "root and branch" ("Stumpf und Stiehl"), the complaint that modern philosophy has become deracinated became a pun: "In Berlin philosophy has been destroyed [through the influence of] Stumpf and Riehl."

For the generation of German philosophers who came of age around the time of the First World War, the philosophical model that had dominated the universities since the last third of the nineteenth century had ceased to arouse enthusiasm. This was particularly true of the older vision of philosophy conceived according to the scientific model. Riehl had argued in a famous essay, "On Scientific and Non-Scientific Philosophy" (1883), that the task of philosophy was first and foremost that of scientific criticism. Stumpf, the "grandfather" of phenomenology, was the teacher of Edmund Husserl, who famously defined philosophy as a "rigorous science" *(strenge Wissenschaft)*.[67] Although one must naturally distinguish between critical idealism and Husserlian phenomenology, Husserl, like Stumpf and Riehl, was a vehement critic of both psychologism and historicism, and his famous call that philosophers return "to the things themselves" was intended as a rejection of the more metaphysical tendencies in German thought, such as neo-Hegelianism and Wilhelm Dilthey's life-philosophy.

Academic philosophy in the Wilhelmine period was predominantly conceived as a critical rather than speculative enterprise. The paradigmatic philosophy of the time was neo-Kantianism. At Marburg, Hermann Cohen and Paul Natorp helped to promote an understanding of Kant's philosophy as a study in the conceptual underpinnings of natural science. And from the last quarter of the nineteenth century until the collapse of the Second Reich, the Marburg school remained one of the most powerful in all of Germany. Hans-Georg Gadamer recalls that in his youth one spoke of a student at last

66. Scholem, *Walter Benjamin: The Story of a Friendship,* trans. Harry Zohn (New York: Schocken Books, 1981), 21.

67. Riehl, "Über wissenschaftliche und nicht-wissenschaftliche Philosophie"; orig. Riehl's *Antrittsrede,* a public lecture upon assuming the Freiburg chair in philosophy in 1883; published in Riehl, *Philosophische Studien aus vier Jahrzehnten* (Leipzig: Quelle und Meyer, 1925). Husserl, "Philosophie als strenge Wissenschaft," *Logos* 1 (1911; J. C. B. Mohr). Republished in book form, Frankfurt am Main: Vittorio Klostermann, 1981. In English: *Phenomenology and the Crisis of Philosophy,* trans. Quentin Lauer (New York: Harper Torchbooks, 1965).

"going to Marburg" as a marker of philosophical arrival.[68] Significantly, Hermann Cohen, the true founder of the Marburg school, was the only unbaptised German Jew to have achieved the status of full professor of philosophy in the German university system. Of Cohen's many pupils, only Ernst Cassirer eventually surpassed his teacher in accomplishment, extending the neo-Kantian investigation of a priori forms into the wider sphere of culture, until at last the older methods were largely unrecognizable.[69]

The dominance of neo-Kantian philosophy in the Wilhelmine period echoed the broader, cultural veneration for Kant. But for younger students, this authority often felt oppressive.[70] Robert Musil's spiritually disoriented hero Törleß is given a copy of Kant's *Critique of Pure Reason,* with the grave announcement, "Here is Philosophy."[71] But while Törleß continues to believe the book contains the ultimate answers, he never dares to look inside. Across the intellectual landscape, one finds similar expressions of discontent. Karl Jaspers recalls finding Husserl's philosophical perspective both "naïve and pretentious"—it had put "an end to everything that could be called philosophy in the great sense of the word." Gadamer writes of the "tortuous" chains of argument that he associated with neo-Kantians such as Cassirer, Eugen Kühnemann, and Julius Guttmann. And Eugen Rosenstock-

68. On the rise of neo-Kantianism, see Klaus Köhnke, *Entstehung und Aufstieg des Neukantianismus* (Frankfurt am Main: Suhrkamp Verlag, 1986). Even the competing school of neo-Hegelian philosophy was opposed as irrationalist. Wilhelm Windelband, a leading neo-Kantian of the Southwestern school, warned his colleagues, "Philosophy that still wishes to be an autonomous science must vanquish its 'metaphysical tendencies.'" "Die Erneuerung des Hegelianismus," in his *Präludien: Aufsätze und Reden zur Philosophie und ihrer Geschichte* (Tübingen: J. C. B. Mohr, Paul Siebeck, 1915), I: 273–89. Gadamer, *Philosophical Apprenticeships,* trans. Robert Sullivan (Cambridge, Mass.: MIT Press, 1985), 7.

69. John Michael Krois, "Cassirer, Neo-Kantianism and Metaphysics," *Revue de Métaphysique et de Morale* 4 (1992): 437–53.

70. See esp. the chapter "Die erdrückende Autorität Kants" in Peter Wust, *Die Auferstehung der Metaphysik* (Leipzig: Felix Meiner, 1920).

71. "Now, in Törleß's hearing the name Kant had never been uttered except in passing and then in the tone in which one refers to some awe-inspiring holy man. And Törleß could not think anything but that with Kant the problems of philosophy had been finally solved, so that since then it had become futile for anyone to concern himself with the subject. . . . At home these men's works were kept in the book case with the green glass in Papa's study, and Törleß knew this book case was never opened except to display its contents to a visitor. It was like a shrine of some divinity to which one does not readily draw nigh and which one venerates only because one is glad that thanks to its existence there are certain things one need no longer bother about." Musil, *Young Törless,* trans. Eithne Wilkins and Ernst Kaiser (New York: Noonday Press, 1955), 115. A similar image is in Gadamer's memoir: "The first book of philosophy I picked up was Kant's *Critique of Pure Reason.* . . . [I]t was in my father's library. . . . Thus was I initiated to philosophy during my first academic vacation. I really brooded over the book, but not the slightest understandable thought slipped out of it." *Philosophical Apprenticeships,* 3.

Huessy, in a 1916 letter to Rosenzweig, expressed a marked revulsion toward the entire panoply of neo-idealist "Schools," which in his view had "laid waste to the noblest of human powers."[72]

In the first decades of the twentieth century this older model of philosophy and its potent combination of German Idealist methodology and modern scientific values began to arouse great frustration. Disillusionment with the older model of idealist thought was especially intense among that generation of German philosophers that had come of age around the time of the First World War. These students were, in Scholem's words, "proponents of radical demands." They regarded their professors with both disappointment and disdain, and they felt an increasing admiration toward the various "outsiders" of the German canon. Against the rationalist tradition (Kant, Hegel, and Schiller), the younger generation drew inspiration instead from its rebels (Schelling, Feuerbach, Kierkegaard, Schopenhauer, and Nietzsche). Against the older values of science, idealism, and critique, they developed a new vocabulary of religion, vitalism, and *Existenz*. Scholem summarized their view as "a positive attitude toward metaphysics."[73]

By the beginning of the First World War, although the neo-Kantian schools still dominated the German universities, many students were now inclined to see their idealist training as mere preparation.[74] It was a common sentiment that one must return to the source-texts themselves, not bothering with previous academic interpretation. Rather than reject the older canon, they aimed to force it to speak in a new way. In a letter to Rosenzweig, Rosenstock-Huessy advanced this proposal, which anticipates what Heidegger later called a "destruction" of the philosophical tradition:

> The root of the scholastic and Kantian errors seems to me to be quickly indicated: they take the truths in which logic is embodied as "purely logical" truths in opposition to others in which logic is *not* embodied. I would like to go

72. Jaspers, *Philosophy*, trans. E. B. Ashton (Chicago: University of Chicago Press, 1969), I: 6–7. Similarly, Scholem writes that "I cannot recall either of us ever speaking of our university teachers with enthusiasm." He recalls being wholly uninspired by Ernst Cassirer's lectures on pre-Socratic philosophy, while Heinrich Rickert's lectures left Benjamin similarly cold. *Walter Benjamin*, 21. Gadamer, *Philosophical Apprenticeships*, 5. Rosenstock-Huessy further complains in his letter to Rosenzweig: "What a veritable hell of timeless, wordless, and countless abstractions these Gorlands, Riezlers, Kroners, etc., bring to light!" *Briefe*, Eugen Rosenstock-Huessy to Franz Rosenzweig ([October 4, 1916]), 662–65; quote at 664.

73. Scholem, *Walter Benjamin*, 21.

74. Rosenzweig confessed to Rosenstock-Huessy: "It is so long since I had any cause to bother myself over the Kantians. Even when I was reading Kant himself (lately it was the *ewigen Frieden*, and in February the *Religion* . . . ), I did not find any reason to turn to them." "One must have passed through one of them," he concluded, "it does not matter which." But "afterwards one need only to bother himself further with the master, the 'good Master,' long since dead." *Briefe*, An Eugen Rosenstock-Huessy (undated, from 1916), 674.

through Kant's Critiques just to see how far, sentence by sentence, they themselves are metaphysical in their formal rhetorical, illogical structure.[75]

Like Rosenstock-Huessy, many writers in the early 1920s began to speak of the new philosophical sensibility as indicating a "resurrection of metaphysics."[76] As I will demonstrate in the chapters that follow, it was clear that they meant something quite different than metaphysics as it had been customarily defined. They no longer believed, as the neo-idealists before them, that the task of philosophy was to provide the human being with an intellectual grasp of the Absolute. They feared what Georg Trakl called "eternity's icy wave," believing that it might drown the individual rather than redeem him.[77] Against idealism's promise of transcendence, many of the new philosophers believed that the true task of philosophy is to help the human being toward a deeper appreciation of his finitude.

One of the first examples of this remarkable new vision and its strategy of reversal is Rosenzweig's *Star of Redemption,* which commences in a tone of grandiose sarcasm:

> From Death, from the fear of death, begins all knowledge of the All. To throw off the fear of the earthly [die Angst des Irdischen], to rob death of its poisonous sting . . . , thus philosophy deceives itself. (SE, 3 [E, 3] my translation)

### METAPHYSICS AND THE NEW THINKING

Two essays, appearing roughly four years apart, help bring into focus the above complaint against traditional philosophy. The first is Rosenzweig's "The New Thinking" ("Das neue Denken") published in *Der Morgen* in October 1925. The second is Heidegger's "Was ist Metaphysik?", which was first delivered as a public lecture at Freiburg in July, 1929 and published later that same year. These texts may be usefully compared, as they are both manifestos, each of them striving to provide a kind of overview of the new type of philosophy born during the 1920s. Moreover, each of these two texts in its own distinctive fashion offers a rejoinder to the older definition of the philosophical task propounded by Husserl and Riehl. Taken together, they provide a vivid portrait of the new philosophical style.

---

75. *Briefe,* (October 4, 1916), 664. This is analogous to Heidegger's efforts in *Kant und das Problem der Metaphysik;* on Heidegger's "reversal" of the neo-Kantian tradition, see chapter 6.

76. See, for example, Ludwig Landgrebe, *Major Problems in Contemporary European Philosophy,* trans. K. Reinhardt (New York: Ungar Publishers, 1966).

77. Trakl warned in his 1914 poem "Lament" that "Eternity's icy wave / Would swallow the golden image / Of man." The original reads: "Des Menschen goldnes Bildnis / Verschlänge die eisige Woge / Der Ewigkeit. An schaurigen Riffen / Zerschellt der purpurne Leib . . . / Sieh ein ängstlicher Kahn versink / Unter Sternen." "Klage II," in Trakl, *Poems and Prose,* bilingual edition, trans. Alexander Stillmark (London: Libris, 2001), 124–25.

What is initially striking is that both essays begin by appealing to science as the ultimate arbiter of truth. Rosenzweig writes of "common sense" *(gesunde Menschenverstand)* that, "[t]he new philosophy . . . does nothing more than make the 'method' of sound common sense into the method of scientific thinking" (ND, 149). Heidegger's essay begins with the insight that "science is exceptional in that, in a way peculiar to it, it gives the matter itself explicitly and solely the first and last word. In such impartiality of inquiring . . . a peculiarly delineated submission to beings themselves obtains, in order that they may reveal themselves" (WM, 96). But upon closer examination, both of these appeals to science *(Wissenschaft)* appear somewhat disingenuous. Rosenzweig is toying with the idea of "science" only because it makes "common sense" seem all the wiser. "All philosophy," he writes, "has asked after the 'essence' [*Wesen*] . . . . This is this question by which it is distinguished from the unphilosophical thinking of sound common sense. [The latter] never bothers to ask what a thing 'actually' [*eigentlich*] is" (ND, 143). In a similar fashion, Heidegger writes, "According to the idea behind them, in the sciences we approach what is essential in all things" *(zum Wesentlichen aller Dinge).* But "no amount of scientific rigor attains to the seriousness of metaphysics. Philosophy can never be measured by the standard of the idea of science" (WM, 25).

Both of these definitions seem to contain oblique (and somewhat disapproving) references to Husserlian phenomenology, which was most often characterized as a "scientific" investigation of the "essence" of the thing at hand. But what truly unites Rosenzweig and Heidegger is not simply their common antipathies for the older methods. Both of them explore what this "scientific" mode of questioning means for the human being. In his whimsical posthumously published *Das Büchlein vom gesunden und kranken Menschenverstand* (The little book of sick and healthy common sense), Rosenzweig showed how this quasi-phenomenological concern for the "essence" of a thing lifts not only the object, but the philosopher as well, from the stream of time. Freezing the world "on the pinpoint of the detemporalizing question," the thinker too becomes paralyzed, and ultimately finds himself in a "hospital," where only the strong medication of "common sense" can cure him of his illness. For Heidegger too, the phenomenological fixation on the "scientific" as opposed to the "natural" attitude has highly negative consequences for the human being who questions. In evaluating the scientific mode, we must take into account "the way scientific man secures to himself what is most properly his" (WM English, 109).

For both Rosenzweig and Heidegger, then, science is ultimately superficial. It enjoys a certain "security" only by remaining stubbornly fixed on beings. Thus Heidegger: "What should be examined are beings only, and besides that—nothing." This "nothing" *(Nichts)* is "rejected precisely by science, given up as a nullity." But what science denies is in fact its unacknowledged foundation. Thought itself does not think the "nothing" so much as find its origin there: "Being held out into the nothing—as Dasein is—on the ground of concealed anxiety makes man a lieutenant of the nothing." Thus it is in the experience of nothing that human existence begins. In the factical (rather than logical) negation of Dasein, "beings as a whole, in accord with their most proper possibility—that is, in a finite way—come to themselves" (WM English, 110). Metaphysics, Heidegger concludes, "belongs to the 'nature of man.'" With this rather abstract conclusion, Heidegger has reversed the idealist order of priorities. It is no longer the human being who "reveals" the world as it is; rather, Being reveals itself only in Dasein when the latter is compelled to realize its own finitude. Similar abstractions introduce Book 1 of Rosenzweig's *Star of Redemption,* entitled, "God and His Being, or, Metaphysics" ("Gott und sein Sein, oder, Metaphysik"). Here Rosenzweig writes: "Of God we know nothing. But this Nothing-knowledge [*Nichtswissen*] is a Nothing-knowledge of God. As such it is the beginning of our Knowledge of him." Rosenzweig protests against the "scientific" *(wissenschaftliche)* mode of questioning, where the "nothing" is little more than negation, and "one concept among many."[78]

There are important differences between Heidegger and Rosenzweig in their discussion of the "nothing." Rosenzweig affirms that "God's freedom is born of the original negation of the Nothing" (SE, 32 [E, 29]). Heidegger objects to this religious definition: "ex nihilo fit—ens creatum" forces the nothing to "become the counter-concept of being" while the actual "question of the nothing" is still not posed (WM English, 110). But it appears that Rosenzweig and Heidegger are at least operating in a common intellectual horizon. For each of them, metaphysics now designates the opposite of science, and only metaphysics can properly discover the "nothing" as the origin of Being. Traditional philosophy-as-science denies this "nothing" has a place and refuses, as Rosenzweig says coyly, to see that the nothing is in fact "something." Philosophy thus creates for itself the illusion that it is self-sufficient, or infinite in scope. But this self-sufficiency is an illusion, as the "nothing" reveals. Even "transcendence" now suffers a reversal of its conventional meaning: "Being itself," Heidegger concludes, "is essentially finite [*endlich*] and reveals itself [*sich . . . offenbart*] only in the transcendence of Dasein which is held out into the nothing" (WM English, 110).

Heidegger and Rosenzweig are much alike in their attempts to lay down a new definition of the philosophical task. The new thinking and the new metaphysics are similar insofar as they return from the realm of transcen-

---

78. Rosenzweig argues: "By denying the dark presupposition of all life, . . . by not allowing death to count as Something but turning it into Nothing, philosophy creates for itself the illusion of lacking all presupposition." SE, 25.

dent thought to that of finite existence. Heidegger's "fundamental on-tology" as expounded in *Being and Time* begins with the insight that the existent human being *(Dasein)* is being-in-the-world and therefore must commence its questioning about Being from where it already is. Similarly, Rosenzweig argues that the new thinking as developed in *The Star of Re-demption* takes life itself *(Leben)* as the insuperable horizon of thought. (The terms are comparable: *life* was in fact the young Heidegger's term of art in his lectures on the phenomenology of religion from 1920 to 1921 before he came upon the more rigorous formulation, *Dasein.*) [79] Both philosophies claim that human existence cannot be dissociated from time:

> The new thinking knows just as the age-old [*uralte*] thinking of common sense, that it cannot have knowledge independent of time. . . . Knowledge is bound in every moment precisely to this moment and cannot make its past unpassed, nor its future unfutured. The times of reality are thus not inter-changeable. Just as every occurrence has its present, its past, and its future, without which it cannot be, and cannot properly be known, so too reality as a whole. . . . [T]he difference between old and new, logical and grammatical thinking lies . . . in taking time seriously [*im Ernstnehmen der Zeit*]. (ND, 149)

With a lexicon that is admittedly more developed, Heidegger also asserted that "temporality" *(Zeitlichkeit)* is constitutive of human understanding. Ro-senzweig tells us that traditional thought asserted its independence from time, but he insists that this is an illusion, dangerous enough that it can be compared to physical paralysis.[80] Rosenzweig and Heidegger further claim that the horizon of philosophy is itself temporal; Rosenzweig calls this a narrative philosophy *(erzählende Philosophie),* while Heidegger speaks of hermeneutics.[81]

For both Rosenzweig and Heidegger, such a hermeneutic or "narrative" method means that language is the unbreachable horizon of understand-ing. Rosenzweig writes that for the new thinking, "the method of speech replaces the method of thinking that was maintained in all earlier philoso-phies" (ND, 151). For Heidegger, "language . . . has its roots in the exis-tential constitution of Dasein's disclosedness" (SZ, 161). Language thus emerges in the course of his analysis as part of the fundamental structure of

---

79. On Heidegger's "Einleitung in die Phänomenologie der Religion," see the discussion in Ernst Tugendhat, *Der Wahrheitsbegriff bei Husserl und Heidegger* (Berlin: Walter de Gruyter, 1970), 265; and the suggestive comments in Charles Guignon, *Heidegger and the Problem of Knowledge* (Indianapolis: Hackett, 1983), 58–59.

80. Strangely, Rosenzweig may have conceived this metaphor *before* he was stricken with amyotrophic lateral sclerosis; see Glatzer's introduction to *Büchlein.*

81. SZ, esp. 335–50, §68, sections *a* ("Die Zeitlichkeit des Verstehens") and *d* ("Die Zeitlichkeit der Rede") respectively.

human existence in its "understanding of Being." For Rosenzweig as well, the break with traditional philosophy was explicit: "Thinking is timeless and wants to be timeless. . . . It regards the last, the goal, as the first. Speech is bound to time and nourished by time, and it neither can nor wants to abandon this element" (ND, 151). Both Rosenzweig and Heidegger argue that thought always occurs in language: Rosenzweig calls it "grammatical" as opposed to "logical" thought; Heidegger similarly insists that "logic" is derivative and language is "original" *(ursprünglich)* (SZ, 166). Both suggest that because language is constitutive of human understanding, so too are speaking and being heard. Thus Heidegger suggests that "Both talking and hearing are based upon understanding" (SZ, 166). Even "[k]eeping silent authentically" is possible "only in genuine discoursing" (SZ, 208).

Despite all of these similarities, there is one element found in Rosenzweig's excursus upon "The New Thinking" that Heidegger's philosophy apparently lacks. Rosenzweig tells us that with the advent of the new philosophy, "theological concerns" have at last made a breakthrough. For many readers, this difference is decisive, and it confirms Löwith's argument that Rosenzweig is in the end a philosopher of eternal revelation, not temporality. But Rosenzweig goes on to warn us against this misunderstanding. The new thinking, he cautions, *"is not itself theological,"* at least, he adds, not "what one has understood by this until now, neither in goal nor in method" (ND, 113; my emphasis). Rosenzweig's emphasis on this single point is rather striking, given that *The Star of Redemption* was commonly taken to be a "Jewish book." But here too, he warns us, appearances can be deceiving: "It is not a 'Jewish book.' . . . Nor does it make any claim to being a philosophy of religion—how could it, when the word religion absolutely nowhere makes an appearance! Rather, it is a simple System of Philosophy" (ND, 140).[82]

Given Rosenzweig's reputation as a Jewish philosopher, it may seem strange to note that he openly resisted labeling *The Star of Redemption* a "Jewish philosophy." Not only does he repudiate this term, he boldly suggests that his book will inaugurate nothing less than a new "Philosophy" as such, which (in a reversal of Kant's meaning) is compared to Kant's "Copernican revolution." The meaning of this revolution is best illustrated by Rosenzweig's claim to have created a radical partnership between philosophy and theology. The point is not that Rosenzweig is a "believing" philosopher or that he has produced a "philosophical" account of religion. The new thinking "does not center on so-called 'religious problems'" but treats them "together with the problems of logic, ethics, and aesthetics." So not only is Rosenzweig claiming his originality as a philosopher, he also claims that his idea of religion is at odds with that of the religious tradition: *"If this is theol-*

82. For further explanation of this passage, see my comments in chapter 3.

*ogy,"* he writes, *"it is, at any rate, no less new as theology than as philosophy."* The true purpose of Rosenzweig's new thinking is to create a partnership between them: "Theology must not debate philosophy to play the part of a handmaid, yet the role of charwomen which philosophy has recently assigned to theology is just as humiliating." The "true relationship," he writes, "is a sisterly one" (ND, 140; my emphasis).

<h3 style="text-align:center">PHILOSOPHY AND FINITUDE</h3>

Given this untraditional account of the relationship between theology and philosophy, one cannot accept without qualification Löwith's claim that Rosenzweig is simply a "religious" thinker. But it is equally misleading to call Heidegger a "pagan" philosopher. As I will show, Heidegger's notion of metaphysics itself has a theological background. Like Rosenzweig, Heidegger develops concepts that represent a "translation" from theology into modern philosophy. Indeed, I hope that the comparison with Rosenzweig will help to bring out this theological provenance more boldly. So while the obvious prominence of theological materials in Rosenzweig's philosophy remains an important point of contrast, it remains to be seen just how substantial that contrast really is.

One should not be deceived into believing Rosenzweig and Heidegger were united in every respect. But from these introductory remarks it seems clear that their work belonged to a common horizon of concerns. Each begins by staging a revolt against what Trakl called "the icy wind of eternity." And each ends by declaring that the new task of thought is a "metaphysics" directed against the metaphysical tradition. From the new perspective, the older idealist philosophy had placed undue emphasis upon the possibility of redemption as an essentially mental possibility. In both Husserlian phenomenology and neo-Kantian epistemology, the old thinking saw the human being as basically cognitive in nature, a being of infinite capacities, spontaneous rather than dependent, eternal rather than bounded by life and death. The new thinking reversed these values, and so revived for philosophy a religious attitude that Schleiermacher had once called "absolute dependence" *(unbedingte Abhängigkeit)*.[83]

For both Rosenzweig and Heidegger, an organizing philosophical principle was finitude, or *Endlichkeit*. By this I mean limitation in life (mortality) and in knowledge (we cannot know all that there is). One of the most fascinating things about this new concept is that it returns philosophy to an insight that is distinctively religious in origin. For as I will show, finitude always appears in contrast to God, who is infinite. Thus a religious sensibility can

---

83. Friedrich Schleiermacher, *Der christliche Glaube* (Berlin: G. Reimer, 1821).

be detected at the edges of the new philosophy even when it is not explicitly religious.[84] As I will demonstrate in the following chapter, it was the question of religious experience most of all that first exposed the limitations of neo-idealism and thereby brought Wiemar philosophy to the precipice of a new metaphysics.

84. On the quarrel between philosophy and religion in Weimar thought, also see Strauss, *Philosophie und Gesetz*. Much of Weimar-era thought, furthermore, is marked by the revival of interest in Kierkegaard. See Hannah Arendt, "Soren Kierkegaard," *Frankfurter Zeitung* No. 75–76 (January 29, 1932); reprinted in *Essays in Understanding: Uncollected and Unpublished Works by Hannah Arendt*, ed. Jerome Kohn (New York: Harcourt, Brace and Co., 1994), 43–49. It is significant that, later in his career, Heidegger complained of *Being and Time* that it was "too Kierkegaardian." See the remarks on this in Dennis J. Schmidt, *The Ubiquity of the Finite: Hegel, Heidegger, and the Entitlements of Philosophy* (Cambridge, Mass.: MIT Press, 1988).

# Chapter 1

# Toward Metaphysics

## *Cohen's* Opus Postumum
## *and the Origins of the New Thinking*

*Die Schüler mit ihrem Schülmeister sterbt. Der Meister lebt.*
—FRANZ ROSENZWEIG, *"Vertauschte Fronten" (1929)*

On April 4, 1918, the great neo-Kantian philosopher Hermann Cohen died. Only six years earlier (on July 4, 1912), he had celebrated his seventieth birthday with great ceremony, accompanied by ennobling speeches and announcements in major papers across Germany. The eminent philosophical journal *Kantstudien* published a special volume in honor of his contributions to aesthetics, ethics, epistemology, and religion. His seminars at the University of Marburg were legendary. His colleague Paul Natorp called them a monument to the "Marburg school." In Jewish circles Cohen was regarded as "the second Maimonides." But for many students his work was "primordially and authentically German." Ernst Cassirer, perhaps the most famous of those students, credited Cohen with nothing less than the "renewal of Kantian philosophy."[1]

Cohen was buried three days following his death. The sarcophagus was laid in a prominent spot among the notables in Berlin's Weißensee cemetery, the largest Jewish burial ground in all of Western Europe. The

---

1. Paul Natorp, "Addresse an Cohen," in *Philosophische Abhandlungen, H. Cohen zum 70. Geburtstag dargebracht* (Berlin: 1912); and Natorp, "Kant und die Marburger Schule," *Kantstudien* (Festheft zu Hermann Cohens 70. Geburtstag) 17, 3 (1912): 193–221. As "second Maimonides," Walter Kinkel, *Hermann Cohen: Eine Einführung in sein Werk* (Stuttgart: Strecker und Schröder, 1924), 93. "Marburg und Umgebung, Der 70. Geburtstag Hermann Cohens," *Oberhessische Zeitung* 47, 156 (July 6, 1912). A biographical sketch is Hans Liebeschütz, "Hermann Cohen and His Historical Background," LBIY, 1968, 3–172. On Cohen's socialism, see Steven S. Schwarzschild, "The Democratic Socialism of Hermann Cohen," *Hebrew Union College Annual* 28 (1956): 417–38; and Timothy Keck, "Kant and Socialism: The Marburg School in Wilhelmian Germany" (Ph.D. diss., University of Wisconsin at Madison, 1975). Ernst Cassirer, "Hermann Cohen und die Erneuerung der Kantischen Philosophie," *Kantstudien* (Festheft zu Hermann Cohens 70.Geburtstag) 17, 3 (1912): 222–51.

gravestone holds much symbolism: a massive granite block, it stands above ground and is enclosed at both ends by tall, peaked stones. On the opposed slopes are paired inscriptions, written by the Orthodox rabbi Nehemiah Nobel of Frankfurt am Main, in the two languages from which Cohen drew his spiritual sustenance, German and Hebrew.[2]

For most of his life, Cohen lived with the comforting and relatively innocent belief that it was possible to forge a synthesis of German and Jewish identity. He was praised, and later attacked, for his unbounded trust in their spiritual affinity.[3] Intellectually, however, his legacy was divided. Toward the end of his life, Cohen was himself consumed with the question of the compatibility between religion and philosophy. His study *Der Begriff der Religion im System der Philosophie* (The concept of religion in the system of philosophy, 1915) demonstrates an earlier stage in his reflections. His last and most enigmatic work of philosophy was published posthumously in 1919 as *Religion der Vernunft aus den Quellen des Judentums* (Religion of reason out of the sources of Judaism). The work immediately met with a storm of debate. For some, Cohen's last book was plainly compatible with his earlier idealism. For others, it signaled a radical break, suggesting that he had abandoned the neo-Kantian problematic for a new kind of religious phenomenology.[4] The interpretative struggle between these two groups over the true sense of Cohen's *opus postumum* quickly escalated to become part of a much larger dispute concerning the status of religion in modern philosophy. As this chapter will explain, Cohen's death thus marked the beginning of an intellectual

2. For a summary of Cohen's life, see *Hermann Cohen, 1842–1918, Kantinterpret, Begründer der "Marburger Schule," Jüdischer Religionsphilosoph,* Eine Ausstellung in der Universitätsbibliothek Marburg vom 1. Juli bis 14. August 1992 (Marburg: Schriften der Universitätsbibliothek, 1992), 171. The German inscription on Cohen's grave lauds his efforts to harmonize Platonism and Kant. The Hebrew calls him a teacher and defender of his people. See Steven Schwarzschild, "Germanism and Judaism—Hermann Cohen's Normative Paradigm of the German-Jewish Symbiosis," in *Jews and Germans from 1860–1933: The Problematic Synthesis,* ed. David Bronsen, (Heidelberg: Carl Winter Verlag, 1979), 129–72, esp. n. 8. On Rabbi Nobel, see Rachel Heuberger, "Orthodoxy versus Reform: The Case of Rabbi Nehemiah Anton Nobel of Frankfurt a. Main," LBIY, 1992, 45–58.

3. For a strongly negative view, see Micha Brumlik, "1915: In *Deutschtum und Judentum* Hermann Cohen Applies Neo-Kantian Philosophy to the German Jewish Question," in *Yale Companion to Jewish Writing and Thought in German Culture, 1096–1996,* ed. Sander Gilman and Jack Zipes (New Haven: Yale University Press, 1997), 336–42.

4. Cohen, *Die Religion der Vernunft aus den Quellen des Judentums* (Leipzig: Fock Verlag, 1919); 2nd corrected ed. by Bruno Strauß as *Religion der Vernunft aus den Quellen des Judentums* (Frankfurt am Main: Kaufmann Verlag, 1929) [RV]. Note the difference in the titles—the initial definite article was never intended by Cohen and was dropped from the second edition. For remarks on the correction, see Strauß's afterword; and VF. Rosenzweig called it a *Heimkehr,* a turn homeward. See his "Einleitung," in JS I: lxiv.

crisis that would ultimately precipitate the birth of a new, post-rationalist philosophy.

The controversy began at Cohen's grave. Ernst Cassirer delivered a solemn eulogy for his departed teacher, recalling both his "incomparable warmth and his scholarly objectivity." For Cassirer, Cohen's most admirable quality had been the "unity of his will and his intellect, his human and his intellectual being." In all Cohen's work, even his studies in logic, there was never a separation between thought and life. The *Religion of Reason,* which Cohen had not lived to see in print, was for Cassirer the culmination of that all-embracing idealist spirit. (In 1918 it was still unavailable to the general public; Cassirer confessed that he had only begun reading it a few weeks earlier.) It was Cohen's "last great religious-philosophical work," which to Cassirer illustrated the "deep inner coherence" between Cohen's philosophical and religious ideas.[5]

This interpretation did not go unchallenged. When Cassirer's eulogy was published the following month, it appeared together with a brief letter, "The Docent: A Personal Recollection" ("Der Dozent: Eine persönliche Erinnerung"), which Franz Rosenzweig had mailed from the front. In it Rosenzweig disputed Cassirer's recollection of the late philosopher as an untroubled and unified man. For Rosenzweig, Cohen was Janus-faced, split between reason and conviction. When Cohen spoke, one witnessed "an entirely unpredictable boiling forth of pathos from its subterranean sources, the narrow togetherness of the coolest thoughts and the hottest heart." Cohen would lecture at first with "rigorous matter-of-factness," delicately carrying his listeners along in the placid flow of his thoughts. But this seeming calm was a ruse: "[A]t any moment, wholly without transition, and never in a manner that was predictable or sensed in advance, the firestorm of [his] personality suddenly broke through." It was "like a volcano flowing under smooth ground." Cohen was split between system and faith, a volatile combination of forces that could not be sustained. Toward the end of his life, the passionate element broke free: "In his final, theological epoch, it drove him over and beyond his system at last to confront those questions with an eye-to-eye immediacy." At heart, Cohen had never been the cultured professor he seemed. He was, in Rosenzweig's view, "ein frommer Mensch," a pious man.[6]

---

5. Cassirer, "Worte gesprochen an seinem Grabe," *Neue Jüdische Monatshefte: Zeitschrift für Politik, Wirtschaft und Literatur in Ost und West* (Sonderheft Hermann Cohen) 2, 15/16 (May 10–25, 1918), 349.

6. Rosenzweig, "Der Dozent: Eine persönliche Erinnerung," reprinted as "Ein Gedenkblatt," in KS, 291–98; quotes at 293. Shortly after Cohen's death, Rosenzweig wrote to Gritli that "All *Nachrufe* for Cohen are unsatisfying. It is almost as if nobody knew him." GB

Interpretation of Cohen's life and work thus split into two opposed camps. One side saw harmony between Cohen's faith and his philosophy, where the other side regarded Cohen's legacy as fundamentally divided. The controversy was only natural, since both camps could find a wealth of corroborating evidence to support their opinions in Cohen's difficult and sometimes obscure final work.[7] But far from condemning the book to oblivion, this instability of meaning actually helped to ensure its continued life well into the 1920s. The debate over the status of religion in neo-Kantianism thus provides a useful point of departure for exploring the striking transformation of German thought in the Weimar era.

FROM METAPHYSICS TO METHOD: *KANT'S THEORY OF EXPERIENCE*

To appreciate Cohen's ambiguous philosophical legacy in the 1920s, one must first understand his original contribution to neo-Kantianism. Cohen's singular importance in the history of philosophy can be traced to the publication of his first major work in 1871, *Kant's Theory of Experience (Kants Theorie der Erfahrung).*[8] His chief contribution to the interpretation of Kant's philosophy was to radically revise the contemporary understanding of the Kantian doctrine of the thing-in-itself *(Ding-an-sich)*. Throughout the 1860s, Adolf Trendelenburg and Kuno Fischer had disputed the status of space and time in relation to things in themselves, as presented in the "transcendental aesthetic" of the first critique. In Trendelenburg's view, Kant was without warrant in concluding that space and time are pure forms of intuition only and can have no further application to things in themselves. It seemed clear that there was a "gap" *(Lücke)* or neglected alternative in Kant's argumentation. In his many rejoinders to Trendelenburg, Fischer pointed out that this objection utterly misses the nature of the Kantian distinction between transcendental and empirical ideality: as the formal con-

---

(15.4.1918), 72–73. He later confessed to Gritli his negative impression of the published graveside addresses delivered by Kellermann and Cassirer (although he praised Natorp for at least recognizing Cohen's particular role in Marburg's reputation). But it was Cassirer's *Nachruf* that especially aroused Rosenzweig's ire. GB (19.4.1918), 78–79. Elsewhere, he announced that "it is truly as if no-one knew him. But it is surely the case that hardly anyone believed him. Perhaps only your . . . Franz." GB (23.4.1918), 81–82.

7. For Steven Schwarzschild, e.g., any existentialist reading of Cohen's work is an "illicit" effort to "re-ontologize" or "re-hypostatize" as really existent entities what for Cohen were concepts of a merely "functional" nature ; see Schwarzschild, "Introduction," in *Ethik*, vii–xxx.

8. Cohen, *Kants Theorie der Erfahrung* [KTE] (Berlin: Harrwitz und Gossmann, 1871), reprinted in *Werke*, vol. I, part 3. Cohen himself significantly expanded this book and the fifth and latest edition is in *Werke*, vol. I, part 1. Unless otherwise noted, it is the fifth edition that is cited.

ditions by which objects are known to us, space and time must apply to all possible experience. As such, they are empirically real. But according to the very meaning of space and time as conditions for the objects of experience, they cannot also be the conditions for things as such. This, Fischer concluded, is precisely what Kant meant by the "transcendental ideality" of space and time: "Regarded as the conditions of things (transcendentally), space and time have no reality [*Wirklichkeit*]."[9]

In *Kant's Theory of Experience,* Cohen disputed both views. Both of the older scholars, Cohen argued, had misunderstood the true character of the thing-in-itself in Kant's philosophy.[10] The distinction between the thing-in-itself and appearance, he argued, is not a metaphysical distinction, it is *methodological.* The rule of method in Kant's philosophy can only be understood when we grasp that his primary objective was not to lay the groundwork for a future metaphysics. Rather, it was to seek the justificatory principles that guide us in the infinite progress of scientific discovery. The realm of appearance is nothing other than the realm of nature as described by science. The status of the thing-in-itself is simply the as-yet-unknown, the unconditioned; it is that which is the goal *(Zweck)* of scientific inquiry and which will one day be integrated into the system of natural-mathematical explanation. Where appearance is the known, the thing-in-itself is the task *(Aufgabe)* of knowledge (KTE, 661–62). Accordingly, the world as a whole is a "problem," to be examined and eventually known through natural-mathematical explanation. In Cohen's words, it is "the task of the thing in itself" (KTE, 662–70). For Cohen, even Fischer had not fully liberated himself from a metaphysical understanding of the transcendental/empirical dis-

9. The Fischer-Trendelenburg debate can be traced back to the first publication of Trendelenburg's *Logische Untersuchungen* (Leipzig: S. Hirzel Verlag) in 1840, with subsequent editions printed in 1862 and 1870; then see Kuno Fischer, *Logik und Metaphysik, oder Wissenschaftslehre* (Stuttgart: C. P. Schetlin, 1852), esp. pp. 175–80; Trendelenburg, "Über eine Lücke in Kants Beweis von der ausschliessenden Subjektivität des Raumes und der Zeit. Ein kritisches und antikritisches Blatt," *Historischen Beiträgen zur Philosophie* 3 (1867): 215ff; Fischer, "Kants Vernunftkritik und deren Entstehung," in his multi-volume work, *Geschichte der neueren Philosophie,* vol. III, 2nd. ed. (Mannheim: F. Bassermann, 1865); and finally, Trendelenburg, *Kuno Fischer und sein Kant: Eine Entgegnung* (Leipzig: S. Hirzel Verlag, 1869). See also Trendelenburg, *Logische Untersuchungen* (Leipzig: S. Hirzel Verlag, 1870), 164–65, n.1. Kant's own discussion of the distinction between empirical reality and transcendental ideality of space and time can be found in KdrV, "Transcendentalen Aesthetik, Zweiter Abschnitt, Von der Zeit," §6, 52–53. For a recent discussion, see Henry Allison, *Kant's Transcendental Idealism: An Interpretation and Defense* (New Haven: Yale University Press, 1983), 111–14.

10. On Cohen's apprenticeship with Trendelenburg, see Thomas Willey, *Back to Kant: The Revival of Kantianism in German Social and Historical Thought, 1860–1914* (Detroit: Wayne State University Press, 1978), 106–7. See the section entitled "Trendelenburg's Ansicht von der 'Lücke' im transcendentalen Beweise," KTE, 1st ed., 62.

tinction. At some level, Cohen suggested, Kant's most eminent interpreters were still beholden to the scholastic (precritical) vision of philosophy as a voyage beyond the sensible world.

In Cohen's opinion, however, Kant's true achievement was precisely to have abandoned the metaphysical worldview so as to set the questions of philosophy on a new, properly scientific foundation. With the publication of the *Critique of Pure Reason,* said Cohen, philosophy first understood that its true task is critical, not constructive. It sets out with the facts of science as they are given at the time, asking not what is known but how such knowing is possible. Once we have grasped this methodological purpose, we can easily see that it makes little sense to speak of time and space, the conditions of objects in appearance, as features of the thing-in-itself as well. For the notion of objective description for a realm beyond experience as it is defined by science is meaningless. Time, like space, is nothing but a "form of scientific sensibility"(KTE, 700).[11] For Cohen, therefore, Kant represented a major turning point in Western thought: "*Before [Kant] there was metaphysics as art; with him for the first time there is metaphysics as science*" (KTE, 732; my emphasis).

Cohen's strongest criticism was reserved for those who misunderstood the Kantian vision as that of "metaphysical fantasy" rather than "methodical criticism" (KTE, 682–700). This misunderstanding, in Cohen's view, commonly grew out of the post-Kantian attempt to collapse the distinction between sensibility and understanding. Kant had insisted on the division between intuitions and concepts, while knowledge is only possible thanks to their synthesis. But many of his successors (notably Schelling, Fichte, and Hegel) had committed a grossly metaphysical error by cutting across these two elements, thereby transforming what was, in Cohen's opinion, Kant's purely regulative notion of an "intellectual intuition" into a real possibility. But this was a violation of Kant's systematic intentions. The thing-in-itself may be thought, but it cannot be known; it is a regulative Idea, or *Grenzbegriff,* necessary for the progress of science (KTE, 645). If the distinction between sensibility and thought is collapsed, there is no longer a place for the unconditioned; all discovery vanishes in the permanence of the Absolute. This, in Cohen's view, is the common mistake shared by pantheism, Spinozism, mysticism, and all varieties of fanaticism: none of them allowed for the proper understanding of the thing-in-itself as the "infinite task" *(unendliche Aufgabe)* of science (KTE, 769–70).

The importance of Platonic themes in this interpretation should not be missed. Cohen often indicated the close affinity, already apparent to Kant

---

11. Further: "The vehicles of the a priori in the Kantian theoretical structure, time and space, like the categories, are to be understood as methods, not as forms of spirit."

himself, between the Platonic theory of Ideas and the Kantian doctrine of regulative Ideas. Both of these doctrines suggest that the ideas prized as reason's greatest possessions do not have their origins in empirical experience. In fact, they both function as conditions for the possibility of sensual knowledge. Cohen therefore went so far as to speak of Plato as the true founder of epistemological criticism *(Erkenntniskritik)* (KTE, 13). The association with Kant is further reinforced through the fact that it was Plato who was largely responsible for turning philosophy toward the question of the specific Being *(Sein)* associated with mathematics (KTE, 21).[12] But here, Cohen insisted, the parallel comes to an end. For Plato, the Idea is not only presumed to be the ground of experience, it represents experience of a superior kind: by transcending the world of the senses for this higher sphere, the philosopher can arrive at a final, perfected station of insight. Yet Cohen perceived that for this reason Plato could easily, though perhaps one-sidedly, be interpreted as a theorist of "intellectual intuition" (KTE, 643). The Platonic theory of ideas laid the foundations of systematic philosophy, but it became overzealous in its appreciation of reason as a faculty that is believed capable of producing knowledge even when it is set free of the "fertile plain" of the empirical world.[13]

According to Cohen, Kant's "theory of experience" presents the solution to this danger, as announced in the famous opening lines of the first critique:

> There can be no doubt that all our knowledge begins with experience. . . . But though all our knowledge begins with experience, it does not follow that it all arises out of experience. (KdrV, "Einleitung," 1 [B1])

In Cohen's view, these phrases inaugurate a new direction for philosophy (KTE, 1st ed., 3). The distinction between where knowledge "begins" *(anfange)* and from what sources it "originates" *(entspringt)* provided Cohen with the basis for his interpretation of Kant, and also anticipated Cohen's own critical method, the "principle of origins." As Cohen explained, Kant understood that the true task of philosophy lies not in the search for new knowledge or "matter." Rather, its task is merely to justify the sensuous, a priori (space and time) elements by which knowledge is first possible. Cohen calls these elements "forms of spirit" *(Formen des Geistes)* (KTE, 1st ed., 243). While the world of the senses is also the world "foundation," this does

12. Also see Cohen's essay, "Platons Ideenlehre und die Mathematik" (1878), reprinted in Cohen, *Schriften zur Philosophie und Zeitgeschichte* (Berlin: Akademie Verlag, 1928), 336–66.

13. Hence Kant's famous "dove" metaphor, which indicated how Platonism transgressed the boundaries of experience and attempted erroneously to find knowledge beyond the senses, like a dove trying to fly without atmosphere. See KdrV, 54; and Cohen's discussion in KTE, 25.

not compel us to surrender ourselves to the senses entirely: the Kantian revolution transforms philosophy into a science of the empirical, but this science is guaranteed of its rights by means of a new, idealist theory of the
a priori (KTE, 270). This doctrine, in Cohen's view, represented a revolution
in philosophy that Kant himself had justly compared to the Copernican revolution in astronomy.[14] Cohen believed that this insight had radically transformed the modern understanding of the task of philosophy. In fact, one
could credit the *Critique of Pure Reason* with having inaugurated a truly modern vision of the place of the human being in the world. We are no longer
condemned to a role of receptivity, where we are mere spectators confronting an already finished creation. Rather, the knowing subject is granted new
dignity as an spontaneous agent in the production of knowledge. Cohen's
interpretation is not, therefore, confined to an analysis of scientific method.
For Cohen, "experience" in the Kantian lexicon ultimately meant nothing
less than the activity of thought as such (KTE, 1st ed., 3).

From this brief summary one can see that Cohen's fame was due chiefly
to his uncompromising vision of philosophy as science in which metaphysics
no longer enjoyed a rightful place. Although a now-familiar revision of
Kantian epistemology, Cohen's work at the time demanded a dramatic
transformation of the philosophical enterprise. Its radicalism prompted
Rosenzweig to claim that Cohen was at heart a Hegelian, since his "panmethodism" seemed to have robbed the world of its independent being.[15]
The claim was not entirely without warrant: Cohen placed great emphasis
on natural-scientific reasoning as the dominant model for philosophy, and
in the later, revised editions of *Kant's Theory of Experience,* he even strengthened the equation between Kant's critical philosophy and the progress of
modern science. He also radically expanded his treatment of the thing-
in-itself as the task of scientific discovery. Cohen thus surpassed Kant as
an enemy of traditional metaphysics. But this radicalism had its risks: By
conceiving the thing-in-itself as little else than a methodological idea, or
"task," Cohen's new theory of experience threatened the metaphysical independence of the world as such. The beings encountered in sensibility
now seemed to dissolve in a system of intellectual immanence. Cohen took
the decisive step toward this full-blown idealism in his mature theory of
knowledge.

14. See KdrV, "Vorrede zur zweiten Auflage," 28.
15. As early as 1918, Rosenzweig observed in a letter, "One often says that Cohen was far
more a Hegelian than he himself knew—and this is correct. But for me the Hegelian in him
was precisely what I couldn't swallow, as little with Cohen as with Hegel himself." *Briefe,* N.221,
An die Mutter (15.4.1918), 299.

BEING OUT OF NOTHINGNESS: COHEN'S LOGIC

Cohen's *Logic of Pure Knowledge (Logik der reinen Erkenntnis),* first published in 1902, begins by positing the identity of thought *(Denken)* and being *(Sein).* In this claim Cohen already displayed an idealism surpassing Kant, whose critical philosophy sustained thought's relation to something external to itself, an object "given" in intuition *(Anschauung).* Cohen regarded this residual "empiricism" as a moment of weakness in Kant's philosophy. For if the purpose of critique is to discover the pure, a priori element in our knowledge (as illustrated by mathematics), then we must begin with thought alone, taken as a pure and independent faculty. The element of thought that will be our sole concern is thought in so far as it is the condition for the possibility of knowledge, that is, transcendental logic. But "[t]hought must have no origin [*Ursprung*] outside of itself, when its purity is to be without limit and uncorrupted" *(Logik,* 13). Cohen thus insisted that the ideal of philosophy as a science of pure knowledge had been founded with an insight attributed to Parmenides: "Being is the Being of Thought" *(Logik,* 15). In Plato, this insight became fixed in the doctrine of the Idea, as a hypothesis or question: "What is *x?*" is in essence a question regarding the origin *(Ursprung)* of *x.* The being that is in question discovers its origins beyond itself, in thought. In fact, Cohen suggested, theological faith in eternity depends on the doctrine that being is generated in thought: "In this belief there is expressed a willing confidence in the eternity of thought, or, as is meant here, in the sovereignty of thought." But this sovereignty would be thrown into jeopardy if thought were to be compelled to acknowledge that it depends in the slightest measure on a source of givenness outside of itself. "Thought can and must disclose being" *(Logik,* 31).

The heart of Cohen's doctrine concerning the generation of being from thought was to be found in the "principle of origin" *(Ursprungsprinzip).*[16] In his discussion of the historical sources of this principle, Cohen credited Nicholas de Cusa with the crucial "discovery" that there is no element in our knowledge more certain than mathematics *(Logik,* 34). Specifically, the mathematical concept of the infinite *(das Unendliche)* is the linchpin of all our scientific knowledge. Accordingly, Cohen explained the principle of origins as follows: All that can be posited or known is finite. Yet all finite being is first thought by means of the infinite. There is no finitude whatsoever unless it is created in thinking of it as a limitation of the infinite. The

16. On Cohen's *Urpsrungsprinzip,* see Walter Kinkel, "Das Urteil des Ursprungs: Ein Kapitel aus einem Kommentar zu H. Cohens *Logik der reinen Erkenntnis,*" *Kantstudien* (Festheft zu Hermann Cohens 70. Geburtstag) 17, 3 (1912): 274–82; Amos Funkenstein, *Theology and the Scientific Imagination* (Princeton: Princeton University Press, 1986), esp. 351–60, and *Perceptions of Jewish History* (Berkeley: University of California Press, 1993), esp. 257–305.

infinite, therefore, is the "tool and instrument" for the discovery of finite being (*Logik,* 32).

Specifically, the instrument that serves to generate being is the concept of the infinitesimal, or infinitely small magnitude, as it took shape in the calculus of Leibniz. In Cohen's view, infinitesimal analysis is not just "the legitimate instrument of mathematical-natural science." In fact, science as such depends on the infinitesimal for its methodological integrity and its claims to certainty. In physics, the infinitesimal method may be used to demonstrate that being, mass, and force are all functions of motion (*Logik,* 33). In calculus, whose methods form the theoretical basis of physics and geometry, the infinitesimal method allows us, for example, to compute the area under a curve: its area is equal to the sum of an infinite number of rectangles with infinitely small widths, that is, rectangles with bases of lengths approaching zero. In this sense, a magnitude that is given the mathematical definition as tending toward nothing becomes the originating point in thought for the generation of reality as such. Kant, although his achievement was corrupted through his devotion to the doctrine of the sensuous given, was the first to recognize by means of an analysis of the infinitely small, that reality *(Realität)* is generated in thought; it is a category of mind, which, in Kant's words, "represents only that something the very concept of which includes being."[17] The importance of the infinitesimal, therefore, cannot be underestimated. For Cohen, it served as the grand model of philosophical idealism as such, signifying "undiminished certitude, the uninhibited and creative [*schöpferische*] independence of pure thought" (*Logik,* 35).

### LOGIC, NOTHINGNESS, AND NEGATION

For our purposes, the most consequential element of Cohen's critical idealism is indicated by the notion that being is first generated in a logical operation of negation. Cohen discussed the historical and philosophical details of this notion in a section of the *Logik* entitled "The Something and the Nothing" ("Das Etwas und das Nichts") and in those sections that immediately follow.[18] The concept of origin, in Cohen's view, is first discovered in myth: while Thales believed that all is water, Anaximander argued that the infinite itself is the point of origin for being. With this insight, the concept of origin first assumed its character as "spirit" *(Geist)* instead of substance. But unfortunately, the concept of origins here retained a metaphys-

17. KdrV, "Anticipationen der Wahrnehmung," 204–13 (A170/B212–176/B218). This is discussed by Cohen in *Logik,* 35.

18. But see the discussion on the "judgment of origins" in its entirety, in *Logik,* 79–93, esp. §5, 84.

ical rather than logical character, and in the ensuing scholastic disputes concerning the ontological problem, it was debated whether even God's being might be created in thought. For Cohen, the modern logical principle of origins had fully surmounted these metaphysical errors. "Only Thought itself is capable of creating that which qualifies as Being" (*Logik*, 81). For insofar as knowledge is certainty, thought cannot depend upon a sensuous given. For the Greeks, the meaning of the given was that which is derived from thought by means of analysis alone. Thought must accept as given only that which it alone can discover. What it wishes to discover is the "something," that which can be determined: in mathematics, this determinability is denoted by the sign *x*. The question "What is *x*?" summarizes the problem of origins. Since the origins of something *(Etwas)* cannot be discovered in another something (for this merely reiterates the question anew), the origins of a something lay not in another something, but rather in the nothing *(das Nichts)* (*Logik*, 84).

Cohen admits that at first glance this might appear nonsensical: "It seems absurd that in order to find something, one would turn toward the nothing, which seems to constitute the true abyss for thought [*Abgrund für das Denken*]" (*Logik*, 84). But the apparent absurdity is in fact unavoidable. For since something cannot lie at the origin of something without infinite regress, the remaining alternative must be that the nothing is a "station" in the generation of being. This nothing is not erected, as it were, as an "un-thing" that stands in contradiction to the something. Rather, it is the "offspring" of "the deepest logical dilemma" in which thought cannot help but find itself (*Logik*, 84–85). The relationship between nothingness and being is first illustrated in the grammatical association between the particle of privation *(Un)* and the idea of negation *(nicht)*. The proposition "*x* is un-*y*" was called by Aristotle a "privative"—and by Kant an "infinite" *(unendliche)*—judgment. Thus the negation of an attribute can take an affirmative form, and nothingness *(das Nichts)* can thereby assume a role in the determination of an object (*Logik*, 89). Cohen employs a classical example: "The soul is not mortal" is a negative proposition. But "The soul is immortal" employs a privative concept, immortality, which was derived by injecting the negation into the predicate itself. In this fashion, we have not only determined what the soul is not, we have taken a small step toward a positive determination of what the soul is. In sum, we have employed the "nothing" in order to progress toward the determination of a "something." The relationship between the nothing and the something is therefore one of continuity: "Being [*Sein*] itself," Cohen concludes, must receive its origin through not-being [*Nichtsein*]." Nothingness is not a mere correlative concept for being, it is the "springboard" from which Being is born (*Logik*, 93).

Cohen's logical theory provided much ground for criticism, especially by Heidegger. As we have seen, the governing principle of Cohen's idealism was the proposition that being is a methodological, not a metaphysical premise; it is generated from thought alone. For Cohen, the human mind is independent and creative; it is no longer dependent for the most vital element of its knowledge upon a sensual form that belongs to intuition. (This already demonstrated a significant departure from Kant, who sustained the independence of receptive intuition. For Cohen, spontaneity *without* receptivity characterizes human thought.) The element of experience to which one may ascribe actual being is that which is generated purely from thought itself, by means of a logical process that begins with the concept of nothingness *(Nichtsein)*.

This concept of nothingness has little to do with the later, existentialist use of the word. For Cohen, *das Nichts* is significant as a logical operation only. When Rosenzweig appropriated many of the gestures from Cohen's *Logic* for his own philosophy, he read the idealist play of concepts as an allegory: What had been a logical operation became a real description, a narrative concerning the "surging forth" of creation from chaos (SE, 49 [E, 45–46]). As I shall explain later, Rosenzweig's *Star of Redemption* begins by invoking this deeper, pre-cognitive *Nichts* as the rupture between Being and thought. For Rosenzweig, it signaled an ontological difference that philosophy since Parmenides wished to evade. Similarly, Heidegger was to object in his 1929 lecture "What Is Metaphysics?" that nothingness should never be equated with negation, for by doing so we would attain merely "the formal concept of the imagined nothing but never the nothing itself." This was a more or less explicit attack on Cohen's panlogism:

> The nothing is the origin of negation, not vice versa. [Das Nichts ist der Ursprung der Verneinung, nicht umgekehrt.] If the power of the intellect in the field of inquiry into the nothing and into Being is thus shattered, then the fate of the reign of "logic" in philosophy is thereby decided. The idea of "logic" itself disintegrates in the turbulence of a more original questioning. (WM, 37; WM English, 107)

Heidegger's claims concerning the "origin" *(Ursprung)* of negation makes covert reference to Cohen's *Ursprungsprinzip*. While for Cohen Being is generated from thought alone through the logical instrument of infinite negation, for Heidegger this principle illicitly supplants metaphysics with method. For Heidegger and for Rosenzweig as well, this central achievement of neo-Kantian logical theory was intolerable, for it meant that Being had lost its independence in relation to concepts and that authentic metaphysics had thereby been purged from philosophy. The mistaken assumption of Cohen's *Logic* that being originates in cognition alone was to provide Heidegger throughout his career with one of his most reliable targets of criticism: indeed, one senses a satirical edge in Heidegger's allusion to a "more original" *(ursprünglicheren)* inquiry in which Cohen's principle of origins loses its force. Much like Rosenzweig, Heidegger wished to reverse the neo-Kantian achievement, to surmount panmethodism and to inaugurate a new species of metaphysics. Such a reversal of the older, neo-Kantian priorities—method, not metaphysics—is a hallmark of existential ontology. And it is one of the features that most dramatically illustrates the commonality of perspective between Rosenzweig and Heidegger.

### THE KANTIAN MOMENT IN JEWISH THOUGHT

Jürgen Habermas once observed that there is a deep affinity between the spirit of Kant and the spirit of Judaism. For Habermas and many others, the remarkable prominence of theorists in the Kantian tradition who were of Jewish heritage would seem to suggest Kant's essential "attractiveness to the Jewish mind." While such formulations appear unwise, one may of course speculate as to the reasons for the enduring relationship between Kant and modern "Jewish" thought.[19] It seems most likely that it was the emancipatory potential of Kant's Enlightenment idea that best explains the alliance. In German culture, this bond between Jewish and liberal-enlightenment interests held sway from the era of emancipation to the First World War and continued well into the Weimar Republic, when most Jews still identified themselves with the major liberal parties or the majority socialists (not, as some might now imagine, with anarchism or radical-utopianism).[20] But by the end of the 1920s a sizable portion of the younger generation had

●

19. Habermas, "The German Idealism of the Jewish Philosophers," in his *Philosophische-Politische Profile* (Frankfurt am Main: Suhrkamp Verlag, 1971); in English, *Philosophical-Political Profiles*, trans. Frederick Lawrence (Cambridge, Mass.: MIT Press, 1983). On the supposed affinity between Judaism and Kant, see Heinz Moshe Graupe, "Kant und das Judentum," *Zeitschrift für Religions- und Geistesgeschichte* 13 (1961): 308–33; for a social-historical explanation, see Jacob Katz, *Out of the Ghetto: The Social Background of Jewish Emancipation* (New York: Schocken, 1978), and "Kant and Judaism, the Historical Context" (Hebrew), *Tarbitz* 41 (1971–72): 217–37.

20. On Kant's Jewish contemporaries, see inter alia, Kant, *Philosophical Correspondence,* ed. Arnulf Zweig (Cambridge: Cambridge University Press, 1999), esp. the remarks on Maimon and Herz, *passim.* Also on Herz see esp. Ernst Cassirer, *Kants Leben und Lehre* (Berlin: Bruno Cassirer, 1918); on Mendelssohn, see esp. Alexander Altmann, *Moses Mendelssohn: A Biographical Study* (Philadelphia: The Jewish Publication Society of America, 1973). On Kant and Jewish socialists such as Eduard Bernstein, Max Adler, Otto Bauer, and Kurt Eisner, see Peter Gay, *The Dilemma of Democratic Socialism: Eduard Bernstein's Challenge to Marx* (New York: Columbia University Press, 1962). On Otto Liebmann (who coined the phrase "back to Kant"), see his *Kant und die Epigonen: Eine kritische Abhandlung,* Kant-Gesellschaft (Berlin: Reuther und Reichard, 1912). On the Jewish-liberal alliance, see Peter Pulzer, *Jews and the German State: The Political History of a Minority, 1848–1933* (Oxford: Oxford University Press, 1992); for a cultural perspective, see George Mosse, *German Jews beyond Judaism* (Cincinnati: Hebrew Union College Press, 1985).

grown disillusioned with Kantian idealism. For this group, the "inner affinity" that Hermann Cohen perceived between Kant and Judaism was no
longer self-evident.[21]

Cohen's belief that Kant and Judaism are inherently connected may seem
counterintuitive given Kant's own rather negative assessment of Judaism.
But whatever one makes of Kant's admittedly negative perspective, it is by
and large consistent with his greater defense of Enlightenment autonomy.[22]
And it should be remembered that elsewhere Kant articulated a qualified
praise for Judaism's anti-representationalist understanding of God and
even praised the second commandment as "the most sublime passage"
in Jewish law. (Combined with Kant's legislative model of freedom, this
anti-representationalist bias prompted Hegel to quip that Kant's was a "Jewish" philosophy.)[23] So if the strong antipathy to divine representation in
Kant's philosophy did not make the alliance between Judaism and Kant
somehow inevitable, it clearly prompted many thinkers to discern their
"elective affinity."[24]

21. See Cohen, "Innere Beziehungen der Kantischen Philosophie zum Judentum." Orig.
pub. in *Bericht der Lehranstalt für die Wissenschaft des Judentums in Berlin* 28 (1910): 41–61;
reprinted in JS I: 284–305.

22. In *Religion within the Bounds of Reason Alone,* trans. Theodore M. Greene and Hoyt H.
Hudson (New York: Harper Torchbooks, 1960), Kant argued that Judaism is a mere collection
of "statutory laws" founded upon "a political organization." Its laws "relate merely to external
acts" and do not touch upon the "moral disposition" of the individual. And since Kant regarded
Judaism as lacking any "belief in a future life," it was thus "no religion at all" (116). And see
the discussion in Cohen, "Innere Beziehungen," 286. Cf. the largely negative view in Paul
Lawrence Rose, *German Question, Jewish Question: Revolutionary Antisemitism from Kant to Wagner*
(Princeton: Princeton University Press, 1990). A moderate assessment is Cassirer, *Kants Leben
und Lehre,* esp. 414–15. On Kant's infamous reference to the "euthanasia" of Judaism, see
Nathan Rotenstreich, *Jews and German Philosophy: The Polemics of Emancipation* (New York:
Schocken Books, 1984), 5. An excellent discussion is Julius Guttmann, "Kant und das Juden-
tum," in *Schriften der Gesellschaft zur Förderung der Wissenschaft des Judentums* (Leipzig, Buch-
handlung Gustav Fock, 1908), esp. 43–61.

23. On the second commandment and the sublime, see Kant, *Critique of the Power of Judgment,* ed. Paul Guyer, trans. Paul Guyer and Eric Matthews (Cambridge: Cambridge University
Press, 2000) 156, §29. Hegel regarded both Kant and Judaism as denying sensual representation any place in religion. They thereby sustain the dualism between ideal and real at an ar-
rested middle-stage in the dialectic. Hence Hegel called Judaism "the religion of sublimity."
*Lectures on the Philosophy of Religion: The Lectures of 1827,* trans. R. F. Brown et al. (Berkeley: University of California Press, 1988), and JH, esp. 89.

24. Against Judaism's reputation as anti-visual, see Daniel Boyarin, "The Eye of the Torah,"
*Critical Inquiry* 16 (spring 1990): 532–55. On the second commandment and its legacy, see
Moshe Halbertal and Avishai Margalit, *Idolatry,* trans. Naomi Goldblum (Cambridge, Mass.:
Harvard University Press, 1992). Maimonides, perhaps the boldest Jewish critic of divine pred-
ication, developed a theoretical "negation of privations," an inspiration for Cohen's principle
of origins. On this see my "The Erotics of Negative Theology: Maimonides on Apprehension,"
*Jewish Studies Quarterly* 2,1 (1995): 1–38.

Cohen could thereby draw upon Kant's moral philosophy to construct a "pure" ethics that he regarded as an expression of Judaism's inner core. In his 1915 wartime pamphlet *Deutschtum und Judentum,* Cohen argued that the Jewish people owe their primary allegiance to Germany because of the profound cultural bond that unites them, in philosophy, prayer, and music.[25] Most of all this bond was demonstrable in the German Enlightenment's humanist-ethical belief in progress. (The inspiration for Gotthold Lessing's *Education of the Human Race,* for example, was in Cohen's view traceable to the messianic idea in Judaism.) Even Bismarck's decision to inaugurate general voting rights was a "logical consequence" of Jewish messianism, which aims at the redemption of the world as a whole and is therefore a major inspiration for all movements of social reform. Given these affinities between German and Jewish culture, Cohen argued that it was vital that Germany win the war so as to realize its world-historical mission. Here too, it was Kant who provided the crucial idea: "German culture," Cohen insisted, must be at the "middle" of any future "league of states" and must pave the way toward world peace. For it was in German culture most of all that one discovered the true foundations for "world culture." Germany's success in a "just war" was therefore the prerequisite for perpetual peace.[26]

In a famous critique, Martin Buber accused Cohen of naively concentrating on "concepts" and neglecting the "reality" of the Jewish nation. Cohen replied that the spirit of the Hebrew prophets was intimately linked to life in exile: "The realization of Judaism" he argued, in fact depended upon the Jews' dispersion among the peoples of the earth. "This dispersion," he continued, "is our historical reality. The reality of Zionism contradicts the conceptual world of the prophets as well as the entirety of our philosophical rationalism."[27] Cohen's belief that Jews belong to, and must remain within, the sphere of German culture did not imply that Jews should abandon their own religion and convert to Christianity. But it did imply that Ger-

25. Karl Löwith notes that the word "pure" in Cohen's writing combines German Idealism and Jewish purification ritual. "Philosophie der Vernunft und Religion der Offenbarung in H. Cohens Religionsphilosophie," in *Sitzungsberichte der Heidelberger Akademie der Wissenschaften* 7 (Heidelberg: Carl Winter, Universitätsverlag, 1968): 4–34. On allegiance, see, e.g., Cohen's 1883 essay, "Von Kants Einfluß auf die deutsche Kultur," reprinted in Cohen, *Schriften zur Philosophie und Zeitgeschichte* I: 367–96.

26. It followed that Jewish efforts to establish a separate polity were ill-conceived, as Germany itself was already the perfect embodiment of Jewish values. See Cohen, "Religion und Zionismus" (1916), in JS II: 319–27, esp. 326. Also see his "Über das Eigentümliche des deutschen Geistes" (1914), reprinted *Schriften zur Philosophie und Zeitgeschichte* I: 527 ff.

27. Martin Buber, "Begriffe und Wirklichkeit," *Der Jude* 5 (July 1916): 281 ff. Hermann Cohen, "Antwort auf das offene Schreiben des Herrn Dr. Martin Buber an Hermann Cohen" (1916), reprinted in JS II: 328–40.

man Jews were to consider themselves as fundamentally German as those Germans who belonged to the Christian faith. Similarity, not otherness, was the guiding principle of Cohen's cultural vision.[28]

The belief that German Jews are just like other Germans grew increasingly controversial with the rise of Jewish nationalist values.[29] Attacked by Zionists and German nationalists alike, the ideal of cultural belonging was replaced by the notion that Jews are fundamentally distinct and that, even if they should not quit Germany for Palestine, they should cultivate their distinctiveness rather than suppress it. At the very least, their various attempts to hide their "difference" were often interpreted as a kind of false consciousness. The theme of Jewish national difference, which presents so stark a contrast with Cohen's universalist message, would appear prominently in all of Rosenzweig's writing from *The Star of Redemption* to the Bible translation.

Perhaps the most intriguing aspect of this transformation in the way Jews were perceived in relation to Germans is that it was accompanied by a reversal of theological perspective. Cohen, who argued that God lacks all distinguishing characteristics, also argued that German Jews lack features that might have set them apart from other Germans. Rosenzweig, who argued far more forcefully for the distinctiveness of Judaism alongside Christianity, also spoke of the Jewish people as distinguished from all other peoples by blood and destiny. It is therefore significant that Rosenzweig (when compared to Cohen) was also far more appreciative of imagistic description. He embraced anthropomorphism, even the representation of God's "face," without significant quarrel.[30] The emergence of this new trend in Jewish philosophy cannot be explained except as an indication of the waning of Kant's influence. But it is also, perhaps, a reflection on the theological level of changes that were being felt in the realm of politics.

### COHEN'S *RELIGION OF REASON*

Cohen's belief in a deep affinity between Kant and Judaism was to inform his later reflections upon the place of religion in critical philosophy. His treat-

28. See Cohen's arguments against conversion as a response to antisemitism: "Der Religionswechsel in der neuen Ära des Antisemitismus," in JS II: 342–45. And see Amos Funkenstein, "Hermann Cohen: Philosophie, Deutschtum und Judentum," *Jahrbuch des Instituts für deutsche Geschichte*, 6, *Sonderdruck* (Tel-Aviv University, 1984): 355–65.

29. See, e.g., the severe criticism of Cohen in Jacob Klatzkin, "Deutschtum und Judentum: Eine Besprechung," *Der Jude* 2, 4 (1917–18): 245–52.

30. Of course, he distinguished between anthropomorphic description and the doctrine of God's full-blown corporeality; see "Bemerkungen über Anthropomorphismus," FR III: 735–46.

ment of this question began in earnest with the second volume of his independent critical system, *The Ethics of Pure Will* (*Ethik des reinen Willens*, 1904),
and in *The Concept of Religion in the System of Philosophy* (1915). Taken together, these texts demonstrate the evolution of Cohen's thoughts on religion during the final stage of his critical period. While the *Ethics* conceives
God as a "guarantee" between theoretical and practical reason, *The Concept
of Religion* introduces the novel idea that religion has its own "particularity"
*(Eigenart)* in philosophy. It is this idea that Cohen elaborated in his final
work, *Religion of Reason*. We can thus forgo a careful exposition of the earlier texts to concentrate more or less exclusively on the *opus postumum* itself.

The first edition of Cohen's *Die Religion der Vernunft aus den Quellen des Judentums* was published in 1919. In a preface Martha Cohen expressed sad-
ness that her husband had died too soon to see the public appearance of
this book to which "he clung with his entire soul." Cohen had dedicated the
book to his observant father, which Martha Cohen and later Rosenzweig
took as a sign of Cohen's enduring attachment to Judaism. But the first
edition contained significant errors, and Cohen had managed to correct
only the first half of the manuscript before he died.[31] It was not until 1929
that a second, corrected edition appeared under the title Cohen originally
intended: *Religion der Vernunft aus den Quellen des Judentums* (Religion of
reason out of the sources of Judaism; note the lack of the opening definite
article).

As many critics have noted, the title itself appears torn between the
demands of rationalism and the demands of a specific religious tradition.
Throughout the text, the language of Kant exists in uneasy alliance with the
language of the Hebrew Bible, and the combination, however fruitful, produces a certain ambiguity in argument. Indeed, the book's true intentions
remain a matter of controversy. One may argue that Cohen's chief purpose
in the book was to demonstrate that, appearances notwithstanding, there
is in fact no real tension between religion and philosophy. Specifically, he
aimed to show that Judaism itself was in its essential features not only compatible with reason but in fact reason's legitimate offspring. But if this was
indeed his purpose, Cohen's difficulties in realizing this objective are evident throughout.

The long, introductory portion of the text consists in a systematic eluci-
dation of the title and an overview of the chief tasks of the work. The first
challenge is to understand the meaning of a religion of reason, as opposed
to religion as such. The philosophical treatment of religion, Cohen argues,

---

31. Martha Cohen, "Geleitwort zur ersten Auflage," in RV, vi–vii. Cohen had stopped,
oddly enough, in the very middle of the chapter on "Immortality and Resurrection." See
Strauß's afterword to the second edition, 623–29.

is distinct from the merely descriptive methods provided in the history of religion. History, unlike philosophy, has no tools by which to judge the validity of a religious concept. Reason, according to Kant's principles, is our "source" *(Quelle)* of concepts. So rather than derive our concept of religion from some set of historical or literary sources, we in fact possess this concept in advance, and bring it to these sources as the a priori is brought to the world of experience. There is, therefore, a "religion of reason" in the sense that it is born from reason alone. "Reason," wrote Cohen, "is the cliff from which the concept springs, and from which it must first spring for methodical insight, if the course it will assume in the stream of history is to be surveyed" (RV, 6).

Whatever the later disputes over its contents, Cohen's book at least begins with a robust affirmation of the idealist method: not only is history discredited as the source of our religious concepts, "all sensuous qualities" and anything spawned by the imagination must be rejected as well. If religion is to have its origins in our reason alone, it must exclude any trace of "historical naturalism," "contingency," and "facticity." It follows that no one people or culture can suffice as inspiration. Rather, the religion of reason is the joint product of rational humanity as a whole. To this universalist principle, however, Cohen adds a note of qualification: Among the sources for the religion of reason, Judaism alone is the "primordial source" and the "source for other sources" *(Urquelle für andere Quellen)* (RV, 8–10). Judaism, then, enjoys what Cohen will call a unique intellectual advantage, or "headstart" *(Vorsprung),* in the religion of reason. But while he affirms Judaism's "primordiality" *(Ursprünglichkeit),* he assures us that this does not admit an element of contingency into his system. Just as reason is the organum of rules, so too the religion of reason exhibits a fundamentally lawful and necessary character (RV, 10, 12). If religion does provide a legitimate and noncontingent contribution to philosophy, then the correct concept of religion must be one that enjoys its own "share" *(Anteil)* in reason. The task of the book would be to lay out the basic contents of rational religion.[32]

Cohen's chief argument was that religion supplements the ethical concept of the human being (RV, 13). But this presented an immediate threat to his system. As Cohen had argued on many occasions, reason encompasses a single, unified domain. So just as there can be only one reason, there can only be one method for each of its concepts (RV, 15). Moreover, in the *Ethics of Pure Will,* Cohen had argued that ethics categorically denies religion any

---

32. "Matters do not stand such that whosoever has science and philosophy would thereby also possess religion as well. Rather, religion also has its share in reason, and this means: Reason does not exhaust its powers in [creating] science and philosophy." RV, 8.

independent share in reason.[33] But in *Religion of Reason*, Cohen seemed to change his mind. He now argued that religion does indeed lay claim to a unique conceptual sphere.[34] And he suggested that ethics does not generate a fully adequate concept of the human being. Since ethics must safeguard its purity against all sensuous and historical particularity, it is therefore compelled to rescue the concept of the human self as subject from individuality as such. Ethics thus regards the individual as nothing other than a "symbol" or "carrier of humanity."[35] "The 'I' of man," Cohen concluded, "becomes in ethics the 'I' of humanity" and is thus absorbed into the generality, or the "All" *(Allheit)* (RV, 17).

In *Religion of Reason*, Cohen for the first time expressed a certain dissatisfaction with the ethical notion of selfhood. Ethics, he explained, regards the self only from the generic point of view. Each "I" *(Ich)* becomes a third-person, interchangeable subjectivity, and is thereby exhausted within the logic of exemplarity. But Cohen now argued that this ethical perspective missed a crucial aspect of the individual. By theorizing the subject within the universal, its particularity remains obscure. Each "I" must also be regarded as a finite "you" *(Du)*. Here religion makes its unique contribution (RV, 18). Only religion, Cohen suggested, is capable of recognizing the richness of the finite subject, transforming the "he" into a discrete "you."[36] It achieves this transformation by recognizing the unique suffering *(Leiden)* of the individual and feeling "sympathy" *(Mitleid)* (RV, 20; the word play between *Leiden* and *Mitleid* is evident in the German text). The inadequacy of ethics here is apparent. Since pain is not an ethical category, ethics remains unmoved in the face of suffering (RV, 21). Suffering stands "at the limit point" of ethics. It is not ethics but religion alone, therefore, that first "illuminates the horizon of man" (RV, 22).[37]

33. Or, if religion does have some quasi-independence, it is only "as a natural condition, whose cultural fruits fall wholly within the ethical domain." *Ethik* (1907 ed.), 397.

34. On the differences among the three arguments, i.e., in the *Ethik*, the *Begriff der Religion*, and the *Religion der Vernunft*, see the introductory remarks by Andrea Poma in BR, 7–49, esp. 15; also see Mechthild Dreyer, *Die Idee Gottes im Werk Hermann Cohen*, Monographien zur Philosophischen Forschung 230 (Königstein: Verlag Anton Hain, 1985).

35. This is necessary, Cohen argues, if ethics is to function properly as universal legislation. Political ethics follows the very same pattern, by realizing the abstraction of humanity in a state, which is thus defined by constitutional law *(Rechtsverfassung)*, not heritage *(Abstammung)*. The individual "elevates himself" in the state, which in turn "purifies" the individual. RV, 15–17.

36. Here I reproduce Cohen's use of the male pronoun.

37. On Cohen's view, Judaism (especially the Hebrew prophets) is to be credited for introducing the idea that God will one day "vanquish the tears from every face." Christianity, on the other hand, shares with Spinozism and Schopenhauer an erroneous understanding of suffering that is in Cohen's view patently "metaphysical" (in this context a term of disapproval): for

Here Cohen was compelled to address anew the problem he had already posed concerning the relationship between religion and ethics: Are we not confronted with the predicament we wished to avoid, that ethics now appears inadequate to its task and must share its place with religion? And doesn't this predicament mean that philosophy itself is robbed of its unity? Cohen attempted to extricate himself from this difficulty by noting that while there is a certain "lack" in the ethical concept of man, the authority of ethics remains unimpaired (RV, 15). Since the particularity of the religious self itself belongs to "the infinite membership chain of humanity," it is therefore "new, but not foreign." The contribution of religion is indeed "inside" the ethical totality yet it is nonetheless an innovation.[38]

Whether this was truly a solution is doubtful. Significantly, the same potential difficulty reappeared elsewhere, especially in Cohen's remarks on the religious idea of God. In his *Ethics of Pure Will,* Cohen had conceived God as a purely ethical concept embracing humankind as a "totality." And just as from the ethical point of view man is a mere specimen of humanity, so too the ethical God is a mere a "guarantee," a methodological assurance of the compatibility between ethics and nature (*Ethik,* 422, 426).[39] In *Religion of Reason,* however, Cohen now faulted this concept as negligent of individual cases. The ethical transcendence of the particular, he suggested, was symptomatic of "lazy reason" ("Dieser 'faulen Vernunft'") (RV, 24).

The suggestion that reason is lazy was clearly discordant with Cohen's earlier critical philosophy. (Rosenzweig would consider it a sign of Cohen's disillusionment with idealism.) Cohen's new interest in religion, it seems, allowed him to regard his earlier idealist doctrine from an unfamiliar perspective. Seen from the "higher" cognitivist point of view, ethical universalism appeared as a mark of purity. But when seen from the more "earthly" position of the suffering individual, the same universalism now appeared as indifference. Whether this new perspective signaled a true revolution in Cohen's philosophy may be disputed. But Cohen himself continued to insist on the compatibility between religion and ethics. In fact, he found that Judaism forbade any violation of rationalist-ethical principles: "Religion is

---

"[t]he metaphysical sense of suffering [erroneously] makes it into the authentic and sole reality of human existence." RV, 19, 21.

38. This argument is already evident in BR, §23 of the chapter concerning "The Relation of Religion to Ethics," esp. 44.

39. Cohen further argued that the ultimate condition in which the "is" is identical with the "ought," the ideal with the real, can be called "the messianic kingdom." And this "messianic" concept of God is fully explicable within the ethical domain. But in the *Religion of Reason,* Cohen expressed dissatisfaction with this idea: the concept of God that has been "transplanted" *(verplanzt)* from monotheism to ethics remains "an ethical God" only, but not yet "the actual God of religion." RV, 25.

itself an ethical theory, or it is not religion" (RV, 38).[40] It is only pantheism that introduces the idea that Cohen disparagingly termed "the so-called existence of God" *(die so-gennanten Dasein Gottes),* thereby introducing an irrational and metaphysical moment in religion. The way was then open for skepticism to reject religion as bankrupt to the core. Cohen admitted that there are such irrational elements in some of the older Jewish sources. For example, he regarded the notion of the Jewish people as a "community of blood" *(Gemeinschaft des Bluts)* as a materialistic corruption. And even the book of Deuteronomy does not manage to avoid the idea of a sacrificial cult (though in Ezekiel sacrifice is supplanted by repentance—its rational equivalent; RV, 31). For these reasons, Cohen insisted that the religion of reason is grounded chiefly in the Prophetic texts.[41]

The remainder of Cohen's book provides a systematic treatment of those rudimentary concepts in Judaism that lay the groundwork for the religion of reason. The most important of these is the idea of God's uniqueness. Cohen sees the revolutionary nature of Hebrew monotheism in its thoroughgoing rejection of paganism: Greek thought equates the being of God *(Sein)* with the entities of the cosmos *(Seiende);* Judaism alone conceives the being of God as unique. For the Hebrew Bible, the world is mere appearance *(Schein);* God alone is being *(Sein)* (RV, 49–53; also 481–85). This idea is first announced to Moses at the burning bush (Exodus 3:13–14), for which Cohen provides the following translation:

> Da sprach Mose zu Gott: Wenn ich nun aber zu den Israelite komme und ihnen sage: der Gott eurer Väter hat mich zu euch gesandt, und sie mich fragen: was ist sein Name? Was soll ich dann ihnen sagen? Da sprach Gott zu Mose: Ich bin, der ich bin.

> Then spake Moses to God: If I now come to the children of Israel and say to them: the God of your fathers has sent me to you, and they ask me, what is his

---

40. Again Cohen takes pains to show that this concept is derived from religion alone, even while the integrity of ethics remains unimpaired. But once again the argument involves a certain equivocation: "Ethics remains valuable in those theoretical foundations by which it must lead the method toward the determination of the value of the human; but religion has disclosed topical insights, and has derived these from the principles of its thought of God, which insights remain closed to the ethical method. These insights are the foundations for its own special mode [*Eigenart*], which are just as indispensable, as [that] the handling of these concepts is adapted to the general method of ethics." RV, 27.

41. In fact, the Jewish sources display a curious "double-nature" *(Doppelheit)* in that the oldest of these sources (the so-called five books of Moses) are still wrapped in myth, while the prophets are relatively free from the older type of mythological thinking. As messengers of the religion of reason, therefore, "the prophets stand as independent carriers beside Moses, who lay far behind them in darkness, such that it was they who first lifted from him the veil of myth." RV, 31.

Name? What should I then say to them? Then spake God to Moses, I am, that
I am. (My translation of Cohen's German)

Like Buber and Rosenzweig after him, Cohen regarded this passage as a veritable revelation in the history of philosophy. According to Cohen, God's
response, "Ich bin, der ich bin" ("I am, that which I am") meant that God
alone is identical with being.[42] Significantly, Cohen expressed the difference between divine and worldly being in the German words *Sein* (being) as
against *Dasein* (existence): Divine being, he argued, is pure and admits of
no connection whatsoever with "sensual existence" *(sinnlichen Dasein).* It
followed that God is beyond time and "becoming" (RV, 53).[43] (This idealist
reading is precisely what Buber and Rosenzweig found unacceptable, as I
shall explain in chapter 5.)

From these spare beginnings, Cohen derived a rich conception of God.
Here he relied upon the model of the principle of origins introduced in his
*Logic.* Once again, he recalled that our notion of the infinite is the starting
point for the generation of finitude (RV, 76). But he now gave this principle a new, religious meaning. Being, as the infinite negation of all that is
transitory, is also the origin of becoming. Accordingly, God is the creator,
and the world is God's creation *(Schöpfung).* In Cohen's view, this concept of
creation is utterly distinct from the mythological idea of God as an entity
who first fashions the cosmos: the concept of creation arises from nothing
else but the logical idea of God as unique. Accordingly, as a being of spirit,
or *Geist,* God creates human reason. And just as the negation of privations
helps us to generate one concept from another, the concept of creation in

42. The precise translation of the Hebrew—*ehiyeh asher ehiyeh*—was therefore a matter of
some concern. In *Religion of Reason,* Cohen objects strenuously to the translation by Emil
Kautzsch, "Ich bin wer ich bin" (I am who I am) because of its overtly personalist implications
*(Die Heilige Schrift des Alten Testaments,* 4th ed. [Tübingen: J. C. B. Mohr, Paul Siebeck, 1922).
He thus admired Mendelssohn's translation, "I am the eternal" *(Ich bin der Ewige),* which
marked God as "unique, against which the world has no being whatsoever." RV, 49–53.

43. Such claims inform Cohen's richly philosophical interpretation of the second commandment. The ban on visual or plastic representations of God and image worship *(Bilderdienst)* is based upon the idea that sensual representation introduces an impurity into our religious devotion. Where this devotion is not an exclusive service to the one and only God
*(avodath elohim),* we are not only committing an intellectual mistake of categories; we are in fact
supplanting the love of God with worldly slavery *(avodah)* and idolatry *(avodah za'ra).* Remarkably, Cohen's hostility to representation does not extend to linguistic description: while Judaism forbids the plastic arts, it allows for poetry. The prophets were in fact poetic thinkers
*(Dichterdenker).* Apparently, Cohen believed that language is a stimulus for the correct idea of
a thing, while images tend to supplant thought. As Cohen explained, there can be no image
*(Bild)* of God because there is no empirical concept for him. God is not a "copy" *(Abbild);*
rather, God is the "primordial concept" *(Urgedanke)* and the "primordial being" *(Ursein).* RV,
esp. chap. 2, "Der Bilderdienst," 58–67.

turn issues a new concept, that of revelation *(Offenbarung)* (RV, 81). But revelation is not the "unveiling" of God's essence, as this would be a mythological error. Like creation, revelation is a logical idea only—a relation of spirit *(Geistlichkeit).*[44] And this relation is not one-sided. Revelation is the actualization of God as well, who cannot remain in the isolation of his being but must also emerge into the realm of becoming (RV, 109–11).[45] God as becoming is only actualized through human knowledge ("Es ist als ob das Sein Gottes erst in der Erkenntnis des Menschen aktuell würde") (RV, 100–104). The relation between man and God is therefore a "correlation" in which both elements gain actuality through their mutual bond. Correlation, Cohen insists, is therefore the decisive category for understanding man's relation to God (RV, 104).

The remaining chapters of Cohen's study draw out the various consequences of the correlation idea. God's attributes of action are not objective descriptions; they present man with unending ethical tasks. God's holiness is a process, not a feature. And when God is drawn toward the sphere of becoming, his holiness is realized in the midst of humanity, and humanity becomes in turn holy before God (RV, 120). God's holiness is therefore ethical, and has nothing to do with mere "facticity" *(Tatsächlichkeit).* Similarly, man's holiness is an infinite task, realized "only in the abstraction of eternal ethical becoming" (RV, 129).

However, in the introductory remarks to the eighth chapter, Cohen grew impatient: "Man as we have made his acquaintance so far has been known to us only as holy spirit, only as an ethical essence of reason." Here, man is "only an abstraction of religion" that rests wholly "on the ground of its share in reason and in the theory of ethics." He possesses "no relation to historical experience, nor to natural knowledge." The correlation between man and God is so far only a "problem" and the ethical dimension of religion is itself still far from arriving at any experiential content (RV, 131–32). This already indicates a radical shift in tone. Cohen had previously denied that experience has any significant role in laying down the requirements for philosophical investigation. But religion would now address man as an experiential creature and would propose two aspects of human being as yet

44. This helps to explain why Moses, in his encounter with God on Mount Sinai, sees only God's back, not his face. In Cohen's interpretation, this illustrates the difference between monotheism and mythology. Kautzsch's translation of 2. Moses [Exodus] 33:19 reads God's phrase *kol tov'i* as "all meine Schöne" ("all my beauty" or "glory"). Cohen insists that this translation is incorrect. The human relationship to the divine is not one of empirical knowledge. Rather, our relation to God is that of ethical obligation following after the fact of our createdness in reason. RV, 93.

45. On Cohen's concept of correlation, see Alexander Altmann, "Hermann Cohens Begriff der Correlation," in *In Zwei Welten: Siegfried Moses um fünfundsiebzigsten Geburtstag,* ed. Hans Tramer (Tel-Aviv: Verlag Bitaon, 1962), 377–99.

undisclosed to philosophy. One would address the human being as an individual, while the other would describe his membership within a distinctive (non-universal) grouping, that is, under the category of *Mehrheit,* not *Allheit.* Both of these concepts, Cohen admitted, are originally "derived from experience" (RV, 132).

Under the category of the group, religion provides a unique understanding of the human being as "fellow-man" *(Mitmensch).* In the Bible, the fellow-man is potentially each and every human being that one might encounter. Despite the apparently national consciousness of the ancient Hebrews, the Bible clearly grants priority to the idea of all humankind as children of Adam. For Cohen, the tension between this humanistic insight and the more particularist idea of the Israelites as especially privileged, as children of Abraham, is dissolved in the idea of the "neighbor" *(der Nächste),* who is potentially anyone. Despite the struggle against idolatry, even the pagan Edomite is a neighbor, and every foreigner is a fellow-man. Thus respect must be shown for all human beings as "sons of Noah." The neighbor who is singled out most often as the object of prophetic attention is the man suffering in poverty. According to Cohen, the religion of reason wholly rejects any concern for suffering that does not fall under the category of the social. Concern for death, for example, would imply a "metaphysics of suffering" whereas Judaism must direct its attention solely toward "spiritual suffering" (RV, 158).

In this argument, Cohen had not yet overcome his tendency to see all of religion as partaking in the universalist structures of ethical thought. He admitted that the proper response to suffering is "powerful emotion," rather than mere knowledge of the suffering condition, since the suffering of the other goes directly to the "heart." But despite the importance of sympathy, Cohen did not seem ready to admit a personal dimension into the religion of reason: "Every trace of interest in the subjective, individual grounds of suffering must be entirely shut out. . . . Suffering is social, and it therefore follows that its understanding cannot be called forth by means of any insight that touches only the individual"(RV, 160). In fact, even Cohen's account of love seemed constrained by ethical-universalist principles. In the chapter "The Problem of Religious Love," Cohen suggested that it is love that first transforms the human being who is merely nearby *(Nebenmensch)* into a true neighbor *(Mitmensch).* Love in this manifestation is a "primordial form" of humanity, and religion alone is responsible for its genesis. "What ethics could not accomplish, religion can" (RV, 169). Religious love therefore begins with man alone. Here Cohen noted that God merely loves humanity in a generic fashion—"in its infinity"(RV, 172).

The Protestant theologian Wilhelm Herrmann (Cohen's colleague at Marburg), subjected this idealist view of religion to serious criticism. According to Herrmann, Cohen's religious philosophy lacked a fundamental appreciation for the "simple faith of man," who possesses his "very own experiences" of God's "reality." "The reality in which we live is not constituted through the abstractions of science, but rather through that which we experience ourselves." And religion must concern itself with precisely the reality of "our very own existence" *(unserer eigenen Existenz).*[46]

Clearly, such remarks struck at the heart of Cohen's idealism. In *Religion of Reason,* Cohen addresses Herrmann's objection, but the response does little more than repeat the idealist principles of his philosophy: "Reality," Cohen objects, is "a concept of relation between thought and sensation." It is thus indisputable that "God can have no reality whatsoever." Herrmann's complaint, Cohen continues, is really inspired by a Christian expectation that God be represented in human form. But Judaism cannot help but take issue with this tendency toward anthropomorphism. Since its beginnings, Judaism has resisted the confusion between "biological life" and God's purely "ethical reality":

> What the *Idea,* as ethical reality, and only as such, can positively mean and accomplish for reality [*Wirklichkeit*] becomes most clear in the case of love of God, on the foundations of love of God. The realizing power [*realisierende Kraft*] of the idea is nowhere so evident, as it is in the case of love of God. *How can one love an idea?* To this must be answered: How can one love anything but an idea? (RV, 185)

For those who shared Herrmann's preferences for a God of experience, this answer was of course far from satisfactory. Cohen, it seemed, could not conceive of religion except as one element within the sovereign system of rationalist ethics. But this meant neglecting entirely what Herrmann called "the inner life of individual man."[47]

In the chapter entitled "The Individual as I," Cohen admitted that his treatment of religion still lacked a crucial dimension. It is true that the *Mitmensch* first discloses the self, but only as self-for-another, as an *Ich* for a *Du.* He had not yet discovered what this *Ich* might be on its own. The "absolute individual," in other words, had not yet emerged to full determinacy. For ethics must subscribe to categories of universality, and it therefore conceives the self as no more than an example, or "point of relation," within the totality. Here the ethical self is—to borrow Robert Musil's phrase—a "man without qualities."

---

46. Wilhelm Herrmann, "Hermann Cohens Ethik," *Die Christliche Welt,* Evangelisches Gemeindeblatt für Geildete aller Stände, 21 (1907): Part I (January 17), 51–59; Part II (March 7), 222–28; quotes at 225.

47. Herrmann, "Cohens Ethik," Part II, 223.

It was the unique role of religion to discover the human subject in what Cohen termed its "isolation."[48] From the ethical point of view, Cohen explained, the self is "real" only as a successful agent of the universal. But there is a quality to subjectivity that appears only in the universal's absence: Cohen called this our "ethical fragility" (RV, 25). Like Jonah stripped of his protective palm branches, this "fragile" self is disclosed only in those circumstances where we sense our failure before the universal. And this is precisely the notion of selfhood which prompts the idea of sin (especially prominent in the book of Ezekiel; RV, 25–26). Here we have truly arrived at what Cohen called "the boundary of ethics."[49]

The correlation between the God of religion and the finite self provides the unique route to redemption from sin.[50] For Cohen, redemption is not a metaphysical concept, but rather a device of teleology. In fact, it is the act of repentance *(Versöhnung),* in which the individual who is now aware of his sin voluntarily submits before God. To repent can mean only to become free from sin, and from this process of emancipation the subject is disclosed as fully actual—he is the possessor, in the language of Ezekiel, of a new and purified soul: "The human being can become a new human being. The possibility of this self-transformation makes of the individual an 'I'" (RV, 227).[51]

Cohen regards reconciliation as an eternal process. Just as the ethical task is infinite, so the act of repentance is one of "perpetual turning." The

48. Cohen argued already in BR that "the religious person is strictly an individual. And this absolute Individuality is granted to him by means of the correlation with God. Through God the human being becomes an absolute individual [*Individuum*]." BR, 92.

49. Ethical man "knows of no council" that could disburden him of his guilt for membership in what Cohen calls "the empire of ethical being" (*Reich der sittlichen Wesen*). On the indifference of ethics to the concept of guilt, see Cohen's arguments concerning legal judgment and punishment in *Ethik;* and his comparison of the ethical concept of responsibility with that of religion in RV, 194–96.

50. In order to explain the meaning of this redemption, Cohen offers a brief but fascinating excursus concerning the idea of sacrifice in the Hebrew Bible. Contrary to what one might have expected, he does not speak of the sacrifice of animals as wholly irrational. Instead, he suggests that we must accept the continuity between mythology and religion, even while we take care to admit of only those aspects of myth that have fully evolved into legitimately religious concepts. In the discussion of subjective guilt, Cohen places great importance in this evolutionary process; the correlation between man and God that promises release from guilt is in fact the mature expression of the idea of sacrifice. Cohen warns us, however, that there is a crucial difference between the cultic practice and its rationalized equivalent: in its mature form, repentance is a conceptual tool, and no longer a metaphysical act. The notions of sin, guilt, and reconciliation with God as they appear in the religion of reason are to be considered from the "purely methodological" point of view, as "instrument of disclosure" that help us to conceive of the finite individual. RV, 202–11.

51. Cohen thus admired the slogan from Ezekiel 18:31, "Cast off from yourselves [*Werft ab von euch*] all of your misdeeds . . . and make for yourselves a new heart and a new Spirit."

"new beginning" of the subject as a soul is therefore a regulative idea, not a discrete event as in cultic sacrifice (RV, 226–40). Redemption therefore means both the disclosure of the subject as an individual and the release of this individual from sin (both conceived as teleological method, not metaphysics) (RV, 250). But Judaism nonetheless embodies this process in a discrete ceremony of ritual "purification" from sin, in the "day of reconciliation and repentance" or Yom Kippur. In a rational form, this ritual addresses the very same concerns that once preoccupied practitioners of pagan religion: the question of divine judgment and fate. But monotheism has risen above the concept of fate: "What polytheism called destiny and fate [*Verhängnis und Schicksal*] monotheism calls judgment and redemption" (RV, 258).[52]

One of the most striking consequences of Cohen's theory of redemption is that it provides a philosophical justification for the perpetuity of Jewish exile. For just as the freeing of the individual from sin is an eternal process, so too is the suffering of the individual. The people of Israel for Cohen thus functioned as a collective symbol of finitude. The Jews are an individual subject writ large, who must suffer so as to take part in the process of redemption. In the history of the world, the Jews must therefore remain apart as symbols of redemption—they are, in Cohen's phrase, the *Leidenvolk* of world history.[53] But this symbolic function also guarantees that the Jews are an eternal nation, who do not live as the other nations, bounded by states and politics within the "horizon of history" (RV, 273). The Jews, Cohen argues, are "by no means a state, but indeed a people" (RV, 300). Accordingly, they must be isolated so as to symbolize the isolation of the self before God: "Israel," Cohen writes, is "in all its history a prototype of suffering, a symbol of human misery, of human existence as such" (RV, 301).

Cohen's argument therefore confirmed that the Jews remain isolated from history: their exile marks not only their persecution but also their redemption. For the "remnant" *(Rest)* of Israel is a symbol for redeemed humanity, the "Israel of the future" (RV, 303). The perpetuity of both suffering and redemption in Cohen's philosophy therefore demands that we interpret the biblical notion of the messianic age as an ideal, not a concrete reality. In the domain of rational philosophy, Cohen reminds us, "all existence vanishes from the standpoint of the idea." For history must be endless, since it represents for philosophy the "horizon for the infinite devel-

---

52. Because this redemption is perpetual, so too is the notion of suffering from which it emerges. Suffering, Cohen explains, is a "rung toward redemption." And for this reason, "a certain permanence of suffering . . . provides the correct interpretation for the sense of my existence." RV, 266.

53. Borrowing from Lessing, Cohen describes the mission of the Jews as the "education of the human race" *(die Erziehung des Menschengeschlechts)*. RV, 330.

opment of humanity" (RV, 271–72). As the horizon of redemption, history is more than a mere collection of facts. Its futurity, Cohen argues, must be considered the horizon of pure being.[54]

In the philosophical sense, the concept of immortality has nothing in common with the metaphysical notion that the individual, as "mere existence" *(bloßen Existenz)*, may survive beyond death (RV, 355). Eternal life is a "religious expression" not a factical description (RV, 380). Similarly, Cohen finds the meaning of Jewish ritual and law in ethics, not cultic practice as such. Law is therefore *Gesetz,* the positing of an infinite task, and not *Gebot,* an arbitrary command.[55] In analogous fashion, Cohen interprets prayer as the expression through language (which is the medium of reason) of the human being's love for God. Prayer is not the attempt to unify with a God of "reality"; it is instead the true language in which to express the correlation between man and God. Moreover, "the man who is not capable of prayer cannot unburden himself from his finitude [*Endlichkeit*] with all its fears and spoilage." And whoever is capable of prayer thereby "loses earthly fears [*Erdenangst*] and the hardship of this world in a soaring upward toward infinity [*Aufschwung zur Unendlichkeit*]" (RV, 463).

### IS COHEN'S ARGUMENT COHERENT?

At first glance, Cohen's *Religion of Reason* appears to be a powerful and unambiguous expression of religious idealism. At virtually every turn, it rejects a literal understanding of religious notions, supplanting the literal with the philosophical. Indeed, it often appears that Cohen is little interested in religious categories themselves and grants them his attention only if they prove compliant to idealist demands.[56] As we have seen, the neo-Kantian mode of thought, as exemplified in Cohen's studies in logic and ethics, had as its one of its chief aims the expulsion of all residual metaphysical contents from systematic philosophy. It replaced these metaphysical contents with concepts that were purely methodological in character.[57] At times, this re-

54. History is therefore for Cohen *Geschichte* as against *Historie*—a distinction that will play an important role in Heidegger's philosophy as well; see esp. the remarks in SZ, 397–404.

55. For Rosenzweig's inversion of this view and his theory of Jewish law as commandment, see "Die Bauleute," FR III; also see my remarks on law as a practical horizon of meaning in the discussion of Rosenzweig's *Star,* in chapter 3. Also see *Briefe,* N.342, An Rudolf Hallo (Frankfurt a.M., 27.3.1922), 425.

56. At times, his interpretation is so vigorous that it results in laughable anachronism, as when he compares the Prophets to the cosmopolitans of the eighteenth century. RV, 283.

57. This habit of thought is even apparent in the title of Cohen's *Religion der Vernunft.* The genitive implies that religion is one of the possessions "of reason," suggesting that Cohen was more stringent in his rationalism than Kant, whose *Religion innerhalb der Grenzen der bloßen*

quirement yielded jarring comparisons; hence Cohen's remark that "there must be one God, valid for all peoples, just as there is one mathematics, valid for all" (RV, 295).

But one may justifiably ask if such methods are at all appropriate to the study of religion. Some would argue that what is most real in religion dissolves when exposed to rational scrutiny—hence the principle, "Credo quia absurdum est."[58] Clearly, Cohen rejected this view; he held that one cannot believe what has not passed before the court of reason. But one cannot therefore dismiss him as a dogmatic rationalist. As noted above, Cohen insisted that religion possesses concepts peculiarly its own—indeed, he called this religion's "peculiarity" *(Eigenart)*. One may object, however, that this does not yet grant religion a legitimacy alongside reason. For as noted above, Cohen expressly denied religion its full independence *(Selbständigkeit)*. It remained little more than a province within the domain of rationalized ethics.

Following Rosenzweig, many critics have wondered whether this account of the relationship between ethics and religion can be sustained. As discussed above, Cohen saw ethics as capable of generating only concepts of universal meaning. The ethical individual is therefore a mere representative of the totality. In fact, Cohen claims that "this dissolution of the individual is for ethics its highest triumph" (RV, 208). The very same notion of the individual is evident in the social teachings of the biblical prophets, who, in their zeal to speak of humanity, lose sight of the finite person:

> The individual, as a solitary person [*Das Individuum, als Einzelmensch*] disappears in [the ethical] gazing upon humanity from a distance. "Think nothing of man, for of what consequence is he?" Isaiah by no means rejects this Hamlet phrase (Is. 2:22); for his enthusiasm for the unique God brought him to a disregard of man characteristic of his age. With this judgment . . . however, one does not yet arrive at a proper understanding of the problem posed by the individual, although it might well be worthwhile to soar upward into the totality [*Allheit*]. (RV, 208)

This passage is symptomatic of Cohen's difficulty in binding religion to ethics within the confines of a single rational system. Both ethics and reli-

---

*Vernunft* demanded only that religion be regarded "within the boundaries of" reason. On this see Nathan Rotenstreich, *"Religion within Limits of Reason Alone and Religion of Reason,"* LBIY 1972, 179–87.

58. But the idea is not only premodern. It was the "irrational" aspect of religion that Rudolf Otto (the professor of theology who was a colleague of Cohen and Natorp at Marburg) made the object of his 1917 study *The Idea of the Holy;* significantly, it was subtitled *On the Irrational in the Idea of the Divine and Its Relation to the Rational.* Otto, *Das Heilige: Über das Irrationale in der Idee des Göttlichen und sein Verhältnis zum Rationalen* (Breslau: Trewendt und Granier, 1917).

gion speak to the human longing for transcendence, though they do so in quite distinctive ways. Ethical transcendence allows the individual to "soar upward into the totality." (Significantly, Cohen describes this as the "resurrection" of the individual in humanity—a religious metaphor that is provocative to say the least, since Cohen is trying to distinguish ethics from religion.) But religious transcendence allows the individual a release from sin. (Cohen considers this the true, "non-metaphysical" meaning of redemption.)

Now at first glance, it may seem that religious redemption can occur alongside the "triumph" of ethics. The process by which God recognizes the individual in his sin seems to have little to do with ethical concerns. But neither does it appear to bar ethical satisfaction. Ethics and religion are, it seems, more or less indifferent spheres. But as we have seen, Cohen insists that ethics is incomplete and lacks the concept of individuality only religion can provide. Furthermore, he argues that the concepts of religion are wholly its own but find their full meaning only in relation to ethics. In this sense the two systems cannot survive in mutual indifference and are in fact mutually dependent for their success. On closer inspection, however, this cannot be the case, because the success of the one system seems to demand the failure of the other: ethics must cancel out the finitude that religion regards as the proper sphere of redemption, but religion must resist the eclipse of the individual that ethics sees as a necessity for universalization.[59] Indeed, religion first discovers the individual only in its moment of ethical failure. In this sense, religion and ethics are not only incompatible, they are locked in opposition.

It would be wrong to characterize this moment of dissonance in Cohen's argument as fatal. Cohen was clearly aware that the unstable relationship between ethics and religion threatened the unity of his philosophical system, and he took great pains to arrive at a correct formula to describe their relationship. But the result was at best an uneasy truce, achieved largely at religion's expense. Ethics could tolerate its alliance with religion only because Cohen had defined the essence of religion in such a fashion that most, if not all, of its nonrational elements, which he called "mythical" or "metaphysical," were banished from the start. This is particularly true of the paired elements in the correlation between God and man, which Cohen defined as religion's unique contribution to philosophy. At various points in the text it appears as if Cohen too felt dissatisfied with his solution: There is a defensive note to his remark that the individual as disclosed by religion is

---

59. Of course, Cohen was aware of the problem this posed to the coherency of his philosophical system. He wished to ensure religion its "share" (*Anteil*) in reason. But he believed that the methodological integrity of philosophy demands that each of its various domains make its own unique contribution to the whole. RV, 14.

neither "a mere abstraction" nor a "specter" (RV, 238–39). And there is an evasive quality to his defense against Herrmann's suggestion that God should be real, not an idea. Cohen responded, as noted above, with a rhetorical question—"How can one love anything other than an idea?" This was an unfortunate *petitio principi* and was cited by several of Cohen's later critics to highlight what they considered his aggravating disregard for the nature of religious experience.[60]

But the suggestion that Cohen was too much of an idealist fully to appreciate religion is misleading. The often tortuous quality of his attempts to distinguish between religious and ethical concepts is a symptom of the great difficulty he experienced in negotiating between the two poles of his thought: the idealist methodologies he cherished and the religious phenomena whose reality he wished somehow to preserve. In the quality of its writing, the *Religion of Reason* presents a thinker confident of his views. But in the subtlety of its distinctions, the work betrays a thinker caught between two equally powerful commitments. Cohen seemed resigned to the fact that few readers would accept his attempt to make idealism capture the full meaning of religion. "But here too," he wrote, "abstraction is my fate."[61]

## RECEPTION AND CRISIS

On April 15, 1918, Rosenzweig, at that time stationed at the Macedonian front, read the public announcement of Cohen's death in a newspaper obituary. In a letter to his mother, Rosenzweig observed that "Cohen's philosophy of religion hardly follows as a smooth consequence of his previous system, but is rather something of a new phase."[62] For Rosenzweig, the appearance of religious elements had shattered, not supplemented, the system of critical philosophy that Cohen had taken such care to construct. It was obvious that the "individual" that had appeared in Cohen's religious philosophy was no longer an example but instead a unique creation, as

60. See, e.g., Guttmann's claim that "God remains for Cohen an Idea, even in this last phase of his thought." PJ, 361–62.

61. Quoted from a letter of March 27, 1907, in Siegfried Ucko, *Der Gottesbegriff in der Philosophie Hermann Cohens* (Berlin: Siegfried Scholem, 1927), 31–33.

62. *Breife*, N.221, An die Mutter (15.4.1918.), 299. The first reference to Cohen's death in Rosenzweig's published letters is from April 7, 1918 (*Briefe*, N.215, An die Mutter, 291–92). Rosenzweig had only recently read the manuscript of chapters from Cohen's still unpublished *Religion der Vernunft*. He discusses them, inter alia, in a letter to Rudolf Ehrenberg from March 5, 1918 (*Briefe*, N.210, 281ff). Rosenzweig's letter to Cohen himself about the manuscript (March 9, 1918) is a fascinating illustration of their differences. Rosenzweig especially disputes Cohen's tendency to use technical-sounding philosophical language such as "correlation," where simpler language would suffice. The complaint illustrates Rosenzweig's greater sense of ambivalence regarding academic philosophy. *Briefe*, N.212, 286–88.

unique as the God who had created him. This individual, according to Rosenzweig, was not only in tension with but had in fact burst the bounds of reason, and had emerged, like Cohen himself, from the constraints of the older system into a new, "metaphysical," reality.[63]

In his extended introduction ("Einleitung") to Cohen's *Jüdische Schriften* (Jewish writings), Rosenzweig popularized the notion that there was a split in Cohen's soul between the philosopher and the religious individual. "The man Cohen," Rosenzweig wrote, had succeeded in keeping from view the "hidden treasures" of his religious belief, hiding them from the "treasure-digging spade of the systematician." Only at the end of his life, in the *Religion of Reason* did he finally bring these treasures to light: "The care for systematic organization" that had defined all of his previous work up to the *Concept of Religion* in 1915, was at last silenced, and now, despite the great effort expended in the exposition of concepts, the whole work betrayed a new quality of piety and "naïveté." Whatever respect was owed to reason's majesty, reason was now forced to acknowledge that it was like a dam in a river, which, fed by a far more ancient source, "overflowed the whole of the earth." Rosenzweig therefore ascribed great significance to the fact that Cohen had dedicated the book, not to any "school" of philosophy, but rather to the man to whom he owed his deep feelings of connection with the "homeland of blood and spirit"—his father.

Rosenzweig's interpretation of Cohen involved more than a touch of romanticism. While he was correct to discern in Cohen's thought a potential conflict between philosophy and religion, he had also bent Cohen to his own purposes. (The reference to Judaism as a "homeland of blood," for example, is a phrase wholly alien to Cohen's manner of thinking.) Given this tendency to dramatize and perhaps even distort Cohen's work, it is not surprising that one could find many interpreters of the neo-Kantian tradition who disputed the accuracy of Rosenzweig's portrait. Most of all, they objected to the implication that Cohen himself had grown dissatisfied with his critical system and had perhaps even taken steps toward abandoning it. From the neo-Kantian perspective, Rosenzweig was inattentive to the philosophical continuities between the "early" and the "late" phases in Cohen's career. When one examined the *opus postumum* against the background of neo-Kantian method, Cohen's treatment of religion appeared fully consonant with his previous work in logic, ethics, and aesthetics.[64]

---

63. Julius Guttmann speaks of the possibility in Cohen's work of an unnoticed "breakthrough into the metaphysical," PJ, 361; against this view, see Altmann, "Cohens Begriff der Correlation," esp. 397.

64. For a similar perspective, see Altmann, "Cohens Begriff der Correlation," 399; and Emil Fackenheim, *Hermann Cohen—After Fifty Years*, Leo Baeck Memorial Lecture (New York: Leo Baeck Institute, 1969), 23.

The most prominent representative of this argument was Walter Kinkel, a professor of philosophy in Gießen and a strong partisan of Marburg idealism. In 1924, the same year as the publication of Rosenzweig's introduction to Cohen's *Jüdische Schriften*, Kinkel published his study, *Hermann Cohen: An Introduction to His Work*, a sophisticated and thorough treatment of all Cohen's major writings, including the *opus postumum*. While disagreeing with Rosenzweig, Kinkel believed that Cohen himself had probably inflated the status of religion in his system beyond what was warranted by rational necessity. The celebrated idea that religion enjoys its very own peculiarity *(Eigenart)* was shown to be incorrect according to Cohen's own principles. As Kinkel explained, Cohen's exposition of religious concepts in the *Religion of Reason* had not yielded any novel concepts not already satisfied by ethics. The question whether the last book addressed concepts that belong more properly to religion or to ethics was therefore, from the standpoint of the system, a matter of indifference.[65]

Surveying the larger intellectual landscape, one can see that this dispute was hardly an isolated affair. The status of religion and its relation to modern, idealist philosophy was a subject of great interest throughout the 1920s.[66] Dozens of writers joined in the debate surrounding the meaning of the religious turn in critical philosophy. For many, Cohen's study of religion was the paramount illustration of a far greater transformation taking place in the discipline of philosophy. For others it was a lamentable failure, proving once and for all that neo-Kantianism was now obsolete.[67] Those who believed in the continued viability of neo-Kantian methods complained that the Marburg school had been unfairly branded as "rationalizing," and, accordingly, they tended to read Cohen's final work as the crowning achieve-

65. Kinkel argues that "one must assume not only a connection, but in fact an identity between religion and ethics." *Cohen: Eine Einführung,* 272–73. The argument of "indifference" aroused Rosenzweig's ire. In a revised version of his introduction to JS, which was included in the 1926 collection of essays, *Zweistromland,* Rosenzweig wrote that "before finishing [this introduction], Kinkel's book on Cohen came to my attention. . . . The strict-believing Marburgian denies his own master any adherents subsequent to the theological transition after 1912. In the peculiarity [*Eigenart*] of religious life which the final Cohen defended, Kinkel sees self-deceit. Here only one can be correct: Kinkel or—Cohen." "Einleitung," in *Zweistromland: Kleinere Schriften zur Religion und Philosophie* (Berlin: Philo Verlag, 1926). The "Einleitung" originally appeared in JS I: xliv, and was also reprinted in KS, 299–350 (with the remark on Kinkel then added as a new footnote at 299), and in FR III: 205.
66. The place of religion in Kant's corpus received significant attention as well; see, e.g., Horst Stephen, "Kant und die Religion," *Kantstudien* 24, 1 (1924): 207–32.
67. Johannes Hessen, *Die Religionsphilosophie des Neukantianismus* (Freiburg: Herder Verlag, 1924), 114. In 1947 Hessen wrote a study of Heidegger's thought. Albert Lewkowitz judged Cohen's rationalism as inadequate for addressing religious concerns; *Religiöse Denker der Gegenwart: Über die Verwandlung des modernen Lebensanschauungs* (Berlin: Philo Verlag, 1923).

ment of his idealism.[68] Even among Marburgians, however, some argued that Cohen's engagement with religion represented an unsatisfactory approach to a task that was nonetheless vital to idealism's eventual success. Others in the neo-Kantian tradition felt that Cohen's treatment of religion contained discordant elements or was even superfluous to his critical system, but they nonetheless applauded Cohen's earlier achievements.

Clearly, the debate over the place of religion in neo-Kantianism was not a marginal event. Because religion represented a potential challenge to the character of modern philosophy, the neo-Kantian attempt to come to terms with religious phenomena played an important role in the larger debate over philosophy's future direction.[69] At issue was whether the philosophy of religion presented in Cohen's final work was consonant with critical methods. Ernst Troeltsch, for example, expressed some dissatisfaction at Cohen's "strictly 'scientific' monotheism." The entire treatment of religion seemed confined to a relation between ideas that had been "generated according to a process of necessity from autonomous thought." Through these methods, Cohen had seemingly prohibited not only every form of "metaphysics" but also denied to the individual "every real community with God."[70]

Many proponents of neo-Kantianism as well as transcendental phenomenology insisted that the philosophy of religion remain on wholly rationalist foundations.[71] While admitting that Cohen had not succeeded, some took it upon themselves to complete the study of religion with "the systematic spirit of critical idealism."[72] One scholar went so far as to argue that religion is not only a unique source of concepts within the greater edifice of philosophy; it is in fact "the central problem of thought as such." This was evident in all "religiously minded" philosophers, "from Job to Kierkegaard, [down to] Cohen and his school." Modern philosophy was therefore com-

---

68. Heinz Graupe, *Die Stellung der Religion im systematischen Denken der Marburger Schule,* Inaugural Dissertation for the Philosophical Faculty of the Friedrich-Wilhelms-Universität (Berlin: Thuringia Druckerei, 1930).

69. Some neo-Kantians planned their new "tasks," e.g., Kurt Sternberg, "Der Neukantianismus und die Forderungen der Gegenwart," *Kantstudien* 25, 4 (1920), 396–410.

70. Ernst Troeltsch, "Cohen, Hermann: *Der Begriff der Religion im System der Philosophie* (Besprechung)," *Theologische Literaturzeitung* 43, 4/5 (February 23, 1918): 57–62. But Troeltsch also saw that there was discord between Cohen's rationalism and his "earnest, deeply religious personality" (58, 61).

71. See, e.g., Heinrich Scholz, *Religionsphilosophie* (Berlin: Verlag Reuther und Reichard, 1922), esp. 23–83. Scholz argued that reason "cannot allow that one sacrifice one's self to unreason" and there is thus no such thing as a philosophical validation of religion" (320). But his explicit references to Cohen were spare; see, e.g., 279.

72. See, e.g., the extensive, systematic study by the Cohen and Natorp student Albert Görland, *Religionsphilosophie als Wissenschaft aus dem Systemgeiste des Kritischen Idealismus* (Berlin: Walter de Gruyter Verlag, 1922), 1–3, and 26.

pelled as if by inner necessity toward the ultimate questions of religion.[73] But for many neo-idealists, Cohen's investigation of religion was suspect precisely because it seemed to have strayed beyond the bounds of critical philosophy. For these scholars, the great advantage of Marburg idealism was that it had guarded against "any kind of metaphysics," and one could only lament its later corruption by "religious-metaphysical" belief."[74]

The debate over Cohen's religious thought brought together a diverse group of theologians and philosophers who were deeply concerned with the question of how religion coordinated with the rationalist methods prevalent in the German idealist tradition. Many argued that idealism failed to recognize the true force of religious experience.[75] Several critics from a Christian-Protestant perspective expressed strong misgivings about Cohen's work, alluding to what they perceived as its characteristically "Jewish" qualities. The theory of God as mere "Idea" seemed a startling case of intellectualism; it bespoke blindness to the "reality" of a living redeemer and thus typified Judaism's rejection of the incarnation.[76] Admittedly, Cohen's philosophy of religion did little to discourage such criticism. The neo-Kantian hostility toward any "metaphysical" account of experience sanctioned the

---

73. Graupe, *Die Stellung der Religion*, 1–3, and *passim*.

74. See, e.g., Albert Lewkowitz, who claimed that in the *Religion of Reason* Cohen had ascribed to God a worldly existence (*Dasein*), thus transgressing critical principles. "Die Religionsphilosophie des Neukantianismus: Ein Beitrage zur kritischen Lehre von der transcendenten Realität," *Zeitschrift für Philosophie und Philosophische Kritik* 144, 1 (Leipzig: Verlag Johann Ambrosius Barthin): 10–34. Similarly, see Johannes Hessen, *Die Religionsphilosophie des Neukantianismus*, 2nd ed. (Freiburg im Breisgau: Herder, 1925); and Kurt Kesseler, *Kritik der Neukantischen Religionsphilosophie der Gegenwart* (Leipzig: J. Klinkhardt, 1920). For a neo-Kantian perspective on Hessen, see Kurt Sternberg, "Johannes Hessen, *Die Religionsphilosophie des Neukantianismus*" (review), *Kantstudien* 30 (1925): 206-7. Against them, see Ucko, *Der Gottesbegriff*, esp., 31–33. Like Lewkowitz, Ucko suspected that Cohen had begun to theorize God as a "transcendental reality" (40, 21–28). He was nonetheless regarded as defending Cohen against the charge of metaphysics, and thus he "helped to destroy, against Rosenzweig, the legend of a break and theological transformation starting around 1912." See Heinz Graupe, "Ucko, *Der Gottesbegriff*" (review), *Der Morgen* 5, 6 (February 1930): 361.

75. See, e.g., Karl Bornhausen, who argued that Cohen's earlier work on religion celebrated reason as a fully sovereign power over "all appearance." Hence there was "no real redemption" and "no real God" (*keinen wirklichen Gott*), a deficiency Cohen overcame in the *Religion*. "Das Problem der Wirklichkeit Gottes: Zu Cohens Religionsphilosophie," *Zeitschrift für Theologie und Kirche* (ed. D. W. Herrmann and D. M. Rade, Professoren der Theologie in Marburg) 27 (1917): 55–75, quotes at 68, and "Die Religion der Vernunft," *Kantstudien* 29, 3 (1924): 377–85.

76. Hinrich Knittermeyer asked whether in Cohen's system "reason does not become lord over God himself." "Hermann Cohens Religion der Vernunft," *Die Christliche Welt*, Evangelsiches Gemeindeblatt für Gebildete aller Stände (Marburg) 36, Parts I-II, 42/43, (October 22, 1922): 792–97; Part III, 44/45 (November 9, 1922): 818–24. Also see Wilhelm Herrmann, "Der Begriff der Religion nach Hermann Cohen," *Die Christliche Welt* 30, 44 (November 2, 1916): 839–42.

widespread opinion that Cohen's philosophy made no accommodation for a God of "transcendental reality."[77] It seems clear that in such opinions, growing disillusionment with German idealism and commonplace Christian misunderstandings about Judaism became hopelessly intertwined.

The 1920s brought increased disenchantment regarding the viability of the idealist approach to religion. As neo-Kantian methods declined, hostility toward metaphysical meaning yielded to calls for a "resurrection of metaphysics." This dispute between idealists and partisans of a new metaphysical philosophy was one of the central preoccupations in the so-called "crisis" of interwar German thought. The neo-idealists were inclined to view their opponents as a great danger to philosophy conceived as a systematic science.[78] But it was a widespread perception that neo-idealism was in decline. "[O]ne seeks God behind the things," one scholar lamented. "Intuition and metaphysics are the slogans of the day."[79] For the younger generation, however, the Marburg school now seemed "tyrannical and spiteful." Cohen's principle of origins, once a model of reason's ability to spawn being from thought, was now rejected; the new philosophies saw concepts as bound by a prior finitude. The "task of the coming philosophy," would no longer be primarily conceptual; it would restore to man his immediate contact with "the abysses of Being."[80]

---

77. Cohen's reflections on Judaism thus seemed in accord with the commonplace prejudice that while Judaism was an ethical religion, it was deficient in passion and imagination. Thus Ernst Renan argued that Judaism is a religion without myth: born in the desert, it lacked imagination and obeyed, in Renan's view, "le principe d'un formalisme étroit." By contrast, Western Christianity possessed a "profondeur de sentimentalité" that was "justement l'opposé du génie sémitique, essentiellement sec et dur." "De la part des peuples sémitiques dans l'histoire de la civilisation" (Discours d'ouverture du cours de langues hébraïque, chaldaïque et syriaque au Collège de France prononcé le 21 février 1862) (Paris: Michel Lévy, 1862), reprinted in Renan, Qu'est-ce qu'une nation?, ed. Joël Roman (Paris and London: Presses Pocket, 1992), 182–200.

78. See e.g., Peter Wust, Auferstehung der Metaphysik (Leipzig: Felix Meiner, 1920); and Heinrich Kerler, Die auferstandene Metaphysik: Eine Abrechnung, 2nd ed. (Ulm: Verlag Heinrich Kerler, 1921). This crisis brought a "battle of decision" (Entscheidungskampf); see Ucko, Gottesbegriff, 8. This was anticipated by an earlier "crisis" pitting Lebensphilosophie against neo-idealism; see Albert Lewkowitz, "Die Krisis der modernen Erkenntnistheorie," Archiv für systmatischen Philosophie 21, 2 (May 1915): 186–96. For the neo-idealist view, see Görland, Religionsphilosophie.

79. See Walter Kinkel: "Our age, moved by a thousand storms of every political and religious variety, is all too willing to yield to the metaphysical longing for knowledge of what the world holds in its innermost secrets." By contrast, Cohen had become a symbol of reason spurned. His work was "a singular call that one take stock of human freedom" despite "the burdens and struggles of existence [Schwere und Last des Daseins]." "Hermann Cohens Religionsphilosophie," Jüdisch-liberale Zeitung 5, 46 (November 13, 1925): 1–3.

80. Albert Lewkowitz, "Zum 10jährigen Todestage Hermann Cohens (4. April 1928)," Monatsschrift für Geschichte und Wissenschaft des Judentums 72, 3/4 (March–April 1928): 113–16. Wust, Auferstehung der Metaphysik, 84, 277–78.

## SYSTEM AND PERSON

To grasp the true significance of Rosenzweig's new thinking within the context of Weimar philosophy, it is not sufficient to survey merely the *philosophical* disputes that erupted upon the death of Marburg's most famous philosopher. For Cohen had been an enormously charismatic teacher as well—the sheer force of his personality would inspire various posthumous portraits.[81] Indeed, there is a significant connection between the way Cohen himself came to be remembered *as an individual* and the new prominence of the *concept* of the individual in Rosenzweig's philosophy. Before turning to summarize the lessons of this chapter, this link deserves further exploration.

In all of his mature reflections upon Cohen, Rosenzweig combined biographical and philosophical observations in order to reinforce Cohen's own insights concerning the discovery of the religious self. Cohen's *Religion,* which traces the emergence of a selfhood beyond universal concepts, seemed to recapitulate Cohen's very own life, in which, as Rosenzweig saw it, Cohen had abandoned the confinement of the critical system in order to embrace the faith of his father. (Rosenzweig also seems to have regarded Cohen as a kind of surrogate father for his own philosophy.)[82] Cohen's biography thus seemed to realize the lessons of his own posthumous work.

Rosenzweig's attention to biographical facts and personal anecdotes when writing about Cohen was not accidental and must be regarded as itself of philosophical significance.[83] The most famous anecdote was the fol-

---

81. Others beside Rosenzweig wrote memory sketches of Cohen. See, e.g., Robert Arnold Fritzsche, *Hermann Cohen aus persönlicher Erinnerung* (Berlin: Bruno Cassirer, 1922).

82. Rosenzweig's father died on March 19, 1918; Cohen passed away some two weeks later. The close proximity of these two events seems to have made a deep impression on the younger Rosenzweig. See, e.g., the letter to his mother, *Briefe,* N.214 (April 5, 1918), 290–91. In a subsequent letter to his mother, he speaks of his "double farewell." *Briefe,* N.215 (April 7, 1918), 291–92. Oddly, he admits that he feels a sense of "recovery" in fleeing from "the constant pressures of the one tragedy into the other," since his feelings toward Cohen are "freer and more objective." He also requests, a few days later, that his mother send him Cohen's *Logik,* explaining that "I now want to read Cohen's system, just so soon as I can write a large review upon the appearance of the new book. [i.e., the *Religion der Vernunft*]." *Briefe,* N.222 (16.4.1918), 299–300. It seems likely that in Rosenzweig's imagination Cohen played the role of surrogate father, toward whom he may have felt less conflicted emotion than toward his own father. See, *Briefe,* N.45, An den Vater (Freiburg, 1.7.1910), 52–53. If so, Rosenzweig's unusual interpretation of Kafka's *The Judgment* (see Introduction, at n. 56) takes on added significance as a parable for the split within Cohen's personality between the values of the father (science) and the son (religion).

83. As Rosenzweig explained, the "gap" in ethics can only be filled by "the Biographical as such [*das Biographische*]." Cited from notes for a lecture, "Über Hermann Cohens 'Religion der Vernunft,'" in FR III: 225–27. Rosenzweig was at times criticized for this biographical emphasis. See, e.g., Graupe, "Ucko, *Der Gottesbegriff,*" 651.

lowing, published in Rosenzweig's commentary upon Jehuda Halevi's poem "Der Name" (The name):

> When Hermann Cohen was still in Marburg, he once confronted an old Marburg Jew with the idea of God as propounded in his *Ethics*. The latter listened respectfully, and when Cohen was done, asked him, "And where is the *B'aure Aulom* [the Creator of the World]?" But Cohen said nothing and broke out in tears. (FR, IV: Band 1, 71)

This anecdote has been related on several occasions.[84] While one may question its veracity, it helped Rosenzweig to illustrate the victory of the new philosophy, since it dramatizes Rosenzweig's claim that philosophy cannot successfully capture the meaning of God without recourse to robustly religious language. When Cohen falls silent and begins to weep, it is as if all of idealism has confessed defeat.

As further illustration, Rosenzweig cited a letter Cohen wrote in 1890 to an associate, the neo-Kantian August Stadler, on the occasion of the death of the novelist Gottfried Keller.[85] Here Cohen struck a note of unusual cynicism: It is possible, he suggests, to "free oneself from the thoughts of bourgeois scholars," who "regard the intellectual transport into eternal culture as the highest . . .value of the poor, human individual." But then one has missed what is "truly of value in the human being":

> [F]ar more remains behind, in what was unsaid and passed over, in the mood, and . . . in the sensibility of fellow-feeling, [in that] which is esteemed as the eternal in the earthly. . . . It is already religion where one decorates the futility of the earthly with the glory of the eternal. What kind of ethics ever said to us that we shall not immediately abandon the ruins of an erstwhile reason to its . . . fate, that we shall tirelessly fulfill our duties to other respective scarecrows of the ethical law? Oh the time we have . . . lost, crying tears to human frailty![86]

With uncharacteristic irony, Cohen seemed here to convey his growing disenchantment with idealism and "bourgeois" culture. Despite the triumph of ethics, Cohen alludes to the "individual-nonetheless" *(Individuum quand-même)*, a solitary self who "remains behind" in silence. Here for Rosenzweig

---

84. See, e.g., Martin Buber, "Die Tränen," *Jüdische Rundschau* 33 (27/28): 4. It is also related in Strauss, *Philosophie und Gesetz*. Against the veracity of such stories, see Steven Schwarzschild, "Franz Rosenzweig's Anecdotes about Hermann Cohen," in *Gegenwart im Rückblick: Festgabe für die Jüdische Gemeinde zu Berlin 25 Jahre nach dem Neubeginn* (Heidelberg: Lothar Stiehm Verlag, 1970), 209–18, esp. nn. 10 and 13.

85. See Cohen's *Nachruf* for Stadler, *Kantstudien* 15, 3 (1910): 403–20; and for Cohen's letter to Stadler, see Cohen, *Briefe*, sel. and ed. Bertha and Bruno Strauß (Berlin: Schocken Verlag, 1936), N.2, An August Stadler, 1890.

86. Quoted in Rosenzweig, "Einleitung" to JS, FR III: 205.

was the beginning of a finitude beyond ethics and incapable of the "intellectual transport" idealism has promised. The Stadler letter thus represented Cohen's "first steps" toward the basic insights of his later philosophy of religion.[87] Furthermore, for Rosenzweig the letter was proof of Cohen's importance for the new thinking. In his 1929 commentary on the Davos debates, Rosenzweig would again cite the letter as a precedent for Heidegger's "new thinking."[88]

Significantly, Rosenzweig's first evidence in comparing Cohen and Heidegger is really biographical and not philosophical; it depends upon the informal remarks of a private letter. But Rosenzweig also corroborated his contemporaries' suggestion that Cohen and Heidegger were similar in their style of instruction.[89] In his short text, "The Docent: A Personal Recollection," Rosenzweig recalls his first meeting with Cohen in the autumn of 1913. The philosopher had just retired from his Marburg post to join Berlin's Institute for the Study of Judaism. Rosenzweig knew little of his work excepting some "occasional writings" on Jewish themes, which, he writes, "had left me with little besides a cold and gray impression, [and] . . . fundamental distrust against everything on the marketplace of German academic philosophy." But finally he attended Cohen's lectures in November:

> Here I experienced a surprise beyond compare. Accustomed to finding nothing but cleverness in philosophical posts . . . here instead I found a philosopher. Instead of tightrope-walkers, showing off their . . . leaps on the high-wire of thought, I saw a man. . . . Here one had the indestructible feeling, this man must philosophize. . . . That which, misled by the contemporary trends, I had given up looking for except in the writings of the great dead, that rigorous and scholarly mind surging over the abyss . . . I now confronted in speaking life, face to face.[90]

Such narratives are common among the first generation of scholars that turned from idealism to existentialism in the hope that at last they had

87. See the citations in FR III, "Einleitung," as well as in VF. Incidentally, Kasimir Edschmid's 1919 manifesto for expressionist poetry cites Keller as the great representative of the vanishing, bourgeois world: "Keller's great tradition," he wrote, had vanished in "bourgeois decadence," and with Expressionism, the "Revolution in spirit" had at last created "a new form." *Über den Expressionismus in der Literatur und die neue Dichtung,* (Berlin: Erich Reiß Verlag, 1919), 31.

88. Compare Heidegger's remarks on the "lazy" philosopher (in DVS, 291) to Cohen's remarks concerning "lazy" reason, in RV, 24.

89. Nicolai Hartmann, for example, having just attended Heidegger's very first lecture in Marburg, is purported to have remarked to the young Hans-Georg Gadamer that "he had not seen such a powerful performance since Hermann Cohen." Gadamer, *Philosophical Apprenticeships,* 48; for a similar comparison, see Jacques Derrida, "Interpretations at War: Kant, the Jew, the German," *New Literary History* 22 (1991): 39–95, at 48.

90. "Der Dozent," KS, 291–93.

found the authentic voice of philosophy. Like Heidegger, Cohen too had a "primordial" *(ürsprungliches)*, not merely "acquired" relationship to "the ultimate questions" *(letzten Fragen).*[91] The "close juxtaposition" in Cohen's personality between "the coolest thoughts and hottest heart" made for a certain element of drama in his delivery. Rosenzweig's shock at having discovered in Cohen a true "thinker" was all the stronger as Cohen's published writings contained little hint of his personal charisma.[92] But "face to face," Rosenzweig heard in Cohen a rare intellectual force that "surged over the abyss" *(über den Abgrund . . . brütete).*[93] Rosenzweig recalls hearing Cohen speak:

> A gesture only for a moment, . . . a single word, a short sentence of five or six words, and the flow of speech had broadened into an overflowing ocean, and through the web of thoughts the reborn world of the human heart would be illuminated.[94]

For Rosenzweig, there is an analogy between thought and thinker. Just as the *Religion of Reason* thematized a correlation between man and God that flowed from the hidden "sources" of Judaism to burst the boundaries of the critical system, so too in Cohen's personality one witnessed an impersonal "web of thoughts" from which burst forth a "reborn world" of personal belief. (An irrepressible sense for the "primordial" drove Cohen "over and beyond his system," toward an "eye-to-eye immediacy" with the questions in "his last, theological epoch.")[95] Cohen was therefore a perfect example for

---

91. Rosenzweig may have heard similar rumors about Heidegger from Leo Strauss, who attended Heidegger's seminars in Marburg; see Schwarzschild, "Rosenzweig's Anecdotes," 216, n.13. Compare Karl Jaspers's memories of disillusionment with Husserl in *Philosophy*, trans. E. B. Ashton (Chicago: University of Chicago Press, 1969), I: 6–7. Rosenzweig wrote to Gritli about Cohen, "Since Schopenhauer and Nietzsche he [Cohen] is indeed the first, and he stands so near to me, or rather me to him, that I can hardly read him. . . . What a person! [*Was für ein Mensch!*] I still wonder at the fact that I came to him, indeed, truly at the twelfth hour." GB (29.12.1918), 207.

92. See, e.g., Hannah Arendt's dramatic description of the young Heidegger as a teacher, in "Martin Heidegger at Eighty," orig. pub. *New York Review of Books,* October 1971; reprinted in *Heidegger and Modern Philosophy: Critical Essays,* ed. Michael Murray (New Haven: Yale University Press, 1978), 293–303.

93. In the Buber-Rosenzweig Bible, one reads: "Und die Erde war Wirrnis und Wüste / Finsternis allüber Abgrund / Braus Gottes brütend allüber den Wassern." *Schrift, Das Buch Im Anfang,* 1:2–4. Note the common terms, "surging" *(brütend)* and "abyss" *(Abgrund)*; and compare Heidegger, *Vom Wesen des Grundes,* 3rd German ed. (Frankfurt am Main: Vittorio Klostermann, 1949), 49.

94. "Der Dozent," 292.

95. "Der Dozent," 292. In a letter to Gritli written shortly after Cohen's death, Rosenzweig confirmed that Cohen's "philosophy of religion itself obviously no longer belongs to the system." GB (23.4.1918), 80. The same observation is found in other commentaries of the period. See, e.g., Lewkowitz, in *Religiöse Denker;* and Knittermeyer, "Cohens Religion der Vernunft," passim.

Rosenzweig's claim in the *Star* that after Nietzsche, "the biographical" had become a philosophical principle in its own right (SE, 10 [E, 9–10]).

## THE BIRTH OF THE NEW PHILOSOPHY

As I have shown, Cohen provided Rosenzweig with a dramatic illustration of the self-overcoming of idealism, a theme exploited in *The Star of Redemption*.[96] Much like Heidegger, Rosenzweig characterized the metaphysical tradition as a "flight" from finitude; and both regarded neo-Kantianism as the paradigm of this evasion. (I shall discuss this parallel at greater length in my comments on *The Star*.) More intriguing perhaps, Cohen also bequeathed Rosenzweig a distinction between religion and ethics that verged on polarity. Cohen's account of religion's special contribution to philosophy suggested that religion could accomplish what ethics could not. But this prompted the suspicion that religion considered alone was not in itself ethical. As discussed above, Cohen's defense against this suspicion—the argument that religion generates its concepts "for the sake of" ethics—was barely sustainable. I would therefore suggest that in Cohen's posthumous work Rosenzweig found support for the view that *religion appears only where ethics has vanished*. It is this view that may help to explain the broader *absence* of ethical themes in Rosenzweig's mature philosophy.

Cohen's specific ideas about Judaism and Jewish life also appear in Rosenzweig's mature philosophy (though Rosenzweig may have developed them without Cohen's influence). As we have seen, Cohen had argued that the Jews' isolation and their eternal wandering are necessary for the religion of reason, in that their suffering reiterates the pain of the individual on a world-historical scale.[97] Their laws serve, in Cohen's phrase, as "an instrument of isolation" (RV, 418). And their redemption becomes a sign for the redemption of each and every individual. Jewish "purity" for Cohen therefore expresses the idealist principle that regulative ideals remain isolated from politics. Similarly, Rosenzweig affirms the necessary isolation of the Jews from the "life of the peoples" *(Leben der Völker)*.[98] Here, the wretched condition of "Ahasverus," the wandering Jew, is no longer a mark of Christianity triumphant but instead a badge of pride for Judaism. In relation to this-worldly politics, Rosenzweig writes, the Jews remain "merely dutiful." But in contrast to this "external life" there is a "pure inner Jewish

96. Lewkowitz, in 1915, spoke of the "overcoming of rationalism" through the recognition by idealist philosophy itself that it must ultimately resort to metaphysical categories. "Die Krisis der modernen Erkenntnistheorie."

97. Recall Cohen's use of *Menschenleid,* esp. RV, 173.

98. These claims are already evident in Rosenzweig's famous correspondence with Eugen Rosenstock-Huessy on Judaism and Christianity, circa 1916. *Briefe,* 637–720.

life in all that serves the maintenance of the people, of its 'life' insofar as it is not purchased from without, but must be worked out from within."[99]

It is difficult to suppress the thought that the argument about Jewish suffering and election in Rosenzweig's work bears traces of Cohen's idealism. But there is an important difference. What for Cohen was chiefly a conceptual distinction became for Rosenzweig a metaphysical difference. To be "outside of the state" is a metaphor, but it expresses a civic problem. To be "outside of history," makes no sense without recourse to metaphysical categories. Similarly, for Cohen eternity characterized the ethico-messianic *idea* of ethics and the "eternal task" of theoretical reason, while for Rosenzweig it characterized the special *being* of the Jews insofar as they felt themselves uniquely redeemed. Cohen's conceptual categories became in Rosenzweig's philosophy the names for an ontological predicament.

In such examples, one may discern the transition from philosophical idealism to philosophical expressionism. Cohen had labored throughout his career to extinguish the last remaining flames of metaphysics from philosophy. Rosenzweig now revived them, and, not without warrant, cited Cohen himself as justification. Most of all, Rosenzweig helped to popularize the image of Cohen as a man who had struggled between his public reason and his more inward faith. Cohen thus became, in Rosenzweig's hands, a prophet of the coming philosophy. It was, however, the ambiguity in Cohen's work itself that was chiefly responsible for this curious legacy. As Julius Guttmann was to explain, Cohen's treatment of religion led in two very different directions: on the one hand, toward a critical interpretation of God as an idea, the contents of which are fully explicable according to ethical principles; and, on the other hand, almost without intention, toward a "breakthrough into the metaphysical."[100]

As I have shown, this ambiguity was illustrative of a broader crisis of purpose that seized German philosophy during the 1920s.[101] Over the next decade, the lines of stress first exposed in the debate between philosophy and religion became increasingly apparent, until what had been an ambiguity internal to the school of idealism erupted as a struggle between rival modes

99. *Briefe*, e.g., 659 ff. and esp. 691.

100. In German, "Durchbruch ins *Metaphysische*." See Guttmann, PJ, 361. The theme of a *Durchbruch* is a common in German expressionism. See Walter Sokel, *The Writer in Extremis* (Stanford, Calif.: Stanford University Press, 1959), 78.

101. One critic noted that among Cohen's younger followers were some who wished to build a "bridge" between critical idealism and a more "speculative" idealism like that of Schelling. Such departures would have been impossible, "had there not been influential and readily available in Cohen's system itself principles, points of view, or tendencies, that inwardly made such transformations possible." Arthur Liebert, "Cohen, Hermann. *Kants Theorie der Erfahrung*, 3. Auflage; 1918. Berlin, Bruno Cassirer" (review), *Kantstudien* 25, 1 (1920): 59–61.

of thought. In 1929, when Rosenzweig surveyed the previous ten years, he saw this very same struggle being played out in the Davos encounter between Martin Heidegger and Ernst Cassirer. Rosenzweig saw Cassirer as the last scion of the "old philosophy" and Heidegger as the triumphant voice of the new thinking. But he would also claim that Heidegger embodied the "metaphysical" perspective hidden within Cohen's late philosophy of religion. It mattered little that Cohen himself had died over ten years before. The counter-idealist tendencies of his final period had at last emerged, though Cohen's Marburg disciples refused to recognize it. Thus Rosenzweig's remark: "The schoolchildren die, together with their schoolteacher. The Master lives" (VF, 87).

Chapter 2

# Hegel's Fate

## *The Emergence of Finitude*
## *in Rosenzweig's* Hegel and the State

*What is most one's own in humanity is one's fate.*
—ROSENZWEIG, *The Star of Redemption*

"This book that I could no longer have written . . . " This was the provocative phrase Rosenzweig applied to his doctoral dissertation, *Hegel and the
State (Hegel und der Staat)*. Written in Freiburg under the direction of Friedrich Meinecke, it was largely complete by 1913, but first saw publication in
1920, just a year before his astonishing effort in original philosophy, *The Star
of Redemption (Der Stern der Erlösung).*[1] At first glance the two books belong to
seemingly different worlds. *The Star* is generally regarded as the work of a
mature philosopher who has at last outgrown the training of his youth. Various comments by Rosenzweig himself only strengthened this impression.
Before the publication of *Hegel and the State,* he appended a retraction to
the ending pages of its preface, condemning his imposing two-volume work
as mere "scholarship" that now spoke only to antiquarian concerns. "Scholarship survives," he wrote, "even where the German life it once knew does
not" (HS, I: xii). The war had rendered the book's doctrines and hopes
obsolete; it was little more than a record of "spirit of the prewar years," while
in 1919 one could no longer speak of "Spirit" at all. It was therefore his
"nevermore-book."

The change of perspective was indeed dramatic. When he had com-
menced his research, Rosenzweig had shared the widespread belief of his
generation that a coming world war could serve as a theater for the triumph
of German ideals. Like his *Doktor-Vater* Friedrich Meinecke, he had trusted

---

1. Rosenzweig completed his doctorate in 1912. After the war he emended his dissertation, which was published in two volumes as *Hegel und der Staat* (München and Berlin: Verlag
R. Oldenbourg, 1920). A one-volume edition was prepared for publication in 1937 but was destroyed by the Gestapo. It was later printed in photostat (Aalen: Scientia Verlag, 1962). In what
follows I cite the 1962 edition, hereafter identified as HS.

in the path from thought to action. This was the sentiment of Hölderlin's poem "An die Deutschen," which Rosenzweig appended as an epigraph to the cover of his book:

> Aber kömmt, wie der Strahl aus dem Gewölke kömmt
> Aus Gedanken vielleicht geistig und reif die Tat?
> Folgt der Schrift, wie des Haines
> Dunkelm Blatte, die goldne Frucht?

> But shall there come, like rays from the cloud,
> out of thoughts, perhaps, the Deed, ripe and full of spirit?
> From the written word, as dark pages from the bough;
> does there follow golden fruit?[2]

By the time the dissertation was published, however, Rosenzweig had lost his confidence in history as bringing the ideal to reality. The twentieth century had spawned a new kind of nationalism, which, lacking Hegel's inheritance of Enlightenment reason, had devolved into a force of merciless destruction. When Rosenzweig surveyed the German empire, he now saw a "field of ruins." Updating the dissertation seemed impossible. In the preface, Rosenzweig writes, "This book, which today I could no longer have written, I could just as little revise. There remained only the possibility of publishing the book just as it was" (HS, I: xii).

Surely one of the greatest curses a book can bear is the disdain of its own author.[3] Rosenzweig's decision to publish his Hegel study under his own rueful disclaimers meant that his first great foray into philosophy would be considered in isolation from his later work. Robbed of its paternal blessing, the book has endured an Ishmael-like misfortune: with few exceptions, it has been widely regarded as the offspring of the system Rosenzweig abandoned. The illusion of a break in his development was later perpetuated by existentialist interpreters who regarded Rosenzweig as a philosopher in the Kierkegaardian tradition—and, like Kierkegaard, as a rebel against

---

2. Rosenzweig's epigraph cites an unusual variant of the poem with several earlier word choices; he also modifies the old spelling. The text of the poem in the critical edition reads: "Aber komt, wie der Stral aus dem Gewölke komt, / Aus Gedanken vieleicht geistig und reif die That? / Folgt die Frucht, wie des Haines / Dunklem Blatte, der stillen Schrift?" Hölderlin, "An die Deutschen" (zweite Fassung), in *Sämtliche Werke: Kritische Textausgabe*, Band 4, Oden I, ed. D. E. Sattler (Darmstadt: Luchterhand Verlag, 1985), 146–57.

3. Perhaps the most compelling testimony for Rosenzweig's change of perspective is found in a letter addressed to his mother in October 1918, when he was in Belgrade, a witness to the collapse of the Second Reich. "In 1914," he wrote, " I would never have believed in such ruin, at most . . . a persistence of Bismarck's results. Until this very year. And now all is gone: the world as I pictured it is no longer there. . . . [Y]ou are concerned for the Hegel book with the paper shortage, but I'm concerned about something entirely different: the reader shortage. Who is supposed to read this book about this 'bloody German'?" *Briefe*, N.261, (Belgrad. 19.10.18.), 351–52.

Hegel. More recently, the prejudice has been confirmed under the pressure of postmodernist critics for whom Rosenzweig is seen as a philosopher allergic to any talk of holistic plenitude. Even today *Hegel and the State* is perceived as the obligatory exercise of a young scholar still shackled by the methods of conventional research. It thus suffers the shadow-fate of a negative model: both for Rosenzweig himself and for many of his interpreters, it is taken a sign of what he left behind—a model of the "old" thinking as against the "new."[4]

But the contrast is overdrawn. The illusion of a radical break gains much of its plausibility as a convenient narrative device. And it is especially tempting when the author himself denies any significant continuity.[5] Surreptitious debts are less obvious, but for that very reason may exert a stronger influence upon one's thought. To be sure, Rosenzweig strenuously argued for a revolution against German idealism. But holding a philosophy in contempt is not the same as liberating oneself fully from its grasp.[6]

In this chapter, I shall argue that Rosenzweig's *Hegel and the State* represents his earliest sustained reflection on the philosophical themes that would predominate in his later work. The book is officially a study in the origins of Hegel's mature political thought; it traces the gradual evolution of the idea of the state from his earliest writings forward to its culmination in the philosophies of right and history. From the perspective of the later Rosenzweig, Hegel's mature theory of the state was the final expression of a panhistorical metaphysical tradition that celebrates the triumph of social reality over the individual. But in *Hegel and the State,* Rosenzweig locates a critical break in Hegel's early theological writings.[7] The young Hegel as

---

4. Best readings are Shlomo Avineri, "Rosenzweig's Hegel Interpretation: Its Relationship to the Development of His Jewish Reawakening," in Kassel, II: 831–38; Otto Pöggeler, "Rosenzweig und Hegel," in Kassel, II: 839–53; Ulrich Bieberich, *Wenn die Geschichte göttlich wäre: Rosenzweigs Auseinandersetzung mit Hegel* (St. Ottilien: Verlag Erzabtei St. Ottilien, 1989); Gérard Bensussan, "Hegel et Rosenzweig: le franchissement de l'horizon," in *Hegel et l'Etat* (French translation of *Hegel und der Staat*), trans. Gérard Bensussan (Paris: Presses Univeritaires de France, 1991), xix–xliii; and Paul-Laurent Assoun, "Avant-propos, Rosenzweig et la politique: postérité d'une rupture," in *Hegel et l'Etat*, v–xvii.

5. Also see the criticism of facile opposition in Bensussan, "Hegel et Rosenzweig," xix–xliii. In his later letters to friends Rosenzweig professed more than once about his dissertation that "even as I began to write it, I already considered Hegel's philosophy pernicious." *Briefe*, N.365, An Rudolf Hallo (4.2.23), 476.

6. Not all readers experienced so unbridgeable an divide. In 1929 Walter Benjamin characterized the *Star of Redemption* as "a victorious outbreak of Hegelian dialectic in Hermann Cohen's *Religion of Reason out of the Sources of Judaism.*" "Bücher, die Lebendig Geblieben Sind," *Die Literarische Welt* 5, 20 (May 17, 1929): 6; reprinted in Benjamin, *Gesammelte Schriften* (Frankfurt am Main: Suhrkamp Verlag, 1972), III: 169–71.

7. Myriam Bienenstock is one of the very few recent interpreters to suggest an intimate relationship deeper than antipathy. Rosenzweig's Hegel book, she writes, "embodies an

Rosenzweig presents him was preoccupied with the problem of religious unworldliness. Hegel identified this problem by the special term *Schicksal*, or fate, which he considered the definitive mark of Judaism and early Christianity. Fate in this special sense accounted for the tragic division between Jesus and the Jews; ultimately it explained the "fate" of Christianity as well. Surprisingly, in *Hegel and the State* Rosenzweig discerns a path leading directly from this idea of fate to Hegel's mature philosophical vision. To Rosenzweig, the state, conceived as a rational-social whole, is the place wherein Hegelian subjectivity first overcomes its division for the sake of a higher, "superior" reality. Rosenzweig therefore regarded fate as a site of theological protest within Hegel's own philosophy. As I shall argue below, this protest would later inform Rosenzweig's reflections upon the nature of Jewish existence.

## HEGELIANISM AND *LEBENSPHILOSOPHIE*

Rosenzweig's study of Hegel's political thought must be understood within the context of the so-called Hegel Renaissance, which emerged toward the end of the nineteenth century. While it took many forms, the Hegel Renaissance was widely seen as expressing a new "longing for metaphysics." Opponents ridiculed its "nonscientific" aspiration to "Weltanschauung." Some detected a Hegelian strain in neo-Kantianism itself. But most neo-Kantians feared the Hegel Renaissance would end by destroying the critical spirit they had championed. More often, it was explained with reference to the rising spirit of discontent among Germany's younger generation just before the First World War. Most of all, however, the renewed interest in Hegel's philosophy emerged in tandem with the rise of *Lebensphilosophie,* or "the philosophy of life."[8]

---

understanding of political and historical life which departs quite significantly from Hegel's own conception" and is therefore based on a fundamental misinterpretation of Hegel. But nonetheless "some of the ideas Rosenzweig ascribes to Hegel in *Hegel und der Staat* recur, almost word for word, in his later masterpiece of Jewish philosophy, *The Star of Redemption.*" But she understates Rosenzweig's interest in the young Hegel's theology. "Rosenzweig's Hegel," *The Owl of Minerva* 23, 2 (spring 1992): 177–82.

    8. Wilhelm Windelband, "Die Erneuerung des Hegelianismus," in *Präludien: Aufsätze und Reden zur Philosophie und ihrer Geschichte* (Tübingen: J. C. B. Mohr, Paul Siebeck, 1915), I: 273–89. In his 1883 lecture, "Scientific and Nonscientific Philosophy," delivered at Freiburg as his Antrittsrede, Alois Riehl had explicitly rejected Hegel, together with all thinking that aspired to "Weltanschauung." "Über wissenschaftliche und nichtwissenschaftliche Philosophie," published in *Philosophische Studien aus vier Jahrzehnten* (Leipzig: Quelle und Meyer, 1925). In his 1927 study of the Hegel Renaissance, Heinrich Levy argued that the metaphysical tendencies of neo-Kantianism were most evident in Cohen's claim that the system of scientific explanation was a dynamic, self-generating whole spawning being from thought. There was also a certain Hegelian strain in "the dominant ethical meaning that Cohen ascribed to the state," since "he

It was the late nineteenth-century philosopher and historian Wilhelm Dilthey who was chiefly responsible for the development of Lebensphilosophie. Because Dilthey exerted a powerful influence upon Rosenzweig, it is important to gain a sense of his philosophical contributions. Generally speaking, Dilthey's method involved a "re-experiencing" *(Nacherleben)* of the inner life of a thinker. By this he hoped to arrive at an interpretative, empathetic understanding of a thinker's perspective upon the world. (He called this kind of empathic understanding *Verstehen,* which has remained a touchstone of philosophical hermeneutics). When a thinker's ideas were properly regarded in this fashion, they were recognized as "manifestations of life" *(Lebensäusserungen).* Now for Dilthey, this method of hermeneutic understanding rested upon a quite basic assumption that human beings are rooted in particular historical contexts—he called this "historicality" *(Geschichtlichkeit).* To properly study a given thinker's concepts thus required a historical reconstruction of that person's inner life as a whole. Understanding the formal philosophical work was but one element in the larger practice Dilthey called "life interpretation" *(Lebensauffassung).*[9]

The key term in Dilthey's method was *life.* Despite its simplicity, this was a highly charged concept, grounded upon the assumption that a philosopher's work takes shape within a greater, holistic framework determined by personality and history. Such a life framework, however, is itself unstable. The ongoing experiences of individuals themselves undergo transformation within history and culture. But this life framework forms a necessary background for all meaning, and philosophy itself cannot be understood apart from its temporal frame: "Life," wrote Dilthey, "is the basic element or fact which must form the starting point for philosophy. It is known from within. It is that behind which we cannot go. Life cannot be brought before the bar of reason."[10]

The idea of *life* as a holistic, temporal context of meaning was to become a central theme in the writings of both Rosenzweig and Heidegger. *The Star of Redemption* places great emphasis upon the principle that religious experience must remain within the bounds of the human life-horizon. (As I

---

presented ethics within a superior and all-embracing totality [*Allheit*]." *Die Hegel-Renaissance in der deutschen Philosophie,* ed. Kant-Gesellschaft (Charlottenburg: Pan-Verlag, Rolf Heise, 1927). Also see Hermann Glockner, "Hegelrenaissance und Neuhegelianismus: Eine Säkularbetrachtung," *Logos* 20 (1931): 169–95. Windelband feared the new philosophy, in its turn toward "metaphysical reality," risked hypostatizing the Kantian ideas. "Philosophy that still wishes to be an autonomous science," he concluded, must remain "cautious in the face of Hegelianism's metaphysical tendencies." "Die Erneuerung," 279, 287. On Lebensphilosophie, see Heinrich Kleiner, "Neuhegelianismus," *Historisches Wörterbuch der Philosophie* 4 (1984): 741–48.

9. See Richard E. Palmer, *Hermeneutics* (Evanston, Ill.: Northwestern University Press, 1969), 98–123.

10. Quoted in Palmer, *Hermeneutics,* 120.

shall later explain, *life* is one of the most frequently recurrent terms in the book.) [11] Similarly, in the lesser-known work *The Little Book of Sick and Healthy Common Sense (Das Büchlein vom gesunden und kranken Menschenverstand)*, Rosenzweig argues that philosophy must not and indeed cannot abstract itself from the *Lebensstrom,* or "life-stream." For Rosenzweig, life is the temporal context within which all experience finds its true meaning. Dilthey's influence upon the early Heidegger is well-documented. In *Being and Time,* Heidegger claimed that philosophy occurs within a hermeneutic sphere of human temporal existence, or *Dasein.* But as I have noted already in the introduction, Heidegger had earlier designated this sphere as "life" (for example, in his 1920–21 lectures on the philosophy of religion).[12]

Dilthey's principle of "life" as a holistic, temporal context of meaning is a key theme in his famous 1905 study, *The Young Hegel's History (Der jugendgeschichte Hegels).* For the earlier biographers, the theme of "life" had been obscured, largely because they had devoted the greater share of their attention to Hegel's mature system. What was most revolutionary in Dilthey's study was its emphasis on Hegel's youth, especially the period of his early theological studies in Tübingen, Bern, and Frankfurt (during which time Hegel had developed a close friendship with Hölderlin).[13] Given this emphasis, Dilthey was predisposed to regard the mature Hegel's political thought as the expression of earlier theological, or even metaphysical, concerns. As Rosenzweig explained in his own prefatory survey of Hegel schol-

---

11. On the importance of the concept of *life* in Rosenzweig, see Amos Funkenstein, *Perceptions of Jewish History* (Berkeley: University of California Press, 1993), 330, n. 59. Also see chapter 3 below, esp. the section on "The Hermeneutics of Life," (174–82).

12. In *History of the Concept of Time,* Heidegger writes that "Dilthey was the first to understand 'the aims of phenomenology.'" *History of the Concept of Time, Prologomena,* trans. Theodore Kisiel (Bloomington: Indiana University Press, 1985) 118. As Charles Bambach notes, "What Dilthey brought to his study of 'life' was a keen interest in the contextualized relations and temporal continuity that make up the experience of living." *Heidegger, Dilthey, and the Crisis of Historicism* (Ithaca, N.Y.: Cornell University Press, 1995), 239. Also see Karl Löwith, "Phänomenologische Ontologie und protestantische Theologie," *Zeitschrift für Theologie und Kirche,* Neue Folge 11, 5 (1930): 365–99. The work of Hermann Glockner, in which fate is a dominant theme, represents an attempt at mediating between Heidegger and Hegel. On this see Käte Nadler, "Hermann Glockner: Hegel (Notizen)," *Logos* 20 (1931): 118–20. On Heidegger's "Einleitung in die Phänomenologie der Religion," see the discussion in Ernst Tugendhat, *Der Wahrheitsbegriff bei Husserl und Heidegger* (Berlin: Walter de Gruyter, 1970), 265; and the suggestive comments in Charles Guignon, *Heidegger and the Problem of Knowledge* (Indianapolis: Hackett, 1983), 58–59.

13. As Heinrich Levy explains, Dilthey's relation to Hegel is guided by the principle "to understand life in terms of life itself" (das Leben aus ihm selber verstehen zu wollen). Dilthey's study of Hegel thus "revealed the moment of life . . . in the young Hegel's philosophy, a philosophy not yet permeated by panlogism . . .[a theme that] became a powerful factor in the Hegel Renaissance." *Die Hegel-Renaissance,* 19. But see also Julius Klaiber, *Hölderlin, Hegel, und Schelling in ihren schwäbischen Jugendjahren* (Stuttgart: Minerva Verlag, 1877), reprinted 1981.

arship, previous interpreters had missed this metaphysical dimension of Hegel's thought. Dilthey's Hegel was distinguished from most of his contemporaries "in that he early on concentrated the whole of his thought for a series of years on Christian religiosity," and this fundamental training continued to nourish his thought throughout his later life.[14] In fact, according to Rosenzweig, Dilthey's book traced "first and foremost the development of the Metaphysician, and only secondly the philosopher of history." Thus, Rosenzweig emphasized, Dilthey conceived of the political and historical facets of Hegel's thought as *more a part than a fundamental power in his development.*" On Dilthey's view, Hegel cared little for "power-state" *(machtstaatlich)* politics. Rather, he conceived of politics itself in a *cultural,* and ironically *nonpolitical* fashion, as a "cultural-national [*kulturnationaler*] wish." And for Rosenzweig, this interpretation of Hegel was evidence of German scholarship's "inner turning away from the state" (HS, I: 50).

As we shall see, Rosenzweig's summary of Dilthey's place in the Hegel Renaissance proved a remarkable anticipation of Rosenzweig's own later philosophy. Indeed, Rosenzweig's mature thought exhibits just the "inner turning away from the state" that he had already discerned in Dilthey's work. Moreover, it was in reading Dilthey's book that Rosenzweig first developed an acute appreciation for the suppressed theological dimension of German Idealism. To grasp the importance of Rosenzweig's own encounter with Hegelianism thus demands a richer understanding of Dilthey's interpretation.

For Dilthey, Hegel's political and social thought were rooted in a deeper and more comprehensive worldview *(Weltanschauung),* which he characterized as "mystical pantheism" (JH, 39). The origins of Hegel's pantheistic doctrine, Dilthey claimed, could be traced all the way back to Hegel's early years of apprenticeship with the Lutheran Orthodoxy at the Tübingen seminary, where he had first immersed himself in "the entire sphere of consciousness of Jewish and Christian religiosity" (JH, 10). Most of all, Hegel became aware of a fundamental contrast between the Jewish theory of "punishment" and the Christian doctrine of "reconciliation" *(Versöhnung).* For Hegel (wrote Dilthey), Jewish legality expressed an entire manner of life: punishment as the Jews conceived it could not reconcile the crime with the law; rather, punishment "calls forth only the feeling of powerlessness before a master." But "[t]he forgiving of sins belongs . . . to a religion that lay beyond Jewish morality"; and such a forgiveness is "fate reconciled by means of love" *(durch Liebe versöhnte Schicksal)* (JH, 10–15).

14. Rosenzweig argues that for Rosenkranz, Hegel had been primarily a philosopher of religion, while Haym had seen chiefly "the political man." HS, I: 45–50. Dilthey writes that Hegel was distinguished from his youthful companions in that "he concentrated the full power of his thought for a continuous span of years upon the Christian religion." JH, 5.

According to Dilthey, the basic structure of Hegel's "mystical pantheism" was already expressed in his early theological narrative of fate as reconciled through love. "Fate" *(Schicksal)*, or division, was the defining mark of the Jews' *Lebensauffassung*, and informed their legalistic understanding of morality. For Judaism on Hegel's view presents a perpetual oscillation between crime and punishment, and the "superior" Christian interpretation of life offers the only true remedy for this condition. Jewish division *(Trennung)* is overcome in Christianity, and Jewish fate is reconciled in the higher unity of Christian love. According to Dilthey, Hegel's narrative of "reconciliation with fate through love" was thus the earliest expression of his later, philosophical ideal of knowledge as the rational *Allheit*, or totality.[15]

Dilthey's interpretation of Hegel exercised a profound effect on Rosenzweig and his intellectual generation. In the preface to *Hegel and the State*, Rosenzweig writes, "in Dilthey a new generation of youth found its leader." Here was an established scholar—Rosenzweig called him a "contemporary of Nietzsche"—who had "already long since struggled to hold open the path leading back to the past" and who "renewed the historical memory of Hegel for a generation that, out of a newer, different longing, sought the way back to the old idealism."[16] Rosenzweig concludes that

> it was an entirely new Hegel that Dilthey's book introduced, [and] a highly responsive sense for soulful reality as such. So Dilthey recognized, and he first, how that connection between Hegel and Hölderlin was more than a biographical curiosity and more than a sign . . . for later, organic development. He first raised . . . the veil to show how, in the rigid, gigantic portrait of the historical Hegel, that in [the earlier biographies] remained soulless and opaque, there raged from youth onward a stream of secret suffering and passion. (HS, I: xii)

Some intellectuals, however, dissented from this renewal of enthusiasm for Dilthey's work. In *The Young Hegel (Der junge Hegel)*, completed in 1938, Georg Lukács famously attacked Dilthey's book for its "irrationalist" and "reactionary" strains. "Dilthey meets the imperialist and reactionary revival of Romanticism halfway," Lukács complained, "[and] by ignoring or distorting the most vital historical facts . . . he brings Hegel within the orbit of

---

15. "Love is the process of unifying what is divided, the dissolution of oppositions in unity. The religion of Jesus is thus, as the religion of love, also the experience of unity between human and the divine Spirit. . . . *[T]his metaphysical interpretation of Christianity expresses . . . the core of Hegel's philosophy of religion*" (my emphasis). According to Dilthey, the young Hegel shared this romantic ideal with his friend Hölderlin, as shown the final lines of *Hyperion:* "Versöhnung ist mitten im Streit, und alles Getrennte findet sich wieder." JH, 77, 140.

16. "[W]e who were younger then," writes Rosenzweig, "still vividly remember in what a surprisingly immediate and contemporary way [Dilthey's oldest essays] seemed to address us." HS, I: x–xii.

philosophical Romanticism" (TYH, xix). Even worse, the "postwar period [of] neo-Hegelianism proceeded along the paths laid down by Dilthey," in order to "make apparent use of Hegel's approach to the philosophy of history [and] to exploit his concept of 'reconciliation,'" so as to eventually achieve "a 'synthesis' of all contemporary philosophical movements (including fascism)."[17]

Despite his obvious rancor, Lukács was in a sense correct that Dilthey had portrayed the young Hegel as indifferent to politics. (The very suggestion that Hegel had passed through an "early theological period" was for Lukács "a legend created and fostered by the reactionary apologists of imperialism"; TYH, 16). But for Lukács any apparent indifference to politics betrayed a deeper political commitment (a judgment that is hardly surprising given Lukács' strongly partisan views on philosophy, and given, too, the overwhelming pressure of events in the late 1930s.)[18] There was some measure of truth in his judgment. As we have seen, Dilthey's Hegel was a thinker who considered politics derivative of deeper, more "metaphysical" concerns. Significantly, Lukács ranged Rosenzweig among the many disciples of Dilthey's irrationalism, and he claimed that Rosenzweig, too, embraced an imperialist vision (TYH, esp. 16–31). The judgment is clearly extreme. But it is true that Rosenzweig's *Hegel and the State* followed Dilthey's example. Ironically, Rosenzweig's study of Hegel's political theory was in this sense an apolitical work, and thus offered a foretaste of Rosenzweig's later philosophical resistance to politics and history.

Rosenzweig, of course, was not alone. Dilthey's work helped to spawn a new generation of Hegel scholarship in the early twentieth century. Scholars such as Richard Kroner, Hermann Glockner, Jean Wahl, Jean Hippolyte, and Alexandre Koyré all drew inspiration from Dilthey's example. The definitive characteristic of the Hegel Renaissance, then, was its pronounced interest in the less "rational" and more "metaphysical" dimension of Hegel's

17. "It is no accident that Dilthey's monograph, which focuses its attention on Hegel's *youth*, should stand at the beginning of this whole development. Dilthey believed that he had discovered certain motifs in Hegel's transitional phase . . . which were susceptible to exploitation by an irrationalist, mystical interpretation. . . . [In Dilthey's] book the figure of the young Hegel, who had [once] been peripheral . . . now moved steadily into the forefront of attention. Increasing use was made of Hegel's sketches and notes, most of them not intended for publication, and they were interpreted in such a way as to give birth to a 'true German' philosopher, i.e., a mythical, irrationalist figure palatable to Fascism." TYH, xix.

18. As Lukács writes: "The unprejudiced and attentive reader will find precious little to do with theology in them, indeed as far as theology is concerned the tone is one of sustained hostility.[On the contrary,] the point of Hegel's interest in religion is a covert political interest. . . . [T]his indirect political quality inherent in religion and the attack on religion existed to the same extent in the period of Hegels' *Early Theological Writings*. . . . Their main thrust is directed against the Christian religion." TYH, 31.

early writings. Wahl and Hippolyte, for example, resembled Rosenzweig in their fixation upon the themes of fate and dissatisfaction in Hegel's thought.[19] For most of them, it was Dilthey above all who was credited for having "lifted the veil" to reveal Hegel's true character.

## HEGEL'S THEOLOGICAL WRITINGS

Rosenzweig's academic research was facilitated by the publication of a complete scholarly edition of Hegel's young theological writings (edited by Dilthey's student, Hermann Nohl) in 1907. Three essays, the fruit of Hegel's youthful days of study at Tübingen, Bern, and Frankfurt, proved especially important: "The Life of Jesus," "The Positivity of the Christian Religion," and "The Spirit of Christianity and Its Fate." Quite at odds with his mature, official reputation, they portrayed Hegel as a philosopher preoccupied, not by political concerns, but by questions of a metaphysical and religious nature. As I shall explain, what most aroused Rosenzweig's interest was Hegel's emerging concept of "fate" as metaphysical division.

The early essay "The Life of Jesus" ("Das Leben Jesu," 1795) reflects Hegel's Kantian interpretation of Jesus. According to Hegel, Judaism is a religion of "positivity," consisting in external laws that are imposed upon the individual from without. In Hegel's imaginative reconstruction, Jesus ad-

---

19. See, e.g., Wahl, who saw "the unhappy consciousness" as the moment of subjectivity in division or fate: "Fate, as . . . conceived by Schiller and most of all Hölderlin, illustrated at once the notion and the abolition . . . of the sentiment of the unhappy consciousness." Fate was "Being itself" (*l'être lui-même*), "the consciousness that Being has of itself as something hostile" and yet "something which can be reconciled." *Le Malheur de la Conscience dans la Philosophie de Hegel*, 2nd ed. (Paris: Presses Universitaires de France, 1951; orig. pub. 1929), esp. 170–74. Praising Wahl's focus upon Hegel's religion, see Georges Gurvitch, "Die neueste französiche Literatur über den nachkantischen deutschen Idealismus (Notizen)," *Logos* 20 (1931): 105–18. Paul Hönigsheim suggests that renewed interest in the young Hegel was motivated most of all by a certain "yearning for metaphysics [*Wunsch nach Metaphysik*]." "Zur Hegelrenaissance im Vorkriegs-Heidelberg," *Hegel-Studien* II (1963): 291–310. And Richard Kroner regarded Hegel as "without doubt the greatest irrationalist known in the history of philosophy." But he attempted to heal the divide between the life-philosophical and panconceptualist dimensions of Hegel's work, thus fusing neo-Kantian methods with an "irrationalist" interpretation of Hegelianism inspired by Lebensphilosophie. In Kroner's view, "No thinker before [Hegel] had been so capable of both irrationalizing the concept [*den Begriff so sehr zu irrationalisieren*] and of illuminating that which is most irrational by means of the concept." *Von Kant bis Hegel*, 2 vols. (Tübingen: J. C. B. Mohr, Paul Siebeck, 1921, 1924), II: 271 and ff. And Levy wrote that "With Kroner the ring was closed, the synthesis complete: The philosophy of reason explicated itself as the philosophy of life." *Die Hegel-Renaissance*, 83. On Kroner, also see Glockner, "Hegelrenaissance." On Wahl and Hippolyte, see Levy's notes on the Hegel conference of 1930: "Der Hegel-Kongreß, der im Haag am 23. und 24. April 1930 tagte. (Notizen)." *Logos* 19 (1930): 419–28.

monishes the Jews, "When you regard your ecclesiastical statues and positive precepts as the highest law given to mankind, you fail to recognize
man's dignity."

> That which a human being is able to call his self, that which transcends death
> and destruction and will determine its own just deserts, is capable of govern-
> ing itself. It makes itself known as reason; when it legislates, it does not depend
> on anything beyond itself. . . . This inner law is a law of freedom, which man
> gives to himself and to which he freely submits; it is eternal, and in it lies the
> feeling of immortality. . . . You however, are slaves. You stand yoked by a law
> imposed on you from without; and this is why you are powerless to wrest your-
> self free of bondage to your inclinations. (Nohl, 89)

Hegel's criticism of Judaism anticipates his later, more systematic concept
of fate. Jewish positivity means diremption—law-giver and law-receiver
are split. In the Kantian (that is, "Christian") notion of legislation, however,
reason "does not depend on anything beyond itself." At this point, then,
Hegel cast the basic concepts of division and unity as a Kantian distinction
between heteronomous and autonomous action. There were the roots,
though barely recognizable, of Hegel's later distinction between fate and
reconciliation.[20]

In "The Positivity of the Christian Religion" ("Die Positivität der christlichen Religion," 1795), Hegel moved beyond his early infatuation with the
Kantian ideal of freedom as self-legislation. He now found Judaism and
Christianity prone to the same error of "positivity." From one perspective,
this fact in itself is a remarkable testament to Hegel's integrity in matters of
religious judgment. Drawing on Mendelssohn's distinction between associations of contract and associations of belief, he argued that "[t]he special characteristic of the Jewish religion—that bondage to law from which
Christians so heartily congratulate themselves on being free—turns up
once more in the Christian church. . . . [W]hile, in Judaism, only actions
were commanded, the Christian church goes farther and commands feelings" (Nohl, 209; English, 140). The emphasis on an interiorized "belief,"

20. The specific term "fate" (*Schicksal*) occurs only once and with the rather vague sense of
"tragic destiny." (Jesus' last counsel to his disciples is that, rather than regret his crucifixion,
they should instead "respect the fate [*Schicksal*] that the Divine has determined for me." Nohl,
128.) But Hegel interprets the crucifixion itself as a return to God and thus as an overcoming
of division: "The spirit soars more uninhibitedly toward the fountainhead of all goodness and
enters into its homeland, the realm of the infinite [*in das Reich der Unendlichkeit*]. . . . Then Jesus lifted his eyes toward heaven. 'My father, he said, my hour has come, the hour in which I
am to manifest in its complete dignity the spirit whose source is your infinity, the hour in which
I return home to you . . . above everything that has a beginning and an end, above everything
that is finite [*über alles, was endlich ist*].'" Nohl, 127.

which Hegel had once regarded as a mark of Christianity's superiority, was now seen as a sign of its descent into paradox, since Christianity commanded what should have been an uncoerced condition of faith.

It would be wrong, however, to conclude that the positivity essay represents Hegel's advance beyond anti-Jewish parochialism. He still regarded Judaism as inferior to Christianity insofar as it demanded national as well as divine isolation—the Jews were dissociated from other peoples just as their God remained apart from the world. It is this two-fold separation that Hegel characterizes as "fate."

> The Jewish people, which utterly abhorred and despised all surrounding peoples, wishes to remain on its solitary pinnacle [*hocherhaben*] and persist in its own ways, its own manners, and its own conceit. Any equalization with others or unification with them . . . was in its eyes a horrible abomination. . . . But this obstinacy could not hold out against the fate [*Schicksal*] which was falling on them with ever increasing speed and with a weight which grew heavier from day to day. (Nohl, 148; English, 178)[21]

Significantly, Hegel characterized this condition as *hocherhaben* (literally, "highly sublime"). Sublimity *(Erhabenheit)* would later name that moment in the narrative of Spirit which Hegel conceived as peculiar to Judaism. Following Kant, sublimity (as against beauty) was Hegel's technical term for the failure of the finite mind adequately to embrace its object of representation: when the mind confronts the Infinite without mediation, it experiences the Infinite as an awesome and inassimilable Other.[22] The theme of sublimity is already implicit in Hegel's critique of Jewish separation, construed as both a metaphysical and a social predicament: "[The Jews'] mania for segregation had been unable to resist political subjection" and "the Whole was once and for all torn asunder [Das Ganze war einmal und auf ewig zerrissen]" (Nohl, 148).

"Fate" in Hegel's special sense means tornness—a dissociation from one's surroundings as well as from the divine. It was admittedly an unusual term, in that Hegel did not employ it in the customary sense as destiny or "tragic end." But it was not without affinities to this everyday meaning, since it described *the particular way* that division determines destiny. Indeed, Hegel used the fate concept to name the specific political consequences

---

21. I have amended the Knox translation somewhat, as it obscures the philosophical sense.

22. On the idea of sublimity in Judaism, see Hegel's *Lectures on the Philosophy of Religion. One Volume Edition: The Lectures of 1827*, trans. R. F. Brown et al. (Berkeley: University of California Press, 1988), and Yirmiyahu Yovel, "Hegel's Concept of Religion and Judaism as the Religion of Sublimity," *Tarbiz* (in Hebrew) 16, 3–4 (April–September 1976): 303–26. See Hegel, *Lectures on the Philosophy of Religion*, 366.

(national separateness) that appeared to follow upon a deeper, metaphysical condition (diremption between humanity and God). Significantly, this argument would reappear in Max Weber's idea that the Jews' conception of a transcendent God correlates with their continued status as a "Pariah-Volk."[23] Despite the boldness of this argument, however, Hegel still conceived of "fate" apart from any explicitly political consequences.

It was only in Hegel's later essay of the Frankfurt period, "The Spirit of Christianity and Its Fate" ("Der Geist des Christentums und sein Schicksal," 1798–99) that "fate" came to describe a more generalized, metaphysical predicament. "With Abraham, the true progenitor of the Jews," writes Hegel, "the history of this people begins," Abraham's character "governs the entire fate of his posterity [die alle Schicksale seiner Nachkommenschaft regierte]." But for Hegel, fate is already more than a feature of Jewish history; it is a fundamental moment in world-spirit: "Submission to the fetters of the stronger; this . . . is called fate" (Nohl, 243). Fate is not merely a separation *(Trennung)* but a relation of subordination—power juxtaposed with incapacity. It thus falls under the category of the sublime (as against Greco-Christian beauty):

> The first act which made Abraham the progenitor of a nation is a *disseverance* [*Trennung*] which *snaps the bonds* of communal life and love. The entirety of the relationships in which he had hitherto lived with men and nature, *these beautiful relationships of his youth . . . he spurned.* (Nohl, 245–46; my emphasis)

Judaism for Hegel is thus a religion of division; it sets finite man over and against an all-powerful, infinite God. "In the spirit of the Jews," he writes, there was to be found "an impassable gulf, an alien court of judgment [eine unübersteigliche Kluft, ein fremdes Gericht]." Judaism, he continues, "always presupposes an ideal over against a reality which fails to correspond with the ideal, . . . the indigence of the Jews was such that . . . they had renounced all nobility and all beauty" (Nohl, 290). In relation to God, the human sphere is degraded to the point of nothingness: "[T]he non-being of man [*das Nichtssein des Menschen*] and the littleness of an existence maintained by favor was to be recalled . . . in every human activity" (Nohl, 251;

23. See the fine essay by Hans Liebeschütz, "Max Weber's Historical Interpretation of Judaism," in LBIY, 1964; 41–68, and Arnaldo Momigliano, "A Note on Max Weber's Definition of Judaism as a Pariah-Religion," *History and Theory* 19, 3 (1980): 313–18. And most recently, Gary Abraham, *Max Weber and the Jewish Question* (Urbana: University of Illinois Press, 1992). Rosenzweig expressed great admiration for Weber's "Pariah" concept: "I'm now reading Max Weber's *Judaism,* which I actually wanted to read during the war. It's a shame, that I didn't, as I could have worked with it in [*The Star*]; it is historically the same as what I've expressed philosophically." *Briefe,* N.316, An die Mutter, ([Kassel], 15.8. 21), 405.

English, 192). God's being is all-powerful and sublime, surpassing human cognition: "On God the Jews are dependent throughout, and that on which a man depends cannot have the form of a truth," for "truth is beauty intellectually represented," while with the Jews, God is "outside them, unseen and unfelt" (Nohl, 252; English, 293).[24] And "however sublime the idea of God . . . there yet always remains the Jewish principle of opposing thought to reality, reason to sense." Judaism, Hegel concludes, is characterized by "the rending of life and a dead connection of God and the world" (Nohl, 308; English, 259).

The fate idea thus describes Jewish history as well as Jewish doctrine. In Hegel's view, the act of geographical dislocation that inaugurates the biblical history—God says to Abraham, "Get thee out of the land of thy fathers . . . "—is of decisive importance. For his withdrawal is at once historical *and* metaphysical. Abraham's departure is therefore an expression of his life and exhibits what will be the tragic condition of the Jews from that day forward.[25] The fate of the Jews can only be annulled if their religious separation from God is annulled as well:

> The subsequent circumstances of the Jewish people up to the mean abject, wretched circumstances in which they are still to be found today, have all of them been simply consequences and elaborations of their original fate [*ihres ursprünglichen Schicksals*]. By this fate—an infinite power [*unendlichen Macht*] which they set over themselves and could never conquer—they have been maltreated and will be continually maltreated until they appease it by the spirit of beauty [*Geist der Schönheit*] and so annul it by reconciliation [*durch die Versöhnung aufheben*]. (Nohl, 256; English, 199)

Clearly, Hegel's concept of fate is one of the earliest articulations of his notion of dialectical reconciliation. Indeed, one could argue that the relationship between Jewish fate and (Christian) beauty is a template of the dialectic itself. Judaism's fate is one moment in what will eventually become

24. "The existence of God appears to the Jews not as a truth but as a command." Nohl, 252; English, 293.

25. Here one glimpses Hegel's theories regarding the tragic hero: "Destruction of life is not the nullification of life but its diremption [*Trennung*] and the destruction consists in its transformation into an enemy. It is immortal, and, if slain, it appears as its terrifying ghost which vindicates every branch of life and lets loose its Eumenides. The disembodied spirit of the injured life comes on the scene against the trespass, just as Banquo who came as a friend to Macbeth was not blotted out when he was murdered but immediately thereafter took his seat, not as a guest at the feast, but as an evil spirit. The trespasser intended to have to do with another's life, but he has only destroyed his own, for life is not different from life. . . . In his arrogance he has destroyed indeed, but only the friendliness of life; he has perverted life into an enemy." Nohl, 280; English, 229.

Hegel's interpretation of world history as a narrative that moves from primitive and beautiful unity through the turbulence of sublime division, eventually to be *aufgehoben,* at once preserved and annihilated, at a higher plane of reconciliation *(Versöhnung).*[26] At every stage, infinite Spirit works away at its own potential, struggling toward its own realization in the finite world through a process that is both logical and irreversible. Judaism thus exemplifies the historicity that belongs to all finite being, which, having once contributed its share in the theater of time, must irrevocably collapse: "[W]hen the genius of a nation has fled," Hegel writes, "inspiration cannot conjure it back." For no amount of effort can "enchant away a people's fate, though if it be pure and living, it can well call a new spirit forth out of the depths of its life." And so, although "the Jewish prophets kindled their flame from the torch of a languishing genius" and tried desperately "to restore its old vigor" and "its old, dread sublime unity [*seine alte schauernde erhabene Einheit*]," their efforts were doomed to failure. They could become only "cold fanatics, circumscribed and ineffective when they were involved in politics and statecraft." They could afford only "a reminiscence of bygone ages and so could only add to the confusion of the present without resurrecting the past" (Nohl, 259; English, 203). Thus "History is the fate of Spirit."[27]

It would be misleading to suggest that Hegel's "Spirit of Christianity" is primarily concerned with the fate of Judaism. As the title suggests, Hegel wants to explain Jesus' "failed" encounter with the Jews and Christianity's broader inability to triumph over Jewish fate. As Hegel explains, Jesus could not but adopt the Jews' own stance of division: "Jesus did not fight merely against one part of the Jewish fate. . . . [R]ather, he set himself against the whole [*sondern stellte sich dem Ganzen entgegen*]." But "even his sublime effort [*erhabener Versuch*] to overcome the whole of the Jewish fate must therefore have failed with his people [and he became] its victim himself" (Nohl, 261; English, 205). Thus Jesus' "tragedy" (a term Hegel withholds from Judaism itself) could not have been otherwise.[28] Jesus' struggle against the very principles of his age required that he either succumb directly or, through his re-

---

26. The Jewish mind according to Hegel was one of abstraction, or *Verstand,* capable of dissection but not synthesis. (In the *Phenomenology, Verstand* is "the activity of dissolution.") Judaism was wholly incapable of grasping in Jesus the unity of the finite and infinite: it could only perceive "two natures of different kinds, a human nature and a divine one, . . . remaining as two because they are posited as absolutely different." From the Jews' "intellectualistic point of view," Hegel observes, they could not help but "elevate the intellect, absolute division, destruction of life, to the pinnacle of spirit." Nohl, 311; English, 264.

27. On this point, see Michael Foster, *Die Geschichte als Schicksal des Geistes in der Hegelschen Philosophie* (Tübingen: J. C. B. Mohr, Paul Siebeck, 1929).

28. Significantly, Hegel refuses to characterize Jewish fate itself as "tragic," presumably because this term implies a certain nobility he is unwilling to grant the Jewish condition. See, e.g., Nohl, 260; English, 204–5.

sistance, again exhibit the disunity that is itself the mark of fate. His life thus describes a *world-historical necessity*.[29]

For Hegel, the fate of Judaism and early Christianity is part of the broader narrative of overcoming division. Whereas the essay on positivity upheld the Kantian distinction between Jewish heteronomy and Christian "duty," in "The Spirit of Christianity" it was now supplanted by the distinction between Jewish "division" (fate) and Christian "reconciliation."[30] The change in perspective was striking. Hegel now criticized the Kantian idea of autonomy he once prized. And he no longer regarded Christianity as internalizing law, but instead as transcending law entirely. From this new perspective, Hegel denied the Kantian idea that self-legislation under the aegis of reason yields freedom, since such self-legislation merely imports into the subject the division (between law and inclination) that it had earlier condemned as unfreedom between subjects. Submission to the laws of one's own reason, Hegel concluded, merely makes a man "his own slave" (Nohl, 267; English, 212). Judaism, as a religion of positive legislation, could only appeal to the categories of generality, applying universal rules to particular instances. Against this model of legislation, Jesus brought something "totally foreign"—namely, Jesus introduced "*the subjective*" (Nohl, 264; English, 209; my emphasis).[31]

According to Hegel, the Christian gospel of pure subjectivity is innocent of any concepts having to do with universalist legislation or politics. Indeed, Christianity and Judaism are opposed as forms of life. Judaism is the "division" that only Jesus can heal: "In fate . . . the hostile power is the power of life made hostile; hence fear of fate is not the fear of an *alien* being." Fate is life, only regarded as an opposing force. "Only through a departure from that united life . . . only through the killing of life, is something alien produced" (Nohl, 283; English, 232). Clearly, Hegel conceives of the opposition between Judaism and Christianity as more metaphysical than political.[32] But as a metaphysical condition, its solution presents a greater

29. Lukács correctly sees in Hegel's concept of fate "the contours of his view of historical necessity and his theory of tragedy." TYH, 95.

30. Hegel now equated Judaism and Kantianism. As Dilthey notes, "the identification of Kantian morality with Old Testament law is now . . . complete. And as a consequence of this new legal position . . . reconciliation is now longer possible." JH, 89.

31. As Hegel explained, the essence of Christianity is "reconciliation" *(Versöhnung)* in which "the law loses its form" and "the concept is displaced by life." Nohl, 269; English, 215. Jesus thus focused his attention upon the finite individual: "Over and against the positivity of the Jews," Hegel concludes, "Jesus set *man*." Nohl, 276 ff., English, 224–29; my emphasis.

32. "The trespass of a man regarded as in the toils of fate is therefore not a rebellion of the subject against his ruler, the slave's flight from his master, liberation from subservience, not a revivification out of a dead situation, for the man is alive." Nohl, 280; English, 229.

challenge: "A reconciliation with fate seems still more difficult to conceive than one with the penal law, since a reconciliation with fate seems to require a cancellation of annihilation. . . . Fate . . . occurs within the orbit of life, . . . the law is later than life and is outranked by it" (Nohl, 281; English, 230).

Christian love represents the solution to this metaphysical condition.[33] Indeed, one could argue that Hegel provides a philosophical portrait of Christian penitence:

> [L]ife can heal its wounds again; the severed, hostile life can return into itself. . . . When the trespasser . . . knows himself . . . as disrupted, then the working of his fate commences, and this feeling of a life disrupted must become a longing for what has been lost. . . . In fate . . . the man recognizes his own life, and his supplication to it is not supplication to a lord but a reversion and an approach to himself. (Nohl, 271; English, 218)

The difficulty, however, is that for Christianity in its formative phases such a "return" to life was impossible. According to Hegel, Jesus is born into a world that will oppose him.[34] He is therefore forced to "flee" the world for the security and seclusion of the Christian fold. The early Christians attempt to dwell "above the whole sphere of justice or injustice." They must "surrender their rights," since "in love there vanish not only rights but also the feeling of inequality and the hatred of enemies" (Nohl, 271; English, 218).[35] While this may appear to offer a solution, the Christian principle of

33. Christian "love" is for Hegel the vehicle of reconciliation: "To love God," he writes, "is to feel one's self in the 'all' of life, with no restrictions, in the infinite." Nohl, 296; English, 247. Only Christianity can grasp the whole as a whole, can seize the infinite and the finite as one; their unity is a "holy mystery," because "this connection is life itself." Christianity thus provides "the feeling for the whole," which overcomes "the diremption of man's existence." Nohl, 270; English, 271. But the incarnation of Jesus represents a truth beyond the capacities of reflective thinking *(Verstand)* and thus beyond Judaism. Also see JH, 138.

34. Hegel's remarks upon the Jewish failure to acknowledge Jesus' divinity are brutal: "How were [the Jews] to recognize divinity in a man, poor things that they were, possessing only a consciousness of their misery, of the depth of their servitude, of their opposition to the divine, of an impassable gulf between the being of God and the being of men? Spirit alone recognizes spirit. They saw in Jesus only the man. . . . More he could not be, for he was only one like themselves, and they felt themselves to be nothing. The Jewish multitude was bound to wreck his attempt to give them the consciousness of something divine, for faith in something great, cannot make its home in a dunghill. The lion has no room in a nest, the infinite spirit none in the prison of a Jewish soul, the all of life none in a withering leaf." Nohl, 312; English, 265. Scholars disagree whether Hegel was able to surmount this negative view for a more nuanced and "enlightened" perspective. On the change of perspective, see Nathan Rotenstreich, "Hegel's Image of Judaism," *Jewish Social Studies* 15, 1 (January 1953): 33–52; and more recently, Stephen B. Smith, "Hegel and the Jewish Question: In between Tradition and Modernity," *History of Political Thought* 12, 1 (spring 1991): 87–106.

35. "By giving up its right, as its hostile fate, to the evil genius of the other, the heart reconciles itself with him, and thereby has won just so much for itself in the field of life, has made

apolitical reconciliation and love requires that Jesus separate himself utterly from his world.[36]

Hegel calls the early Christian's seclusion "beauty of soul" *(Schönheit der Seele),* anticipating the "beautiful soul" theorized in *The Phenomenology of Spirit.*[37] For Hegel, the beautiful soul is imperfect, since it "cannot attain to an objective existence." It remains pure only to "waste itself in yearning" (a criticism, apparently, that Hegel directed at the Moravians, a sect of pietistic Christianity), and it enjoys only "the potentiality of renouncing everything in order to maintain one's self" (Nohl, 286; English, 236).[38] That is to say, Jesus himself suffers the fullest burdens of fate. "This restriction of love to itself, its flight from all determinate modes of living even if its spirit breathed in them, or even if they sprang from its spirit, this removal of itself from all fate, is just [itself] *its greatest fate*" (my emphasis). "Here," Hegel concludes, "is the point where Jesus is linked with fate, linked indeed in the most sublime way, but where he suffers under it." Thus the paradox—Hegel quotes Matthew 39—"Yet the man who seeks to save his life will lose it" (Nohl, 324; English, 281).

As one can now see, Hegel's actual aim in "The Spirit of Christianity" was to explain the tragic seclusion of the early Christians: they live as if in a "Kingdom of God" that is "not of this world." They find themselves "set over against a hostile state," and they "become private persons excluding themselves from it." For Jesus himself and those who follow him, wrote Hegel, faith requires "a loss of freedom, a restriction of life, passivity under the domination of an alien might which was despised, but which ceded to Jesus without conditions the little that he wanted from it." In sum, the Christians followed their savior's example and restricted themselves wholly to "existence among his people [*Existenz unter seinem Volke*]"[39] As Hegel explained,

---

friendly just so much life as was hostile to it, has reconciled the divine to itself; and the fate it had aroused against itself by its own deed has dissolved into the airs of night." Nohl, 286; English, 236.

36. "[B]y . . . setting an absolutely total fate over against himself, the man has *eo ipso* lifted himself above fate entirely. Life has become untrue to him, not he to life. He has fled from life but done no injury to it. . . . Rather than make life his enemy, rather than rouse a fate against himself, he flies from life. Hence Jesus required his friends to forsake father, mother, and everything in order to avoid entry into a league with the profane world and so into the sphere where a fate becomes possible." Nohl, 286; English, 236.

37. Assoun also notes an affinity between Rosenzweig's description of Judaism and Hegel's "beautiful soul," which is dissociated from the social world. "Avant-propos." See Hegel, *The Phenomenology of Spirit*, esp. §632 ff.

38. In German: "Die höchste Freiheit ist das negative Attribute der Schönheit der Seele, d.h. die Möglichkeit auf alles Verzicht zu tun, um sich zu erhalten."

39. "The Kingdom of God is not of this world, . . . thus the fate of Jesus in common with those who remained true to him was . . . a limitation [*Beschränkung*] of life, a passivity [in

this "separation from the world" was to remain a definitive mark of Christian fate, most especially its indifference (actually its subordination) to the state (Nohl, 328; English, 287). Ultimately, then, the Christians fall victim to the same divisions that mark Judaism itself: "The covenantal community [*Bund der Gemeine*] found no reconciliation of fate, but only attained the extreme opposite of the Jewish spirit, not the middle course of beauty." The Christian condition, Hegel concludes, was "*as poor as the Jewish spirit itself*" (Nohl, 330; English, 288; my emphasis).

In sum, the young Hegel regarded the distinction between Judaism and Christianity as a quarrel over two irreconcilable modes of life. Judaism exhibits the most violent aspects of fate, as it suffers division both internally (as a theological principle) and externally (as a social antipathy to other nations). Against Judaism, Christianity holds out the promise of complete reconciliation. It offers a metaphorical baptism within the oceanic "all" of life, healing the divisions of Judaism both theologically (in the incarnation) and socially (in the universalist gospel). But on Hegel's view, Christianity did not achieve the reconciliation it promised. His mission unrealized, Jesus bequeaths his disciples a life "in but not of the world." Christianity forswears any true reconciliation and promotes a life of isolated purity, thereby sustaining the antinomy between religion and politics.

Hegel's young theological writings exerted a strong influence on Rosenzweig. As we shall see, *The Star of Redemption* wages an uneasy struggle against dialectical totalization, but without abandoning the ideal of "life" itself as the final stage of reconciliation. Like the young Hegel, it articulates a philosophy of "subjectivity" against the language of ethics and legislation. But unlike Hegel, Rosenzweig found lasting virtue in the tension between religion and politics. Indeed, the metaphysical dissociation between the Jews and humanity became for Rosenzweig a mark of their redemption. Of course, before Rosenzweig could develop these concepts with any rigor, he had first to discover the specific connection between Hegel's young theological writings and his later idea of the state.

### ROSENZWEIG'S *HEGEL AND THE STATE*

At first glance, Rosenzweig's dissertation, *Hegel and the State,* seems to be a study in political thought. Rosenzweig traces Hegel's idea of the state from its origins to its final expression, with a chronological linearity that seems unbroken and, except for an occasionally grandiose note, in a style of ex-

---

relation to] a foreign power one despises, which, however, left to Jesus the minimum that he needed, . . . existence among his people." Nohl, 327–38; English, 283.

emplary restraint.[40] One might find it difficult to discern in this vast two-volume study any significant themes shared in common with the Hegel Renaissance. There is no talk here of Hegel's "mystical pantheism," no attempt to make of Hegel a great "irrationalist," and little of the darker allusions to Romanticism prominently featured in the works of Dilthey, Kroner, Glockner, and Wahl. But at the deepest level, Rosenzweig's book exhibits the characteristic fascination of Lebensphilosophie with the metaphysical and theological dimension of Hegel's thought. According to Rosenzweig, the Hegelian theory of politics was itself a response to the predicament of "fate" found in the young theological writings. To understand this connection, some background on Rosenzweig's book is necessary.

Rosenzweig's dissertation betrays the strong influence of his advisor, the historian Friedrich Meinecke. Rosenzweig first hit upon the guiding argument of the dissertation when he read Meinecke's *Cosmopolitanism and the National State,* which remarks passingly upon the question of Hegel's contributions to modern theories of the nation-state (HS, I: foreword). In Meinecke's view, Hegel belonged, along with Leopold von Ranke and Otto von Bismarck, to the triumvirate of German thinkers whom Meinecke considered the "great liberators of the state" from Enlightenment cosmopolitanism. But although Hegel stood at the threshold of modern nationalism, he failed to appreciate its true power. His continued allegiance to the German Enlightenment prevented the "liberation of [his] political thinking from nonpolitical, universalistic ideas." Ultimately, Meinecke criticized Hegel as insensitive to historical and national particularity. For while Hegel had built "a massive structure of thought arching above the historical world," he "did history a disservice," by violating "the unique character of historical life that he seemed to have acknowledged so clearly." Thus "the old universalistic tendency . . . deprived all historical individualities of their proper rights," thereby "making them mere unconscious instruments and functionaries of the world spirit." And so, Meinecke concluded, whoever surrendered to Hegel's vision of history "stood in danger of transforming actual life in this world into a phantasmagoria."[41]

Rosenzweig's initial impressions of Meinecke were enthusiastic. By the spring of 1909 he seems to have hit upon the themes of his projected dis-

40. "Ses fastes parfois pompeux"—a judgment I share with Gérard Bensussan, the French translator of Rosenzweig's dissertation. See his "Hegel et Rosenzweig."

41. Meinecke, *Cosmopolitanism and the National State,* trans. Robert B. Kimber (Princeton: Princeton University Press, 1970), 197 ff. For Meinecke's account of historicism in German thought, see his *Die Entstehung des Historismus* (Munich: R. Oldenbourg, 1959); in English, *Historism: The Rise of a New Historical Outlook,* trans. J. E. Anderson (New York: Herder and Herder, 1972).

sertation: he would write a pre-history of German imperialist ideas before the Bismarckian founding of the Reich. Like Meinecke, he wanted to explain how nationalist ideals are intimately tied to political consequences: "From 'Culture' to canons," wrote Rosenzweig, "is a small step."[42]

The published text of *Hegel and the State* portrays the emergence of Hegel's political thought according to the historicist method. It is an unabashedly evolutionist narrative, couched in the language of anticipation.[43] (Hegel is "not yet" arrived at his full idea of the state, Hegel is "still" beholden to older concepts he will later abandon, and so forth.) Following Meinecke, Rosenzweig sees Hegel as spanning two epochs: his roots lay in the cosmopolitanism of the eighteenth century, while his final years stretched toward the era of German liberalism, without, however, having followed the evolution of the idea of the state to its conclusion. Hegel's thought, writes Rosenzweig, "did not describe the entire arc of the nineteenth century, but "only served rather to open its path" (HS, II: 240).

Hegel's idea of the state, writes Rosenzweig, was "forged from the metal of freedom," and bespeaks a theory of will that was itself a "witness to the eighteenth century, . . . to Rousseau and the Revolution." For Hegel, the state remained the highest theater for the realization of individual will. And it was this "liberal element" in his theory, according to Rosenzweig, that made Hegel unable fully to recognize a more robust variety of national-

---

42. *Briefe,* N.33, An Hans Ehrenberg (6.8.1909), 43. In a letter from Freiburg, Rosenzweig writes, "Meinecke mehr-als-gefällt mir." *Briefe,* N.30, An die Mutter (30.10.1908), 40. But by October of 1917, Rosenzweig was convinced that Meinecke's national emphasis blinded him to the true consequences of the war, that blocs of states in alliance had surpassed individual nation-states as the vehicles of history. See *Briefe,* N.187, An die Eltern (1.10.17), 245. In the autumn of 1908, quite early in his period of study with Meinecke at Freiburg, Rosenzweig observed that "throughout the book one sees those features of today, now become self-evident, in their moments of initial development. . . . The presentation is classic. To have written such a book I would well give ten years of my life." *Briefe,* N.32, An die Mutter. (13.11.1908, Freiburg), 41.

43. While Meinecke's own politics were nationalist, he did not necessarily succeed in passing this perspective along to his students. In fact, Rosenzweig considered himself lucky to have been raised in the "quiet, untroubled atmosphere" of Meinecke's historicism, partly, he later confessed, because Meinecke was a guide without being truly an inspiration. *Briefe,* N.180, An die Eltern, [20.9.1917], 229. Despite being warned by the historian Max Lenz in Berlin that Meinecke's "idea-historical method" might need amendment, Rosenzweig demurred: "There is nothing more stupid than a historian—philosophers, of course, excepted—I told him that Meinecke's dangerous book remains quite plainly my ideal." *Briefe,* N.47, An Hans Ehrenberg (Berlin 28.10.10.), 56. Rosenzweig confessed, "I too have the philological tic and must hold fast to the path of the history of ideas." Yet he could also find truth in Victor Weizäcker's caricature: "Weizäcker says: *Ideengeschichte* à la Meinecke asks always one question: Did he and he 'have' this and that idea? He's right to mock this method, of course, if at this point the questioning is supposed to have come to an end." *Briefe,* N. 233, An Hans Ehrenberg (11.5.1918), 318.

ism.[44] Only in later works of the nineteenth century, in the theories of Friedrich Christoph Dahlmann and Friedrich Julius Stahl, would Hegel's theory of the individual will be eclipsed by a theory of the nation; and, with Heinrich von Treitschke, the nation itself would come to fruition only by surrendering its sovereignty to the state. And so, Rosenzweig concludes, the individual had to recede if the nation was to emerge, because individual and nation occupied the very same position in the nineteenth century's evolving theory of the state. Hegel was still too strongly a partisan of contractually fortified individualism and therefore had not truly grasped the nation as a meta-individual.[45]

For those most acquainted with Rosenzweig as an author of *The Star of Redemption* and related texts on the new thinking, it may seem remarkable that he was also the author of so "academic" a work. *Hegel and the State* is indeed a descriptive and historicist piece of scholarship, not a work of philosophy. And unlike Rosenzweig's later writing, it is more or less dispassionate in tone. In fact, the book was criticized (by Hermann Glockner) for its quasi-objective, "deeply un-Hegelian" character.[46] To this charge, Rosenzweig readily agreed:

> Glockner considers the Hegel book a failure precisely in what I intended to show. This generation of *Privatdozenten* can no longer imagine with what contempt one once held Hegel; when I began writing, the slightest interest in Hegel could be considered a barrier to doctoral status, and upstanding

44. Lukács misunderstood both Rosenzweig and Dilthey on this score, writing that they did not grasp Hegel's differences from Bismarckian nationalism: "The imperialist apologists find their way out of the impasse by dismissing his [Hegel's] republicanism as an 'infantile disorder.' Franz Rosenzweig, for example, regards Hegel as a precursor of Bismarckian politics. Distorting and suppressing the available evidence in a completely anti-historical fashion, he firstly obscures the fact that even in his old age Hegel was never a precursor of Bismarck and that even his reactionary views were quite different." Hence the "worthlessness of the modern theories of Meinecke, Rosenzweig . . . [etc.], which attempt to turn Hegel into a forerunner of Ranke." TYH, 31–33.

45. "Hegel was never adequately to safeguard for the Nation its own unrestricted right" since "he felt too strongly in the state itself . . . the restless fulfillment of the longings of the individual." HS, II: 245. Later in this chapter I shall touch upon this theme of the nation as a "meta-individual" and how this idea might relate to Rosenzweig's own thoughts about Jewish identity.

46. For Glockner Rosenzweig's book was "a mass of valuable items of discrete information," chiefly concerned with "the development of the material, rearrangements, changes of opinion." It seemed "as if Hegel had progressed in the form of aphorisms, sketches, prefaces, and individual bits of assertion, as if he possessed no philosophical method at all; in a word, as if he philosophized as the Pygmies do today." The book was "an arrangement of learned citations and wretched reflections," and generally "a deeply un-Hegelian and overall unphilosophical product." "Hans Wenke, *Hegels Theorie des Objektiven Geistes* (Notizen)," *Logos* 17 (1928): 229–36.

people such as Kroner cleansed themselves of the suspicion of Hegelianizing with the very same zeal as their partners in belief had cleansed themselves of the charge of Judaising in the Spain of a couple of centuries ago.[47]

Here Rosenzweig offered the provocative suggestion that true Hegelians would find their "faith" as little accepted in polite society as the Spanish Marranos their secret Judaism. The analogy, while appealing, overstates the case. Rosenzweig saw that the German university was no longer hospitable to philosophical convictions of any sort (though "Hegelianizing," given its metaphysical and life-philosophical associations, may have been especially shunned). Its "secular" character notwithstanding, however, Rosenzweig's Hegel book anticipates many of the ideas found in his later, "theological" philosophy. To explain this connection requires closer study.

Following the precepts of German historicism in its concern for origins, *Hegel and the State* identified a surprising continuity between Hegel's earliest writings on religion and his later theory of the state. This grand narrative met with much approval and was regarded as an innovative synthesis of Dilthey's Lebensphilosophie and Meinecke's historical methods.[48] Specifically, Rosenzweig argued that Hegel's mature idea of the state first appeared as a "reconciliation" to the theological and metaphysical problem of fate.[49] The connection was not at all obvious, and it required a complete reconstruction of Hegel's path of intellectual development from the first years in Tübingen to the later lectures on history and law in Berlin, in order to show that his earliest struggles with religion were in fact preliminary attempts at laying the "metaphysical" groundwork for his later theory of the state. A good portion of the first volume discusses Hegel's young theological writings.

47. *Briefe*, N. 529, An die Mutter (2.10.28), 622.
48. Dilthey, however, had hinted at such a link in Hegel's work in the closing lines of *Die Jugendgeschichte Hegels;* JH, 186. In praise, the sociologist Ferdinand Tönnies, for example, wrote that "more and more," historical writing on philosophical and related literature has learned that to know a subject means this: *to know its origin and development* [*Ursprung und Entwicklung*]"; (my emphasis). And while Rosenzweig's portrait of the young Hegel as fundamentally a "poet" followed "in the tracks of the earlier biographies and Dilthey's *Jugendgeschichte Hegels,*" his book had succeeded in explaining the connection between the young theologian and the mature theorist of the state "more deeply and with greater comprehension than it has been ever previously." "Franz Rosenzweig, *Hegel und der Staat* (Besprechung)," *Zeitschrift für Politik* 13, 2 (1923): 172–76.
49. As Tönnies observed, "[T]his theory [of the state] stands in connection with [Hegel's] studies in the philosophy of religion; *he grasps the state as one part of "fate."* . . . He struggles against the private-law violation of the state-idea. [Rather,] it should be justified by means of the state's own legislative power: *only then shall the individual subordinate himself to it* [*dann unterwerfe sich ihnen der Mensch*]." "Franz Rosenzweig," 172–76; quote at 173, my emphasis.

Rosenzweig's interpretations of Hegel's "Life of Jesus" and "Positivity" are unremarkable. He describes especially the latter as a study in the contrast between Christianity, the ascendant "religion of reason," and "the dead positivity of Judaism" (HS, I: 32–33). While it therefore marks the beginning of Hegel's "historical" thinking, Rosenzweig finds it politically without interest. At this stage, he writes, Hegel's idea of the state is "poor" and "soulless," since it enjoys no greater role than to protect the natural rights of man: it is as if "the state were only the unmoving mountain cliff over which the proud longing of humanity pours forth and onwards across the plains— with a strengthened force, but otherwise in essence unchanged." The human element does not as yet "circulate as a life-giving blood through the body of the state, so as to create an independent, breathing existence" (HS, I: 39). Rosenzweig suggests that at this early stage, Hegel regarded the state in much the same fashion as did his friend Friedrich Schelling, the author (so Rosenzweig claimed) of the so-called "Oldest System-Program of German Idealism." According to this curious document, there could be "no idea of the State," just as there is no idea of a machine; for the state too is a "mechanical thing." Hegel also, in Rosenzweig's determination, would not yet acknowledge the state as the living actualization of human freedom, but saw in it merely the guarantor of human-centered needs.[50]

For Rosenzweig, the turning point in Hegel's political development is found in "The Spirit of Christianity and Its Fate." Here for the first time Hegel introduced the theme of the "unity of life."[51] Jesus was no longer "the teacher and prophet of Kantian morality," but instead "the personal carrier of the new ethical system which Hegel substituted for the Kantian ethics of 'division'" (HS, I: 63–65). As Rosenzweig explains, division is a wound in

50. Thus the manuscript's exhortation: "We must therefore rise out and beyond the state!" ("Wir müssen also auch über den Staat hinaus!") For Rosenzweig's relationship to Schelling, consult his study, "Das Älteste Systemprogramm des Deutschen Idealismus: Ein handschriftlicher Fund" [ASP], in KS, 230–77; quote at 233. Rosenzweig's judgment that Schelling was the author of the "Systemprogramm" has been widely disputed. See, inter alia, the various essays found in the special volume of *Hegel-Studien*, "Das älteste Systemprogramm, Studien zur Frühgeschichte des deutschen Idealismus," 9 (1973). Rosenzweig's relationship to Schelling is a guiding thread in Else-Rahel Freund, *Die Existenzphilosophie Franz Rosenzweigs* (Leipzig: Felix Meiner, 1933).

51. Lukács criticizes Rosenzweig, along with Dilthey, for paying too much attention to "life" in this essay. He accuses them of "senselessness and the lack of scientific rigor," for only this can explain how the "imperialist neo-Hegelians" manage to "lump Hegel's Frankfurt period together with vital tendencies of the day." TJH, 162. Against Lukács, one has only to read Hegel's essay to see that "life" was a category of great philosophical importance; his charge of "imperialism" is simply bizarre.

the midst of "life." It does not touch "a foreign God who threatens the world from an infinite remove, nor is it a violation of a categorical law that stands in sublime unattainability over and against the reality of a life ruled by drives and inclinations." Rather, the division touches the violator himself, since all of life is one:

> The fate of man does not remain forever unreconciled, as the wounded law that is outward or inward, Jewish or Kantian. Rather, just as the fate grew forth directly out of the guilty division of man from "life," so too his reconciliation comes directly through his reunification with life, the replacement of the torn relation: love. Life can heal its wounds, for life is nothing other than the movement from guilt to fate. The individual cannot extract himself from this movement; precisely because he is an individual [*Einzelner*] he cannot be free of guilt; and if he were to wish to be so, were he to save himself out from the stream of life and cast himself upon its banks, this very innocence he has longed for, just this desire to hold himself back from life, even this would be his guilt. He who had hoped to remain free of fate [*Schicksallos*] thereby meets the greatest fate. (HS, I: 64–65)

Such in gross outline is what Rosenzweig calls Hegel's "ethical metaphysics" of the early Frankfurt period (ca. 1799). According to Rosenzweig, the themes of fate and its overcoming were to prove "decisive." In their relation, "one could already sense how [Hegel's] intellectual relationship to the state would [soon] develop" (HS, I: 75, 65).

The development happened gradually. Paying careful attention to Hegel's monthly sketches for the "Spirit of Christianity" essay, Rosenzweig distinguishes two phases of development. In the earlier phase, Hegel presented a theory of Jewish fate for which there was as yet no solution. Here, claims Rosenzweig, Hegel had not yet developed the tools with which he could fully break out of his earlier Kantianism. The fate of Abraham thus lacked a higher theory of reconciliation.[52]

It is noteworthy that Rosenzweig seemed at this point quite uninterested (at least outwardly) in Hegel's remarks on Judaism. Neither in the printed dissertation nor in Rosenzweig's letters from the period does one find him roused to defend Judaism against Hegel's often invidious remarks. In fact, Rosenzweig reiterated without comment Hegel's various descriptions of Judaism as an inhibited phase of Spirit, and he seemed almost to agree with Hegel that "nations ruled by division" must be left behind for "a higher form of human existence" (HS, I: 52–53). Even more striking, perhaps, it is specifically *the fate of Jesus* that occupies pride of place in Rosenzweig's

---

52. It was, Rosenzweig admits, the "first probative fragment" in what was to be Hegel's mature manner of writing history, "but little else." HS, I: 81.

commentary. As I shall explain below, Hegel's Jesus later served as a model for Rosenzweig's theories of Jewish existence.[53]

In the first phase of composition, the figure of Jesus in "The Spirit of Christianity" represents for Hegel an image of "supreme subjectivity" that stands opposed to the world. Here Jesus is a heroic but isolated individual, in Rosenzweig's words, poised "in struggle against the eternal Death" of Judaism and the state. (In Jesus, Hegel has represented "Man" retreating from "the enemy world" and confronting it in "animosity." "All of life is on the side of man"; HS, I: 73.) Jesus flees from the world into absolute, eternal "solitude," and he cannot conceive of any possible resolution for his condition. Indeed, "he wants his suffering." His condition, as Rosenzweig takes care to note, is not merely sociopolitical; it represents a metaphysical principle: "[Jesus] cannot achieve unity with the objects that surround him." He "shudders before the infinite."[54]

To underscore the metaphysical dimension of Jesus' predicament, Rosenzweig draws a connection between Hegel's vision of isolated human existence and his early, human-centered theory of state. Both indicate Hegel's rejection of Kant, for whom Church and State remain mutually indifferent. Against Kant, Hegel objects that it belongs to the nature of the Church to grasp human life "as a Whole" *(als ein Ganzes)*. Thus Kant's dualism was not simply unworkable in life, it was metaphysically impossible. Along with the dualism of law and inclination, Hegel rejected Kant's dualism of "State-person and Church-person," and thus disdained the state-idea that this "fractured" *(zertrümmert)* model of humanity made possible.[55] The individual yearned for "dissolution" of the self in the "Whole." But the best Hegel could offer was a theory of Christian love that provided private consolation for the lonely believer. As Rosenzweig explains, love was "an event that still occurred only within the windowless four walls of the 'I.'" It did not yet truly

53. There is perhaps no greater evidence than this to show how Rosenzweig's later monument to Judaism was built out of the debris of previous philosophy, and often from the most unlikely sources. Hence Gershom Scholem's remark that in Rosenzweig's philosophy, Judaism displays a "strangely churchlike aspect." "On the 1930 Edition of Rosenzweig's *Star of Redemption*," in his *The Messianic Idea in Judaism and Other Essays in Jewish Spirituality* (New York: Schocken Books, 1931); orig. pub. *Frankfurter Israelitisches Gemeindeblatt* 10 (1931): 15–17.

54. Rosenzweig's precise phrasing is worth quoting: "Als Leiden nämlich wird dieser Zustand empfunden, aber als ein Leiden, gegen das es kein Mittel, keinen Kampf gibt noch geben darf, eben weil der Mensch das Leiden will; er sucht sich von der Welt rein zu erhalten, seine Fremdheit gegen sie zu bewahren." HS, I: 76. And in the final phrase quoted, "ihm graut vor dem Unendlichen." Here Rosenzweig quotes a letter by Hegel in which he notes that, "the highest Subjectivity" is "to fear the object, the flight from it, the fear of Unification." HS, I: 75.

55. Rosenzweig calls this Hegel's "new, anti-Kantian vision of man as an indivisible unity." HS, I: 75–77 He explains that, at this point, "man is still the measure of the state." HS, I: 77–79.

reach beyond the subject and into the world. Rather, it "happened only in the blind storm of individual feeling" (HS, I: 79).[56]

From this astonishingly subtle and complex interpretation, Rosenzweig concluded that Hegel's new theory of the state could only emerge in tandem with a metaphysical solution to the predicament of finite subjectivity. Thus the solution to fate was (in Rosenzweig's words) the "decisive turning point" in Hegel's thought, although it endured "a brief instant" (HS, I: 75). The new Christian solution to fate would allow a true "overcoming" [*Überwindung*] of finite individuality, and the new unity of subject and world would then allow for the appearance of a new kind of state no longer confined to "the measure of man."[57]

In the second phase of writing "The Spirit of Christianity," notes Rosenzweig, Hegel came to recognize that the only possible solution to fate was a new theory of politics conceived on an unprecedented metaphysical scale. From this new perspective, Hegel regarded the state as a suprasubjective entity with its own purposes beyond those of the individual. In fact, the state was "life"; so Jesus' dissociation from the political world was nothing less than a "renunciation" of life itself.[58] Rosenzweig's concludes:

> Here we grasp in our hands the turning point of Hegel's vision of the state. The state as an element of fate! And fate in the most expansive sense that Hegel had at the time developed: The Whole of Life, which the individual encounters. (HS, I: 87–88)

The state is no longer an expression of human will, nor a guarantor of individual rights. It is, writes Rosenzweig, "an Unavoidable thing from which [the subject] cannot extricate himself" (HS, I: 86–88). Newly conceived as

---

56. Hegel had not yet arrived at an understanding of the world such that it might confront man in all its "brightly lit contours," and not as "inhumanly monstrous."

57. Lukács too observes this transformation in Hegel, but interprets it as Hegel's victory over a false subjectivism: "Fate, which had been seen before as a social necessity, now becomes a feeling, a sensing; it becomes the individual's experience of the necessity that has overtaken him. . . . [T]he reconciliation of fate through love is the path along which Hegel arrives at the mystical objectivity of his religious life." Such language "soon vanishes from Hegel's philosophical vocabulary" and the "fruitful elements are absorbed into his theory of dialectics, but the word 'fate' is no longer used to describe them. The idea of a reconciliation through love disappears entirely, once Hegel has begun to look at social phenomena exclusively from a sociohistorical standpoint, and no longer from the perspective of the individual." TYH, see esp. 179–208.

58. As illustration, Rosenzweig cites the following fragment from the Nohl edition, at 305: "The Fate of Jesus: Renunciation of the relations of life [Schicksal Jesu—Entsagung der Beziehungen des Lebens]—a) civic and civilian, b) political, c) life together with others—family, relations, subsistence. The relationship of Jesus to the world partly flight, partly reaction and struggle against it. So long as Jesus had not changed the world he had of necessity to flee it." HS, I: 85.

the whole of "life," Hegel's idea of the state provides the solution to a basically metaphysical dilemma:

> This is the instant, where every vision of the state that would see the individual standing against the Whole [*vor dem Ganzen*] has now become a nullity. It is unthinkable that "fate" in this enormous sense could still be considered as a matter of contract. The state is there, . . . grown beyond dependency on the individual man. And so [Hegel] will now find in the state something more, something altogether different than the guarantor of the rights of man; he will no longer constrain himself to believing that justice should be the highest measure of its rule. (HS, I: 88)

Hegel's solution (according to Rosenzweig) was to discern in the "fate" of Jesus the symptomatic isolation attending a basically liberal model of the state as a created thing. For as long as the state is conceived as something artificial (hence lifeless), Christianity could persist in the illusion of a life beyond politics. But once the state is itself recognized as the greater sphere of life, Christianity cannot remain apolitical without introducing a fateful division within life. As Rosenzweig explains,

> It is not, then, a mere "covenant" [*Bund*] with the world that first creates the "possibility of fate"; fate also meets whosoever thwarts it, whoever is sublimely above fate also meets fate; and the most sublime of all, the fate of this, the highest guilt that is born in the highest guiltlessness: Whoever would save his life, he shall lose it.

Since the state was now conceived as the highest theater of life, incidental human concerns such as those of contract and justice were (in Rosenzweig's words) "cast aside." But in submitting to the state, the individual had no guarantee that it would act on her subjective behalf. Fate was therefore "something unavoidable" from which the individual "cannot—and . . . *should* not, extricate himself." "It stands there in all its greatness, and," Rosenzweig concludes with palpable satisfaction, "*an element of this fate is the state!*" (HS, I: 88; emphasis in original)

The novelty of this interpretation lay in its claim that Hegel's political theory was a direct outgrowth of his early theological concerns. The idea of the state was born, according to Rosenzweig, from the "struggle between part and whole" that had first appeared in Jesus' struggles against an inhospitable world. But in the space of a few months, the struggle had come to an end—in Rosenzweig's words, "the whole had definitively won." The state now represented "the power of the general over the individual," lending sovereignty its "necessary character."[59]

---

59. Compare Lukács, who writes, "Even though the fate of the individual remains a kind of leitmotiv throughout the period and as such is one of the factors responsible for the

A conceptual puzzle in Rosenzweig's interpretation was that it represented the state as both a component of fate and simultaneously its solution. Like Hegel's idea of the Jewish God, the state had become a manifestation of sublime power; it was the final form of that "monstrous" world that once opposed the unhappy consciousness. The encounter between state and subject was therefore radically unequal, for even as it healed the one-sided life of finite subjectivity, the state also put an end to the subject's hopes to encounter the world as an expression of his own subjective will. The state was therefore at once a reconciliation of fate and fate's final manifestation. In this sense, it expressed the structural paradox of Hegel's dialectic; it was both redemption and tragedy.[60]

### THE ECLIPSE OF THE POLITICAL

The accuracy of Rosenzweig's account remains open to debate. Georg Lukács suspected an alliance with German "irrationalism," while Ferdinand Tönnies welcomed the "theological" emphasis.[61] Neither view is decisive. In any case, one should be wary of drawing any explicitly political conclusions from Rosenzweig's approach. The influence of Lebensphilosophie was so pervasive that it bridged political divides. Even Lukács, who excoriated it as a symptom of political reaction, followed its initiative in his attention to the young theological writings.[62] Still, from the summary above it may be pos-

---

culmination of his thought in religion, the entire period is marked by an unbroken striving to break out of the subjectivity such an approach must engender. And if his solution is a sort of mystical pseudo-objectivity of the religious life, this internal debate does nevertheless prepare the way for his later more objective, dialectical approach to both history and society." TYH, 186.

60. Bensussan writes, "[L]a Raison intégrative de Hegel va trouver dans l'État le lieu de cette unification et . . . l'État est en effet l'espace de 'la réconciliation devenue objective.'" He concludes that Hegel's idea of the state is "la théorisation achevée de la puissance du monde et, ajoutera *L'Étoile,* de l'impuissance de l'individu singulier face au monde." "Hegel et Rosenzweig," xxxiii, xxiv.

61. Tönnies's approval is unsurprising. He was convinced that the consolidation of social order threatened to extinguish local and ethnic-communal life, hence his famous distinction between *Gesellschaft* and *Gemeinschaft,* which expressed a rueful mistrust of the social totality much akin to the antipolitical features of Rosenzweig's later philosophy. That Rosenzweig belonged to the distinctively *Germanic* school of historical pessimists is readily apparent from his observation in 1919 that Oswald Spengler, author of *The Decline of the West,* was "the greatest philosopher of history since Hegel." *Briefe,* N.269, An Rudolf Ehrenberg (5.5.1919), 359.

62. Lukács admitted that although the emergent social philosophy was still "mystified" and "chaotic," one could already discern that "in Hegel's view fate represents the dialectical movement of the totality of life, of society as a whole," and since fate "encompasses [both] the self-destruction and re-creation of that life, . . . it is the uninterrupted dialectical self-reproduction of society." TYH, 195.

sible to draw certain preliminary conclusions about how Rosenzweig's *Hegel and the State* relates to his later philosophical as well as political thought.

First, it seems clear that the state had come to be associated for Rosenzweig with the eclipse of the individual. As we have seen, the fate of Jesus was for Hegel a model for the predicament of finitude in general; the struggle between Jesus and his society showed that any engagement in the political world demanded surrender in the face of irresistible authority. From this story, Rosenzweig appears to have concluded that finite subjectivity and the state are necessarily opposed. Since the full realization of the state's purposes on earth demands the eclipse of the individual, Rosenzweig came to believe that the preservation of finitude required a life *elsewhere than politics.*[63]

This conclusion had further ramifications for Rosenzweig's understanding of the Jews. In *Hegel and the State* Rosenzweig does not explicitly suggest an analogy between the fate of Jesus and that of the Jewish people. But his care in addressing Hegel's discourse on Judaism and "fate" naturally encourages readers to perceive a resemblance between them. Clearly, the early Christians suffer the same tragic isolation that Hegel saw as an intrinsic feature of Judaism. Indeed, in Rosenzweig's own philosophy the Jews would come to occupy the very same structural position of messianic exemplarity and isolation as Hegel had assigned to Jesus. Thus in *The Star of Redemption* Rosenzweig would characterize the sufferings and isolation of the messianic people as "Jewish fate" ( *Jüdische Schicksal)* (SE, 331–39 [E, 298–305]). Leo Strauss was in this sense correct in his observation, "The dogma of Israel's chosenness [thus became] for Rosenzweig 'the truly central thought of Judaism' because, as he makes clear, he approaches Judaism from the Christian point of view, [and] because he looks for a Jewish analogue to the Christian doctrine of Christ."[64]

The resemblance is surprisingly close: Hegel's Christians find themselves "set over against a hostile state; [they] become private persons excluding themselves from it." The fate of Jesus and those who follow him was in Hegel's words, "a loss of [political] freedom, a restriction of life" and "passivity under the domination of an alien might which was despised, but which ceded to Jesus without conditions the little that he wanted from it—existence among his people."[65] Both Christ and the Jewish people are thus vic-

---

63. Compare Rilke's definition in the *Duino Elegies:* "Dieses heißt Schicksal: gegenüber sein und nichts als das und immer gegenüber." (That is what fate means: to be opposite, to be opposite and nothing else, forever.)

64. Leo Strauss, *Spinoza's Critique of Religion,* trans. E. M. Sinclair (New York: Schocken Books, 1965), 13. Note that Strauss dedicated this book to the memory of Franz Rosenzweig.

65. The description is worth citing in full: "The fate of Jesus was that he had to suffer from the fate of his people; either he had to make that fate his own, to bear its necessity and share

tims of dissociative fate (although Christ is crucified, while the Jews suffer a life of permanent dispersal). And like Hegel's early Christians, Rosenzweig's Jews seek to live out their lives in a "Kingdom of God" that is "in but not of this world."[66]

As I have already suggested, Hegel's interpretation of the state as the culmination of fate may help to explain Rosenzweig's later indifference to politics. But it also may account for Rosenzweig's aversion to dialectics. As noted above, Rosenzweig's focus upon the "theological" and metaphysical themes animating Hegel's thought followed the example of Dilthey, for whom Hegel had been primarily a metaphysician and not a political thinker.[67] And like Dilthey, Rosenzweig regarded Hegel's political theory as at core the culmination of a dialectical drama relating part to whole, and finitude to totality. The most "true reconciliation," writes Hegel in the *Philosophy of Right*, "discloses the state as the image and actuality of reason."[68] Reconciliation itself, then, was the metaphysical principle behind Hegel's politics. So Rosenzweig's awakening skepticism regarding the salvific potential of state-life seems to have been motivated by a deeper antipathy to dialectical reconciliation as such.[69]

Most of all, Rosenzweig's encounter with Hegel seemed to have played a critical role in the development of a new, post-metaphysical concept of redemption. As I will explain, the abandonment of dialectics allowed for a deepened appreciation of finitude, propelling Rosenzweig away from Hegel and toward Nietzsche as the "first" philosopher of subjectivity. Given this

---

its joy, to unite his spirit with his people's, but to sacrifice his own beauty, his connection with the divine, or else he had to repel his nation's fate from himself, but submit to a life undeveloped and without pleasure in itself." Nohl, 327–28; English, 283.

66. Strauss was wrong to conclude that Rosenzweig had substituted a worldly idea of national distinction for the medieval Jewish idea of the centrality of divine law, as if "the same change would have been effected if the starting point had been mere secularist nationalism." This cannot be true. Rosenzweig embraced an idea of Jewish national distinction that lacked any obvious secular-political consequences. Indeed, he could only embrace the Jewish "nation" because he regarded it as innocent of Hegel's "metaphysical" politics. See Strauss, *Spinoza's Critique of Religion*, 13.

67. On the aversion to dialectics, see Assoun, who writes, "On peut penser que la politique est en quelque sorte noyée dans cette considérable presque métaphysique qu'est *L'Etoile de la Rédemption*—comme si ce texte faisait droit à cette décision de parler d'*autre chose*... que de politique.... Cet 'échappement latéral' au monde de la politique n'est pas un banal apolitisme, mais un repositionnement du politique dans la totalité anthropologique, quelque chose comme une 'transmutation des valeurs.'" "Avant-propos," xii; emphasis and first ellipsis in original.

68. Hegel, *The Philosophy of Right*, §360. Cited from the English translation, trans. T. M. Knox (London: Oxford University Press, 1952), 222–23.

69. On the traces of dialectical thinking in Rosenzweig's work, see the interesting dissertation by Bieberich, *Wenn die Geschichte göttlich wäre*.

new perspective, it is not surprising that that *The Star of Redemption* regards the sheer fact of mortality as Hegel's defeat. For Rosenzweig, the nonrelational and nontransferable experience of possible death would become the conceptual instrument for exposing the falsity of idealist totalization. Rosenzweig thus refused to follow Hegel's idea that the death of the particular should be considered a moment of tragedy in an unfolding narrative of redemption. To be sure, Rosenzweig's refusal is partly anti-Christian: he rejects the logic that enabled Hegel to read the crucifixion of Jesus as a historical necessity. But at a deeper level, it is anti-metaphysical: he rejects any logic of reconciliation whatsoever insofar as it claims to find in death a higher and salvific purpose. One might even say that this is the polemical intent behind *The Star of Redemption:* it refuses to see redemption as "beyond" death. If, as Rosenzweig believed, Hegel's attempts to grapple with the theology of the crucifixion lies at the heart of Hegelian statism, then one can only conclude that an abiding mistrust in "metaphysics" lies at the core of *The Star.*

## NATIONALISM WITHOUT STATISM

Perhaps the most paradoxical consequence of Rosenzweig's encounter with Hegel was that it prompted a new philosophical interest in the nation. This shift from a statist to a nationalist understanding of individual fulfillment is a crucial aspect of Rosenzweig's philosophical development. Already anticipated in Tönnies's distinction between society and community, Rosenzweig's abandonment of Hegelian statism can be understood as a shift from public and rational-contractualist political theory anchored in the Enlightenment to a communal and affective political theory that is far more sensitive to the cultural grounds of identity, even to the neglect of actual political institutions.

As has already been shown, the general argument of *Hegel and the State* was that Hegel's political theory contained a fatal insufficiency. In the closing pages of the dissertation, Rosenzweig again noted that Hegel's enduring fidelity to the Enlightenment had prevented him from fully appreciating the role of the nation in politics. In the era of Bismarck, Hegel was therefore doomed to fall into obscurity. Yet even Bismarck, Rosenzweig notes, ultimately frustrated German nationalism more than he realized its highest aims. (Despite German unification, the dream of the nation "yet remained only a hope.") And by 1914, the longing for national realization had reemerged like a sleeping giant: Rosenzweig's contemporaries looked for fulfillment *"not in the state, but in the nation"* (HS, II: 244; my emphasis).[70]

---

70. By 1914, the state itself gradually assumed "the face of national community [*das Gesicht der nationalen Gesittungsgemeinschaft*]." HS, II: 244.

But by the end of the war, Rosenzweig recognized that the longing for national community had ended in disaster. When he turned back to his dissertation, he emended the text so as to better capture both his disillusionment with nationalism and his newly ambivalent relationship to Hegel.[71] The most significant amendment was the addition of a second epigraph, taken, like the first (quoted earlier in this chapter) from Hölderlin's poem "An den Deutschen" and placed on the cover of volume II:[72]

Wohl ist enge begrenzt unsere Lebenzeit,
Unserer Jahre Zahl sehen und zählen wir,
Doch die Jahre der Völker,
Sah ein sterbliches Auge sie?

Our time of life is so narrowly bound
We witness our numbered years and count them
Yet the years of the nations,
did a mortal eye ever yet see them?

The contrast is startling. If the first epigraph seemed unabashedly idealist, the second appears conflicted. It describes the human life span as finite, but then suggests the years of the "nations" *(Völker)* are countless, perhaps immortal.[73]

It is unclear what to make of this change. One reading would be that the nation had now assumed the mantle of reconciliation once reserved for the state. But this seems unlikely given Rosenzweig's well-documented disillusionment with German nationalism. (The dissertation ends with the rueful remark that "today, as the book appears, in the hundred-and-fiftieth year after Hegel's birth, the hundredth year since the publication of his *Philosophy of Right*" the dream of a new, vigorous nationalism seemed "irrevocably

71. Ambivalence, but more love than hatred. In a minor review, Rosenzweig noted his dissatisfaction with Georg Lasson's recently published preface for the new edition of Hegel's *Lectures on the Philosophy of History*. Rosenzweig judged Lasson too undiscriminating an admirer of Hegel: "Love surely belongs to all historical presentations," Rosenzweig admitted. "But . . . the highest love is not the kind that identifies with its object." Rather, the highest love for the historian is "the sort where one knows one's difference" from what one studies, where it is precisely "the feeling of a divide [*Kluft*] that exacts a love of the fullest power." Review of *Hegel, G. W. F., Vorlesungen über die Philosophie der Weltgeschichte,* ed. and with introduction by Georg Lasson, in *Kantstudien* 27 (1922): 183–84.

72. Rosenzweig had selected the first epigraph as early as 1909. As noted above, this passage captured the developmental logic of both historicism and idealism, expressing the belief that "deeds" now "ripe and full of Spirit" originate in thoughts, and that world history unfolds as if organically, like "golden fruit" from the "written word."

73. Incidentally, Heidegger used this very poem to emphasize human finitude in his essay "The Age of the World Picture." See "Die Zeit des Weltbildes," in GA, 5, *Holzwege,* 75–113. For Heidegger, Hölderlin knew that man "belongs to Being and yet remains a stranger [*ein Fremdling*] among beings" (96).

lost in the froth of the waves now flooding all life.") [74] Here Rosenzweig seemed to provide an ironic rejoinder to the Hölderlin stanza first quoted: if deeds are the fruits of ideas, the fallen tree yields no fruit. But in the concluding lines of *Hegel and the State*, Rosenzweig provided the reader with his own gloss on the second Hölderlin epigraph:

> Today, in the darkness that surrounds us, only a glimmer of hope still shines from out of that hardly noticeable concluding portion from Hölderlin's poem, the beginning of which was initially chosen in better days as the leading epigraph of the work. Only a glimmer, and yet to the prisoner in his cell it irresistibly compels his glance. (HS, II: 246)

I would like to suggest that these lines indicate a hidden continuity in Rosenzweig's political thinking. Let us suppose that the "prisoner" alone in his cell is the finite individual of Hegel's philosophy. Naturally, the reference to "today" can only be Europe after the First World War. If so, then the "darkness that surrounds us" is the sense of despair felt by so many in Rosenzweig's generation upon their return from the front. But what, then, is meant by the "glimmer of hope"?

The prisoner still seems to believe that redemption from his isolation is a real possibility. And nationalism provides the only light in his dark cell. For as the second epigraph makes clear, only belonging to a national community offers salvation: "the years of the nations" seem to stretch toward eternity, beyond the vision of "mortal eyes." The closing lines hint at an unfulfilled and still-living hope in the salvific powers of a certain people, even while the *German* people no longer provided a viable solution.

A major claim of this book is that one cannot understand Rosenzweig's philosophy apart from its German context. This is especially true of Rosenzweig's theoretical attachment to the idea of the *Volk*, or people. As I will show in the following two chapters, Rosenzweig's abandonment of German nationalism as a philosophical principle should not be mistaken for a wholesale rejection of its theoretical grounds. The striking thing about the *Star of Redemption* is that it expresses an attachment to the Jewish people by means of a logic that is clearly borrowed from his earliest engagement in German political philosophy. The "glimmer of hope" for the prisoner in his cell signifies a mode of national attachment beyond German nationalism, yet also dependent upon the lessons of German politics. For even while the war had irrevocably damaged the dream of German national redemption, it had not fully extinguished the hope for national life of a different order.

---

74. Hegel's dream of the state cannot be revived, but neither can the nationalist hope of 1914: "When the structure of a world collapses, so too the dreams interwoven with it must be buried in the wreck." HS, II: 246.

In this sense Rosenzweig's philosophical embrace of the Jews is a twofold thought, combining transference with retreat. On the one hand, it represents a continuation of German nationalism in a new form—so one might say that Rosenzweig did not so much abandon his nationalist hopes as project them upon an unexpected entity. On the other hand, the defeat of the German state introduced a violent discontinuity, confirming Rosenzweig's belief that a new *kind* of identification was required. Because the Jewish people rested in suspension beyond the vicissitudes of political life, the idea of Jewish redemption remained largely immune from the widespread climate of political pessimism following the First World War.[75] Rosenzweig's faith in the Jews therefore survived where his faith in the German state could not. Friedrich Meinecke's 1930 obituary for his former student was accurate: "The World War gave the lie to his first line of pursuit, researching the heights of German-Protestant culture," and when the initial dream lay in ruins, Rosenzweig "fled into the world of his blood."[76]

In this chapter I have suggested that Hegelian categories survived in Rosenzweig's philosophy, despite (even against) Hegel himself. In this sense, Rosenzweig remained a Hegelian in the very fashion he opposed him.[77] In Rosenzweig's emerging, independent philosophy, Judaism came to represent a form of collective life without the metaphysical dangers of statehood. But this meant that Jewish existence was now fate itself; it was (in Hegel's terms) the preserve of finitude in the moment preceding its Christian-dialectical reconciliation. As Hölderlin observed, "only the Gods are without fate [*Schicksallos*]."[78]

Rosenzweig's idea of Jewish identity clearly reflects the broader trends in Weimar philosophy. For "fate" could easily serve as another name for finitude. Its prominence as a philosophical category in the 1920s thus indicates

75. On the idea of transference between Jewish messianism and German romanticism, see Michael Löwy, *Redemption and Utopia: Jewish Libertarian Thought in Central Europe, A Study in Elective Affinity*, trans. Hope Heaney (Stanford, Calif.: Stanford University Press, 1992.) On the question of transference, see as well Avineri's suggestive essay, "Rosenzweig's Hegel Interpretation."

76. Meinecke, "Franz Rosenzweig—Nachruf." *Historische Zeitschrift* 142, 1 (1930): 219–20.

77. Cf. Bienenstock's claim that Rosenzweig misunderstood the place of religion in Hegel's philosophy and therefore felt compelled (mistakenly) to reject Hegel.; "Rosenzweig's Hegel," 182.

78. Hölderlin's observation was to inspire Walter Benjamin's 1921 essay "Fate and Character," in *Reflections: Essays, Aphorisms, Autobiographical Writings*, ed. Peter Demetz, trans. Edmund Jephcott (New York: Schocken Books, 1978), 304–11. Dilthey notes a possible historical connection between Hölderlin and Hegel in developing the idea that fate is a distinctively human as opposed to divine problem. JH, 111.

the distinctively post-Nietzschean tenor of the new thinking. Heidegger, for example, was particularly drawn to Hegel's notion that "time appears as the fate . . . [of] spirit." But he objected that "spirit" does not "fall" *into* time, as if, *per impossibile,* it might otherwise have managed to surmount it (SZ, 436).[79] Like Rosenzweig, Heidegger no longer entertained the older theological longing of release from human limitation. Instead, he looked for the "authenticity" of human existence in what he called "the simplicity of its *fate*" ("die Einfachheit seines *Schicksals*"; SZ, 384; emphasis in original).[80]

Given the centrality of the concept of fate for the young Hegel, as well as for Lebensphilosophie, its theological sense was obvious. One of the greatest challenges of the new thinking was that in using such ideas, it had first to conceive them in a modern, post-Nietzschean register. As Theodor Kisiel has recently indicated, Heidegger's earliest engagements with Christian theology fixed upon the problem of worldly redemption. In his mature philosophy, however, Heidegger conceived the Christian stance as "witness" before God in nontheological terms as an "authentic" understanding of Being.[81] "Redemption" now became a category of immanence, premised upon the seizing of one's fate and living from—and out of—the tradition in which one is thrown (SZ, 383–84).

Rosenzweig, too, understood "fate" as a concept of demonstrably Christian-theological origin. But as I shall explain in the following chapters, he then applied the lessons of Hegel's "fate" to what he regarded as most dis-

79. Compare this rejoinder to the position of Michael Foster, in his neo-Hegelian study, *Die Geschichte als Schicksal des Geistes in der Hegelschen Philosophie* (Tübingen: J. C. B. Mohr, Paul Siebeck, 1929). According to Foster, Hegel's concept of the state is "völlig durchchristet und versöhnt."

80. Richard Kroner's opening remarks at the 1930 Hegel congress in Berlin described "our contemporary philosophical thinking" as exhibiting a "pull toward metaphysics" *(Zug zur Metaphysik),* which in Hegelian terms allowed the human being "to recognize and overcome his own finitude and thrownness under fate [seine eigene Endlichkeit und Schicksalunterworfenheit als solche zu erkennen und zu überwinden]." As quoted by Käte Nadler, "Bericht über den 2. Internationalen Hegelkongreß in Berlin vom 18.–22 Oktober, 1930," *Logos* 19 (1930): 443–48. By contrast, Rosenzweig wrote, "[H]uman life crawls along, in God-fearing weakness and bound to the earth, with humble prayers it attempts to turn aside the will of heavenly powers . . . yet never capable of overstepping the limits of the human; the dark powers of the earth . . . press low his proud neck: how, then, should he have presumed himself master of earth and fate [der Erde und des Schicksals Herr zu sein]?" SE, 93.

81. Kisiel comments that Christianity (for Heidegger) announced an "awake and sober" disposition, one that does not allow itself to become "caught up in the *en-theos* which transports us out of this world." Thus the "enormous difficulty" of the Christian life was "to remain very much in this world while taking its bearing 'before God.'" *The Genesis of Heidegger's Being and Time* (Berkeley: University of California Press, 1993), 191. On Heidegger's youthful theological period, see most recently John van Buren, *The Young Heidegger: Rumor of the Hidden King* (Bloomington and Indianapolis: Indiana University Press, 1994).

tinctive about the Jewish way of being-in-the-world: the sublimity of isolation, the truthfulness of a life set free of the false attachments of land and state, an "existence with one's people" that seemed the only possible sign of redemption within the bounds of finitude.[82] As Rosenzweig wrote in *The Star of Redemption,* "What is most one's own in humanity is its fate" ("Das Eigenste des Menschen ist eben sein Schicksal"; SE, 314).

82. See Rosenzweig's illuminating remarks on the *Christian* sources of philosophy: "Philosophy was once a Greek maiden; . . . with Schopenhauer and Nietzsche [however], she is a Christian, who knows just about as little about Christianity as—most Christians, but who is stuffed to the ears with Christian concepts: conversion, overcoming, . . . the holy, rebirth, pity, [etc.]. What philosopher had ever had such words in his mouth?" *Briefe,* N.201, An Rudolf Ehrenberg (1.12.17), 263. And see Heidegger: "Once one has grasped the finitude of one's existence, it snatches one back from the endless multiplicity of possibilities . . . and brings Dasein into the simplicity of its *fate."* SZ, 384 (emphasis in original).

# Chapter 3

# Beyond Metaphysics

*Rosenzweig's* Star *(Part I)*

> *To head toward a Star—this only.*
> —MARTIN HEIDEGGER, *Aus der Erfahrung des Denkens (1947, 1954)*

Rosenzweig's first and only systematic work of philosophy, *The Star of Redemption,* was first published in 1921. Walter Benjamin would later remember it as one of "the great works of German scholarship." But from the very beginning it met with an uncertain reception. Both within and beyond a small circle of loyal readers, it was often misunderstood as a work that addressed exclusively Jewish concerns. To take only one example, Friedrich Meinecke, the historian of ideas who served as doctoral advisor to Rosenzweig for *Hegel and the State,* seems never to have considered the possibility that his student's mature work might enjoy wider appeal. Upon Rosenzweig's death, in a Nachruf for the eminent journal *Historische Zeitschrift,* Meinecke praised Rosenzweig's study of Hegel as "a work of enduring value to German intellectual history" that addressed the "heights of German Protestant culture." But he noted with seeming regret that after its publication Rosenzweig had then "fled into the world of his blood."[1]

Such comments were not unique. They illustrate a widespread perception that Rosenzweig's philosophy falls into two distinctive periods—the German research of the young academic and the Jewish works of a mature thinker. Thanks to this distinction, much scholarly work on Rosenzweig has taken it for granted that one may understand the philosopher of Judaism

---

1. Benjamin, "Bücher, die Lebendig Geblieben Sind," *Die Literarische Welt* 5, 20 (May 17, 1929): 6; reprinted in Benjamin, *Gesammelte Schriften* (Frankfurt am Main: Suhrkamp Verlag, 1972), III: 169–71. Meinecke, "Franz Rosenzweig—Nachruf," *Historische Zeitschrift* 142, 1 (1930): 219–20.

apart from his earlier work, thus ignoring the deeper continuities between the Hegelian youth and the later philosopher of Judaism.[2]

The misunderstanding seems especially tragic given the author's hopes. Writing to Rudolf Hallo in early 1923, Rosenzweig predicted that "one day the *Star* will be seen, and rightly so, as a gift which the German spirit owes to its Jewish enclave."[3] But this was not its fate. Although Rosenzweig hoped that the *Star* would cast light upon its native surroundings, the importance of his work in the transformation of German ideas has been largely neglected. By the end of the 1920s, Walter Benjamin would list it among the ambiguous category of "books that have remained alive." It endured only in the "hiddenness" of specialist's libraries—a condition Benjamin called "a special kind of forgetting."[4]

In this chapter, I will suggest some ways one might go about reading Rosenzweig's *Star of Redemption* in order to restore it to its proper setting among developing patterns of German thought in the Weimar era. Perhaps the most important consequence of this reading will be to show how the very idea of an authentic Jewish philosophy dissociated from the German horizon was in fact a modernist invention. For Rosenzweig as for a number of other Weimar Jewish intellectuals, Jewish philosophical and national "distinctiveness" was the fruit of imagination, a performance of difference that gained its very identity in borrowing from the German philosophical tradition; it was not the somehow natural expression of a self-sufficient Jewish identity and an integral Jewish canon of ideas. Thus a careful investigation of Rosenzweig's philosophy must leave behind any commitment to the idea that it truly belongs to an isolable canon of modern Jewish thought. Or

2. An exception is the excellent volume edited by Paul Mendes-Flohr, *Philosophy of Franz Rosenzweig* [PFR] (Hanover, N.H.: University Press of New England / Brandeis University Press, 1988), esp. the editor's introduction, "Franz Rosenzweig and the German Philosophical Tradition," 1–19. Rosenzweig himself may be judged partly responsible for this perception, but it caused him much disappointment. In "The New Thinking" he complained that his work had suffered a certain "social misapprehension." Though widely regarded as a "Jewish book," he objected that "[i]t is not a "Jewish book" at all. . . . It does deal with Judaism, but not any more exhaustively than with Christianity and barely more exhaustively than with Islam." Elsewhere he wrote that he "received the new thinking in these old [Jewish] words," while for a Christian "the words of the New Testament would have come to his lips [and] . . . to a pagan . . . perhaps entirely his own words." The passage indicates that Rosenzweig considered the new thinking not as intrinsically Jewish, but only incidentally so. ND, 140 and 154–55.

3. *Briefe*, N.364, An Rudolf Hallo (Ende Januar, 1923), 474: "Und der Stern wird wohl einmal und mit Recht als ein Geschenk, das der deutsche Geist seiner jüdischen Enklave verdankt, angesehen werden."

4. Benjamin, "Bücher, die Lebendig Geblieben Sind." Benjamin mentions four books in all; the others are Alois Riegl, *Die Spätrömische Kunstindustrie nach den Funden in Österrich-Ungarn* (Vienna, 1901); Alfred Gotthold Meyer, *Eisenbauten: Ihre Geschichte und Ästhetik* (Eßlingen, 1907); and Georg Lukács, *Geschichte und Klassenbewußtsein* (Berlin, 1923).

rather, it does belong to such a canon, but only because it performs this isolation as a philosophical doctrine. Perhaps the most famous argument of the *Star* is that the Jews are a unique and separate people, dwelling alone in the light of redemption. This argument has encouraged interpreters to read the book as a unique and separate document belonging to a special Jewish canon. However, the very idea of its dissociation from the horizon of German thought cannot be the ground of the book's meanings, since its dissociation is merely the most powerful *effect* of those meanings.

In the course of this chapter and the next, I shall offer a detailed reading of Rosenzweig's *Star,* paying specific attention to the concept of *redemption.* This is no easy feat, since redemption is arguably the organizing concept of the system, yet like many terms in this extraordinarily challenging book it is not always entirely clear what it is supposed to mean. My interpretation is necessarily extensive and inevitably experimental. It takes the reader along some of the thorniest paths in Rosenzweig's philosophy, but it eschews comprehensive exposition. It is not a "guide" to *The Star.* Instead, it travels through *The Star* in thematic units. My reading is divided into four main parts, two in this chapter and two in chapter 4. The first part speaks to questions of style, structure, and method; the second addresses the general argument of *The Star;* the third fills out the precise meaning of redemption; and the fourth turns to the comparison with Heidegger. In each of these sections, I address some of the book's most comprehensive concerns, but always with the aim of elucidating the concept of redemption. Here, I shall argue, the comparison with Heidegger is of considerable aid. As I will show, Heidegger's philosophical project in its early phases—chiefly as developed in *Being and Time* (1927) but also in earlier seminars from the period as assistant professor in Marburg (from 1923 to 1928)—displays a profound if surprising resemblance to Rosenzweig's nearly contemporaneous magnum opus. Accordingly, each section makes frequent nods in Heidegger's direction that will help to bring out the various similarities between them, so that by the end of chapter 4, the reader may see why Rosenzweig's perception of intellectual kinship with Heidegger was in many respects correct.

Before launching the argument, however, I offer a few preliminary remarks, chiefly for those readers who remain skeptical regarding Rosenzweig's status as a philosopher. Simply put, my immediate topic below is the sheer strangeness of Rosenzweig's *Star.* I suspect this is a quality that is quite obvious to almost any reader, but it has been infrequently noted in the secondary literature. It should be plainly stated that the following remarks are meant in a positive spirit; to honestly appreciate Rosenzweig's success, one must also acknowledge his occasional deficiencies.

STYLE, STRUCTURE, AND METHOD IN *THE STAR*

*On the Difficulty of* The Star

Reading Rosenzweig's chief work of philosophy demands great patience. Those more accustomed to an analytic style will find that it does not often accord with familiar standards of rigorous argument. The book is mostly in a declamatory mode—it does not argue, it simply states—and it is written in a grand and self-confident style that does very little to encourage the reader's confidence in Rosenzweig as a philosophical authority. What readers have come to expect as the customary etiquette of modern philosophy—gestures such as statements of purpose, exposition, and proof—are generally absent; disparate topics often follow one after another with a deeper purpose seemingly apparent to the author yet whose concealment from the reader conveys, perhaps by design, an impression of sacred meaning. Indeed, the style alone conveys a hidden directive. Since the book promises as much "wisdom" as philosophy, a reader may feel that she is expected simply to absorb its truth with the same faith she might grant a book of revelation. Of course, such a directive is by definition never stated; an esoteric text asserts its rules for reading precisely by not asserting them at all.

The strangeness of *The Star* does not disqualify it from being considered a genuinely philosophical text. But readers interested in sober interpretation approach it at a considerable disadvantage, since they immediately find themselves in the unpleasant position of acting against the spirit of the text. To read a quasi-sacred text in an exoteric fashion can seem rude, an act of desecration. Yet Rosenzweig, much like Heidegger, may appeal especially to those readers who believe that thinking demands piety even at the cost of precision. The profundity of the *Star* is also a performance. By this I mean that its strangeness is an aesthetic choice and that, paradoxically, its esotericism is also an exoteric effect. If this is so, then a healthy dose of skepticism may help the reader to better discern what is philosophically of value. In this introductory section, I will address some of the ways the *Star* is an unusually challenging book, and I will suggest some reasons why this is so.

What is most immediately strange about the *Star* is its structure. Without knowing anything else about the book, the reader realizes at a single glance that it pays peculiar homage to the traditional philosopher's ideal of a conceptual scheme. Like Hegel or Spinoza, Rosenzweig arranges his text according to an "esprit de système" that asks one to believe that the order of exposition and the order of things really are one and the same. And while the esotericism of the *Star* is episodic, its structure urges itself upon the reader at every turn—the triangle shapes are printed in the text, and the six-pointed star was even embossed with black lines upon the cover of the first published edition. The structure is also conveyed through chapter headings, volumes, divisions, and various figurative devices, all confirming Rosenzweig's claim that *The Star* is a "system of philosophy."

Briefly, the system is as follows. The book consists in three volumes, which are arranged in an ascending, geometrical fashion, moving from the primal elements of philosophy (God, Man, and World), to their three possible combinations (creation, revelation, and redemption), and finally, to the modes of life in which these religious phenomena inform community experience (in Judaism, Christianity, and in the experience of "eternal Truth"). The volumes are interlocked in a curiously centripetal design. The three points of the first volume come together with the three points of the second volume finally to create the eponymous six-pointed star of David— a shape that in the third volume Rosenzweig likens to God's face.[5]

But the appearance of systematicity is not altogether convincing. Some readers may indeed find the star configuration almost too clever; there is a touch of wizardry about it, a Kabbalistic symbol-mongering that a philosopher of greater prudence, though perhaps less imagination, might have thought best to avoid. But this is largely a question of standards. One can decide only with deference to the codes of professional philosophy what kind of order should be tolerated and what should be dismissed as mere idiosyncrasy. Intended or not, Rosenzweig's claims to systematicity lapse occasionally into parody—at times, one suspects that he is out to explode the ideal of a self-grounding philosophical structure from within. But it seems clear that for Rosenzweig the star shape was a sincere attempt at conceptual exposition and not a merely convenient device. He seems to have considered it at least as vital to the success of his philosophy as Hegel considered the structure of the *Phenomenology,* of which he boasted that the "true form" *(wahre Gestalt)* must coincide with how "truth exists."[6]

But just why there is this precise kind of structure remains unargued, and it asserts its plausibility chiefly through metaphor—the book has a "fire," as well as "points" and "rays"—and (in an unacknowledged figurative shift borrowed from the Yom Kippur service) a concluding "gate." It does not help that Rosenzweig mixed metaphors when borrowing from the vast lex-

5. One of the most succinct explanations for this tripartite scheme can be found in the introductory remarks by Else-Rahel Freund, in her *Franz Rosenzweig's Philosophy of Existence,* ed. Paul Mendes-Flohr, trans. Stephen L. Weinstein and Robert Israel (The Hague: Martinus Nijoff, 1979), esp. 5, where Freund explains, "The three parts of *The Star* treat three modes of human existence: the solitary human being, the human being before God, and the human being in community. From a methodological standpoint they answer the questions 'How is existence to be conceived, how is it to be experienced, and how is it to be envisioned *(schauen)*?'"

6. Hegel, "Vorrede," in *Phänomenologie des Geistes,* in *Sämtliche Werke,* vol. 5, ed. Johannes Hoffmeister (Hamburg: Felix Meiner, 1952), 12.

icon of past philosophies: there is talk of a "kingdom," but also of a "threshold," a "Psychologik" (psycho-logic), "miracles," and the "sleep of the world." The variety is bewildering. All of it seems to suggest that Rosenzweig had violated the a priori necessity Kant called the "architectonic of pure reason" (KdrV, 685 ff). Indeed, architecture is the more common simile for philosophical systematicity: Descartes in the second discourse writes of demolishing old houses in order to construct better ones straightened by the "plumb-line of reason." And Hegel, though claiming that "spirit is ... never at rest but always in ... movement," nonetheless characterized the System as a rational "construct" *(Bau).*[7]

But a star has no right angles. Unlike a foundation, a system, or a house (all metaphors for how arguments cohere) it is more symbol than geometrical shape, and it is not easily plotted like an equation upon a Cartesian grid. More importantly, unlike the ladder-like movement of the older systems, a star also lacks a definitive sense of spatial orientation. Its symmetry suggests that the book follows a centripetal argument that may be grasped meaningfully from any direction. (Rosenzweig was unclear on this point. Though arguing that there is an "above" and a "below" to *The Star* despite the "dis-oriented" indifference of the visual shape, he also noted that the star is constructed from "mutually isolated points, none of which could serve unambiguously as point of reference for the others.")[8] Interpreters have shown remarkable ingenuity in attempting to find the philosophical meaning in the book's shape—perhaps the most convincing is the recent claim that each of the three volumes presupposes the one that follows as its hermeneutic horizon, so the book should actually be read backwards.[9] Whatever the merits of this claim, it seems clear that *The Star* does not exhibit a philosophical structure in the sense of a necessary conceptual scheme. Having rejected the Hegelian unity of being and thought, Rosen-

7. Descartes, *Discourse on Method and the Meditations,* trans. and with Introduction by F. E. Sutcliffe (London: Penguin Books, 1968), 37. Hegel, *Phänomenologie,* 15. It is worth noting that Rosenzweig's *Star* was published just seven years before Rudolf Carnap's *Der logische Aufbau der Welt* (Berlin: Weltkreis Verlag, 1928). For an interesting discussion of the relationship between the metaphor of building in analytic philosophy and architecture, see Peter Galison, "Aufbau/Bauhaus: Logical Positivism and Architectural Modernism," *Critical Inquiry* 16, 4 (summer 1990): 709–52.

8. The star-shape for Rosenzweig is clearly a relic of ancient Judaism, even while he thought of his work as exemplifying the new thinking. Here one already encounters the historical indeterminacy of his philosophy; it is at once modernist and backward-looking. On the meaning of the star-shape, see Rosenzweig's extended discussion concluding Book II, "Threshold," esp. the sections meaningfully entitled "The New Unity," "The New Totality," "The New Relationship," "The New Interconnection," and "The New Order," in SE, 283–91 (E, 254–61).

9. Leora Batnitzky, *Idolatry and Representation: The Philosophy of Franz Rosenzweig Reconsidered* (Princeton: Princeton University Press, 2000), 64.

zweig could not claim that *The Star* is the very scaffolding of things as they are. The star shape is thus a manifestation of structural contingency—a gesture of order, but without the idealist's confidence that the order of things and the order of ideas are the same.

Recognizing the moment of contingency in Rosenzweig's star structure opens up the possibility that it may have aesthetic as well as a philosophical motivations. From one perspective, the ideal of a system may be an artifact of Rosenzweig's training in German Idealism. All of the book's introductions and transitions and various attempts at symmetry demonstrate that its author may have been still enchanted with Hegelian system-building, despite his protests to the contrary. His program for Jewish education, for example, written in 1917, displays the same impulse toward structuring the education of spirit, and the very same impulse governs his description of the need for Gymnasium reform a year earlier.[10] A first draft of the projected divisions and section titles for *The Star,* which Rosenzweig included in a letter to Rudolf Ehrenberg in September 1918, reveals a thinker enraptured by his "system." Yet he also confesses to feeling overwhelmed by disorder— "I sit under a shower of thoughts." "Actually all that is in me has gone into it," he continues, "thus naturally also all that has influenced me."[11] A system makes a poor dam when the current of ideas is so powerful. On the other hand, there is an unmistakably literary feeling to *The Star,* which reveals it to be a child of German expressionism. While Rosenzweig insisted that his book was a "system" of philosophy, it is a system of slanted walls and twisted corridors, like something sprung from the imagination of Caligari.[12]

The sheer strangeness of *The Star* demands an aesthetic as well as a philosophical explanation; but it is not easy to tell one from the other. Admittedly, *The Star* sometimes reads like a work of literature. In a letter from 1926, Rosenzweig described only its three introductions as "lectures," and only the first volume as "scholarly." He characterized the second volume as "lyrical" and even suggested that it was best read "cum grano salis." The final volume, in which Judaism is interpreted as the "fire" of the star and Christianity as its "rays," Rosenzweig called "monumental."[13]

---

10. "Zeit ist's . . . ," KS, 56–78; "Volksschule und Reichsschule," KS, 420–66.

11. *Briefe,* N.256, An Rudolf Ehrenberg (4.9.18), 345–47. On the composition of *The Star* as the culmination of many years of "dispersed thoughts," also see GB (4.9.1918), 144.

12. A study could be written of the prominence of star imagery in German expressionism. By sheer coincidence Martin Heidegger's well at Todtnauberg had a wooden star shape on its handle. On this "Sternwürfel" see the poem by Paul Celan, "Todtnauberg," from *Poems of Paul Celan,* trans. Michael Hamburger (New York: Persea Books, 1972), 292–95. On German expressionism in the Caligari film and in Weimar film generally, see Lotte Eisner, *The Haunted Screen* (Berkeley: University of California Press, 1973), and the Weimar-era study by Rudolf Kurtz, *Expressionismus und Film* (Berlin: Lichtbildbühne, 1926).

13. *Briefe,* N.472, An Joseph Rivlin (24.10.26), 566.

A less cordial reader might dismiss any philosopher who suggests that his book be taken with a grain of salt. But it is obvious that a poetic and fundamentally "lyrical" quality pervades *The Star,* and rather than letting this quality pass without comment, it is important to inquire into its possible philosophical meaning. As is well known, Rosenzweig was deeply enamoured of German literature—he was especially knowledgeable regarding Goethe and the poets of German classicism.[14] The most important stylistic influence upon Rosenzweig, however, was undoubtedly Friedrich Schelling. During the period in which Rosenzweig's philosophical insights were first taking shape, he came across the "Oldest System Program of German Idealism," a document whose authorship Rosenzweig credited to Schelling (as noted in chapter 2, this surmise remains disputed). In the fragment one finds the following passage:

> I am now convinced, that the highest act of reason, which, while it comprises all ideas, is an aesthetic act, and that *truth and goodness, are only* become siblings in beauty—the philosopher must possess as much aesthetic power as the poet. . . . The Philosophy of Spirit is an aesthetic philosophy. . . . Poetry receives through it a . . . higher esteem, she becomes in the end that which she was in the beginning—*Instructress to Humanity.* (as quoted by Rosenzweig, ASP, 233–34)

In his philological notes, published along with a transcription of the fragment, Rosenzweig offered a commentary that proves quite revealing of his own nascent philosophical sensibility. Summarizing the fragment's celebration of poetry as an educative force, he then traces this idea back to a comment in Schelling's philosophy of art, where Schelling predicted that, "just as in the childhood of science she was born and nourished from poetry, after her completion she will flood back into the general ocean of poetry" (ASP, 249). Rosenzweig notes that this high estimation of poetic education would have been unthinkable without the influence of Novalis and Schiller, as well as Kant's idea in the first critique (though only half-explicit there) that the imagination is the hidden yet "common root" of practical and theoretical reason, and, by inference, the primary medium for thought. Summarizing the various interrelations of poetry and philosophy, Rosenzweig claimed that Schelling had brought these various ideas to this unanticipated conclusion:

> the question of the ending point in philosophy can only be solved together with the question of its point of departure, [and] . . . the question concern-

14. See e.g., *Briefe,* N.29, An Hans Ehrenberg (11.10.1908), 38–39; and the projected book on "The Hero, a History of Tragic Individuality in Germany since Lessing," in N.52, An Gertrud Oppenheim (28.9.1911), 60–61.

ing the object of philosophy or its content, and the question concerning its essence or its form, is really one [*nur eine ist*]. (ASP, 250)

From Schelling, Rosenzweig inherited the philosophical argument that poetry must be considered a more "original" mode of understanding. More than a decade later, in the essay "The New Thinking," he could still approvingly cite Schelling's prediction that the philosophy of the future would be a "narrative philosophy" *(erzählende Philosophie),* a phrase that legitimizes both literature and temporality.

Rosenzweig specifically followed Schelling's idea that the original and future poetry of humanity is a primordial structure of meaning. In other words, poetry is myth. To support this idea, Rosenzweig cites Schelling's *System of Transcendental Idealism* (1800), which argues that "what should be the instrument for the return [*Rückkehr*] of science to poetry, is . . . not hard to say, since *such an instrument exists in mythology,* before this now seemingly irreparable separation occurred" (ASP, 253; my emphasis). If philosophy emerges and returns to myth, then all of modern thought must represent an extended detour from the unified field of meaningfulness that once structured the world in mythological systems. Rosenzweig again cites Schelling: "the oldest Ur-wisdom [*Urkunden*] of all peoples begins with mythology," since mythological traditions "brought harmony and unity to uncultivated human groups and became a gentle cord by which the social family was bound to a single teaching, a single belief, a single activity" (ASP, 254). He further cites Hölderlin's *Hyperion* that "the first child of divine beauty is art. . . . The second daughter is religion." Rosenzweig concludes that, "without poetry," "the poetic religious people of Greece . . . would never have become a philosophical people" (ASP, 272).

Such arguments help to explain why Rosenzweig's own philosophy can announce at once a future-directed "overcoming" of modern thought and a past-directed "return" to Jewish origins. For the Jews are here conceived as the authentic people of myth, thus occupying that privileged space of origins that German thinkers such as Hölderlin most customarily reserved for the Greeks. The final fruit of this argument would be Rosenzweig's turn toward the Bible as a Jewish "myth" analogous in many respects to Homeric saga—an analogy evident to several of Rosenzweig's contemporaries. In *The Star* Rosenzweig would explain that "the Jew alone . . . possess the unity of myth which the nations lost through the influx of Christianity, which they were bound to lose, for their own myth was pagan myth . . . [while] [t]he Jew's myth, since it leads him into his people, also brings him face to face with God who is also the God of all peoples" (SE, 365 [E, 329]). And all of this is to affirm Hölderlin's claim that "poetry is the beginning and the end" of philosophy. "As Minerva from Jupiter's head, she springs forth from the poetry of an infinite divine Being and so too runs in the end together in the secret source of poetry [*Quelle der Dichtung*]" (ASP, 272).

Myth is thus regarded as a fundamentally poetic structure, which is born from the imagination and which lays the grounds for the basic meaningfulness of ancient life. This idea came to special prominence among many of Rosenzweig's intellectual contemporaries, German and Jewish alike.[15] One of the most striking moments in this Weimar-era philosophical discussion of myth is found in Heidegger's comments on Ernst Cassirer's 1925 *Philosophy of Symbolic Forms*, volume II: *Mythical Thought*. Both Cassirer and Heidegger drew upon Schelling's *Philosophy of Mythology*, where myth is seen not merely as a cultural appendage but is considered "the fate of a people." In Schelling's words, myth is a "shaping power" born of the imagination, or *Einbildungskraft*. Cassirer and Heidegger shared the insight that myth must be examined as a symbolic "system" that provides the conditions for the intelligibility of ancient, myth-bearing cultures. But Heidegger objected to Cassirer's fundamentally Kantian argument that myth is therefore a projection of "symbolizing consciousness." This objection arose from Heidegger's broader commitment to the notion that the conditions for meaning are not in essence "representations" projected from a spontaneous understanding (hence, like Rosenzweig, Heidegger's much-repeated acknowledgments of Kant's claims that the imagination is the dark root of consciousness). To conceive of myth as a "form of thought" is to miss the thrownness *(Geworfenheit)* that constitutes meaning well before it reaches out to the world in a cognitive fashion. Thus, "[t]he essential interpretation of myth as a possibility of human Dasein remains contingent and directionless, so long as it cannot be grounded upon a radical ontology of Dasein in light of the problem of Being overall."[16] (In a footnote to *Being and Time*, Heidegger praised Cassirer's "ethnological research" and his treatment of myth within "the phenomenological horizon as disclosed by Husserl." But he doubted whether Kantian methods were adequate. For Heidegger, myth was not a representational or formal system, but merely the most "primitive" example of those existential structures underlying "everydayness" as such [SZ, 51 and n. xi]).

As we shall see, Rosenzweig, too, was interested in poetry, ritual, and myth, not because they are cultural inheritances, but rather because they lay

---

15. For a summary of this theme in Jewish intellectual work, see Steven M. Wasserstrom, "A Rustling in the Woods: The Turn to Myth in Weimar Jewish Thought," chapter 7 in *Religion after Religion: Gershom Scholem, Mircea Eliade, and Henry Corbin at Eranos* (Princeton: Princeton University Press, 1999).

16. See Heidegger's review, "Ernst Cassirer: *Philosophie der symbolischen Formen. 2 Teil: Das mythische Denken*. Berlin 1925," *Deutsche Literaturzeitung* (1928); reprinted as the second appendix to KPM, 255–70, quotes at 265–67.

down the meaningful structures that comprise the conditions for Jewish life. Rosenzweig's later turn to the poetry of Jehuda Halevi and the Bible demonstrates a strong belief that these are not mere texts but sedimented understandings, which articulate meaning in a more "original" fashion than idealist philosophy can perceive. *The Star of Redemption* thus investigates poetry and mytho-poetic structures such as ritual with an eye toward the way these constitute a specific way of being human. Here we are very close to the motivations that drew Heidegger to "ethnology"—not as a positive science but instead as material for thematizing what he called the "ontological structures" of Dasein's world (SZ, 51). Both philosophers were disciples of Schelling; but in *The Star*'s close attention to biblical verse, one might argue that Rosenzweig anticipated Heidegger's idea that "primitive language is poetry, in which Being is established."[17]

The deeper philosophical meaning of poetry in Rosenzweig's mature thought should not be missed. But one must also recognize that he was in some ways a captive to his own literary talent. Rosenzweig's later translations of poetry (from Jehuda Halevi and the Bible) was only the external sign for an inner poetic skill already very much on display in his philosophical writing.[18] The elegance of *The Star* can be appealing, but at times it does more to inhibit than to facilitate a clear sense of the argument. Here Rosenzweig's remarks on the "lyrical" and "monumental" style of his book are significant, and they suggest that even the author felt that he had crafted something strange—a philosophical work verging on anti-philosophy. As Nietzsche said, "one must still have chaos in oneself to be able to give birth to a dancing star."[19]

On the question of style Rosenzweig and Heidegger may seem to have little in common. The sometimes bombastic and richly metaphorical language of *The Star* is quite different from the rudely artisanal yet somehow scholastic language of *Being and Time,* which Heidegger himself in the second introduction criticized for its "awkwardness," "inelegance," and even "harshness." But unlike Rosenzweig, Heidegger at least offered an explicitly philosophical excuse for his style: he noted that customary language might be sufficient for describing entities, but for ontological description "we lack not only most of the words but, above all, the 'grammar'" (SZ, 38–39; BT,

---

17. The line is from Heidegger as cited in John Macquarrie, *Heidegger and Christianity* (New York: Continuum Books, 1999), 89.

18. In his commentary on Luther's Bible translation, Rosenzweig admits that "all speech [is] already dialogical and thus—translation." *Die Schrift und Luther* (Berlin: Lambert Schneider, 1926), 5. (I discuss this idea at greater length in chapter 5 .)

19. Nietzsche, *Also sprach Zarathustra: Ein Buch für alle und keinen.* In *Sämtliche Werke in zwölf Bänden* (Stuttgart: Alfred Kröner Verlag, 1964), VI: 13.

63). In Rosenzweig's various allusions to his own style, he never claims that his philosophical perspective is simply too difficult to find accommodation within the lexicon of traditional philosophy. Instead, in the spirit of Schelling and Nietzsche, he claims that the older philosophy had proven itself an inadequate form of expression, and that the new thinking must therefore fuse with poetry. As I will explore further in the next chapter, Rosenzweig's contemporaries noted a similarity between his philosophical style and that of literary expressionists such as Stefan George. And more recently one commentator has described *The Star* as a case of "Jewish romanticism," a term that opens up the intriguing possibility of comparison with German romantic poets such as Novalis and Hölderlin.[20]

Heidegger adopted a similarly poetic voice in his later writing, when he had concluded that the language of scientific analysis belonged to the armature of technology and was unacceptably metaphysical. He then saw that *Being and Time* had exaggerated human pragmatic activity and had neglected our receptive "openness" to Being. As Heidegger awakened to this idea in the period of the so-called "turning," his works grew increasingly fragmented and prophetic, reflecting the influence of Christian mystics (such as Eckhart) and German romantic and expressionist poets (especially Hölderlin and Trakl). Even the structure of Heidegger's later work revealed a new appreciation for poetry. His second (though much neglected) treatise from 1937, the *Beiträge zur Philosophie,* begins with the announcement, "The time of 'systems' is over." Heidegger explained that because linear accomplishment is no longer his ideal, his book could not make "an introductory ascent from what is below to what is above." Accordingly, instead of chapters the *Beiträge* has six "joints" (an unintended homage to the fanciful, six-fold structure of Rosenzweig's *Star*).[21]

Despite some obvious differences of style, Heidegger and Rosenzweig were aesthetic cousins, both emerging from the intellectual ferment of German expressionism. Each of them represents a peculiarly post-Nietzschean moment in philosophy, when the ideal of a system grew less and less attractive and when the very distinction between poetry and philosophy—already weakened by Schelling's philosophical defense of myth and having absorbed the deeper meaning of Nietzsche's dictum that philosophers must write well—began finally to dissolve. But this explanation presents cold

20. Ernest Rubinstein, *An Episode of Jewish Romanticism: Franz Rosenzweig's "The Star of Redemption"* (Albany: State University of New York Press, 1999).

21. Heidegger, *Beiträge zur Philosophie (Vom Ereignis),* ed. Friedrich-Wilhelm von Herrmann (Frankfurt am Main: Vittorio Klostermann, 1989). Now in English as *Contributions to Philosophy (From Enowning),* trans. Parvis Emad and Kenneth Maly (Bloomington and Indianapolis: Indiana University Press, 1999), quote at 4–5.

comfort for those who would prefer to read Rosenzweig as a traditional philosopher. If Rosenzweig had something truly important to say, so the objection might go, he might have said it better and in a more convincing fashion had he edited out the occasional grandiosity of expression and pruned back the overly dense structures that pay lyrical homage to the ideal of an all-encompassing "system." There is an undeniable quality of literary excess in Rosenzweig's writing. What one makes of this excess can only be decided after one has already taken a leap of faith that the philosophy is intelligible. If the ideas succeed, then the poetic indulgence is forgiven. But if the ideas seem unconvincing, Rosenzweig's efforts will be condemned as kitsch.

Can Rosenzweig's *Star* be rescued from the skeptics? I will not offer a strong conclusion on this point. But it is instructive that here Rosenzweig and Heidegger share a significant disability in common. Both meet with a lukewarm reception among readers who mistrust any elevation in tone and who value above all the ideal of lucid presentation.[22] These readers may even doubt whether the dense language has any philosophical meaning at all. For Rosenzweig such loss of any wider readership may have seemed a necessary sacrifice, since he was proud of having written (in his words) "this great world-poem [*dies große Weltgedicht*]" (ND, 150).

The same might also be said of the many readers who confess a powerful mistrust of Heidegger's work. Stronger skeptics will simply deny that Heidegger has a legitimate place in philosophy at all. Ironically, the perception of a historical rift between modern academic philosophy and so-called original thinking was a beloved, even self-congratulatory theme for both Heidegger and Rosenzweig. Opponents of the poetic style only reconfirm their belief that a rift has actually occurred. Like Rosenzweig, Heidegger seems to have gained an enhanced sense of his own profundity from the very antagonism directed his way by logicians and philosophers in the analytic tradition. The case in favor of taking Heidegger seriously has hardly been helped by those Heideggerians who simply mimic his often frustrating jargon to the point where argument is supplanted by the mere reproduction of linguistic effects. A similar danger awaits Rosenzweig's philosophy. The pre-philosophical belief that his corpus is a cherished inheritance of modern Judaism tends to encourage only appreciation and may inhibit a critical examination of his work. But the sole way to demonstrate respect for Rosenzweig is to subject his work to clarificatory interpretation. One of the un-

22. A typical judgment regarding Heidegger's style is by Richard Wolin: "Heidegger's thinking . . . appears to be afflicted" by "a disdain of traditional methods of philosophical argumentation, which emphasize the non-esoteric, generalizable character of philosophical contents and judgements [etc.]." In Wolin, ed., *The Heidegger Controversy: A Critical Reader* (Cambridge, Mass.: MIT Press, 1993), 12.

avoidable risks of this project, however, is that Rosenzweig's philosophy may be stripped of the strangeness that was initially responsible for much of its appeal.

## Some Problems of Categorization

Characterizing even the most rudimentary philosophical aims of *The Star* can be an enormous challenge. Not surprisingly, there has been only the broadest agreement among interpreters as to its chief purposes. It has been categorized as a "philosophy of religion," but also as an example of "messianic" and "dialogical" thought, and as a "pensée juive moderne." It is found under the rubric of "existentialism" (in English), but also "existenzialism yehudi" (in Hebrew), and "Existenzphilosophie" (in German), each of these naming a distinctive national canon.[23] Others have characterized *The Star* as a species of "experiencing-philosophy," or in variations upon this theme it has been called a "philosophy of dialogical experience" and a "Jewish-theistic philosophy of revelation."[24] Less probable, perhaps, is the attempt to find "libertarian" or "anarchist" strains in Rosenzweig's mature thought, despite his general indifference to politics and (at least on one occasion) his confession of monarchist sympathies.[25] Scholars have also explored Rosenzweig's affinities with a great variety of other philosophers, including Schelling, Wittgenstein, Buber, or Gadamer. There have also been at least two major works that explore how Rosenzweig's thought both anticipates and informs the philosophy of Emmanuel Levinas. Finally, in the most recent literature one finds startling comparison to traditions as distinctive as both Kabbalah and psychoanalysis.[26]

23. See Zeev Levy, *Mevasser Existenzialism yehudi: Mishnato shel Franz Rosenzweig* (Merhavia: Sifriyat po'alim, 1969); Joseph Carlebach "Die Religionsphilosophische Stellung Franz Rosenzweigs," *Jeschurun* 17 (1930): 1–11.

24. Gotthard Fuchs and Hans-Hermann Hendrix, eds., *Zeitgewinn: Messianisches Denken nach Franz Rosenzweig* (Frankfurt am Main: Verlag Joseph Knecht, 1987); Reinhold Mayer, *Franz Rosenzweig: Eine Philosophie der dialogischen Erfahrung* (München: Kaiser Verlag, 1973); Otto Gründler, "Eine jüdische-theistische Offenbarungsphilosophie" (review), *Hochland* 19, 5 (February 1922), 62 ff. For Rosenzweig's comments on Gründler, see *Briefe*, N.340, An Gertrud Oppenheim (14.3.1922), 422–23.

25. Michael Löwy, *Redemption and Utopia: Jewish Libertarian Thought in Central Europe: A Study in Elective Affinity*, trans. Hope Heaney (Stanford, Calif.: Stanford University Press, 1992), esp. 58–60. On Rosenzweig's monarchist tendencies, see, e.g., the 1918 letter in which he writes: "I have now for the first time marked, how monarchist I am." *Briefe*, N.261, An die Mutter (19.10.1918.), 351.

26. On Schelling, see Freund, *Rosenzweig's Philosophy of Existence*, and Mendes-Flohr, "Franz Rosenzweig and the German Philosophical Tradition." On Wittgenstein, see Hilary Putnam's introduction to Rosenzweig, *Understanding the Sick and the Healthy: A View of World, Man, and*

A generous conclusion to be drawn from this great variety of interpretation is that Rosenzweig's work, like that of Nietzsche or Walter Benjamin, is sufficiently rich to sustain many disciplines and diverse perspectives.[27] A less broad-minded inference would be that Rosenzweig failed to convey his philosophical purposes with adequate precision. Evidence for this failure may be found in Rosenzweig's decision four years later to write "The New Thinking." This essay consists chiefly of an effort to clarify the main themes of the book—it is subtitled "a few supplementary remarks to *The Star of Redemption*"—and it is thus an indispensable resource for readers who wish to discover to which category of contemporary thought Rosenzweig's work most properly belongs.

In the opening lines of "The New Thinking," Rosenzweig compares the essay to Kant's *Prolegomena* (1783), which addressed the lingering doubts plaguing some readers of the first critique (first published in 1781). Kant began his shorter "introductory" text in a spirit of sarcasm, directed toward contemporaries who bemoaned "a certain obscurity" and a "want of popularity, entertainment, and facility" in the earlier book.[28] Similarly, Rosenzweig begins "The New Thinking" with a complaint about *The Star*'s reception: he notes with evident mockery that "even the tranquil Kant" included a preface, a luxury Rosenzweig first abjured, as he considered it "cackling after the egg had been laid." So having first complimented himself on having avoided such "discourteous invectives" against his own readers, Rosenzweig then calls the omission a mistake. Lacking the author's advice, some buyers of the book were helplessly confused. They believed they had purchased a "nice Jewish book" and only afterwards, like one of the earliest critics, discovered to their disappointment that it is not for "everyday use." Rosenzweig concludes sharply:

*God,* trans. Nahum Glatzer (Cambridge, Mass.: Harvard University Press, 1999), 1–20. On Buber and Jewish-Christian dialogue, see esp. Mayer, *Franz Rosenzweig.* On Gadamer, see Batnitzky, *Idolatry and Representation.* On Levinas, see Richard Cohen, *Elevations: The Height of the Good in Rosenzweig and Levinas* (Chicago: University of Chicago Press, 1994) and Robert Gibbs, *Correlations in Rosenzweig and Levinas* (Princeton: Princeton University Press, 1992). (I suggest limits to this comparison in the Introduction.) Comparisons to Kabbalah can be found in Moshe Idel, "Rosenzweig and the Kabbalah," in PFR, 162–71; and Gershom Scholem, "Franz Rosenzweig and His Book *The Star of Redemption,*" in PFR, 20–41. A graceful study on Rosenzweig's affinities to psychoanalysis is Eric Santner, *On the Psychotheology of Everyday Life: Reflections on Freud and Rosenzweig* (Chicago: University of Chicago Press, 2001). Rosenzweig himself once offered the fascinating suggestion that the *Star*'s characterization of Judaism was the same as could be found in Max Weber's *Antike Judentum,* except that the *Star* articulated the concept philosophically, and Weber historically. *Briefe,* N.316, An die Mutter ([Kassel] 15.8. 21.), 405.

27. Amos Funkenstein calls Rosenzweig's system "eclectic." *Perceptions of Jewish History* (Berkeley: University of California Press, 1993), 303.

28. Kant, Introduction, *Prolegomena* (Indianapolis: Bobbs-Merrill, Library of Liberal Arts, 1950), 9.

I cannot describe *The Star of Redemption* more correctly than that critic has done with . . . brevity: it is really not intended for the everyday use of every member of the family. It is not a "Jewish book" at all, at least not what those buyers who were so angry with me take for a Jewish book. (ND, 140)

The denial that *The Star* is a Jewish book seems controversial. It is clearly a book in which Jewish themes are prominent and in which the doctrine of Jewish redemption plays the central if not decisive role. Whether it may or may not be considered a Jewish book is of course one of my chief concerns in this study and should not be decided prematurely. But Rosenzweig's objection is obviously significant. As justification, he asks the reader to note the frequent appearance of other, non-Jewish themes, such as Greek tragedy, Christian history, German Idealism, and Islam. But even if one accepts this rather superficial proof that the book is not Jewish, one remains at a loss as how it is best characterized. What kind of argument is it making? What category, what method or school best describes its claims? The essay on the new thinking offers several useful definitions, which may be addressed in turn.

### Against Religion

Perhaps most controversial is Rosenzweig's claim that the book is not intended as a philosophy of religion. To clarify this point, Rosenzweig asks rhetorically, "how could it do that when the word 'religion' does not occur in it at all!" Strictly considered, Rosenzweig was not entirely correct on this point. As Ernest Rubinstein has observed, Rosenzweig's original subsection titles were restored in the revised 1930 edition, one of which reads "Idealistic Religion." But this remains the sole instance of the term in the entire book.[29] And since in the original 1921 edition these titles had been omitted, Rosenzweig's claim in 1925 that the word "religion" cannot be found in *The Star* was literally true at that time. Its absence is somewhat surprising, since so many other closely related or synonymous terms appear with great frequency, such as faith, theology, scholasticism, the Church, the ecclesia *(Ekklesia)*, paganism, Judaism, or Jewry *(Judentum)*, Christianity *(Christentum)*, dogma, and being faithful *(Gläubigsein)*. Given such a variety, one could suspect that Rosenzweig's objection to the term "religion" was overly fastidious. But, as it turns out, there is a very important reason for his objection.

In a crucial passage of "The New Thinking," Rosenzweig suggests that Judaism and Christianity enjoy a unique place in the history of religion, in

---

29. Rubinstein, *An Episode of Jewish Romanticism,* 38.

that both modes of faith were in origin "something wholly 'unreligious.'" Judaism was "originally" *(ursprünglich)* a "fact "*(Tatsache)*, while Christianity was originally an "event" *(Ereignis)* (ND, 154). Rosenzweig admits that each of them could become "specialized," and as such they became "religions." But each could also boast of the capacity "to free themselves from this religiosity," such that "from out of their specialization and self-enclosure behind walls" they could "find their way back again to the open field of reality." For Rosenzweig, Judaism and Christianity were unique in their "unreligious" beginnings, while "[a]ll around them they saw religion, religions." In fact, they "would have been highly astonished" to find themselves characterized as religions.[30]

These arguments are only half convincing. Clearly, Rosenzweig's definition of religion is idiosyncratic, and by more customary standards of usage his objections seem unwarranted.[31] But Rosenzweig's definition of religion is an indispensable part of his general philosophical method. Throughout *The Star,* he is always and exclusively concerned with the primordial moment of a tradition. His claim that Judaism and Christianity were in origin unreligious, only later becoming specialized "religion," and that they may even today be able to escape their religiosity and to return to "the field of reality," suggests that Rosenzweig rejects the term "religion" as naming a degraded and specialized form of faith, while he embraces what can be characterized as faith's "original" *(ursprünglich)* element. *The Star of Redemption,* then, may be characterized as a philosophy of religion, but only insofar as it is a philosophy that dedicates itself to overcoming the degraded tradition of religion while turning toward the "unreligious" moment of origin.[32]

### A Revolutionary Conception of Philosophy

Along with but simultaneously against this "restorative" notion of religion, Rosenzweig promotes a robustly modernist conception of philosophy. In "The New Thinking" he famously described *The Star* as "merely a system of philosophy [*bloß ein System der Philosophie*]" (ND, 140). But Rosenzweig

---

30. For Rosenzweig, only Islam was truly a religion in origin and as such it must be regarded as a mere parody of both Judaism and Christianity. Thus only where *The Star* addresses Islam might it be accurately characterized as a philosophy of religion. ND, 154.

31. Furthermore, the characterization of Islam is both inaccurate and offensive. See the remarks by Alan Udoff in his essay, "Retracing the Steps of Franz Rosenzweig," in *Franz Rosenzweig's "The New Thinking,"* ed. and trans. Alan Udoff and Barbara Galli (Syracuse: Syracuse University Press, 1999), 153–73, esp. n. 22, 186–87.

32. Also see the remark to Gritli: "The plural 'religions' is actually even more impossible than the singular. To be sure, with someone who speaks about 'religion,' really one cannot speak about it." GB (27.11.1918), 200–201.

was not content to play the role of one philosopher among others. Rather, he seems to assert a very special role for himself in the transformation of the contemporary intellectual landscape. Throughout his writings, one can find remarks to the effect that all traditional philosophy has reached an end. One also finds the accompanying explanation that traditional philosophy is defunct because it was characterized by a single and comprehensive error. Often Rosenzweig will characterize this error as "Idealism" (a term that will no doubt raise the eyebrows of anyone who recognizes the true plurality of the history of ideas). Elsewhere he does not even name the tradition; he calls it simply "Philosophy" *(die Philosophie)*. In Rosenzweig's view, philosophy in this idealist sense has reached a point of collapse and will be supplanted by "the new thinking" *(das neue Denken),* a mode of thought ostensibly immune from the errors of the philosophical tradition.

Rosenzweig's self-understanding of his own place in this process may seem grandiose. In the famous opening pages of *The Star of Redemption,* he suggests that he will "throw down the gauntlet to the whole honorable society of philosophers from Ionia to Jena." Elsewhere he selects a particular target, accusing various philosophers of having mistakenly believed they had surmounted the errors of the past. In "The New Thinking," he compares his efforts to Kant's Copernican revolution, adding that Kant's achievement was insufficient, since Kant "sees all things turned around—yet still only the same things that he has seen before." But Rosenzweig objects to studying "the same things." Rather, he saw it as his task to achieve "the complete renewal of thought [*des Denkens, vollkommene Erneuerung*]" (ND, 140). In another passage, he suggests that the philosophy articulated in *The Star* has surpassed all traditional epistemologies and should be called a "messianic theory of knowledge" (ND, 159). He concludes boldly that *The Star* represents "nothing other than the reductio ad absurdum [*Adabsurdumführung*] of the old philosophy, and simultaneously its salvation [*Rettung*]" (ND, 142).

This conception of philosophy is best characterized as revolutionary.[33] In *The Star,* one reads that in recent times philosophy had begun to feel "its ancient throne tottering." The "dynasty which Thales and Parmenides had founded, and which was more than two millennia old, seemed headed for a ruin as brilliant as it was sudden" (SE, 104 [E, 94]). And in "The New Thinking," Rosenzweig again likens his philosophical innovation to bringing down an ancien régime (ND, 141). The metaphors here imply a dramatic, even catastrophic transformation. Given that for Rosenzweig the entire philosophical tradition is united in error, the "new thinking" sees itself

---

33. See, for example, Rosenzweig's reference to the "nachhegelschen Revolution der Philosophie." SE, 18 (E, 16).

as assigned the task of overcoming this erroneous tradition for the sake of genuine thought.[34]

The history of German philosophy in particular proffers a rich succession of thinkers who announced both the demise of metaphysics and the beginning of a new, superior philosophy (for example, Kant's "Copernican revolution," Hegel's knowledge at "dusk," and Nietzsche's "death of God"). Precisely because one can find so many important predecessors for Rosenzweig's claims suggests that his remarks cannot be dismissed as exaggeration, but must be considered as part of an ongoing tendency in German thought. Moreover, Rosenzweig himself provides the reader with a genealogy of this specifically German phenomenon in *The Star*'s introductory chapter, which discusses in chronological succession the philosophical contributions of Hegel, Kierkegaard, Schopenhauer, and finally Nietzsche. The discussion of Nietzsche is especially illuminating, insofar as Rosenzweig seemed to take seriously Nietzsche's announcement that he had overcome the nihilism of the West. In Nietzsche alone there was really "something new" *(etwas Neues)*, since he was the first philosopher who became in his very person "a power over philosophy" (SE, 10 [E, 9]). A more detailed discussion of this argument below will demonstrate that Rosenzweig was attempting, in the wake of Nietzsche, to write his own philosophical work into this narrative as both its destruction and its salvation.

A revolutionary conception of philosophy is one of the broadest points that Rosenzweig and Heidegger shared in common. Like Heidegger, Rosenzweig saw philosophy as both a destructive and a constructive enterprise. Necessarily, the new thinking emerged from an intense struggle with the philosophical tradition which then was to provide both the tools and the occasion for its own destruction. Though hardly of great consequence, it is interesting to note that at least in one place Rosenzweig and Heidegger selected the same terminology to describe the novelty of their efforts: both described the philosophical tradition as an *Irrweg*, an errancy or path of error (ND, 144).[35] Furthermore, Rosenzweig distinguished between the philosophical tradition and his own new mode of thought with terms *die Philosophie* and *das neue Denken*, respectively. The first implied a scholarly

34. The "overcoming" of traditional philosophy in *The Star* was a prominently noted theme in early reviews. See, for example, S. Stern, "Rosenzweig, Franz. Dr. phil. *Der Stern der Erlösung*. Frankfurt a.M., J. Kauffmann, 1921. 532 S" (review), *Kantstudien* 33 (1928): 326–28. On Stern's assessment, Rosenzweig's claim in *The Star* was that "pure philosophy" as such "must be overcome [*muß . . . überwunden werden*]" (326).

35. Heidegger uses the term with greater frequency; see the discussion of the idea of an *Irrweg* and the related notion of "epochs of errancy" in Werner Marx, *Heidegger and the Tradition*, trans. Theodore Kisiel and Murray Greene (Evanston, Ill.: Northwestern University Press, 1971), 163–71.

discipline, a preserve of great ideas. For Rosenzweig, all canonical thought of this sort was associated with morbidity. (In "The New Thinking," he withheld from his readers any easy label for his doctrines lest it become a "sign planted in the cemetery of his general education" [ND, 160].) When Rosenzweig used "Philosophy" in this special sense of the Western tradition, he meant to name something hopelessly defunct. By contrast, the word *thinking (Denken)* in Rosenzweig's usage implied process, movement, temporality. It was therefore well suited to designate his ideal of an ongoing thinking in time, as opposed to the static philosophy of the tradition. As is well known, this same terminology and its accompanying conceptual distinction would survive in the late Heidegger's sharp distinction between the philosophical tradition and the "piety" or gratitude *(Danken)* that he saw as intrinsic to genuine "thinking" *(Denken)*. A similar distinction provides the framework of discussion in Heidegger's late essay "The End of Philosophy and the Task of Thought."[36]

### A Phenomenology of Religious Experience

If one now compares Rosenzweig's revolutionary conception of philosophy with his restorative idea of primal religion, the difference between them is perplexing. The two attitudes would appear to work at cross purposes—one looks forward, the other backward. But the fruitful union of these two perspectives and the reader's consequent sense of disorientation is in fact characteristic of Rosenzweig's mature thought. Indeed, as I will show in chapter 5, it is this very union that produces the unusual aesthetic of the Buber-Rosenzweig Bible translation, which I will call "archaic modernism." Just how Rosenzweig succeeds in making the revolutionary and restorative impulses cohere is the key to understanding his general method in *The Star.* Like Heidegger, Rosenzweig employs what may be considered a *phenomenological* method—a systematic study of the "original" structures of religious experience. To understand Rosenzweig's use of this innovative method first requires a brief summary of Heidegger's phenomenology.

Heidegger famously introduced his early magnum opus, *Being and Time* (1927), as an attempt to "revive" *(wiederholen)* the question of Being. In his view this question had become either trivialized or simply "forgotten" despite, he despairingly admitted, popular talk in his day concerning the need for "metaphysics" (SZ, 2). Heidegger therefore sought to renew a question

---

36. Heidegger, "Das Ende der Philosophie und die Aufgabe des Denkens," in *Zur Sache des Denkens* (Tübingen: Max Niemeyer Verlag, 1969), 61–80. Translated as "The End of Philosophy and the Task of Thinking," in Heidegger, *On Time and Being*, trans. Joan Stambaugh, (New York: Harper and Row, 1972), 55–73.

that had been forgotten. This renewal, however, simultaneously required a "destruction" of the philosophical tradition since it was the tradition itself that was responsible for obscuring the question.[37] The destructive enterprise could only proceed through a creative rereading of the canon, emphasizing those moments that the canon had passed over in silence and bringing to light what had remained "unthought" in the Western tradition. As Heidegger explained, such a tradition "blocks our access to those original 'sources' [*ursprünglichen 'Quellen'*]" from which the philosopher may rediscover the concepts and categories necessary for raising the question of Being. Moreover, the tradition "makes us forget" that they have such an origin and "makes us suppose that the necessity of going back to these sources is something which we need not even understand." Heidegger concluded with the paradoxical-sounding observation that we have been "uprooted by tradition" (SZ, 21; BT, 43).

According to Heidegger, the revival of the question of Being is no easy task, since human existence *(Dasein)* "no longer understands the most elementary conditions that would alone enable it to go back to the past in a positive manner and make it productively its own" (SZ, 21; BT, 43).[38] Heidegger thus adopts for the first part of his philosophy a radically new method that would allow us first to understand these basic conditions, and thereby let Being be understood as well. Borrowing his method from Husserl, Heidegger called this mode of preparatory investigation a "phenomenology" that was designed "to let that which shows itself be seen from itself" (SZ, 34; BT 58).

For Heidegger, the chief characteristic of the phenomenological method consisted in a purely descriptive investigation oriented toward "the things themselves." The point would be to understand the basic structure of intuited phenomena prior to any cooked-up conceptual schemes that an idealist would claim must mediate our access to phenomena. According to Heidegger, the basic structure of intuited phenomena is not conceptual but existential; Dasein's being lies in its "existence." That is to say, our very status as being-in-the-world has its own meaningful structure, embedded in language, social roles, practical activities, and so on. But one cannot hope to discern the way these meaningful structures lend our world its intelligibility if one simply analyzes concepts, since all of these structures are more "original" than any concepts. Instead, one must analyze the constitutive features of our being in the world and only in this way describe its structures of intelligibility. The published portion of *Being and Time*, especially its first di-

---

37. See § 6, titled "Die Aufgabe einer Destruktion der Geschichte der Ontologie." SZ, 19–27.

38. My translation revises the BT version.

vision, is just such an analysis of existence, which Heidegger called an "existential analytic." Methodologically, it is like an internal anatomy; it purports to describe the fundamental and precognitive structures of Dasein's "being-in-the-world," since it is only on the basis of such structures that any understanding of Being can first arise. The question of Being was thus posed first in a "phenomenological" manner, such that Being might then show itself in its "original" status (SZ, 35; BT 60).[39]

Given this summary, one may now discern an important resemblance between Heidegger's idea of phenomenology and Rosenzweig's basic methodological approach in *The Star.* Just as Heidegger attempts to bypass the philosophical tradition to retrieve the original sense of Being, Rosenzweig attempts to liberate both Judaism and Christianity from the specialized "religiosity" of tradition, so that they may "find their way back again" to their origins (as fact and event, respectively). Both of these claims are destructive in Heidegger's sense, since they seek to wrest a primal truth from the errors of tradition. Specifically, what Rosenzweig calls religious "origin" is a name for what is most basic to the lived experience of the faith. Throughout *The Star,* Rosenzweig attempts to understand the most basic features of religious phenomena as constitutive elements in the way human beings live their lives. But such constitutive elements are so fundamental that "religion" in an institutional sense is of little use; in fact, religious traditions will tend to obscure the meaning of these basic elements as they are actually constituted in experience. Concepts about religion are therefore unreliable and have little role to play in Rosenzweig's analysis of religious phenomena. His method thus represents a dramatic departure from Hermann Cohen's reconstruction of a "religion of reason" on the basis of Jewish sources: Where Cohen invoked an a priori and rational religion and thus reconstructed biblical meaning only insofar as it conformed with this idea, Rosenzweig wanted to let biblical meaning show itself "from itself" without the intervening constraints of reason.

Much like Heidegger, Rosenzweig believed that only a radically new kind of philosophy could perform the requisite retrieval of original religious meaning as it is embedded in the experiential structures of life. Rosenzweig's method was to analyze the original phenomena of religion—such as creation, revelation, and redemption, and also ritual, prayer, song, and poetry—in such a fashion that one might understand how they all make up the bedrock of our experience. Of course, for such a goal the mere analysis

---

39. On Heidegger's phenomenological method in relation to Husserlian phenomenology, see the discussion in Herbert Spiegelberg, *The Phenomenological Movement: An Historical Introduction* (The Hague: Martinus Nijhoff, 1960) esp. vol. I, chap. 6, "Martin Heidegger as a Phenomenologist," 271–353.

of religious concepts could not do, since "experience" for Rosenzweig—like "intuited phenomena" for Heidegger—is prior to any conceptual schemes the religious tradition might yield. As if to underscore the "precognitive" nature of these themes, Rosenzweig begins the book by first examining Man, God, and World as dissociated from any philosophical precepts. As he explains, "We mean to restore [*wiederherszustellen*] them, not as objects of a rational science but just the opposite, as 'irrational' objects" (SE, 21 [E, 19]). What was required was a style of analysis that could take these religious themes as primal phenomena, as the constitutive structures of religious experience.[40]

Methodologically, then, Rosenzweig's *Star of Redemption* is best understood as an exercise in the phenomenology of religion. It is important to recognize that this approach to religion was not unique; it was a part of the wider abandonment of idealist methods and the turn "toward the Concrete" (as Jean Wahl entitled his important 1932 survey of contemporary trends in philosophy). A similar turn toward thematizing the "deeper" and "irrational" foundations of religious experience may also be found in Rudolf Otto's *The Holy,* first published in 1917. And while Heidegger could hardly be considered an unqualified champion of religion, he believed that many of its chief experiential categories—such as anxiety, fallenness, mortality, conscience, and guilt—could be salvaged for his existential analytic, since they signaled a deep and precognitive structure of human existence best excavated with the tools of phenomenology. Lacking these modern tools, the primal structures of experience were likely to remain buried and forgotten beneath the philosophical tradition.[41]

40. Significantly, after having composed *The Star,* Rosenzweig met Edmund Husserl and related to Gritli: "And now Husserl. A person in any event. Apparently in his books a bad philosopher, precisely because in speaking [he is] a good one. . . . Surely for young people very appealing; I would surely have gone to him, were he at that time where I was. He . . . expects . . . chaos . . . a return to originality [*Rückkehr zur Ursprünglichkeit*] (this goes along with his 'phenomenology,' *which wants to return abstract and formalistic thinking to the simple and immediate 'phenomenon'*)." The meeting left Rosenzweig with the impression that he was himself *not* a philosopher, something he noted "every time I am with professionals." He thus concluded, somewhat precipitously, that "The *'Star'* [star-sign in letter] is not philosophy." GB (7.2.1919), 231–32. Two years later, Rosenzweig told Gritli of an afternoon gathering at which he was "in a big duel with a Husserlian." But the encounter ended in a "reconciliation" *(Versöhnung)* and "we almost fell into each others' arms." GB (1.5.1921), 744, my emphasis.

41. Wahl, *Vers le Concret: Études d'Histoire de la Philosophie Contemporaine* (Paris: J. Vrin, 1932). Among the most significant parallels to Rosenzweig's book was Otto's *Das Heilige: Über das Irrationale in der Idee des Göttlichen und sein Verhältnis zum Rationalen* (Breslau: Trewendt und Granier, 1917). Without succumbing to what he calls "irrationalism," Otto argues that the "deeper" *(tieferer)* aspect of religion is its experiential or preconceptual dimension, which nonetheless admits of conceptual treatment. On the general relation between

## *A Modernist Turn to Religious Origin*

As shown above, the method of Rosenzweig's *Star* represents a fruitful union between modernism and archaism; it promises both philosophical revolution (an overcoming of the entire intellectual tradition "from Ionia to Jena") and religious restoration (a return to primal religious experience before its modern decay). The comparison with Heidegger may now help us to understand that these two sensibilities were not truly opposed. Like Heidegger's phenomenological method for raising the question of Being, Rosenzweig seems to have believed that only a new mode of philosophy was capable of grasping the original meaningfulness of religious experience. This may help to explain his constant pleas in *The Star* for a "new type" of thinker who would be *"situated between theology and philosophy."* More precisely, it helps to explain why Rosenzweig declared that the "new philosophy" needed "theologians, *yet likewise in a new sense*" (SE, 118 [E, 106]; my emphasis). Only through the revolutionary methods of a new philosophy, could one hope to reveal the original phenomena of religion in their unfamiliar—even "unreligious"—meaning.

Rosenzweig's *Star* thus exemplifies the modernist turn to religious origins; it performs an aesthetic and philosophical gesture characteristic of some of the most fascinating products of Weimar culture. As noted in the introduction, Walter Benjamin's angel of history, with its face turned backward while it is propelled forward, is emblematic of this dual orientation and its strange combination of modernism and nostalgia. For understanding Rosenzweig's *Star,* the comparison with Heidegger is especially illuminating, since *Being and Time* also invoked the need for new and revolutionary methods, so as to retrieve what was most "primordial," and neglected in the philosophical tradition. Like Heidegger, yet in an even more pronounced fashion, Rosenzweig's mature work thus embodied the specific tension between philosophical modernism and religious origins.[42]

---

phenomenology and religion in Weimar thought, see Karl Löwith, "Phänomenologische Ontologie und protestantische Theologie," *Zeitschrift für Theologie und Kirche* (Neue Folge) 11, 5 (1930): 365–99; and in the same issue of this periodical, Karl Heim, "Ontologie und Theologie," 325–38; and Rudolf Bultmann, "Die Geschichtlichkeit des Daseins und der Glaube," 339–64. Also, Kurt Leese, "Vom religiösen Apriori," *Zeitschrift für Theologie und Kirche* (Neue Folge) 11, 2 (1930): 81–99; Martin Heidegger, "Phänomenologie und Theologie," in his *Wegmarken* (Frankfurt am Main: Vittorio Klostermann, 1967), 45–78; and Hans-Georg Gadamer, "Martin Heidegger and Marburg Theology," in his *Philosophical Hermeneutics,* trans. David E. Linge (Berkeley: University of California Press, 1976), 198–212.

42. Kafka's relationship to Judaism was similar, as Gerhom Scholem observed: "Kafka gave expression to *the borderline between religion and nihilism,* and so his writings possess . . . in the eyes of certain readers of our era, something of the rigorous light of canonicity." "Ten Ahistorical Theses on the Kabbalah," in *'Od Davar* (Tel Aviv: Am Oved, 1989), 37; my emphasis. The passage is quoted by Robert Alter, who later notes that for Scholem, Kafka sustained "endless

Given this preparatory exposition, I can now present a quick sketch of Rosenzweig's task in *The Star of Redemption*. As a philosophical heir to Nietzsche, Rosenzweig was committed to the view that the metaphysical tradition had reached a point of collapse. But as a theologian (albeit in a "new" and unprecedented sense), he was also dedicated to reviving an original experience of religion that had been traditionally understood on metaphysical terms. But Nietzsche had already proclaimed that God is dead. How, then, could one articulate a viable philosophy of religion in Nietzsche's wake? What could it mean to be faithful to one's tasks as both a theologian, who must affirm the origins of religion, and a modern philosopher, who must affirm with equal certainty that metaphysics has reached its end? This is the dilemma that perhaps best characterizes *The Star of Redemption:* it represented a philosophical attempt to articulate the fundamental concepts of religious experience without recourse to the language of the metaphysical tradition. The challenge was extraordinary, since the revolutionary demands of Rosenzweig's philosophy threatened at almost every turn to transfigure the religious concepts beyond any recognizably traditional meaning. But the risk was perhaps unavoidable, since Rosenzweig wished to surpass Nietzsche in the overcoming of the philosophical tradition. This may help to explain a curious remark by Margarete Susman in an early review (*Frankfurter Zeitung,* June 1921), which characterized *The Star of Redemption* as a philosophy that had "already gone beyond the zenith of atheism."[43] To see how Rosenzweig fared in this extraordinary effort, I now examine the substance of his book.

## THE ARGUMENT OF *THE STAR*

### *"Frei von jeder Zeitgewalt": Schiller's Dream*

The opening lines of *The Star of Redemption* are perhaps the most frequently cited of all Rosenzweig's philosophical oeuvre:

> From death, from the fear of death, there commences all Knowledge of the All. *To cast off the fear of the Earthly [Die Angst des Irdischen abzuwerfen],* to take

---

interpretability rather than absolute truth as the principal criterion of the canonical." *Canon and Creativity: Modern Writing and the Authority of Scripture* (New Haven: Yale University Press, 2000), 76–77. For the broader claim concerning ongoing interpretation in Jewish literature, also see my remarks in the Conclusion.

43. "A . . . highly significant book, which now however is entirely and directly concerned with redemption, *The Star of Redemption,* by Franz Rosenzweig . . . has already gone beyond the zenith of atheism." Susman, "The Exodus from Philosophy," *Frankfurter Zeitung,* June 17, 1921; 1 Morgenblatt, N. 441; reprinted in Udoff and Galli, eds., *Franz Rosenzweig's "The New Thinking."*

from Death its poisonous sting and from Hades its pestilent breath, in this Philosophy deceives itself [des vermißt sich die Philosophie].

A wealth of interesting commentary has been generated concerning this passage. But no critic so far as I am aware has remarked on the fact that it contains an unacknowledged citation (which I have italicized above). Rosenzweig borrowed this line—"to cast off the fear of the Earthly"—from Friedrich Schiller's poem "The Ideal and Life" ("Das Ideal und das Leben"). The line occurs in the third stanza, reproduced here:

Nur der Körper eignet jenen Mächten,
Die das dunkle Schicksal flechten,
Aber frei von jeder Zeitgewalt,

.  .  .  .  .  .  .  .  .

Göttlich unter Göttern, die Gestalt.
Wollt ihr hoch auf ihren Flügeln schweben,
Werft die Angst des Irdischen von euch,
Fliehet aus dem engen dumpfen Leben
In des Ideales Reich!

Only the body owns those powers
That bind our dark fate,
But free from all time's force,

.  .  .  .  .  .  .  .  .

The divine amongst divinities, is form.
If you would soar upon your wings
Cast the fear of the earthly from you,
Flee from the narrow, dull life,
Into the Ideal's Kingdom.

To understand the significance of Rosenzweig's citation, it is useful first of all to know several facts concerning the history of Schiller's poem. When first composed in 1795, it was titled "The Empire of Shadows," later amended to "The Empire of Forms."[44] It was apparently among the poet's own favorites, and its philosophical qualities made it an object of special devotion among later critics. The Kantian philosopher Kuno Fischer published a short work titled *Schiller als Philosoph* (1859), which treated this poem as the most significant expression of Schiller's "poetic philosophy." F. A. Lange (Cohen's Marburg predecessor) regarded it as "the most difficult" of all Schiller's poems and the greatest example of his "poetry of ideas"; a careful reading would demand "a complete propadeutic course" all its own. And the neo-Kantian Karl Vorländer, writing in 1894, selected

44. From Schiller, *Werke*, vol. III: *Gedichte, Erzählungen* (Frankfurt am Main: Insel Verlag, 1966), 99–103. On the composition of the poem, see the editor's remarks, 498–99.

"Das Ideal und das Leben" as the "most philosophical" among the so-called philosophical poems, which he praised as the "ripest blossoms of Schiller's genius," embodying "in sublime language . . . the highest philosophical ideas as had not been achieved since Plato's day."[45]

It is perhaps no accident that, of all Schiller's poetry, "The Ideal and Life" in particular struck a Kantian chord. Like much of Schiller's work, it bears the imprint of German Idealism. The third stanza is especially rich in language that recalls Kant's distinction between sensible and intelligible worlds. It juxtaposes two spheres—life *(Leben)* and the kingdom of the ideal *(des Ideales Reich)*. The sphere of life is narrow, a nexus of bodies in time and space. Subject to "time's power" the human creature knows himself to be ruled by fate *(Schicksal)*. The kingdom of the ideal, however, is "entirely free from time's force" *(frei von jeder Zeitgewalt);* it promises refuge from life, through it we transcend space and time and we embrace the divinity of "form" *(Gestalt)*. Schiller's language is clearly idealist. A helpful comparison is the *Critique of Practical Reason* (1788), where Kant distinguishes between "the external world of sense" and "my invisible self." The visible world "annihilates, as it were, my importance as an animal creature, which must give back to the planet (a mere speck of the universe) the matter from which it came, the matter which is for a little time provided with vital forces, we know not how." The invisible world, however, "infinitely raises my worth . . . —at least so far as it may be inferred from the purposive destination assigned [to me,] . . . a destination which is not restricted to the conditions and limits of this life but reaches into the infinite."[46]

The parallel between Schiller and Kant, however, is not precise. Within the Kantian framework, the dignity of the human being is at once annihilated and infinite. As was demonstrated in the antinomies, there is no resolving the contradiction between these two perspectives, since the human being must necessarily be understood as simultaneously an inhabitant of both the phenomenal and the noumenal worlds. In Schiller's poem, the necessity of this dualism is lacking. Schiller urges, "Cast off the fear of the earthly" ("Werft die Angst des Irdischen von euch") and encourages us to flee the confinements of temporal life so as to dwell purely in the realm of form. Such language, however vague and lyrical, suggests that salvation is a

45. Kuno Fischer, *Schiller-Schriften* (Heidelberg: winter, 1891). Friedrich Albert Lange, *Einleitung und Kommentar zu Schillers Philosophischen Gedichten* (Bielefeld und Leipzig: Velhagen und Klasing, 1919), xv. Karl Vorländer, "Schiller's Verhältnis zu Kant in seiner geschichtlichen Entwicklung" *Philosophischen Monatshefte* 30 (1894), reprinted in *Kant—Schiller—Goethe: Gesammelte Aufsätze,* 2nd ed. (Leipzig: Felix Meiner, 1923; orig. pub. 1906).

46. Kant, *Critique of Practical Reason,* trans. Lewis White Beck (New York: Macmillan / Library of the Liberal Arts, 1956), 166.

real possibility. And this represents a significant departure from Kant: what
was for Kant merely a transcendental distinction—that is, between two ways
of knowing—became for Schiller a poem of transcendence.[47]

If one now turns to the famous passage that opens *The Star of Redemption*,
one sees immediately how Rosenzweig incorporated significant elements of
the poem. In fact, the opening paragraph of *The Star* presents a disorga-
nized assault upon Schiller's metaphorical world. The line, *"to cast off the fear
of the earthly"* (*"Die Angst des Irdischen abzuwerfen"*) is an obvious reference to
Schiller's "Werft die Angst des Irdischen von euch." Rosenzweig's phrase
"the free soul flutters above and away" makes mockery of Schiller's line "if
you would soar upon your wings." A less obvious but equally significant connection is hidden in Rosenzweig's phrase "the fear of death knows nothing
of such a separation of body and soul," which offers a retort to the first line
in Schiller's third stanza, "Only the body owns these powers." Other references are scattered at random throughout the opening paragraph. Rosenzweig bitterly observes that each of us awaits his journey "into darkness" *(ins
Dunkel),* a phrase reminiscent of Schiller's "dark fate" *(dunkle Schicksal).*
At the bottom of the page (if one follows the format of the first edition),
Rosenzweig makes allusion to the "grand opportunity" of philosophy when
it urges us to slip free from the "narrow of life" *(Enge des Lebens)*—an ironic
echo for Schiller's exhortation "Flee from the narrow, dull life."

There is little evident structure in the way Rosenzweig plays upon Schiller's poem. It is strewn across the page almost as if to suggest the remnants
of an exploded shell. The martial metaphor is appropriate, as death is manifest in the opening paragraph in the "fast-approaching volleys" of enemy
fire, while the victim crawls terrified through a landscape that recalls the
trenches of the First World War—"the naked folds of the earth." Of course,
more learned Germans of the time would have known the source Rosenzweig failed to name. But Rosenzweig's point is that Schiller's values have
grown as anonymous—and as powerless—as the ruins of the philosophical
tradition.[48]

47. On Kant's distinction between "transcendental" and "transcendent," see KdrV, esp.
A296/B253, 316. The possible difference between Schiller and Kant is perhaps best indicated
in one of Kant's "reflections," in which he uses language akin to Schiller's but describes the *Critique* as "a preservative against a malady which has its source in our nature. This malady is the
opposite of love of home (homesickness) which binds [*fesselt*] us to our fatherland. It is a longing to pass out beyond our immediate confines and to relate ourselves to other worlds [Eine
Sehnsucht, uns ausser unserm Kreise zu verlieren und andere Welten zu beziehen]." *Reflexio-
nen Kants zur kritischen Philosophie, Aus Kants handschriftlichen Aufzeichnungen,* ed. Benno Erd-
mann, Neudruck der Ausgabe Leipzig 1882/1884 (Stuttgart-Bad Cannstatt: Friedrich From-
mann Verlag, 1992), 373.

48. This is not the only place in Rosenzweig's work that he cites this poem without naming
its author. See, e.g., the lecture notes from 1924, "Glauben und Wissen," first published in FR,

One may therefore read the entire opening passage of *The Star of Redemption* as an ironic commentary on idealism as it is embodied in Schiller's poem. Schiller's language serves only as a vehicle by which to overcome its values. But the poem is important not merely because it provides Rosenzweig with a picturesque vision of idealism. Far more significant is the way it allows Rosenzweig to build up an association in his reader's mind between idealism and metaphysical release. As we have seen, Schiller seemed to depart from modern idealism where he implied that it is possible for human beings to gain actual transcendence from their lives through intellection. When the mind seizes upon form *(Gestalt)*, Schiller describes this as a moment of deliverance from time and the corporeal world. The unity of being and thought *(Sein und Denken)* now seems to suggest the notion of being-in-thought, a notion against which Rosenzweig wages battle on behalf of the "empty" being-prior-to-thought *(das Sein vor dem Denken)* that appears in the "short, hardly graspable moment" before it can be seized upon by the mind (SE, 22 [E, 19]). The notion that our mental effort alone transports us to a higher stratum of being introduces a new, vigorously metaphysical dimension into the idealist framework.

One may now better understand why Rosenzweig would have chosen to begin with this unacknowledged citation. What Schiller's poem illustrates is nothing less than the idea of redemption as proffered by all of Western philosophy since the pre-Socratics. And it is this idea—that idealism promises a quasi-religious deliverance from life—that is the crucial target in Rosenzweig's introduction. Rosenzweig thus employs the poem so as to pursue a dialogue with the metaphysical tradition. Because he pursues this dialogue in an ironic fashion—that is, within, yet against its metaphors—the opening passage of *The Star* provides us with a perfect example of what Rosenzweig called "the reductio ad absurdum of the old philosophy." This reductio bears an obvious similarity to what Heidegger calls a "destruction"—the attempt to dismantle the entirety of the metaphysical tradition—again, since Parmenides—by recalling us from the "flight" that perpetually lends the tradition its legitimacy.[49]

III: 581–95, and recently translated as "Faith and Knowledge," in Rosenzweig, *God, Man, and the World,* ed. and trans. Barbara Galli (Syracuse: Syracuse University Press, 1998), 97–121. Here Rosenzweig argues extensively with the poem, breaking it into fragments and subverting their meaning just as he does in the introductory passage of the *Star.* Once again he does not name the source, but at least here the quotation marks make it evident that he is citing another work of literature; e.g. his remark that "Doubt could laugh it off. The kingdom of ideals would be *really* a 'kingdom of shadows' [recall the earlier title of Schiller's poem]—*if not* for the arts: 'But presses into the sphere of beauty.' 'Through the quiet shadowy land of beauty.' 'Divine among gods the form.'" Cited from the Galli translation, 118, and also see 120.

49. Even in 1929, Schiller's poem was still a favorite in the neo-Kantian imagination. In the confrontation at Davos, Rosenzweig felt a natural alliance with Heidegger, especially when

## On Wishing to Remain in the World

Given this summary of *The Star*'s opening passage, we are now better positioned to grasp the relationship between Rosenzweig's theological purposes and his antagonism toward traditional metaphysics. It may first prove helpful to return briefly to the opening sentences of the book. Note the phrase "des vermißt sich die Philosophie." In the first English edition this line was translated "Philosophy takes it upon itself." But this misses the crucial sense of "vermißt sich," which also implies self-deception. Another translation might be "in this philosophy deceives itself." The difference is significant. Rosenzweig's argument is that philosophy in its traditional form has been captive to an illusion. It has assigned itself the special task of our redemption from the world, and, in believing too securely in the power of the intellect, it has proffered the sham-consolation that despite our obvious finitude, our true existence lies in thought alone, and that while our bodies may fall into the abyss, our minds nonetheless rise toward the infinite, which we have merely to think so as to find ourselves released instantaneously from what Schiller called time's force *(Zeitgewalt)*. This is the philosopher's idea of immortality—redemption as metaphysics.

According to Rosenzweig, the old dream of metaphysics is ludicrous, a philosophical hoax. The deceit of metaphysics becomes most obvious when an individual comes face to face with death as a real possibility. In such moments, the human being becomes enveloped by anxiety *(Angst)* for his this-worldly being *(Diesseits)*. But philosophy responds by pointing to a "beyond" *(Jenseits)* for which the human being can have no concern. To each and every creature threatened with annihilation, philosophy offers nothing but a "vacuous smile," a metaphysical panacea that only falsifies our earthly fears. But once we have come to recognize our life for what it truly is, we will also have arrived at the paramount truth that the kind of redemption we have inherited from the metaphysical tradition holds no real meaning. We can neither possess, nor should we wish for, an existence beyond our lives in time. No human being, Rosenzweig tells us, actually wishes to flee the fetters that bind him to the world. Against all promises of worldly release, the human being wants only to remain ("er will bleiben"). In other words, "he wants—to live" (SE, 3 [E, 3]). The first paragraph of the book ends by offering a direct rejoinder to Schiller, which again calls upon the poet's own imagery:

---

Cassirer resorted to the very idealist inheritance Heidegger now characterized as flight. When asked about the answers of philosophy when confronted with human anxiety, Cassirer spoke first: "Werft die Angst des Irdischen von Euch," ("Cast off the fear of the earthly") he said, "That is the position of idealism with which I have always been acquainted." KPM, 291; English 182–83.

Man is not to throw off the fear of the earthly; he must remain in the fear of death, but he must remain." [Der Mensch soll die Angst des Irdischen nicht von sich werfen; er soll in der Furcht des Todes—bleiben.] (SE, 4 [E, 4])

This brief passage contains what is perhaps the clearest statement of Rosenzweig's philosophical purpose in *The Star of Redemption. Rosenzweig's chief aim is to expound a new concept of redemption that accords with the post-metaphysical human desire to remain in the world.* The crucial though deceptively modest word in this statement is "remain" *(bleiben)*. At the end of the book, Rosenzweig repeats that the affirmation of life "remains [*bleibt*] always within the bounds of creatureliness" (SE, 463 [E, 416]). Thus the book ends where it begins. The desire to remain is fundamental, in that even when we are threatened with the possibility of our own death, we should not be awakened to longings for an otherworldly realm. Death therefore serves merely to disclose the radical priority of life. We may remain in "the fear of death," but this is naturally true insofar as our finitude is constitutive of our human being. The idea of remaining indicates that we do not and cannot give over what is constitutive of our human being, as if we could trade one nature for another and somehow profit by the exchange. Rosenzweig devotes great energy to criticizing Schiller's dream for good reason, since it amounts to a denial of our fundamental wish as human beings to conceive of our earthly being as the space wherein we may achieve ultimate fulfillment. Philosophy in the traditional sense denies this wish and nourishes the deceptive thought that such fulfillment may be found in a metaphysical "beyond."[50]

*The Star* thus begins by distinguishing between two opposed concepts of redemption. According to the traditional model, redemption is best conceived as a kind of metaphysical departure from the world. In Rosenzweig's opinion, most of Western philosophy (up to what he calls the post-Hegelian revolution) has subscribed to this model in one fashion or another. And because of its overwhelming authority, most if not all of Western theology has also construed redemption along similar lines. In fact, Rosenzweig suggests, philosophy and theology have become mutually intertwined to such a degree that any attempt to speak religiously about redemption ends by distorting its original meaning in accordance with the metaphysical model. But as a modern philosopher and an heir to the post-Hegelian revolution, Rosenzweig argues in a Nietzschean vein that we should reject this model as encouraging a faulty idea of what it means to be human. In its place, Rosenzweig promises to develop an alternative model of redemption, based upon the fundamental premise that to be human is to remain in the world.

50. In a letter to Gritli, Rosenzweig states emphatically that "Idealism simply *knows* nothing at all of redemption." GB (27.11.1918), 200–201; emphasis in original.

This is of course a daunting assignment, since it calls into question some of the deepest and most cherished beliefs, which have determined how Western theologians and philosophers alike have conceived ultimate fulfillment. Already one may discern a moment of irony in Rosenzweig's project: the notion that philosophy and religion are expected to help us toward achieving some kind of ultimate fulfillment may seem to imply that their chief business is to help us toward transcending any and all existential constraint. But as I have shown, Rosenzweig rejects this kind of transcendence as impossible, since he regards existential constraints as constitutive of human being. Yet in Rosenzweig's new understanding of redemption, the expectation that one may achieve ultimacy remains somehow intact, despite the collapse of the metaphysical tradition that gave that achievement its original meaning. The new model thus borrows much of its energy surreptitiously from the ideal it outwardly rejects. In *The Star*, then, Rosenzweig's idea of redemption becomes a mode of fulfillment within the bounds of finitude, the achievement of ultimacy without recourse to metaphysics. *The Star of Redemption*, then, may be read as an answer to Nietzsche's question: "Alas, where is redemption from the flux of things and from the punishment called existence?"[51]

## Metaphysics, Traditional and Modern

I have suggested above that Rosenzweig is a post-Nietzschean philosopher. By this I mean that he takes seriously the philosophical message in Nietzsche's dictum that "God is dead" (or, if one prefers, the equally metaphorical claim that humanity has "wiped away the infinite horizon.") Both dicta appear in Nietzsche's famous aphorism "The Madman," from *The Gay Science*. When the term *God* is used in this metaphorical sense, it is perhaps best construed as naming the space of metaphysics. For Nietzsche, this idea, which he calls "the infinite horizon," has proved so bewitching that since Plato philosophers have dedicated themselves to explaining "How the Real World Became a Myth" (as described in the celebrated parody from *The Twilight of the Idols*).[52]

A potential source of confusion is that Rosenzweig also uses the term *metaphysics* in a second, more positive fashion. In a section of the introduc-

51. "O, wo ist die Erlösung vom Fluß der Dinge und der Strafe 'Dasein'?" Nietzsche, "Erlösung," in *Also sprach Zarathustra*, 150–56; quote 154.

52. Nietzsche, *The Gay Science*, trans. Walter Kaufmann (New York: Vintage Books, 1974), Book 3, Aphorism 125, 181–82; and "Wie die 'wahre Welt' endlich zur Fabel wurde. Geschichte eines Irrthums," in *Sämtliche Werke*, vol. VI: *Der Fall Wagner, Götzen-Dämmerung* (Berlin: de Gruyter, 1988), 80–81; "How the 'Real World' at Last Became a Myth, History of an Error," in *Twilight of the Idols*, trans. R. J. Hollingdale (London: Penguin, 1968), 50–51.

tion entitled "The Metaphysical" ("Das Metaphyisische"), Rosenzweig acknowledges the possibility for confusion arising from this terminological
ambiguity. "Concerning God," he writes, "there has long been a science of
'Metaphysics'" *(eine Wissenschaft, "Metaphysik").* Metaphysics in this older
sense is the science of supersensible and intelligible being. While some philosophers such as Kant used it to designate the larger discipline of *Meta-
physica Specialis,* that is, the set of entities within the metaphysical realm
(God, freedom, and the immortal soul), Rosenzweig applies it to the traditional science of God alone.[53] It is this older sense of metaphysics as a science that according to Nietzsche is now defunct.

But Rosenzweig also affirms, with evident approval, that one may speak
of God as "the metaphysical" (SE, 43 [E, 41]). And to compound the reader's difficulties, Rosenzweig also borrows the prefix *meta* to name the two
other distinctive elements of his system—the metaethical (which names the
human being prior to morality) and the metalogical (which names the cosmos prior to natural science).[54] Thus the three central terms of Rosenzweig's philosophy—the metaphysical, the metaethical, and the metalogical—may be easily confused with metaphysics in the older, pejorative sense.
They are, Rosenzweig admits, "created according to the meaning that this
word has taken on in the course of history." As a consequence of this terminological ambiguity, Rosenzweig alerts us to the fact that readers who are
interested in metaphysics of the new sort should be wary of "confusion with
the age-old philosophical concepts" (SE, 18 [E, 16]).[55]

The overlap in terminology is especially vexing if one tries to understand
why Rosenzweig sees fit to reject the concept of God as it has been customarily understood by the metaphysical tradition. Here, at least, one might
have expected that his thinking would be in accordance with older views.
For one might suppose that any bona fide theology must necessarily subscribe to metaphysics in some fashion. (How else could God be preserved
as a distinctive ontological category if he does not lie beyond physical being?) But Rosenzweig defeats this expectation. God, he affirms, is "the metaphysical" but not "aphysical" *(aphysisch).* To conceive of God as lying wholly
outside the cosmos is an error, since any "acosmism" *(Akosmismus)* is merely
"pantheism in reverse" (SE, 19 [E, 17]). Only the idealist would conceive of

53. On the distinction between general and special metaphysics, see the helpful comments
in Heidegger, KPM, §2.

54. See the useful comments in Rotenstreich, "Rosenzweig's Notion of Metaethics," in
PFR, 69–88.

55. In German, "die Verwechslung mit den uralten philosophischen Begriffen fürchten."
Thanks to Rosenzweig's selection of terms, such confusion is, as he admits, "even harder to
avoid."

God as a supersensible being, but the idealist immediately jumps to the conclusion that God's existence must be that of pure intelligibility. According to Rosenzweig, the so-called "ontological proof" for the existence of God is idealist in just this sense, since it depends upon the customary metaphysical notion that Being and Thought are identical. Traditional theology, he concludes, has all too eagerly accepted the idealist account of God as a being known through the intellect. This conclusion yields a rather unusual image: "Philosophy has fed theology [with the doctrine of] the identity of Thought and Being, like a nursemaid placing a pacifier in the mouth of a hungry child so that it will not cry" (SE, 19 [E, 17]). The point of this metaphor is to suggest that in their effort to articulate an adequate concept of God, religious thinkers have often relied upon the very same erroneously metaphysical notions of the world that have bedeviled philosophers since ancient Greece. Because theology remains caught in these "age-old philosophical concepts," Rosenzweig must combat metaphysics so as to arrive at an authentic understanding of God.

Ironically, Rosenzweig calls this authentic concept of God "the metaphysical." But in contrast to the presumption of divine intelligibility that underlies the older metaphysical idea, Rosenzweig employs his new term in order to name precisely that which *escapes* intelligibility. God is "metaphysical," then, in the sense that divine being exceeds the capacities of thought. To buttress this claim, Rosenzweig calls attention to the technical distinction between existence *(Dasein)* and being *(Sein)*. Whereas being is the category of traditional metaphysics, existence is Rosenzweig's name for the newly "metaphysical" nature of God. Such terminological subtleties may seem frivolous, but they are crucial to understanding the global values of Rosenzweig's system. Moreover, the distinction between *Sein* and *Dasein* would later play an organizing role when Rosenzweig began the task of translating the Bible—a topic I will address in chapter 5.

The distinction between these two terms first arose on the basis of the ancient metaphysical prejudice that worldly entities have no true independence. Plato's participationist theory, for example, is traditionally metaphysical since it suggests that sensible objects are not independent—they rely for their being upon a higher, supersensible realm of which they are mere shadows. In German, Plato's intelligible forms are customarily said to enjoy the sovereign status of "Being" *(Sein),* as against mere "existence" *(Dasein).* According to Rosenzweig, the traditional idea of God is likewise metaphysical, since God is assigned a nonphysical essence grasped only as pure intelligibility. In *The Star,* however, Rosenzweig proposes that philosophers revise this definition of metaphysics. He argues that for something to be truly metaphysical, it must enjoy its own "natural, existing essence" *(daseiendes Wesen).* God is metaphysical in this revised sense only in so far as his ontological status cannot be reduced to that of a being that is wholly present for thought. Rosenzweig concludes that God's "ownmost existence" *(Eigenexistenz)* is that mode of "divine existence" *(göttlichen Daseins)* that remains "independent of the being-in-thought and being of the totality" ("unabhängig vor aller Identität von Sein und Denken") (SE, 19 [E, 17]).

The surprising thing about this explanation is that it reverses customary usage. According to the older language of metaphysics, God is a being whose existence is absolutely necessary *(per se necessarium)*. As such, God is independent through and through.[56] The point of this traditional definition was to reinforce the distinction between the unique ontological status of God on the one hand and the dependent ontological status of worldly entities on the other. Accordingly, scholastic philosophers called God the most real *(ens realissimum)*, whereas they considered worldly being as a degraded reality. However, for Aquinas (who expressed these ideas most characteristically), it did not follow from this distinction that divine being, simply because it is ontologically higher than worldly being, is also more intelligible. Rather, Aquinas believed that to the human intellect, the divine essence will remain forever unintelligible—hence his "negative theology." Rosenzweig, however, seems to have construed the doctrines of traditional metaphysics rather differently. His discussion of divine being *(Sein)* seems to assume that for past philosophers, ontologically higher categories always end up getting equated with pure intelligibility. Only this assumption can explain why throughout *The Star of Redemption* the term *Idealism* is used to name the entire metaphysical tradition. Rosenzweig also adopted the corollary assumption, that for traditional metaphysics worldly entities are epistemologically the most opaque.[57] What is most unusual in this use of the term *metaphysical* is that it simultaneously attacks and depends upon the traditional doctrines. In calling God metaphysical, Rosenzweig means something very much like the ontological status that in traditional metaphysical systems was assigned to the rude and unrefined stuff of the world preexisting our concepts of it. For Rosenzweig divine being is the "most real" insofar as it is more like worldly existence than it is akin to thought. But at the same time it represents just that negativity within the world's lining that phi-

---

56. Aquinas, *Summa Theologica*. A fine discussion of the relevant arguments can be found in F. C. Copleston, *Aquinas* (London: Penguin Books, 1955), chap. 3.

57. In much of this argument, Rosenzweig follows the path of Friedrich Schelling. On Schelling's influence, see Mendes-Flohr, "Franz Rosenzweig and the German Philosophical Tradition," esp. 7–8. This "opaqueness" may be an accurate characterization of at least some traditional doctrines. The Aristotelian theory of perception (e.g., in the *Physics*, 192a 22–34) tells us that worldly entities impress their form upon the mind, but not their matter. This substrate of entities therefore remains as the unintelligible residue, the underlying stuff of being.

losophers have typically characterized as resistant to any and all conceptual representation.[58]

Thus Rosenzweig's new definition of God's nature (although he calls it "the metaphysical") is in fact a willful rejection of traditional metaphysics. Although it emerges from the framework of the older philosophy, it falls into just that category that philosophers customarily reserved for what was not metaphysical at all. When seen against the backdrop of traditional metaphysics, Rosenzweig's name for God as "the metaphysical" must be understood partly in irony. Where traditional theology (in Rosenzweig's somewhat misleading characterization) cherishes the notion that God is intelligible, Rosenzweig insists that "the metaphysical" names precisely that element in God's nature which escapes cognition. However, this means that traditional theology believes in a mere phantom—an exact concept of what is not God. Paradoxically, the theological tradition is a canon of unbelief.

### Parmenides and the Errancy of Tradition

To better appreciate Rosenzweig's sense of the place of metaphysics in relation to the religious tradition, it is first necessary to understand his general characterization of the philosophical canon from ancient Greece to the present day. For Rosenzweig, the history of philosophy presents a more or less unified path of thought stretching "from Parmenides to Hegel." In Hegelian fashion, as we have seen, Rosenzweig famously describes this path as a westward geographical movement—"from Iona to Jena."

Each of these two phrasings is quite common in *The Star of Redemption.* Parmenides (a representative of the "Ionian school") is mentioned at least six times in the book; and even where he is not explicitly named, Rosenzweig clearly has him in mind, especially when he makes allusion to the doctrine of "the identity of being and thought." Hegel (who is associated with Jena) appears with even greater frequency. Just as Kierkegaard's philosophy emerged in resentful dialogue with Hegelianism, Rosenzweig's philosophy is unthinkable without Hegel as its foil. (*The Star*'s first sentence—with its disapproving, backwards glance toward the "All" of philosophical tradition—is only the most famous example.)[59] Throughout *The Star,* Parmen-

58. This resolutely anti-idealist theme explains why Rosenzweig in one place calls his new thinking "absolute empiricism" (ND, 161). For an explanation of how this differs from empiricism in the usual sense, see Reiner Wiehl, "Experience in Rosenzweig's New Thinking," in PFR, 42–68, esp. 56.

59. See SE, 13 (E, 12–13); 14 (E, 15); 22 (E, 19); 50 (E, 47); 56 (E, 52); 104 (E, 94). (One should note that the English translator at least once misreads "Sein und Denken" as "being and reasoning," rather than "being and thought," which constricts Rosenzweig's criticism to *rationalist* cognitivism when in fact he means to criticize cognitivism as such. See, e.g., SE, 14 [E, 13].) When Rosenzweig has completed his exposition of the new "totality" *(Allheit)* formed

ides and Hegel function as convenient markers for the beginning and ending points of the philosophical tradition Rosenzweig wishes to surpass. Yet he is often ambiguous about just what it would mean to surpass the tradition. On the one hand, Rosenzweig wishes to overcome Hegel and move "beyond" traditional philosophy along the path first charted by Nietzsche. On the other hand, he wishes to think back "before" Parmenides to an "original" path of speculation first disclosed in Judaism (which, as noted above, was not "originally" an institutional religion). There are thus two ways to understand Rosenzweig's complaint against the philosophical tradition—either in its inception (where Parmenides figures as chiefly responsible) or in its supposed collapse (where Hegel represents its apogee and Nietzsche its end). In this section, I shall address Rosenzweig's account of Parmenides and the inception of philosophy; and in the section that follows I shall turn to Rosenzweig's account of Nietzsche.

For Rosenzweig, the chief characteristic of the philosophical tradition inaugurated by Parmenides lay in the principle concerning the "identity of being and thought" *(die Identität von Sein und Denken)*.[60] Rosenzweig does not inform his readers that this doctrine derives from a line from Parmenides' didactic poem, customarily entitled "On the Essence of Beings" ("Vom Wesen des Seienden"). The poem describes the narrator's ascent on a chariot, his passage through a special "gate," and his initiation by the Sun-maidens into the secret of the two ways, the way of truth and that of mortal opinion. Along the first of these two ways, a goddess tells the narrator, that "it is the same thing that can be thought and that can be" *(to gar auto noein estin te kai einai)*. This phrase may be crudely translated as "thinking and being are the same."

Rosenzweig sees this dictum as anticipating modern philosophical idealism. According to Rosenzweig, Parmenides provided the earliest expression of the traditional principle that what seems contingent exhibits its inner truth when it is taken up in rational reflection. This is accompanied by the

---

by the six elements of Part I (God, World, and Man) and Part II (Creation, Revelation, and Redemption), he is careful to note that the new unity of his own system has nothing in common with the self-sufficient and rational totality that was embraced "with naive candor" in the "first beginnings" of ancient philosophy (presumably a reference to Parmenides) and that remained characteristic of all Western thought all the way down to "its conclusion in Hegel." SE, 283 (E, 254).

60. But here a small qualification is necessary. Rosenzweig also mentions Thales as an earlier exponent of this very doctrine. As Rosenzweig explains, in the dictum, "All is water," there "already lurks the presupposition of the possibility of conceiving the world." This dictum is thus the "first sentence of philosophy." But Rosenzweig quickly turns from Thales to address Parmenides as the explicit founder of the philosophical tradition. A useful English-language introduction to these thinkers is John Burnet, *Early Greek Philosophy* (London: A. & C. Black, 1930), 192–226.

(rather controversial) assumption that nothing of importance remains as a pre-reflective residue once reason has cooked up the given in a conceptual fashion. Traditional philosophy therefore begins with the assumption that the sheer "thatness" or quiddity of the world is at its core already fully structured in a rational fashion, since only this inner structure warrants the philosophical claim that the actual is the rational. Rosenzweig summarizes this assumption by saying that "the contingent changes itself into something necessary" (SE, 13 [E, 12]). For Rosenzweig, the problem with this idea is that it conflates two distinctive kinds of unity. On the one hand, thought has its own distinctive kind of being, which is indifferent to what is being thought about. In this sense, thought can refer to itself without ever venturing outside of itself. This is the "unity" of thought that is at the same time its power of self-reflexivity—Rosenzweig calls this its "diversity." While thought "refers to being," it also must have a "diversity in itself because it also, at the same time, refers to itself." On the other hand, when thought seizes upon the world, it may lend the world a certain rational structure. This is the "unity" of thought and being when they are considered together. According to Rosenzweig, one trouble with Parmenides and all later developments in idealist philosophy down through Hegel is that these two distinctive unities were conflated when they are in fact distinct. Rosenzweig explains that "the identity of thinking and being presupposes an inner nonidentity [*eine innere Nichtidentität*]." While thought may come into the world and construe it in a rational fashion, the world is contingent and remains external to thought: "[T]hus the world is a beyond as against what is intrinsically logical" (SE, 14 [E, 13]).

As a useful metaphor for this idea, Rosenzweig suggests that we imagine a wall on which there hangs a painting. If the wall illustrates the inner unity of thought and the painting illustrates the outer unity that binds thought with being, then the task is to understand what relationship obtains between the wall and the painting. Rosenzweig suggests that the true problem with idealism lies precisely in its attempt to elide any relationship whatsoever, since it asserts a primal unity that admits of no differentiation: "According to the notion prevailing from Parmenides to Hegel, the wall was in a certain sense painted alfresco, and wall and picture therefore constituted a unity." So the world as it is seized in thought "knows nothing and acknowledges nothing outside of itself." For Rosenzweig, the difficulty with this model of the relationship between thought and being is that it denies the very contingency whose existence philosophy was first called upon to explain. Of course, philosophy depends upon the world, but this point is trivial if we mean only that there would not be thought about a world if there were no world to think. Rosenzweig admits that it "would be impossible to hang the picture but for the wall." But "the wall has not the slightest connection with the picture itself." The world as it was imagined "from Parmenides to Hegel" believed in an intrinsic unity "inside the walls of the world." But this denies thinking its distinctive character, which merely comes to rest in the world. As Rosenzweig explains, "Thought [*Das Denken*] is entitled to a home in the world [*in ihr heimatsberechtigt*], but the world is not itself the totality, rather a home [*eine Heimat*]" (SE, 14 [E, 13]).

This is an exceptionally difficult argument to grasp. An illuminating comparison may be found in Heidegger's various writings on Parmenides, chiefly the concluding chapter of *An Introduction to Metaphysics* (1935), the later lecture "Moira (Parmenides, Fragment VIII, 34–41)" (1954), and the larger text of which this lecture was originally a part, *Was Heißt Denken?* (1954). In all three texts Heidegger develops a philologically sustained reading of Parmenides' dictum that "thinking and being are the same." Much like Rosenzweig, Heidegger objects to the idealist meanings customarily ascribed to this phrase. Unlike Rosenzweig, however, Heidegger suggests that the idealist interpretation itself is incorrect, since it does not capture the original sense of Parmenides' dictum. Only the "crude translation" of this phrase, Heidegger tells us, has yielded the apparently idealist doctrine that "Thinking and being are the same" ("Dasselbe aber ist das Denken und das Sein"). Heidegger considers this a "misinterpretation" and fundamentally "un-Greek" (EM, English, 136; EM, 104). He considers it wrong to attribute the idealist doctrine concerning the unity of being and thought to Parmenides, and he explains that if we look more closely at the original Greek version of the phrase we will see that for Parmenides "the same" *(to auto)* did not mean "sameness" *(Selbigkeit)* nor "an empty being of one piece" *(leere Einerleiheit)*. Instead, for Parmenides "unity is the belonging-together of antagonisms [*Zusammengehörigkeit des Gegenstrebigen*]" (EM, English, 138; EM, 106).

Like Rosenzweig before him, Heidegger advanced a "disunity thesis," insisting that the genuine relation between being and thought was not that of identity but was instead a unity of distinctive elements. Rosenzweig says that "the identity of thinking and being presupposes an inner nonidentity," and Heidegger says that their unity is "the belonging-together of antagonisms." Both express an obvious preference for the disunity thesis as the only genuine basis for a new, post-traditional philosophy. Heidegger, for example, insists that while thought is not "the same" as Being, it must still be understood "for the sake of Being" and "must belong to Being" (EM, English, 139; EM, 106). Rosenzweig expresses this same idea when he writes that while a disunity obtains between thought and being, thought must nonetheless regard the world "as a home [*eine Heimat*]." Both Rosenzweig and Heidegger assign Parmenides a central if not unique place in the originating moment of the philosophical tradition. Both claim that the philosophical tradition begins with Parmenides' doctrine concerning the "identity" of being and thought. Both further argue that this identity has been a baleful inheritance for the philosophical tradition and has remained an essential mark of the errancy of modern philosophy right down to Hegel.

Yet Rosenzweig and Heidegger part company on a crucial point. For Rosenzweig it seems self-evident that Parmenides himself equated being and thought and was therefore an idealist *avant la lettre*. Here Rosenzweig was merely repeating one of the customary assumptions in the history of philosophy as practiced by his German contemporaries.[61] Among the German Idealists themselves, Hegel found it especially gratifying to think of Parmenides as his predecessor. In the *Lectures on the History of Philosophy*, Hegel writes that "Thinking [for Parmenides] is thus identical with its Being; for there is nothing outside of Being, this great affirmation." He concluded that "genuine philosophizing began with Parmenides."[62] Rosenzweig, a follower of Hegel in many respects, seems to have accepted this judgment. He did not ask whether Parmenides might not have meant something quite different from the doctrine later idealists imputed to him.

Heidegger, however, opposed the customary scholarly view of Parmenides as a forerunner to German Idealism. This view, he claimed, misses Parmenides' actual intent. For Heidegger, "The earlier thinking is thus, as it were, deprived of its own freedom of speech." Heidegger therefore proposes engaging in a true "dialogue" with Parmenides, which would require openness to real differences between early Greek thought and the modern tradition.[63] Through such a dialogue, Heidegger found that Parmenides did not assert a simple identity between being and thought as would later animate German Idealism. Parmenides and Hegel were, in fact, starkly opposed:

> The dissimilarity between the two is so far-reaching that through it the very possibility of comprehending the difference is shattered. By indicating this difference we are at the same time giving an indication of the degree to which our own interpretation of Parmenides' saying arises from a way of thinking utterly foreign to the Hegelian approach.[64]

61. The historian of philosophy Karl Joël, for example, makes precisely the same point in his *History of Ancient Philosophy* (1921), where he writes that "the theory of the unity of thinking and being is ontology, a theory which Parmenides founded and pursues with all the fanaticism of a founder [and] . . . [w]ith this unity [he] is a forerunner of . . . Hegel." *Geschichte der Antiken Philosophie* (Tübingen: J. C. B. Mohr, Paul Siebeck, 1921), I: 427–29.

62. Hegel, *Sämtliche Werke*, XII: 274, as cited in Heidegger, "Moira (Parmenides, Fragment VIII, 34–41)," in *Early Greek Thinking: The Dawn of Western Philosophy*, ed. David Farrell Krell and Frank A. Capuzzi (San Francisco: Harper and Row, 1975), 79–101, quotes at 82.

63. Heidegger, "Moira," 85: "All depends on whether the dialogue we have undertaken first of all and continually allows itself to respond to the questioning address of early thinking, or whether it simply closes itself off to such an address and cloaks early thought with the mantle of more recent doctrines."

64. Heidegger, "Moira," 83–84.

The differences between Heidegger and Rosenzweig concerning the place of Parmenides in the history of philosophy are noteworthy for two reasons. Because Rosenzweig inherited (from Hegel) the customary assessment of Parmenides as a proto-idealist, it was only natural for him to perceive an uninterrupted idealist tradition "from Parmenides to Hegel." And since he considered this tradition a source of error, he felt licensed to abandon it entirely and to pursue sources of insight elsewhere. This is a crucial point, since it helps to explain his wholesale rejection of Greek philosophy along with all of its modern variants. For Heidegger, however, such a conclusion would have appeared to rest on a misunderstanding of ancient Greek thought. Parmenides' dictum, he wrote, "became the guiding principle of Western philosophy *only when it ceased to be understood because its original truth could not be held fast*" (EM, English, 145, my emphasis; EM, 111). Thus "falling away from the truth of this maxim began with the Greeks themselves immediately after Parmenides," and the misinterpretation of his doctrine became "the fundamental attitude of the Western Spirit" (EM, English, 145; EM, 111).

The seemingly minor dispute between Rosenzweig and Heidegger concerning Parmenides' possible relation to idealism was therefore symptomatic of a much deeper disagreement concerning the origins of Western thought. Here one can recognize the old quarrel between Athens and Jerusalem. Since Heidegger resisted the modern interpretations of Parmenides as an idealist, he found it possible to glimpse a subterranean strain of ontology in the pre-Socratic tradition that could then be retrieved for productive dialogue. He could return to Greece in order to rethink what he called "the other beginning" of philosophy. But since Rosenzweig found no such refuge from idealism in ancient Greece, he therefore felt it imperative to resist the traditional narrative that grounds philosophy in ancient Greek thought. Alternative origins for the "new thinking" were to be found in the more "original" inheritances of Judaism. Rosenzweig's turn to Judaism thus gains greater philosophical legitimacy since he regarded the intellectual tradition of the Hellenistic West as corrupt from its inception.[65]

## *Nietzsche, Atheist and Man of Faith*

To understand *The Star*'s basic perception of the history of metaphysics, one must examine its more sustained account of how these "Greek" metaphysi-

---

65. The early Heidegger, however, was still markedly anti-Hellenistic. See, e.g., his 1920 allusion to "the necessity of a critical engagement with Greek philosophy and a transformation of Christian existence by means of that critique" thus opening a path toward "an original Christian theology—free of the Greek world." GA, 59, *Phänomenologie der Anschauung und des Ausdrucks,* ed. Claudius Strube (1993), 91.

cal beginnings are supposed to have brought about the theological crisis of modernity. According to Rosenzweig, the first signs of this crisis were already visible with Kant, who rejected the traditional validation of God's existence, the so-called ontological proof. By distinguishing between being *(Sein)* and existence *(Dasein)*, writes Rosenzweig, Kant "criticized to death" the older metaphysical assumption that divine existence is proven by the fact that we can think God. But it was Hegel who dealt theology its "death-blow." For Hegel, the ontological proof was merely a theological expression for the deeper, idealist doctrine that reason and reality are the same. Hegel thus exposed the Parmenidean heart of traditional religion, which according to Rosenzweig utterly neglects the preconceptual core of divine reality. For Rosenzweig, what was missing in all traditional philosophical concepts of the divine was precisely the "metaphysical" (in its post-traditional sense) insight that there must be something that exceeds intelligibility. "God must have existence [*Dasein*]," writes Rosenzweig, "prior to any identity of being and thought [*Sein und Denken*]" (SE, 21 [E, 19]). The older metaphysics neglected this non-identity, and so ended in atheism. Rosenzweig concludes that, if a partisan of the new thinking were to again attempt a deduction of God's reality after the fashion traditional metaphysicians, such a thinker would succeed only by inverting their categories. "[I]t were better the derivation of being from existence [*des Seins vom Dasein*]" than the "ever-repeated attempt to derive existence from being as was the habit of ontological proofs" (SE, 19–20 [E, 17–18]).[66]

For Rosenzweig, the metaphysical and religious tradition reached a moment of modern crisis with Nietzsche. Although it would be natural to assume that Nietzsche's declaration "God is dead" spelled the end of any and all philosophical faith, paradoxically, Rosenzweig sees Nietzsche's atheism as having opened up for the first time the possibility of a truly believing philosophy.[67] The explanation for this apparent paradox lies in the fact that Nietzsche was the very first philosopher who did not ground his rejection of God upon traditional metaphysical assumptions. "The history of philosophy had not yet beheld an atheism like that of Nietzsche," writes Rosenzweig. Nietzsche is "the first thinker who does not negate [*verneint*] God" but instead actually "denies" *(leugnet)* him "in the theological sense of that word" (SE, 20 [E, 18]). Nietzsche's atheism is thus no longer the expression

66. Schelling's late philosophy, Rosenzweig tells us, first showed the signs of adopting this latter alternative of deriving being *from* existence.

67. Here Rosenzweig may have inherited Nietzsche's own fundamentally ambivalent position between modernity and nostalgia for Greek religion. As Karl Löwith observed, Nietzsche's critique of Christianity involved "the paradoxical attempt to recapture antiquity at the extremity of modernism." *From Hegel to Nietzsche: The Revolution in Nineteenth-Century Thought*, trans. David E. Green (Garden City, N.Y.: Holt, Rinehart and Winston, 1964), 365.

of the traditional philosophical assumption that the mind embraces all that there is. Rather, Nietzsche for the first time contemplates what divine reality would mean for human experience, asking, "If God existed, how could I bear not to be God?" According to Rosenzweig, this question is unprecedented in the history of philosophy, since "[n]ever before had a philosopher thus stood, as it were, eye to eye before the living God." The vigor of Nietzsche's rejection lies in the fact, that unlike the metaphysicians before him, Nietzsche construes being as freedom. God's status as "mere Being" *(bloßes Sein)* was no longer of any concern—Nietzsche could simply "laugh it away even if he did 'believe' in it." But such is not the case of divine freedom. For Nietzsche, the very idea of God's freedom presented an obstacle in the path of his own philosophy of the human will to power as infinite. Nietzsche's atheism thus emerged from an unprecedented idea that any recognition of God's freedom must place our own sovereignty over the world in jeopardy. Rosenzweig concludes: "The first real human being among the philosophers was also the first who beheld God face to face— even if it was only in order to deny him" (SE, 20 [E, 18]).

Rosenzweig's arguments concerning Nietzsche and the end of traditional metaphysics present considerable confusion, since (as I have noted above) "metaphysics" for Rosenzweig indicates both the tradition of metaphysics (the older science of intelligible being) and the new, post-Nietzschean rejection of that tradition. The end of the older metaphysics is thus also the beginning of an authentically metaphysical concept of God.[68] For Rosenzweig, Nietzsche thus enjoys a unique and pivotal role in the historical "failure" of the philosophical tradition. On the one hand, Nietzsche's is the first attempt to confront the ramifications of a God who truly exists. But on the other hand, Nietzsche found just this possibility intolerable. His atheism is thus the last expression of the older principle that even the divine must disclose its secrets to the human being. In this sense, Nietzsche stands in Rosenzweig's argument at the boundary line between the two opposed notions of philosophy.

A remarkably similar ambivalence toward "metaphysics" characterizes Heidegger's early thought. Here, too, the fissure between the old metaphysics and the new is located within Nietzsche's ambiguous declaration that

---

68. Here the term *metaphysical* indicates a mode of existence that precedes thought. As I have already noted, this novel use of the term is somewhat ironic. For Rosenzweig metaphysics as traditionally understood attempts to seize upon a realm of being in thought alone. (It thus describes a positive capacity of the mind.) But the metaphysical in Rosenzweig's sense designates just that dimension of God in which we discover resistance to our concepts. (And it thus describes the "disunity thesis," a profound failure of mind.) Indeed, the newly designated "metaphysical" in God simply underscores the broader failure of traditional metaphysics as such.

God is dead; Nietzsche thus becomes both the culmination and the end of traditional philosophy. To grasp this point one must first recall the dual sense of metaphysics for Heidegger. In *Being and Time,* he wrote that "the meaning of Being has become quite forgotten in spite of all our interest in 'metaphysics'" (SZ, 2, and also 21).[69] While this might seem to suggest that that metaphysical speculation, if done properly, remains worthwhile, Heidegger's immediate concern (especially in §6 of the Introduction) is to show how Being has been misunderstood precisely in and through the metaphysical tradition. For Heidegger, then, the term *metaphysics* appears ambiguous. Indeed, in a preliminary note to the third edition of *Kant and the Problem of Metaphysics,* Heidegger confirms that the expression "the problem of metaphysics" has two senses *(doppeldeutig)* (KPM, xvii). On the one hand, it remained "the title for the difficulty of philosophy as such." On the other hand, the development of Western metaphysics since the Greeks followed a course that "hindered the possibility that the original [*ursprüngliche*] problematic can be taken up once again" (KPM, 8). In this sense, metaphysics also named Heidegger's own effort to raise "the question of Being." Much like Rosenzweig, Heidegger felt it necessary to distinguish in his early works between metaphysics in the traditional sense and metaphysics as the name for a new and more fruitful undertaking.[70]

A clear illustration for this second, more positive meaning can be found in Heidegger's 1929 treatise "What Is Metaphysics?" According to Heidegger, "metaphysical inquiry must be posed as a whole and form the essential position of the existence [*Dasein*] that questions." In other words, to ask a metaphysical question immediately casts light on the questioner as well: "We are questioning, here and now, for ourselves" (WM, 24). Heidegger's point is that the way we conduct philosophical investigations into this or that aspect of existence also shapes what kind of existence we may ascribe to ourselves. Science, for example, is solely concerned with worldly entities *(Seienden).* It never asks: "Why are there worldly entities at all, and why not rather nothing?" As a consequence, writes Heidegger, "science wishes to know nothing of the nothing" (WM, 27). But if we, as those who pursue science, thereby concern ourselves exclusively with worldly entities, it follows that a certain understanding of ourselves in terms of "the nothing" is necessarily obscured from view. Metaphysics in the positive sense raises this question of the "nothing." More importantly, it asks us what we learn about ourselves in relation to the nothing. Perhaps the most significant gain of this type of metaphysical inquiry, Heidegger tells us, is that it deepens our

69. Also see the elaborate discussion of the meaning of a "groundlaying" for metaphysics, in KPM, 5–18 and *passim.*

70. On the ambiguity of *metaphysics,* also see Heidegger's 1929 lectures, "Die philosophische Grundtendenzen der Gegenwart," in GA, 28, *Vorlesungen, 1919–1924,* esp. 21 and *passim.*

appreciation for our own finitude *(Endlichkeit)*. We strive for mastery over worldly entities, but despite our conceptual capacities there is a way in which this mastery is an illusion; for our concepts would have little bearing if there were not Being. Thus despite science and logic we are "held out into the nothing" (WM, 35). Moreover, especially in the realm of science and logic we think of ourselves as beings who enjoy an unlimited freedom. But this, too, rubs up against the possibility of the nothing, which exposes the finitude of human existence. Heidegger famously concludes that finitude is so fundamental to our constitution that "our most proper and deepest limitation refuses to yield to our freedom" ("So abgründig gräbt im Dasein die Verendlichung, daß sich unserer Freiheit die eigenste und tiefste Endlichkeit versagt" [WM, 38]).

Certain features of this argument bear an intriguing resemblance to Rosenzweig's own notion of metaphysics. First is the theme of conceptual limitation: like Rosenzweig, Heidegger claims that metaphysics in the new sense is a pursuit that actually takes note of the frustration of our efforts at logical mastery. Just as Rosenzweig calls God "the metaphysical" precisely because divine existence remains conceptually opaque, so too Heidegger finds in nothingness an unsurpassable barrier to thought. Second is the theme of freedom: according to Rosenzweig, Nietzsche was paradoxically the first philosopher to entertain the possibility of an authentic theology (even if he then rejected it), since Nietzsche alone first recognized that conceding any freedom to God would necessarily diminish the human claim of sovereignty in the world. Rosenzweig thus saw Nietzsche's rejection of God as a "curse" *(Fluch)*. This was an unprecedented sort of atheism, since it was born from concern for his own being as it would have suffered in an imagined encounter with a real God. Like Rosenzweig, Heidegger believed that an authentically metaphysical inquiry reveals the finitude at the core of our freedom.[71] And this is so in so radical a fashion that we cannot even bring ourselves before the nothing "through our own decision and will" (WM, 38). But for the most part, human beings are tempted to follow the path of science, which wants self-deceptively to dismiss the nothing "with a lordly wave of the hand." Like Rosenzweig, then, Heidegger blames the metaphysical tradition for having allowed us to evade a deeper understanding of the limitation intrinsic to human freedom.[72]

71. This is one of the central themes of Heidegger's confrontation with Cassirer. For example, Heidegger said there that "freeing" *(Befreiung)* is to be found "in becoming free for the finitude of Dasein." DVS, 284–85.

72. Significantly, Rosenzweig speaks of this evasion as both flight and curse *(Flucht, Fluch)*, an implicit reference to Schiller's dream of metaphysics and an anticipation of Heidegger's definition of inauthenticity as a "flight" *(Flucht)* from Dasein's "ownmost" being. SZ, §40, 184–91.

Finally, and perhaps most importantly, Rosenzweig shares with Heidegger a pronounced regard for the philosophical and historical significance of Nietzsche's atheism. What is perhaps most striking in Rosenzweig's new "theological" philosophy is that it seems somehow to incorporate modern atheism rather than turning tail and seeking refuge in the metaphysical tradition. Rosenzweig's argument takes a brilliant turn; he reads Nietzsche's celebration of human will not as strength but as cowardice: it was only because Nietzsche correctly sensed that the new theology represented a real and unprecedented threat to human freedom that he was repelled from actual belief. Paradoxically, then, Rosenzweig's theology embraces Nietzsche's denial of God. Yet even while Nietzsche himself may have found solace in a doctrine of anthropocentric sovereignty, he at least deserves credit for having discerned the possibility of a theology without metaphysics. The only genuine theology, Rosenzweig suggests, is one courageous enough to surpass metaphysical collapse. In this sense, Rosenzweig's new theology has (in Margarete Susman's phrase) "gone beyond the zenith of atheism."[73]

Heidegger, of course, does not follow Rosenzweig's path "beyond" atheism. But an intriguing similarity can be found if one examines Heidegger's remarks concerning Nietzsche's role in the philosophical tradition.[74] In the 1943 lecture "The Word of Nietzsche: 'God Is Dead,'" Heidegger interprets the "metaphysical meaning" in Nietzsche's atheism as the claim that "the suprasensible ground consisting of the supersensory world, thought as the operative, working reality of everything real, has become unreal." Nietzsche's various assaults on the notion of a suprasensible and intelligible world thus pointed toward the "overcoming of metaphysics" *(die Überwindung der Metaphysik)*. But Heidegger considers Nietzsche's "overcoming" only a partial success. While Nietzsche may have held out the hope of a complete overcoming of metaphysics, he did not successfully follow through on his promise, since he still clung to the human will to power and lodged it in the metaphysical space taken over from traditional theology. Nietzsche's overcoming of metaphysics thus remained "incomplete."[75]

As one can see, this argument closely resembles Rosenzweig's claim that Nietzsche's atheism was also the beginning of an authentic theology. Hei-

73. Susman, "Exodus from Philosophy."

74. Most of Heidegger's interpretation of Nietzsche is found in the notes for lectures delivered between 1936 and 1940, so we must rule out any direct historical connection.

75. See Heidegger, "Überwindung der Metaphysik," originally in *Vorträge und Aufsätze* (Pfullingen: Neske, 1954); reprinted in *The End of Metaphysics,* trans. Joan Stambaugh (New York: Harper and Row, 1973); and also "Die Überwindung der Metaphysik," GA, 67, *Metaphysik und Nihilismus,* esp. 46–50.Elsewhere Heidegger writes that because of his theory of value, Nietzsche is "the most unrestrained Platonist in the history of Western metaphysics." "Plato's Doctrine of Truth," in *Pathmarks,* ed. William McNeill (Cambridge: Cambridge University Press, 1998), 174.

degger, too, indulged the paradox of calling Nietzsche "the sole true believer" of the nineteenth century.[76] Both Heidegger and Rosenzweig seem
to have recognized that Nietzsche's philosophy was the staging-ground for
their own efforts to surmount the metaphysical tradition. Yet both of them
concluded that Nietzsche's jealous concern for the human will to power
prohibited him from bringing his preparatory assault on traditional metaphysics to completion.

Ultimately, these various similarities between Rosenzweig and Heidegger
concerning the Nietzschean "death of God" inform a greater, shared understanding of the tasks of philosophy in the funeral wake of the metaphysical tradition. Like Heidegger, Rosenzweig was concerned to prove his
mettle as a modern philosopher capable of discerning what has gone awry
in the tradition "from Parmenides to Hegel" and possessing the strength
to overcome it, without retreating like Nietzsche to the well-trodden path
of metaphysical error. Rosenzweig clearly perceived himself as a post-
Nietzschean philosopher, yet paradoxically wished to embrace Nietzsche's
atheism for the sake of genuine belief. This required a new mode of thought
courageous enough, in Nietzsche's words, to "wipe away the infinite horizon." In theological terms, Rosenzweig's new thinking would attempt to articulate the concepts of religion but without recourse to the language of the
metaphysical tradition. But along with the death of God, philosophy would
also be required to confront the death of the human being.

### Death, Nothingness, and the Ontological Difference

One of the most significant barriers to understanding the topic of death in
Rosenzweig's *Star* is that it can easily be read in an anthropological mode.[77]
As one of the conventional preoccupations of modern existentialism, it is
easily construed as a *memento mori:* we mortals live in fear and trembling,
and so the chief business of philosophy is to dwell upon the inevitable and
issue all sorts of dark and ennobling thoughts. The temptation to read
Rosenzweig in this fashion is quite strong, thanks in part to his theatrical
exposition:

> Let man creep like a worm into the folds of the naked earth before the fast-
> approaching volleys of a blind death from which there is no appeal; let him
> sense there, forcibly, inexorably, what he otherwise never senses: that his I
> would be but an It if it died; let him therefore cry his very I out with every cry

---

76. See Karl Löwith, "The Political Implications of Heidegger's Existentialism," in Wolin,
*The Heidegger Controversy,* 172.

77. Compare Heidegger's complaints that the themes of "philosophical anthropology"
were often conflated with his own work ; e.g., GA, 28, *Der deutsche Idealismus,* "Die Enthüllung
der Philosophischen Grundtendenzen der Gegenwart," 9–47, esp. 21 and *passim.*

that is still in his throat against that from which there is no appeal, from which there threatens such unthinkable annihilation. (SE, 3 [E, 3])

There is a noteworthy historical reference in this passage. The "folds of the naked earth" may mean trenches, and the approaching "volleys" may indicate gunfire. At first glance, this is indeed a meditation on the ever-present possibility of death as felt by a soldier in the trenches of the First World War. But Rosenzweig uses the experience of mortality in warfare as a philosophical allegory; and it is this deeper purpose that most demands attention.

From the very first lines of the book, death has a self-evidently conceptual status: "From death, from the fear of death, begins all Knowledge of the All." Here Rosenzweig juxtaposes the individual and subjective possibility of death with the philosophical attempt to know the totality. The "All" is a conceptual structure, the Absolute as grasped by the mind. According to Rosenzweig, because philosophy since Parmenides has wished to seize being and thought as a unity, it must necessarily disregard whatsoever threatens to shatter that unity. It therefore attempts to "rid the world of what is singular [*das Einzelne*]." But death in its essence is a phenomenon that necessarily individuates whatsoever it confronts. Death is, in each and every case, death for some specific existence. Man, insofar as he is alive, is singled out by what Heidegger called "Being-towards-death" *(Sein-zum-Tode)*. Death as this future possibility is always something toward which one is moving. Given that, for both Rosenzweig and Heidegger, identity cannot be isolated from the temporal stream, our being-toward-death is constitutive of who we are. And as an inevitable possibility, death resists the philosopher's attempts at evasion, the wish to restore us, in Rosenzweig's phrase, "from death" *(vom Tode)*.

The crucial thing to be noticed here is that, like Heidegger, Rosenzweig is not trying to say something about the actual *experience* of dying. He wishes to take cognizance of death as a possibility, not an event. This is why Heidegger calls human existence being-towards-death, and it is also why Rosenzweig starts with the words "from death." Both philosophers are defining the inner space of human life by its temporal movement toward completion. Notice, then, that Rosenzweig is not a mystic interested in what it might feel like to die. Rather, he construes death as a necessarily constitutive but always potential feature of life: "As long as he lives on earth, he will also remain in fear of Earthly things [soll er auch in der Angst des Irdischen bleiben]."[78]

Philosophy, however, strives to free the human being from recognizing this potential; it wants to envelop the "earthly" in "the blue mist of its

---

78. The prominence of these themes in the *Star* does not mean that Rosenzweig suffered from any kind of morbid fascination with death, as at least one recent critic has suggested.

thought of the totality [*ihres Allgedankens*]" (SE, 4 [E, 4]). But death as a possibility around each particular *life* marks out that life as a particular when it might have seemed otherwise at home within the unified structure of *knowledge*. The possibility of death is thus linked to what Heidegger regarded as the Parmenidean "disunity thesis": it awakens the mind to the existence that must precede thought and calls that existence into question in a way that exceeds the capacities of conceptual speculation. Death is therefore what Heidegger called one's "ownmost" *(eigenste)* possibility, and as such it is "*nonrelational*" *(unbezügliche)* (SZ, 251; my emphasis). In Rosenzweig's words, "*Only what is singular may die*" (SE, 4 [E, 4]; my emphasis). For Rosenzweig, however, this singularity presents traditional philosophy with an impassable obstruction. Philosophy (here, idealism) always strives after unity—it folds the finite into the infinite and subsumes particulars under universals. For this reason, philosophy cannot really acknowledge the nonrelational and singular possibility of death.[79]

Rosenzweig is careful to note that philosophy may sometimes pretend to address death. This happens when death is construed as a generalized and homogeneous "nothingness." But this general Nothing *(das Nichts)* is still not a particular death: "Before the one and universal knowledge of the All," philosophy can only recognize the validity of "the one and universal Nothing." The attempt to universalize death's meaning thus misses precisely the individuating and nonrelational quality that makes death in every case a potential death-for-*someone*. As a possibility that dissociates the particular from its surroundings, the specificity of death will always escape merely conceptual notice. Rosenzweig states this idea with a riddle-like phrase: "The Nothing is not Nothing, it is Something" ("Das Nichts ist nicht Nichts, es ist Etwas"; SE, 5 [E, 5]). For Heidegger as well, the nothing must not be considered as the sheer absence of Being, a blank without consequence. Rather, it is precisely what exposes the gap between the particular and its universal ground. It is a nothing that "does something." Hence Heidegger's claim (echoing Rosenzweig), "the nothing itself nihilates" ("Das Nichts selbst nichtet") (WM, 34).[80]

79. "[A]n All itself," explains Rosenzweig, "would not die, and in the All nothing may die." SE, 4 (E, 4).

80. Rosenzweig considers one alternative, but quickly dismisses it. Let us imagine, he writes, that philosophy were somehow to attempt to recognize death as a particularity. This would require that it refrain from the conceptual transfiguration whereby the death of the fearing individual is subsumed under the general concept of the "Nothing." Philosophy in this new sense could no longer "plug up its ears." It would find itself forced to start from the premise that "every new death-nothing [*Todesnichts*]" is in fact a "something [*Etwas*]," which is "not to be talked or silenced away [*nicht wegzuredendes, nicht wegzuschweigendes*]." But this counterfactual suggestion merely underscores his point that there is no good way for thought to wax

In *The Star of Redemption*, then, death holds a special significance in that it exposes a fundamental insufficiency at the heart of philosophical speculation. As a particularity that cannot be surpassed, death is intrinsically manifold. Each death is yet another singularity, another fact that thus resists being subsumed into a general meaning. "Death," writes Rosenzweig, discloses the "multiplicity of the nothing [*Vielheit des Nichts*]," and this multiplicity dissembles the "foundational thought" of philosophy, the ideal of a "unified and universal Knowledge of the All" ("den Gedanken des einen und allgemeinen Erkennens des All"; SE, 4–5 [E, 4–5]). For Rosenzweig, then, acknowledging the singularity of death helps first of all to discover the human being as an object prior to reason. For each and every finite being, death is a substantive "something"—it is the specific event that *individuates each being in its particularity*. But because this "something" exceeds philosophy, the object it discloses must also exceed universalizing philosophical reason. In this sense, death helps to disclose the human being as what Rosenzweig calls an "irrational" object ("irrational" here meaning that it lacks the articulate bonds with the Universal as reason would demand) (SE, 21 [E, 19]).[81] The individual, regarded as a singularity, must precede any philosophical efforts that would regard her as fungible and subsumable under universalizable, ethical norms. Rosenzweig names this kind of dissociated human being "metaethical."

Following this model, death serves a more general, methodological purpose in *The Star*. For just as its "nothingness" exposes the individual as an irrational object, so too it can function as a kind of wedge to break open the preconceptual facets of all phenomena. At the very least, it names a "something" in being that exceeds reason's grasp. So if death is the specific "nothing" that discloses human being prior to rational reflection, this at least raises the possibility of isolating any element of philosophy as an "irrational object"—a "something" that "does not require thought in order to be." Death is therefore a sign for any object of reflection that philosophy has missed something crucial at the bare and prereflective core of being. The

---

eloquent about death as it simply will not surrender something like a universal "meaning." In short, because there is no "death" in philosophy, there is no "philosophy of death." SE, 4–5 (E, 4–5).

81. Note that "irrational" just means "prior to," in that it is the condition upon which meanings can be taken up for cognitive inspection. Talk about "irrational" objects should not mislead us into regarding Rosenzweig as a philosopher "against" reason. Steven Schwarzschild's comparative study of Rosenzweig and Heidegger polemically concludes that both of them had betrayed the only true "rational" stance in Western philosophy (best embodied for Schwarzschild by neo-Kantianism). A sketch of Schwarzschild's essay was published as "Franz Rosenzweig and Martin Heidegger: The German and Jewish Turn to Ethnicism," in Kassel, II *(Das neue Denken und seine Dimensionen)*: 887–90. The longer document is unpublished; I thank Samuel Moyn for making a copy available to me.

"nothing" thus becomes Rosenzweig's heuristic for seizing upon this naked existence.

Rosenzweig proposes that this methodological use of the "nothing" is first theorized in Cohen's "principle of origins." According to Rosenzweig, this principle explains that when reasoning sets out to understand any phenomenon, it must recognize that the objects available for thought gain their specific being only against the background of an equally specific negation. The mathematical instrument of the differential indicates the entanglement of being with the negativity that exceeds all thought. It thus "teaches us to recognize the origin of the Something in the Nothing." Admittedly, Cohen's logical doctrine appears at first glance idealist, since it conceives of any finitude as having its origin precisely in the *thought* of the infinite—a seeming affirmation of the mind's spontaneity. But Rosenzweig claims that in this respect Cohen's philosophy pointed beyond the magic circle of idealism, since the chief effect of the principle of origins is to challenge the idealist notion that the nothing is an undifferentiated "zero" without consequence for philosophy. Reason, especially in its Hegelian form, conceives of the nothing as unified and thinkable negativity, a blank that cannot disrupt the dialectical union of thought and Being. By contrast, Cohen's principle of origins demonstrates that the nothing is precisely that *particularity* from which all phenomena first gain their differentiation.

Rosenzweig readily admitted that this interpretation of Cohen's philosophy was unorthodox. The principle of origins was widely considered a Platonist doctrine, since it ascribed the highest reality to the entities revealed in mathematical reasoning. But according to Rosenzweig, the Platonist interpretation was incorrect. Cohen "was something quite different from a mere epigone to this movement, which had truly run its course"; in fact, Cohen "took his stand in the most decided opposition precisely to Hegel's founding of logic on the concept of Being, and thereby in turn [broke from] the whole philosophy that Hegel had enjoyed as his inheritance." In Rosenzweig's opinion, then, Cohen's theory of the infinitesimal contained a lesson "at odds with the appearance of his work" and even "contrary to his self-understanding" (SE, 23 [E, 20]).[82]

---

82. Here is a perfect illustration of Rosenzweig's general tendency to read the history of philosophy against the grain. As we have seen in the previous chapters, Rosenzweig found in both Hegel and Cohen moments of dissent—patterns of thought born out of religious speculation that conflicted with the broader idealist purposes of their thought. This is Rosenzweig's most characteristic interpretative gesture, to think the categories of idealism through until they can be made to yield unintended and self-subverting conclusions. In the introduction to *The Star,* he repeats this gesture, wresting even what seems Cohen's most idealist principle from its original framework and applying this principle toward radically new ends. In *The Star,* the principle of origins now becomes an instrument for disclosing the three principal elements of the book—God, Man, and World—in their fundamental "irrationality."

Rosenzweig's reflections on death, nothingness, and negation bear a startling resemblance to themes found in the early Heidegger. First, Heidegger follows Rosenzweig in claiming that death is an event of pure dissociation, which as such individuates the human being. In *Being and Time* death is therefore called "Dasein's ownmost [*eigenste*] possibility." Heidegger's point was to underscore the notion that death is a possibility whose specificity exceeds any generalized concept. As such, death is what he calls "nonrelational" *(unbezüglich)*. There is no way, he explained, that either the death of others or any available, shared notions of death may feasibly "substitute" for our own potential deaths. As existent beings, we each are individuated by its singular possibility. This sort of particularity cannot be overcome. No experiences such as the loss of another, a ritual of public mourning, or an act of commemoration, could ever provide a substitute for the factical disclosure of finitude that is available only for each and every one of us as individuals. We have no real "access" to the "loss-of-Being" of another. And so, while there may be reflection upon death in the fields of biology and psychology, and while there may even be a "theology of death," a truly phenomenological appreciation of the human being demands that one not generalize—in Heidegger's words, one must not "outstrip"—death's possibility as a potential for each and every human being.[83]

These arguments about death speak to its emotional impact as well as its conceptual meaning. Heidegger also seems to share Rosenzweig's suspicion that any attempts to "think" death must somehow ameliorate its impact or cover over the specific state of mind that it arouses. As a philosopher interested in the basic moods that might be said to underlie cognition, Heidegger was very interested in the specific "state-of-mind" *(Befindlichkeit)* that seizes the human being when confronted with his being-towards-death—he famously called it *Angst* (fear, or, more idiomatically, anxiety). He argued that authentic philosophy does not ameliorate but recognizes death, and then uses it to expose the finitude of the human being. In similar fashion, Rosenzweig argues that if thought is to have any integrity it must thematize rather than overcome the fear that accompanies an individual's authentic confrontation with his always-potential death. As Rosenzweig notes, "the Fear of Earthly things [*die Angst des Irdischen*] shall be taken from him only with the Earthly itself." This specific kind of fear is not a simple "emotion," since it is constitutive of being human: "So long as he lives upon the Earth, *he shall remain in the fear of the Earth*" (my emphasis). Both Rosenzweig and Heidegger are aware that human beings have at their disposal a variety of falsifying thoughts and philosophies that would surmount this fundamental fear. But

83. In Heidegger's summary formulation, death thus "reveals itself as that possibility which is one's ownmost, which is nonrelational, and which is not to be outstripped." SZ, 251; BT, 294.

both of them urge us to recognize that any proper understanding of human finitude must somehow gain its nourishment from the encounter with anxiety, since this anxiety is at the core of individual life.[84]

Most surprising, perhaps, is the fact that both Rosenzweig and Heidegger interpret death as pointing to the productive "nothingness" that first allows for the most basic exposure of phenomena in their being. Because death discloses a specific kind of "nothing," it opens up a sphere exceeding all conceptual relatedness, and thus provides a primal encounter with phenomena as objects available for pre-rational consideration. This is the chief lesson in Rosenzweig's rather cryptic talk about the "nothing" and its methodological use in generating a "something" for philosophy. The same idea later appears in Heidegger's "What Is Metaphysics?" Against Cohen and the neo-Kantian theory of logic, Heidegger argued that "the nothing" *(das Nichts)* should never be equated with negation *(Verneinung)*. By doing so we would attain merely "the formal concept of the imagined nothing but never the nothing itself." Indeed, "the nothing is the origin of negation, not vice versa" (WM, 37).[85]

Like Rosenzweig, Heidegger insisted that there is a fatal misunderstanding at the core of the neo-idealist thesis that Being originates in negation. For this doctrine is only possible if one believes in the identity of Being and Thought. Through death, however, we are compelled to recognize a nothing that exceeds all reflection. The "nothing" is not originally a concept; the *concept* of the nothing is born out of *the encounter with the possibility of nothingness*. In the fear of death, man is "held out into the nothing." Logical negation, therefore, is only possible because nothingness itself opens up the prior moment where—as Parmenides first sensed (according to Heidegger only, not Rosenzweig)—thought and being are not originally an inseparable whole.

For both Rosenzweig and Heidegger, Cohen's doctrine of infinite negation was an important example of the unwarranted cognitivism in traditional philosophy. But according to Rosenzweig, what Cohen in fact discovered (though unwittingly) was quite the opposite—he exposed the nothingness

---

84. On the anticipation of death as the highest moment in life, Rosenzweig observed to Gritli: "Not to be ready for death [*todesbereit*] means namely nothing but—not to be wholly living, [for] one is that in the highest life. And what you call piety [*Frömmigkeit*] is indeed nothing but this highest life." GB (8.11.1918), 180.

85. As I noted in chapter 1, this is a more or less explicit attack on Cohen's panlogism. Also see my essay "Science, Finitude, and Infinity: The End of Neo-Kantianism and the Birth of Existentialism," *Jewish Social Studies* 6, 1 (fall 1999): 30–53. On Heidegger's hostility to Cohen, see DVS, esp. 274. On Heidegger's assumption of the Freiburg chair, his departure from Marburg, and his relationship to Cohen, see Heidegger, "Zur Geschichte des philosophischen Lehrstuhles seit 1866," Appendix VI, in KPM, 304–11.

that lies beyond the intellect at the very root of Being.[86] In a similar fashion, Heidegger insists that neo-idealism has matters upside down—nothingness is the origin of negation, not its conceptual precipitate.

Both Rosenzweig and Heidegger were adept at showing how the philosophical tradition contains its own "unthought" negation. Here it is interesting to note how much both Heidegger and Rosenzweig singled out Kantian themes for special attention. Both suggested that Kant's doctrine of the schematism was an unannounced herald for the end of traditional philosophy. In *Kant and the Problem of Metaphysics* (1932), Heidegger would argue regarding the schematism that Kant himself had glimpsed the "irrationality" at the core of his own thought. According to Heidegger, this became obvious in Kant's theory of the imagination, which Kant called the "dark root" uniting sensibility and understanding. This indicated a hidden insight concerning the mutual entanglement of reason and temporality from which Kant—in Heidegger's words—"drew back in fear." Heidegger followed with the curious suggestion that Kant's philosophy "almost" succeeded in understanding a deep truth otherwise hidden from the philosophical tradition. The implication was that in these obscure references to the "mystery buried in the depths of the human soul" Kant only "sensed" the actual meaning of his philosophy. It therefore remained to Heidegger alone to bring about a genuine overcoming of metaphysics.

Rosenzweig anticipates this very same idea in *The Star:*

> the dark terms in which [Kant] occasionally speaks of the mysterious "root" of both [understanding and sensibility] are presumably attempts to grope [*er-tasten*] for a fixed point for the metaphysical Nothing of knowledge. (SE, 24 [E, 21])

Like Heidegger, Rosenzweig makes the point here that what may seem to be the unbridled idealism of the philosophical tradition barely succeeds in masking its deeper failure. Cognitivism itself rests upon a more profound anti-cognitivism, as even Kant's theory of the schematism betrayed an awareness that concepts cannot grasp the human being's primary relation to the world. Heidegger saw Kant's philosophy as an unwitting and ultimately unsuccessful effort to provide a "groundlaying for metaphysics" *(Grundlegung der Metaphysik)*. And much like Rosenzweig, Heidegger meant by "metaphysics" precisely a discipline that begins by recognizing the "nothing" at the root of knowledge and then builds from it an appreciation of the preconceptual groundwork of experience.

---

86. Rosenzweig does admit that Cohen "would be far from admitting" the truth of this discovery. Indeed, the uses to which Rosenzweig has put the master's philosophy run "contrary to [Cohen's] own impression of himself." SE, 23 (E 20).

These observations suggest that Rosenzweig's bewildering reflections on the "nothing" are best understood in light of what Heidegger later called the "ontological difference." To grasp this point, one should first recall that God, Man, and World are meant to enjoy equal primordiality in Rosenzweig's system. But this means they must be evaluated in their factical independence: the world revealed by the nothing is the "metalogical"; the human being so revealed is the "metaethical"; and God is the "metaphysical." The "meta" terminology thus designates the phenomenon as it exists prior to its conceptual relatedness with either of the other elements of the system. In relation to Man and World, for example, God remains metaphysical (i.e., self-enclosed and without relation). So it is specifically the "nothing" that first discloses God's metaphysical being. Thus the very notion of God as the "metaphysical" indicates the ontological rift between God's being and the being of the other phenomena.[87] Rosenzweig goes on to show that the specific "nothing" discloses each of the three elements in its ontological distinction. They are separated, one from another, at the deepest stratum of their being.[88]

This separation bears much resemblance to what Heidegger called the ontological difference. In "What Is Metaphysics?" and the companion essay "On the Essence of Grounds," Heidegger argued that the discipline of metaphysics as traditionally understood had remained wedded to the concept of being as it obtains for worldly entities *(Seiende);* it had thus failed to capture the Being of beings *(Sein des Seienden).* And so, the philosophical tradition as a whole had fallen into the error of thinking about Being as if it were present-at-hand, merely "occurrent" in the objective manner of worldly entities. Furthermore, because worldly being was then construed as a logical category, Being was finally reduced to a little more than a logical relation. For these reasons, Heidegger generally spoke of the history of metaphysics as a path of error. But in the 1929 lectures, he proposed that the discipline of metaphysics could be construed in a different, positive fashion. Rather than dismissing the nothing as the sheer absence of Being, Heidegger suggested that by engaging with the nothing we might be able to seize upon Being prior to any of its conceptual entanglements. He therefore suggested that metaphysics, properly construed, was a discipline deeper than logic. Metaphysics thinks the nothing and thereby allows us to think the difference between Being and beings. The Being of beings is thus ontologically distinct from both conceptual being and the being of the

87. See esp. the comparison to "pagan" metaphysics, at the cost of the ontological differences, at SE, 43 (E, 40).
88. Another critic notes, "Above all, the logical-grammatical form of the *and* is valid for the ontological-methodological multidimensionality of that which is, as impressed upon the particular elements of experience." Wiehl, "Experience in Rosenzweig's New Thinking," 57.

world. And it is the nothing that first discloses this as the "ontological difference."[89]

On the philosophical importance of death, nothingness, and negation, Heidegger and Rosenzweig seemed in close agreement in several respects. Both believed that the only proper kind of philosophy would be one capable of grasping our being-toward-death as a constitutive potential of human life. They further agreed that the philosophical tradition taken as a whole seeks constantly to evade this potential. Both further claimed that "nothingness" appears phenomenologically only when one is most alive to the possibility of death, that is, when seized by anxiety. More specifically, both construed this "nothingness" as a signal that traditional philosophy places undue confidence in the universalizing power of concepts, whereas the nonrelationality of the nothing is more basic than cognition. Most important of all, both Rosenzweig and Heidegger claimed that if, rather than evading the nothing, one begins instead with a sober appreciation of its primacy, it will then be possible to resist the sort of ontological reduction that has been a perennial error in the philosophical tradition.

They disagreed, however, on just what kind of ontological reduction was at issue. Heidegger wished to guard against reducing Being into either worldly or conceptual presence, while Rosenzweig feared any ontological reduction amongst the three primal elements—God, World, and Man. For both Rosenzweig and Heidegger, the effort to flatten out such distinctions—to misconstrue one kind of being as another—was the habitual mistake of the older metaphysics, since it effaced the "ontological difference." For Heidegger this named the distinction between beings and Being. For Rosenzweig, however, the ontological difference was threefold—it named the distinction between the three primal elements. And while Heidegger insisted that "Being" was indeed the ontological condition for all beings, Rosenzweig made it a cardinal principle of his philosophy that no single element could claim ontological primacy—not even God. Despite this important disagreement, however, both Rosenzweig and Heidegger could still agree that is death alone that yields philosophy a glimpse at the nothingness hidden in the fissures of what there is.

### The Hermeneutics of Life

As noted above, Rosenzweig objected to the attempt to make death itself a "topic of philosophy." Rather, it was the *possibility* of death alone that he re-

89. See Heidegger's introductory remarks relating the concept of the "nothing" to that of the "ontological difference" in *Vom Wesen des Grundes* (On the essence of grounds), (Frankfurt am Main: Vittorio Klostermann, 1929; 1949), esp. the "Vorwort zum dritten Auflage," 5. Also see WM, 46.

garded as helpful in illuminating certain features of life. It is therefore life itself that provides *The Star of Redemption* with its basic interpretative horizon. "Life" is indeed one of the most recurrent terms in *The Star*, yet it is also one of the most neglected.[90] Throughout the book, Rosenzweig implies that life holds a salvific meaning, since only if we return to living experience can we at last surmount the errors of idealist speculation. The famous closing lines of the conclusion form a narrowing column of prose that seems intended as an arrow—they return the reader through the "Gate" *(Tor)* of the text and point beyond it "into life" *(Ins Leben)*. To understand the concept of redemption in *The Star* thus requires a deeper assessment of the concept of life and its place in the system's teleological structure.

If "life" is the final word of the book, it is also in a certain sense the first. As already noted above, the opening lines of the introduction describe the self-deception of traditional philosophy, its effort to evade mortality—to escape "from death" *(Vom Tode)*. It would be easy, then, to interpret *The Star*'s structure as a thematic movement "from death" and "to life." But this would be misleading. To be sure, Rosenzweig's aim in the introduction is to confront the specific and irresistible fact of mortality. But he also wants to emphasize how death resists philosophical transfiguration. There is no philosophy of death; there is merely philosophy insofar as it takes shape *within* death's boundaries. Rosenzweig specifies that "man does not want to flee" from his finitude; rather, "he wishes to remain, he wishes—to live." The appearance of this phrase, *"er will—leben,"* at the very beginning of the book (in obvious anticipation of the ending phrase) suggests that the deeper structure of the book is circular, not linear. *The Star* does not move "from death," and "into life." Rather, it describes a circular orbit—from life to life.[91]

The circular structure of *The Star* is confirmed when one glances at Rosenzweig's closing remarks in the penultimate sections of the book (directly before the concluding "Gate"). Here Rosenzweig returns with dramatic emphasis to the opening idea that we are incapable of seizing the truth in its totality. "A direct view of the whole truth is granted only to him who sees it in God. But such an unobstructed vision is beyond life [*jenseits*

---

90. Amos Funkenstein observes: "Rosenzweig became, through his experience as a soldier, a worshipper of life, life as such, life of and in the world. . . . Zest for life is the deepest drive in the *Stern der Erlösung*." *Perceptions of Jewish History*, 300.

91. On the primacy of the life horizon and the impossibility of philosophizing an actual death experience, Rosenzweig wrote to Gritli: " . . . *you have not yet experienced death and birth, only that which lies between them, life. Death remains unconceived*, even if one has experienced it, but birth remains so as well; what is conceived-seized [*begriffen-ergriffen*] is only life." GB (8.4.1918), 68–69; my emphasis; ellipsis in original. And see Freund, *Rosenzweig's Philosophy of Existence*, esp. 3–13.

*des Lebens]*" (SE, 463 [E, 416]). We are creatures *(Geschöpfe)*, precisely insofar as we do not possess the truth as a whole. And as creatures, we remain
"within the boundaries of mortality [*Grenzen der Sterblichkeit*]." If God were
to grant us more than our portion of the truth, this would require that he
wrest us from the "boundaries of the human." But he does not grant us such
a vision, nor do we desire it. We rest and remain "dependent upon our creatureliness" ("Wir hängen an unsrer Geschöpflichkeit"). The language here
is clearly reminiscent of the introduction: "Precisely through and within
these boundaries" we remain who we are. In sum, "We want to *live*" ("Wir
wollen ja *leben)*" (SE, 462–63 [E, 416–17]; my emphasis).

Despite all the philosophical peregrinations of the book, it thus seems
that Rosenzweig has returned in the end to the themes of the very beginning. The concluding lines of *The Star*'s introductory section, "On the Possibility of Knowing the All," offer the reader a clear explanation of the
book's circular structure. We are first required to "disassemble" *(zerstückeln)*
the All, but only as the precondition to discovering it once again *(wieder-
zufinden)* at the end of the inquiry.[92] Thus the reader is urged to conceive of
the book as an interpretative effort that moves "from life" back "to life," following a circular movement that thematizes and then returns to the object
known prior to questioning. This is the familiar structure of the hermeneutic circle, as it is summarized in a closing passage from Part III:

> [I]f the "truly" and even the highest "truly,"—the "Yes" and the "Amen" that
> are collectively spoken . . . in chorus [by those] facing *The Star* of Redemp-
> tion—remain the sign of creatureliness . . . then the end sinks back into the
> beginning [*so sinkt das Ende in den Anfang zurück*].[93]

The hermeneutic and circular structure—from life back to life—was
recognized by various earlier critics of the book. Margarete Susman, characteristically sensitive to the philosophical dimension of Rosenzweig's work,
concluded her 1931 review of the second edition of *The Star* with a reference to the hermeneutics of life. As against the idealist tradition, she
writes, the "inversion" *(Umkehrung)* of thought found in Rosenzweig's book
is guided throughout by its "living question" whereby it "digs itself out and
returns back along the path to its beginning," toward that in which redemptive truth is found, "to life itself."[94]

92. To summarize this process of destruction and recovery, Rosenzweig quotes Goethe's
*Faust:* "Be drowned then! I could also say: Arise!" ("Versinke denn! ich könnt' auch sagen:
steige!"). SE, 24 (E, 22).

93. I have edited this passage; the entire phrase may be found in SE, 463 (E, 417).

94. Susman, "Anzeigen," *Der Morgen* 7, 4 (October 1931): 379–80. Rosenzweig thus remarked to Gritli that he perceived an affinity between *The Star* and a work by Hans Ehrenberg
which they thought to name simply, "Life: An Exegesis." Both books, wrote Rosenzweig, were

Some interpreters have been tempted to read the prominent call to "life" at the end of the text as if it were an exhortation to abandon any further philosophical activity. Hans Ehrenberg, for example, in a 1921 review for the *Frankfurter Zeitung,* expressed dismay at the closing phrase of the book, which he construed as a call to quit philosophy in favor of life.[95] But such a reading is clearly incorrect. In a 1921 letter to Ehrenberg, Rosenzweig explained that the closing phrase was not meant as a principled rejection of all further philosophy: "The 'Life' of the ending word is hardly the opposite of 'philosophy.' . . . In this life there can also be philosophizing; and why not? (I do it myself)." The aim of *The Star,* he concludes, is "anti-mystical, but not anti-intellectual."[96] The emphasis upon the theme of life, then, should not be read as an "exit" from philosophy. Instead, it announces a special type of philosophy, a circular "return" to the grounds of factical life. In this sense, philosophy loses its appearance as a productive discipline and becomes hermeneutic—a thematic investigation of what is implicitly there from the start. In the essay "The New Thinking," Rosenzweig writes that "[a] knowledge, out of which something comes [*herauskommt*] is exactly like a cake into which something has been put [*heineingetan*]." What was put into *The Star of Redemption,* he writes, "was to begin with the experience of factuality [*Tatsächlichkeit*] prior to all facts of real experience." Accordingly, what is "first" in experience "must also return in the last of truth" (ND, 158).

All of this suggests that *The Star* should not be read as a "progressive" argument, but rather as a hermeneutic investigation. As noted earlier, the book's star shape prohibits our finding any easy beginning or end to the system. Rather, it is meant to be considered all at once, with an ever-deepening appreciation of the meanings that are there from the beginning. *The Star* carries out such a hermeneutic reading from the inside of experience, uniting past, present, and future meaning into a particular "life space" that is defined by these three coordinates. For Rosenzweig, "taking time seriously" means that one is never "outside" this threefold horizon. Religious experience, like all life-experience, exhibits a threefold temporal structure, which *The Star* calls creation (past), revelation (present), and redemption (future).

As cited above, Rosenzweig characterizes all such experience as "factuality" *(Tatsächlichkeit).*[97] But what does factuality mean? To answer this ques-

---

to present "life as that between beginning and end [das Leben als das zwischen Anfang und Ende]." GB (25.12.1918), 205.

95. Ehrenberg, "Neue Philosophie, *Frankfurter Zeitung,* December 29, 1921; in English, "New Philosophy," in Udoff and Galli eds., *Rosenzweig's "The New Thinking,"* 112–20.

96. *Briefe,* N.330, An Hans Ehrenberg (Kassel, Ende Dez. 1921), 413–14.

97. Rosenzweig affirmed to Gritli that "Tatsächlichkeit" was "philosophically the most important" topic in *The Star.* See GB (31.1.1919), 226–27.

tion, one must recall that the new thinking habitually distinguishes between our traditional-philosophical understanding of the world and our everyday or "factual" understanding. One of the most often repeated principles of Rosenzweig's philosophy is that thought should not remove itself from the understanding of things that obtains naturally in the flow of everyday life. The most developed discussion of this idea is to be found in Rosenzweig's *Little Book of Sick and Healthy Common Sense (Das Büchlein vom gesunden und kranken Menschenverstand).* This is surely Rosenzweig's most humorous and most polemical work: it offers the allegory of a philosopher who succumbs to paralyzing illness due to excessive philosophizing. He demands to know what the objects of the world "actually" are in isolation from all temporality and worldly context, and eventually this longing for a moment out of time rebounds upon the thinker himself; he finds himself frozen, reduced to his unreal "essence," "detemporalized," and thus paralyzed, lying in a hospital bed unable to move. The title, whose pun has been lost in the English translation, plays upon the fact that the German phrase, "gesunden Menschen-verstand" is the customary translation for the English phrase, "common sense."[98] And it is this "common sense" that presents the "healthy" contrast with the "sick" understanding of the philosopher.

The dominant contrast between common sense and philosophy is easily construed as a polemic against philosophy in toto. Hilary Putnam, for example, has suggested that Rosenzweig meant to argue (with Wittgenstein) that philosophy is like a disease, and that we require only a therapy that will remind us of those common meanings that generally worked for us when we were going about our daily and unphilosophical affairs.[99] The problem with this interpretation is that it underestimates the specifically philosophical point in Rosenzweig's apparently antiphilosophical praise for the everyday. As noted above, he was adamant that the return to "life" did not entail a rejection of philosophy as such, but only philosophy of a particular type. This is evident in the *Büchlein,* where the philosopher is presented as someone who subscribes to a doctrine of "artificial timelessness" *(künstlichen Zeitlosigkeit).* The sickness begins the moment the philosopher demands of the everyday objects around him that they reveal themselves as something other than what they show themselves to be. To ask after the "essence" *(We-*

98. Thus Kant defines "Der gemeine Menschenverstand" as "bloß gesunden" and "noch nicht kultivierten Verstand" in §40 of the *Kritik der Urteilskraft* (Hamburg: Felix Meiner, Philosophischen Bibliothek, 1954), 144.

99. See Putnam's introductory remarks in the recently republished English translation of the *Büchlein,* as *Understanding the Sick and the Healthy: A View of World, Man, and God,* trans. Nahum Glatzer, introduction by Hilary Putnam (Cambridge, Mass.: Harvard University Press, 1999), 1–20.

*sen)* of a thing in this unnatural way is to pose a "detemporalizing question" *(entzeitlichenden Frage).* Such a question then lifts the object out from its meaningful place in the "flow of life" *(Ablauf des Lebens) (Büchlein,* 31). Eventually, the fixation of this philosophical gaze transfigures the philosopher himself, who becomes as rigid and seemingly timeless as the object he sees—hence his paralysis. The cure for the unhappy philosopher is to return him slowly back to the natural understanding of things, the context of lived experience Rosenzweig calls "everydayness" *(Alltäglichkeit) (Büchlein,* 108).

The allegorical, even flippant character of the *Büchlein* may tempt readers to neglect its deeper conceptual point. It is really a philosophical reflection on "everydayness." Rosenzweig here advocates precisely a *philosophy* that remains within the boundaries of everyday understanding. And such an everyday understanding will acknowledge temporality as constitutive of the very being of things. It will reject the idea that the lived, temporal context of things might be momentarily "bracketed" so as to get at some essential nature. For this reason, the new philosophy will cease to be a discipline that transports us into an unfamiliar way of looking at the world. Rather, it will consider "everydayness" as both the beginning and the end of all philosophical inquiry. This is why, as noted above, Rosenzweig's general approach is best considered a nonreductive phenomenology like that of Heidegger. Rosenzweig, too, is searching for a way to develop an enriched appreciation for things that can be developed out of just what they show themselves to be.

Like Heidegger, however, Rosenzweig's phenomenology of the everyday is essentially a hermeneutic investigation of bounded meanings and practices. Even the fanciful story of the philosopher's paralysis and eventual cure reinforces this idea of a closed circle that begins in the everyday and returns to it. The philosopher's "detour" is an error, while Rosenzweig advocates that we always remain *(bleiben)* within the sphere of life's meanings. Once again we see the central theme of *The Star*—that we remain in time and the world.

Incidentally, some readers may notice that Rosenzweig's caricature of philosophy here resembles Husserl's "transcendental" phenomenology. Like Husserl, the allegorical philosopher whom Rosenzweig mocks in his little book is one who wishes to rescue only the "essence" of things by wresting them free of all their empirical and existential characteristics—a tactic that resembles the phenomenologist's method of reduction (*epoché,* or "bracketing"). And like Husserl, Rosenzweig's paralytic philosopher brackets out his own factical, psychological, and existential features to become a pure subject, much like Husserl's "transcendental ego." Indeed, one way to construe Rosenzweig's idea of "life" is to understand it as an equivalent for what Husserl called the "natural" as opposed to the "philosophical" attitude.[100] Of course, for Husserl the natural attitude was precisely what had to be surrendered if philosophy was to be a rigorous science. Rosenzweig not only rejected the idea that philosophy is superior to the natural attitude, he rejected the idea of their contradistinction altogether. Philosophy for Rosenzweig emerges within and returns to life without ever departing from it.

A good parallel is found in Heidegger's early lectures at Freiburg, in the winter semester of 1920–21, under the heading "An Introduction to the Phenomenology of Religion." In laying down the requisite preparatory methodology for a phenomenology of religion, Heidegger began by presenting a contrast between traditional philosophy and his own idea of phenomenological understanding. "The problem of the self-understanding of philosophy," he suggests, "has always been taken too lightly. If one takes this problem radically, one finds that philosophy springs from factical life-experience [*faktische Lebenserfahrung*]. And then it springs right back into this factical life-experience." (The contrast here between Husserl's "transcendental" phenomenology and Heidegger's phenomenology of everyday life could not appear more stark.) Heidegger later repeats that "[f]ormerly philosophers attempted to dismiss factical life-experience as a self-evident and ancillary subject-matter, although philosophizing itself originates from it, and springs back into it in an—altogether essential—reversion [*Umkehr*]."[101]

Like Rosenzweig, Heidegger argues that a true phenomenology of religious experience must follow a circular course within the bounded horizon of factical existence.[102] This claim reappears in *Being and Time*: "Philosophy . . . takes its departure from the hermeneutic of Dasein, which, as an analytic of *existence,* has made fast the guiding line for all philosophical inquiry at the point where it *arises* and to which it *returns*" (SZ, §7C, 38; em-

100. See, e.g., Edmund Husserl, *Experience and Judgement: Investigations in a Genealogy of Logic,* trans. J. S. Churchill and K. Ameriks (Evanston, Ill.: Northwestern University Press, 1973), 331–34; and *Ideas: General Introduction to Pure Phenomenology,* trans. W. R. Boyce Gibson (New York: Macmillan, 1931), 51 and *passim.*

101. GA, 60, *Phänomenologie des religiösen Lebens,* "Einleitung in die Phänomenologie der Religion," Wintersemester, 1920/21, §2, 8. Note that this was a phase in Heidegger's early teaching when he was very much immersed in questions of religious philosophy. A year earlier he had been working on notes for a lecture concerning "The Philosophical Foundations of Medieval Mysticism," while for the summer semester of 1921 he prepared notes for a course on Augustine and Neo-Platonism.

102. Compare Heidegger's 1920 argument that "philosophy is . . . simply the immanent illumination of the experience of life itself, an illumination that *remains in this experience itself without stepping outside it* and making it into some sort of objectivity." GA, 59, *Phänomenologie der Anschauung und des Ausdrucks,* 171 ff.; my emphasis.

phasis in original). Heidegger further specifies that, unlike Husserl, he wants to take up the problem of everydayness as a theme for philosophical exposition. "Dasein's everydayness" *(Alltäglichkeit des Daseins)* is "a positive phenomenal character of its being. Out of this kind of Being—and back into it again—is all existing, such as it is" (SZ, 43). Like Rosenzweig, Heidegger privileged the aspect of things as we encounter them in our everyday affairs. "To the everydayness of Being-in-the-world there belong certain modes of concern." Such modes "permit the entities with which we concern ourselves to be encountered" such that "the worldly character of what is within the world [*die Weltmäßigkeit des Innerweltlichen*] comes to the fore" (SZ, 16–17). Like Rosenzweig, Heidegger argued that factual experience provides the necessary and inescapably bounded context of intelligibility for understanding phenomena. Heidegger calls such experience "the ground of familiarity with the world." Only when such a context breaks down does there emerge that derivative sense of objective presence—Heidegger called it *Vorhandenheit*—that philosophers have customarily privileged as the world "in itself "( SZ, §16, esp. 76).

Now if I am right about Rosenzweig's basically hermeneutic approach, this provides us with a good explanation for *The Star*'s blatant hostility toward any philosophy that claims to know the "All." Rosenzweig was not a postmodernist. But like Heidegger he believed that knowledge is always bounded, local, and finite. As a hermeneutic investigation, *The Star* is interested in the basic structures of lived meaning. But since hermeneutics regards such meaning as local, it denies the relevance of any third-person, neutral account of the totality. Hermeneutics and postmodernism share the insight that knowledge is always partial. But they differ in that hermeneutics regards local knowledge as basically coherent, while postmodernism sees local knowledge as inevitably prone to disruption from the meanings beyond its frame. It seems clear, then, that Rosenzweig was a hermeneutical thinker, since he regarded the life-context as a markedly coherent set of meanings and practices.[103]

Both Heidegger and Rosenzweig refused to accept the claim of traditional philosophers that what is most true can only be arrived at by isolating an essential or transcendental object that is ostensibly beyond time and perspective. Instead, both claimed that the traditional philosophical ideal of "essential" knowing is actually a departure from the local contexts of mean-

103. Affirming the basic coherence of the life-world, Rosenzweig suggested to Gritli that the world of revelation might be called the "Mit- und Umwelt," that is, the "with-world" and the "environment." (GB, 19.11.1918), 195–96. As is well known, Heidegger used both of these terms in *Being and Time* to describe the "social" and "surrounding" aspects of human existence; e.g., on "Mitwelt," see SZ, §26, 118–26; on "Umwelt," SZ, §14–16, 63–77.

ing in which we live. This departure can only be temporary, since it is not the primary mode of understanding. Thus Rosenzweig and Heidegger saw philosophy as a hermeneutical exercise that should always move within a horizon of prior familiarity, since such a horizon is the condition for there being experience at all.[104] As Heidegger explained, "The world is something wherein Dasein as an entity already *was,* and if in any manner it explicitly comes away from anything, it can never do more than come back to the world" (SZ, 76).

## The Primacy of Practice

To call Rosenzweig's thought a hermeneutics is helpful but insufficient; one must specify what kind of hermeneutics is meant. Generally speaking, the hallmark of hermeneutics is that it recognizes there is always a prior, holistic context of meaning at the background of our world, and such a context is always and inescapably at work as the condition for intelligibility for all action and inquiry. Here, however, it is important to distinguish between at least two tendencies in contemporary hermeneutic theory. From Hans-Georg Gadamer we have become aware of how all of human *understanding* is bounded by horizons of tradition. On Gadamer's view, then, hermeneutics is first and foremost a practice of interpretation. Interpretative hermeneutics is primarily a practice of humanistic research that acknowledges the shaping authority of tradition as the inescapable horizon of understanding; it finds its richest application as a theory of how we understand a work of art or literature. And, as Leora Batnitzky has shown, there is undeniably a Gadamerian strain in Rosenzweig's philosophy, especially where it touches on questions of aesthetic experience.[105]

But there is a deeper and distinctive kind of hermeneutic theory best associated with Heidegger, not Gadamer. Heidegger's most distinctive contribution to hermeneutics was to have asked about the ontological *constitution* of the hermeneutical horizon. To be sure, Gadamer elaborated upon the theory of the historicity of meaning (or "tradition") that Heidegger had first introduced in Division II of *Being and Time.* But Heidegger himself had also devoted much of his prior effort in Division I to the thesis that our historically conditioned contexts of meaning are themselves embedded in *ways of being.* To better understand the ontological dimension of Rosen-

104. Hence Rosenzweig's remark in "Das neue Denken" that the vindication of a philosophical argument "occurs in the everyday of life [*Alltag des Lebens*]." ND, 160. This point is emphasized by Freund, *Rosenzweig's Philosophy of Existence,* esp. 12.

105. On the aesthetic dimension of Rosenzweig's *Star,* see Batnitzky, *Idolatry and Representation.*

zweig's hermeneutic theory, the comparison with Heidegger is therefore indispensable.

Heidegger observed that we live in a fashion that is primarily engaged and practical. And he further suggested that such engagements are meaningful only because some understanding of Being is already at play within them. This understanding initially becomes available to us in and through the ways we live. It is of course somewhat misleading to speak here of "understanding." Rather, because such understanding is embedded within pragmatic and concernful *activity*, it is in fact the already-understood, the lived context upon which there can first be anything like an explicit knowledge of the world. Heidegger calls this lived context a "context of assignments" (SZ, §16–18, 83–85). Since this kind of context forms the background of understanding, it comprises part of what Heidegger calls the "Being" of beings. Such "Being" is itself understood as *embedded in practice.* Moreover, for Heidegger this claim is supposedly true both of objects and of ourselves. Objects are first and foremost not objects of knowledge but *pragmata*—objects of practical concern and use. Similarly, "who we ourselves are" is first discovered not through reflection but rather through our purposeful and directed way of living. As Heidegger explains, "[t]he 'essence' of Dasein lies in its existence" (SZ, 42; and BT, 67). Since the general emphasis in Heidegger's hermeneutics is on how meaning is embedded within a lived or existing context, his overall interpretative strategy can be called "existential hermeneutics."

Like Heidegger, Rosenzweig is interested in contexts of meaning that are bound up specifically with our *ways of existing*—of living, of practicing ritual, and of engaging usefully with everyday objects. Rosenzweig's hermeneutic thus shares with Heidegger the existential and eminently *practical* dimension that is noticeably lacking in Gadamer.[106] Throughout Rosenzweig's corpus, one finds innumerable variations on the claim that practical engagement is prior to and provides the lived context for theoretical reflection. This theme is famously dramatized in the *Büchlein*, where, as we have seen, Rosenzweig construes paralysis as an illness that seizes philosophers whenever they abandon what Husserl called the "natural attitude" and imagine that they can isolate the essence of objects only if they are torn from their everyday practical and temporal contexts of meaning. The analy-

---

106. I offer this distinction between Gadamer and Heidegger against the arguments found in Batnitzky, *Idolatry and Representation,* where it is claimed that Rosenzweig is a hermeneutic philosopher in the tradition of Gadamer. While this comparison is helpful, the themes of practice and lived meaning bind Rosenzweig more closely with Heidegger. Ironically, Batnitzky herself emphasizes that Rosenzweig conceives "worship" as *practice* rather than objective knowledge.

sis bears a striking resemblance to Heidegger's discussion of the "dealing" *(Umgang)* in which we primarily encounter the world, as against the decontextualized "presence" of objects when this environment breaks down (SZ, §15, 67–68).

Similarly, in *The Star* Rosenzweig presents a rich interpretation of religious practice as an inherited but ever-renewed context of life. To participate in religious ritual is for Rosenzweig to live in a more or less stable structure of embedded and practical meaning. Rosenzweig therefore calls ritual "earthly repetition" *(irdische Wiederholung;* SE, 323 [E, 291]). The horizon of lived intelligibility is always already forged for us in the repetition of communally accepted meanings and practices as they are handed down from the past. Even the humanly created divisions of time into weeks and seasons and festivals should be understood as the communally accepted contexts that allow for the world to be experienced as meaningful—Rosenzweig calls such divisions "temporal dwellings" (SE, 324 [E, 292]).

Now if one thinks of life as something that always takes place within a horizon of pragmatic engagements and ritual, then one can see that "who we are" might be best discovered upon the basis of what we do. In this sense, the essence of Judaism for Rosenzweig is not primarily cognitive but practical. Against thinkers such as Leo Baeck and Hermann Cohen, Rosenzweig regarded Judaism not primarily as some set of ethical precepts nor as the rational idea of a universal God. Instead, Rosenzweig saw it primarily as a *mode of life.* As he explained in two letters to Rudolf Hallo—one written in 1921, the other in 1922—Rosenzweig calls this condition "Jewish-being" *(Judesein).* "Jewish *life* is the form through which we make Jewish-being tolerable." He took care to emphasize that Jewish life is not reducible to this or that practice or precept. Rather, it is the totality of practices and lived relations, all of which form what Rosenzweig would call the "temporal dwellings" of Jewish identity. He specifies that "Judaism *is not* law. It creates law. But it *is not* law." Rather, Judaism is "being-Jewish."[107] Jewish-being, in other words, is something first discovered not through reflection but through life. To explore the essence of Judaism as Rosenzweig does in *The Star* thus requires a hermeneutic investigation of those distinctive ways of being human that are embodied in the practices, rituals, and festivals of Jewish communal life. As Rosenzweig explained in his critique of Buber's approach to Jewish life, *"man's understanding extends only as far as his doing."*[108]

---

107. *Briefe*, N.342, An Rudolf Hallo (Frankfurt a. M., 27.3.1922), 424–25; and N.306, An Rudolf Hallo (Frankfurt am Main, 15.3.21), 398.

108. Rosenzweig, "Die Bauleute," in KS, 106–21, esp. 113; my emphasis. Cited in Will Herberg, "Rosenzweig's 'Judaism of Personal Existence': A Third Way Between Orthodoxy and Modernism," *Commentary* 10, 6 (December 1950): 541–49. Herberg explains this to mean that

Hermeneutics for Rosenzweig thus presents a challenge to any philosophical approach that would attempt to isolate the essence of an object or a person from the temporal horizon in which it is always realizing what it is. Or, in Heidegger's phrase, noted above, "[t]he 'essence' of Dasein lies in its existence."

This hermeneutic strategy emerges from a specifically modern recognition that there is no permanently founded identity to objects and persons beyond the local contexts of lived engagement.[109] Rosenzweig is a post-Nietzschean philosopher in that, like Heidegger, he denies that human meaning is intelligible independent of a life-context. Temporal hermeneutics thus replaces the transcendental search for essence. For Rosenzweig, to find out what something means requires that one understand it in hermeneutic fashion from within its horizon of temporal existence. This implies that a specific human context rich with practices and community meanings will be a necessary condition for there to be meaningful experience at all. Like Heidegger, Rosenzweig subscribes to the ontological-hermeneutical thesis that it is temporal, human existence itself that first constitutes the ground of meaning. It follows that religious experience cannot be a matter of surmounting temporality. Eternity must happen within time.

### "To Wrest Eternity from Time"

In "The New Thinking," Rosenzweig presents the bold claim that one of the features uniting nearly all of Western thought is its ill-conceived and hopeless effort to transcend temporality. Thinking, he writes, has heretofore been timeless, and has wanted to be so: "Das Denken ist zeitlos, will es sein." But this mode of philosophy is now defunct. A valid mode of philosophy, in Rosenzweig's words, begins in "taking time seriously" *(im Ernstnehmen der Zeit)* (ND, 151, 152). Accordingly, the new thinking will be a revolutionary philosophy in that it will at last recognize time as the primal medium of thought. It can achieve this new recognition by substituting the atemporal "method of thinking" with the temporally bound "method of speech" *(Meth-*

---

"[r]eligious observance is, in effect, the *doing* of one's religious convictions; the two cannot be separated."

109. In *Reflections of a Nonpolitical Man,* Thomas Mann observed, "The *life concept,* this most German, most Goethean, and in the highest, religious sense, conservative concept, is the one that Nietzsche imbued with new feeling, reinvested with new beauty, strength, and holy innocence, elevated to the highest rank, to intellectual dominance. Is not Georg Simmel correct when he claims that after Nietzsche, 'life' became the key concept of all modern world views? In any case, Nietzsche's entire moral criticism stands under the sign of this idea." *Betrachtungen eines Unpolitischen* (Berlin: S. Fischer Verlag, 1918); in English, *Reflections of a Nonpolitical Man,* trans. Walter D. Morris (New York: The Ungar Publishing Company, 1987), 58.

*ode des Sprechens).* For where traditional thought attempted to transcend time, "speech is bound to time" *(zeitgebunden).* Indeed, speech is "nourished by time" *(zeitgenährt)* and it "neither can nor wishes to abandon this nourishing soil [*Nährboden*]." [110]

One might expect Rosenzweig to have concluded that philosophy has no business speculating about putative realms outside of time. Indeed, at first this expectation seems to be justified. Of "everyday matters," writes Rosenzweig, there is no longer much dispute that temporality is the irresistible factum for experience as for thought: "As little as one could just as well begin a conversation with the end, or war with a peace treaty, . . . or life with death, one must learn . . . to keep waiting until the moment comes, and not skip any moment." Similarly, "cognition in each moment is bound to that very moment and cannot make its past not past, or its future not in the future." But God's being seems another matter entirely. The previous methods of philosophy, Rosenzweig grants, seemed best able to address those "last and highest things that one generally believes can be discerned only timelessly." But Rosenzweig insists that the older horizon of timelessness was an illusion, for even when speaking of divine being, temporality must be acknowledged: "What God has done, what He does, what He will do, [just as] what has happened to the world, what will happen to it, what happens to man, what he will do,"—and here is Rosenzweig's bold conclusion—"*all this cannot be rescued from its temporality*" (ND, 150; my emphasis).

The phasing of this conclusion—"*nicht von seiner Zeitlichkeit losgelöst werden*"—is significant. The root term *lösung,* the dissolution of bonds, suggests a contrast between the old philosophy and the new thinking on the idea of redemption. While Rosenzweig ridicules the dream that one can be rescued *(losgelöst)* from temporality, he is also laying the grounds for his own exposition of redemption *(Erlösung).* The reader may presume, then, that the new doctrine of redemption found in *The Star* will not repeat the error of attempting any dissolution (or *Lösung*) of time's force. Accordingly, the concept of redemption found in Rosenzweig's new philosophy must remain within the horizon of temporality, since to seek release from temporality would be simply to fall into the error of traditional thinking.

But many aspects of Rosenzweig's philosophy seem immediately to defeat such expectations. Perhaps most vexing of all is a suggestion—found in the essay "The New Thinking"—that philosophers must try "to wrest eternity from time" *(die Ewigkeit von der Zeit abzuringen* [ND, 156]). This and many other remarks scattered through Rosenzweig's writings are bothersome in

110. For a philosopher of exile, the metaphor of landedness is curious, but perhaps incidental: time, Rosenzweig implies, is as irresistible for the new philosophy as the earth for the nourishment of plants. ND, 151.

that they seem openly to conflict with his programmatic announcement to "take time seriously" (ND, 152). The problem is the following. Rosenzweig seems at many turns intent on debunking all previous philosophies insofar as they have attempted to think beyond the bounds of temporality. Even the movements of God, he insists, "cannot be set free" from time. One would naturally expect, then, to find little positive reference to realms beyond temporality; indeed, one would justifiably expect that for Rosenzweig there just are no such realms. "Frei von jeder Zeitgewalt"—free from any of time's power—is a line found in Schiller's poem. And as we have seen, Rosenzweig seems to scorn every surviving system of the philosophical tradition that remains caught in the self-deception of metaphysical transport. Yet elsewhere in Rosenzweig's writing—especially in *The Star*—we find references to eternity that violate these bold and apparently categorical statements. How, then, is the category of eternity at all compatible with a philosophy that claims time as an unsurpassable horizon?

One possible solution would be simply to read Rosenzweig's more radical claims as nothing more than hyperbole. Of course he meant to "take time seriously," but this does not mean that he meant categorically to deny the possibility of thinking beyond its boundaries. Accordingly, eternity might still be construed as an independent realm untouched by temporality. Because human beings live in time, then, it might also be supposed that philosophical reflection involves an effortful transcendence. Eternity, therefore, is a term we must assign first and foremost to those cognitive truths that do not suffer the constraints of when and where they are the case. On this view, the purpose of philosophy would be to distinguish through arduous mental reflection between the temporal and the nontemporal elements in cognition.

Karl Löwith suggests this reading in his classic essay "F. Rosenzweig and M. Heidegger, or Temporality and Eternity." In a closing passage, Löwith contrasts the notion of eternity found in Rosenzweig's writings with Heidegger's more resolute embrace of temporality. According to Löwith, by his turning away from Christianity Heidegger destroyed "the old tradition so thoroughly that finite time becomes the inmost meaning of being and eternity [becomes] an illusion, whilst up to Hegel the Greek and Christian tradition had been alive, according to which true being was set in the eternal or 'always present.'" Löwith then suggests that "[i]n contradistinction to Heidegger, Rosenzweig, owing to his actual inheritance, his Judaism, and the deliberate return to it—was in the happy position of being able to hold up David's star of eternal truth in the midst of time" (TE, 76–77). For Löwith, then, the contrast between temporality and eternity is fundamental. To underscore this contrast, he alludes in a concluding footnote to one of Heidegger's pupils, who tried to show that mathematics, though customarily considered a repository of eternal truths, in fact rests on existential-temporal foundations. The note seems intended to show that Heidegger's effort to radically temporalize all thought must ultimately fail, since it leads to such patently ridiculous ideas.

But Löwith does not mention the fact that Rosenzweig, like Heidegger, also rejected mathematics as a relevant paradigm for philosophy. To be sure, Rosenzweig employs mathematical instruments in *The Star* in order to expose the "nothing" at the core of being. But one reason mathematics can fulfill this function, according to Rosenzweig, is precisely because "it does not touch the real itself." Even Plato understood that "mathematics does not lead beyond the Something." Precisely because it is a form of truth without temporal determination, it does not inhere in "the chaos of the This." (At most, Rosenzweig cautions us, "it touches upon it.") It is the appearance of purity in mathematics, its seeming to be beyond time, that most explains "the respect which philosophers have accorded it ever since" (SE, 22 [E, 20]). But Rosenzweig does not share traditional philosophers' high esteem for mathematics, precisely because it does not reflect the basic temporality of the world.[111] The truths of mathematics, he concludes, are "hopelessly static" ("die hoffnungslos statischen Wahrheiten, wie die der Mathematik" [ND, 159]).

This remark shows that Rosenzweig did not wish to embrace the paradigm of philosophy that sees it as transcending time through mental effort. The phrase, "to wrest eternity from time" must be construed differently, so as not to identify eternity with an intelligible realm that is atemporal. But if one rejects this reading, what alternatives are available? According to any traditional metaphysics time and eternity are mutually exclusive and exhaustive categories: for any thing, it is either temporal or eternal. Indeed, eternity can even be considered a privative concept, the sheer absence of temporality, just as the infinite is the not-finite. But if this is so, one might conclude that there just are no alternative readings. Rosenzweig's statement that philosophy should wrest eternity from time, if coherent at all, would necessarily be construed as a call to return to traditional metaphysics. But even the most superficial reading of Rosenzweig's philosophy forbids this conclusion. As I have shown, the introductory portion of the *Star* protests against any contemporary effort to rehabilitate the traditional metaphysical project, according to which the mortal being may die while the soul "flutters free" into an eternal beyond. Yet at the same time, Rosenzweig

---

111. As the argument in *The Star* proceeds, Rosenzweig makes it clear that mathematics was afforded only a provisional role. Once one has moved out from the shattered elements of primal phenomena to recover the temporal relations of creation, revelation, and redemption, Rosenzweig insists that one now abandon algebraic reasoning: "The language of mathematical symbols in which we were previously able to demonstrate the evolution of the elements fails us here." SE, 138–39 (E, 124).

claims in the chapter on redemption that life "longs for eternity" (SE, 249 [E, 223]). The reader discovers a seeming affirmation of Schiller's dream, which is elsewhere denied. One might conclude that Rosenzweig's philosophy is hopelessly confused.

## Eternity without Metaphysics

There is, however, a way out of this interpretative difficulty, and it is Rosenzweig's peculiar solution that clears the way for his idea of redemption. As I will show, Rosenzweig was intent upon revising our understanding of the contrast between time and eternity as it has been handed down from the philosophical tradition. It is only if we conceive of time and eternity as logically exclusive terms that we arrive at the impasse described above. For Rosenzweig, however, time and eternity are mutually inclusive. Indeed, the only possible notion of eternity available for the new philosophy is not something to be sought beyond time. Rather, it is discovered within time— it is, or at least can become, *a modification of time.* In this sense, one "wrests eternity from time" only in so far as there is *an eternal way of being within the temporal horizon.* Thus the concluding section of the end piece of Part II ("Schwelle," or "Threshold"), which immediately follows the redemption chapter, is entitled "The Times of Eternity" *(die Zeiten der Ewigkeit).* If eternity were merely the privative of temporality, such a phrase would indeed be incoherent, and the responsible reader could hardly be blamed for suspecting Rosenzweig of mystical wordplay. The peculiarity of the language, however, simply underscores the difficulty of Rosenzweig's attempt to articulate concepts fundamentally at odds with the metaphysical tradition: He writes about "eternity within time" *(Ewigkeit in der Zeit),* and "earthly eternity" *(irdische Ewigkeit).* The introductory portion of Part III asserts that moments of time are "temporal dwellings" *(zeitliche Behausungen)* into which "Eternity is invited." At various points it almost appears as if temporality is supposed to be capable of becoming eternal, a phenomenon Rosenzweig terms the "eternalization of the moment" *(Verewigung des Augenblicks)* (SE, 324 [E, 292]). But mostly Rosenzweig characterizes this event as transforming what is eternal into a modified but still temporal condition. Thus he writes of "the redemptive arrival of the eternal into time" ("das erlösende Kommen der Ewigkeit in die Zeit") (SE, 325 [E, 293]). And he also writes that eternity "by finding acceptance in time, itself becomes—like Time" (SE, 324 [E, 292]).

To better explain these unusual claims one might recall Stefan George's poem "The Star of the Covenant" ("Der Stern des Bundes," first published in 1913, just eight years before Rosenzweig's book). George writes, "Some teach: this is earthly, that eternal, / While another: I am want and you are abundance. / Here is revealed: how the earthly is eternal [*Hier künde sich:*

*wie ist ein irdisches ewig*]." Many of Rosenzweig's early readers alluded to his spiritual affinity with George. Margarete Susman, for example (herself a member of the George Kreis), identified Stefan George as an important literary influence upon Rosenzweig.[112] For both George and Rosenzweig, a central aim is to somehow *bridge* the distinction between "the earthly" and "the eternal." In "The New Thinking," Rosenzweig asserts that one of his chief motivations is "the question of an existing eternity" (*einer seienden Ewigkeit*) (ND, 156). Like George's "earthly eternal," Rosenzweig seems determined to join the eternal and the temporal through the "primary word of all experience"—the "factuality" *(Tatsächlichkeit)* of the "And" (ND, 158).

The notion of a "bridge" should alert the reader to the fact that for Rosenzweig such a union between time and eternity cannot be made absolute. If it were, this would have risked violating the cardinal rule of Rosenzweig's philosophy, which demands that we sustain the ontological difference among *The Star*'s three primordial elements. For Rosenzweig there remains a real distinction between time and eternity insofar as the primal elements do not originally occupy the same ontological ground. Both world and man, of course, live necessarily in time, while divine being has at least one foot in eternity.[113] Rosenzweig is thus careful to indicate that there is an aspect of divine being that is wholly dissociated from time. But the convergence of the two categories takes on bewildering dimensions when he further specifies the meanings of redemption for God, Man, and World. For God, Rosenzweig writes, redemption provides an "assurance of eternity despite the temporality of self-revelation" (SE, 288 [E, 259]). This would seem to mean that revelation entails a certain risk that God might become lost in the flux of the world. It is redemption that overcomes this risk. By joining Man and World together under the sign of eternity, redemption allows for God's return from temporal revelation back into the arms of eternity. Redemption "connects creation with revelation" and is therefore not merely the "assurance of eternity"; it is in fact "the fulfilling realization of eternity" *(die erfüllende Verwirklichung der Ewigkeit)* (SE, 288 [E, 259]). Accordingly, Man and World remain temporal but take on some of the features of eternity. For the World, creation can only give it the quality of existence *(bloß dazusein)* while as "life" the world must turn toward Man for any kind of permanence, stability, or "duration" (SE, 289 [E, 259]). Man alone, however, is uniquely capable of conferring this duration upon the world, since it is Man

112. George, "Der Stern des Bundes" (1913), in *Werke* (München und Düsseldorf: Helmut Küpper, 1958), 380. Susman, "Exodus from Philosophy," in Udoff and Galli, eds., *Rosenzweig's "The New Thinking,"* 107.

113. "God alone," writes Rosenzweig, "plants the sapling of his own eternity neither into the beginning of time nor into its middle, but utterly beyond time into eternity." SE, 290 (E, 260).

who is the recipient of revelation. Thus "God's revelation to man is the guarantee" that is "given to the world for its redemption." And in this redemption the world, like God, finds "entry into eternity" *(Eingehens in die Ewigkeit)* (SE, 290 [E, 260]).

The distinction between time and eternity in the *Star* thus cannot be construed in the manner of traditional metaphysics.[114] Indeed, the concept of redemption seems uniquely designed to overcome their distinction, a convergence that is then applied to each of the three primary elements: For God, redemption means the return to eternity after the self-revelation in time. For the World, redemption comes about through the achievement of "duration," that it continue alongside humankind as the environment of revelation. But for Man, what can redemption mean? In what sense does Man become eternal? Here one confronts a potentially fatal problem in Rosenzweig's thought. If the *Star* is to remain true to its opening statement, then it must lay down a new mode of thinking that acknowledges the unsurpassable fact of mortality. It cannot seek a route whereby the human being might trespass beyond the temporal boundaries that give each life a definite beginning and end, since this would be to adopt the language of traditional metaphysics that Rosenzweig scorns. Unless one dismisses as sheer hyperbole the various programmatic statements found in "The New Thinking," then one must conclude that Rosenzweig considered temporality an unsurpassable horizon. But if so, then in what sense can the category of eternity be meaningfully applied to the human being? What remains of the concept of redemption when it is folded back within the horizon of time? Rosenzweig's proposed answer is the topic of the following chapter.

114. Compare Max Scheler's remarks in *Vom Ewigen im Menschen,* in *Werke,* 4th ed., vol. V (Berne: A. Francke, 1954; orig. pub. 1920); in English, *The Eternal in Man,* trans. Bernard Noble (New York: Harper and Brothers, 1960), 12: "A man has a poor conception of the eternal if, merely grasping its contrast to the flow of time, he is unable to hear the soft voice of eternity in the most momentary demand which is made on the individual in the here and now. For rightly conceived, the eternal is not sealed away from time in a simple juxtaposition: it timelessly embraces the context of time and its fullness, pervading each of its moments. . . . And so the eternal can be no asylum into which a man may flee, thinking himself unable to endure any more of history and life."

# Chapter 4

# Redemption-in-the-World

## *Rosenzweig's* Star *(Part II)*

*[W]e are not fully at home in our interpreted world.*
—RAINER MARIA RILKE, *Duino Elegies*

*To redeem those who lived in the past and to re-create all "it was" into a*
*"thus I willed it"—that alone I call redemption.*
—FRIEDRICH NIETZSCHE, "On Redemption," *Thus Spake Zarathustra*

As I have argued in the previous chapter, both Rosenzweig and Heidegger saw as a chief requirement of the new philosophy that it follow a hermeneutic method, tracing out the meaning of religious concepts along the temporal path of human life. The new thinking would never stray into alien worlds; rather, it would remain faithfully within the bounds of "factical life-experience." For Rosenzweig, however, this requirement cannot be dissociated from his more global effort to develop a new concept of redemption. Because he was a modern, post-Nietzschean philosopher, for him redemption could no longer mean, as it once had for others, the metaphysical move from temporality to eternity. Redemption was now constrained to appear within the life-horizon alone, as a mode of factical existence within time yet not fully of time. Taking Heidegger's language as my guide, I will call Rosenzweig's concept "redemption-in-the-world." As I shall show, this concept bears a striking resemblance to what Heidegger called "authenticity."

### TEMPORALITY AND COLLECTIVITY IN *THE STAR*

#### *The Forms of Life*

Rosenzweig develops the new model of redemption in book three of *The Star*'s second volume, the redemption chapter. He begins by distinguishing between that which in the world displays mere "existence" *(Dasein)* and that which has "living being" *(Lebendigsein)*. The existent is distinguished from the living in that mere existence suffers from the "creaturely weakness" of all created being. It is prone to constant change and decay, and enjoys no stable identity. But this is to construe existence as the condition of any object whatsoever, since all existence is originally mere "appearance." Here Rosenzweig pays homage to the standard epistemological view that worldly things can be thought of as entirely dissociated from the minds that may happen to encounter them. And when such objects do happen to become objects of knowledge, they may still be known in a merely theoretical way, as entities with basic features or identifying characteristics. To emphasize this idea Rosenzweig exploits the root meaning in the term *Gegenstand*, or object, suggesting that an object is what "merely stands against" *(bloß gegenübersteht)* the cognitive subject. For Rosenzweig, this is simply what the world is like when it is conceived in its unredeemed condition—that is, when it is thought of apart from God and man. The unredeemed world never enjoys more than this sort of existence, or *Da-sein*, which according to Rosenzweig means that "[t]here where it is, it is" ("da wo sie ist, ist sie") (SE, 247 [E, 222]).

For a worldly being to be redeemed would first of all require that it "step forth as an entity that is enduring, constant." In other words, the world needs "an enduring content, an individuality which contains in itself something which is imperishable; . . . something which, once there, remains enduring." This would be an individuality that "delimits itself," and *"determines its size and form from out of itself, which can be constrained but not determined by others."* According to Rosenzweig, such an entity does exist "in the midst of the world," although, he cautions, it is in many cases "dispersed" *(verstreut)*. It goes by the simple name of "life" *(Leben)*. Mere "existence" and "life" are therefore two modalities of entities in the world. Where existence is mere appearance, life is "essence." Only "the living" *(das Lebendige)*, moreover, is capable of enduring with a stable identity through time. Life enjoys "its ownmost self," *(die selbsteigene)* as a "necessarily permanent form [*Gestalt*] that it shapes *from within*" (SE, 248 [E, 222]; my emphasis).

At this point Rosenzweig's argument is bewilderingly abstract. It may be helpful to recall that Rosenzweig was attempting to work out a concept of redemption within the constraints of temporality. The key to so-called eternal permanency in this argument is the concept of "form" *(Gestalt)*. Significantly, this is Schiller's name for the "divine amongst divinities." But Rosenzweig reverses its metaphysical sense. Rather than exhorting us to flee temporality to dwell in the eternal, Rosenzweig construes form as a *worldly* refuge. It is a "dwelling" within time, which offers protection from the damages of mere "existence."[1] Form in this new, post-metaphysical sense allows a living being to determine its identity "from out of itself" and free from

---

1. Thus the claim by Hermann Herrigel that "The Eternal must ever and again step into time and assume a finite form." *Zwischen Frage und Antwort* (Berlin: Lambert Schneider, 1930). On Herrigel's role in popularizing the ideas of both Rosenzweig and Heidegger, see my remarks on the Davos encounter in chapter 6.

constraint "by others." Essentially Rosenzweig is developing his account of how a hermeneutic life-horizon may under special conditions allow for an independent island of meaning within time. As we shall see, this is the basis of his view of Jewish life.[2]

The special experience of redemption-in-the-world can only obtain where "life" enters into a certain relation to God. The primal elements of Man and World, explains Rosenzweig, are inseparable; their bond "cannot be dissolved" ("denn Mensch und Welt sind nicht von einander zu lösen"). They can only be re-solved and re-deemed *(erlöst)* through a third element that redeems each for and through the other.[3] In other words, Rosenzweig wants to explain how it could be that life should be able to gain a hold on eternity even while it remains wholly finite. His answer is that life, while wedded to the world, can achieve eternity only in a common relation to God. And it is the commonality of this relation that is "the act of Redemption" (SE, 251 [E, 225]).

### Historicism and Ecstatic Temporality

What is immediately striking about this notion of redemption is that it does not remove the individual from the world. Rather, it binds man and world more closely to each other but in a specific and self-sustaining fashion *(die selbsteigene)* so as to realize the "permanence" of form that all life desires. It is crucial to notice, however, that such a permanence appears within, not beyond time. The terminological distinction underlying this idea of permanence—between existence and life—is one that occurs within the boundaries of temporality. Yet there is admittedly something odd about Rosenzweig's notion of time. The permanence that all life craves is always just arriving. Like Faust's striving, life's satisfaction is never entirely complete. In Rosenzweig's language, it always stands under the sign of the "not yet" *(noch nicht)*. Existence is therefore "yet finite" and its emergence as wholly living being is always a process that is "not yet finished" (SE, 244 [E, 219]).

Such a structure of longing produces a peculiar relationship to time as it is normally conceived. Rosenzweig reinforces this peculiarity by claiming

---

2. The argument on determining identity prepares the way for Rosenzweig's later portrait of the Jewish community: he specifies that *"Everything can be alive, not only living creatures, but also institutions, communities, feelings, things, works."* SE, 248 (E, 222); my emphasis. The drift of the argument is further apparent in his remark that formed life may enjoy "permanence " but is often "dispersed" *(verstreut)*—a term that in German often designated the Jewish Diaspora. SE, 248 (E, 222).

3. Here Rosenzweig indulges in a word-play irreproducible in English: "Sie [Mensch und Welt] können sich selber nicht von einander lösen, sie können nur miteinander—er-löst werden." SE, 251 (E, 225).

that the "growth" of the redemptive "kingdom" has "no relation to time," but this is an obvious hyperbole. It is nonetheless quite a challenge for the reader to gain a clear sense of what kind of temporality Rosenzweig actually has in mind. On the one hand, the "permanence" of redemption is not specified to arrive in one precise moment of the future. In this sense it is not simply a phenomenon in the future tense. On the other hand, redemption is a tomorrow that "could just as well be today." In this sense existence in the present is deeply marked by its future orientation, so redemption must also be a present-tense phenomenon. Redemption is thus characterized by a dual temporality—it is both present and future. As Rosenzweig explains, "the enlivening of existence [*die Verlebendigung des Daseins*] . . . is just as much always already there as it is futural [*immer ebenso schon da wie zukünftig*]" (SE, 250 [E, 224]). Redemption is "not yet there" *(noch nicht da)*. But this does not by any means make redemption into an unrealized and merely futural possibility. Rosenzweig is quite emphatic on this point although his language is strained: redemption is "once and for all not yet there [*einfürallemal noch nicht da*]," and it "comes eternally [*Es kommt ewig*]." The future is thus "first and foremost a matter of anticipating [since] the end must be expected at every moment. Only thus does the future become the time of eternity [Erst dadurch wird sie zur Zeit der Ewigkeit]" (SE, 252 [E, 226]).

Here Rosenzweig has attempted to collapse the distinctions between temporality and eternity in a surprising manner. Because redemption "comes eternally" Rosenzweig characterizes its temporal measure, or *Zeitmaß*, as indeterminate. He concludes that an existence that points toward eternity in this fashion "no longer has any relationship to time." So while life remains temporal through and through, it has simultaneously taken on the qualities of eternity ("Dasein . . . ist ewig geworden") (SE, 250 [E, 224]). Now at this point a less sympathetic reader might conclude that Rosenzweig is playing rather irresponsibly with language. For when he writes that redemption comes "eternally," this just means that it is constantly in arrival, and this notion of being "constantly" in a state of not-yet-arriving is hardly the same as eternity. If something constantly exhibits a certain feature, this still does not warrant concluding that the object itself is independent of time. This objection, I would suggest, is at least partly correct. What Rosenzweig calls the "eternity" of life is really the eternity of a *temporal orientation;* it is a stance toward the future that nonetheless remains within time. This helps to explain the strange phrase, "the time of eternity." Whatever the meaning of eternity, it still cannot efface human finitude.[4]

4. Rosenzweig immediately acknowledges this temporality when he notes again the obvious point that all life must still die. SE, 251 (E, 225). But the permanent directedness that he calls "eternity" demands a third element, an appearance "from without [*aus einem Außen hinzu*]." SE, 251 (E, 225). World and man achieve their eternity only in a common orientation

Perhaps the most significant feature of this argument, however, is that it depends upon a quite distinctive notion of time as continuous, rather than sequential. In Rosenzweig's view, traditional philosophy has failed to "take time seriously," since it has attempted to seize upon the "essence" of any thing as if it could be encountered in a permanent present, a "paralysis" ostensibly independent of time. Rosenzweig's debts to Lebensphilosophie are nowhere more evident than in his profound antipathy to this model of philosophical understanding. To Rosenzweig, the notion that redemption could somehow lift the living being out of the temporal flux is therefore nonsensical, since it imagines that there is a way of achieving a stable identity without reference to the unified ground of meaning that flows from past to future. The philosophical tradition therefore encourages a faulty, "historicist" notion of time as merely sequential rather than continuous. (Whether this accurately describes the historicist view of time is an important question but best left for another occasion.)

Against the historicist sequential understanding of time, for which past, present, and future are arranged as if in a chain, Rosenzweig proposes a continuous understanding of time, for which past, present, and future become mutually informative indices within a given moment.[5] Thus "life" is a unified field in which no temporal aspect can be legitimately isolated from the other. The meanings of one's past are understood to be already the necessary background of present meaning. Accordingly, "creation" in *The Star* is just this past tense of inherited structures. Similarly, "redemption" is the future orientation that is always true of life, since to live is to be oriented with hope toward the fulfillment of one's deepest purposes. Past and future therefore constitute meaning in the present:

> Not in time . . . occurs that which occurs, but rather *time itself occurs.* . . . Just as every single event has its present, its past, and its future, without which it can not be known or at least known only distortedly, *so too reality as a whole.* Reality also has its past and its future, specifically an everlasting past and an eternal future. (ND, 150; my emphasis)[6]

---

toward God. Here it is interesting to note that for Rosenzweig God is not the agent of redemption but its *medium*—he is the object toward which man and world point in common. Thus God is in the "dative," while man and world are "two different nominatives." The linguistic nature of this relation is noteworthy, since Rosenzweig assigns a particular importance to the idea that the joining of elements can only occur through speech. God, though remaining beyond both man and world, is "the dative" that "truly binds." SE, 259–60 (E, 233).

5. On Rosenzweig's understanding of history see Alexander Altmann, "Franz Rosenzweig on History," in PFR, 124–37, and on historicism see the sensitive essay by Paul Mendes-Flohr, "Franz Rosenzweig and the Crisis of Historicism," in PFR, 138–61, where he observes that, "Rosenzweig presents eternity as the future anticipated in the present." Also see David N. Myers, *Resisting History: Historicism and Its Discontents in German-Jewish Thought* (Princeton: Princeton University Press, 2003).

6. Rosenzweig thus affirmed once again that reality must be seized "as a whole" (im Ganzen). For comments, see Else-Rahel Freund, *Franz Rosenzweig's Philosophy of Existence,* trans.

Like Rosenzweig, Heidegger claims that merely "sequential" (or "vulgar") time, while valid in its way, is not "original," since it fails to capture how the present is already constituted only on the basis of past and future meaning (SZ, esp. §81, 420–28). Against such an understanding of sequential time conceived as a mere series of "nows," Heidegger offers his own model of continuous time, wherein its three modes—past, present, and future—are called the "ecstases" of temporality *(Ekstasen der Zeitlichkeit)* (SZ, 424 and 329–31). This term captures Heidegger's idea that any given moment already in its very structure "juts out" into what comes before and after, such that it is really not possible to speak of a simple "moment" as merely present. Heidegger called the past "heritage" *(Erbe* or *Herkunft),* insofar as it "juts out" into the present to ground the always-already structures of meaning in which we live. (In many places Heidegger calls the future "fate" [*Schicksal*], insofar as it makes the present what it is because of its teleological directness toward a definite end [see esp. SZ, 384].)

A similar notion of "ecstatic" rather than sequential temporality is crucial to Rosenzweig's understanding of redemption. Like Heidegger, Rosenzweig opposes merely "sequential" time to a truly ecstatic temporality. For only if time is considered an "original" unity can it then make sense to say that eternity is more than merely the present conceived as a permanent condition. For Rosenzweig, then, the past is not merely what happens to have happened; it *grounds* the meanings we find ourselves in. Because the Jews live in such a grounded present, Rosenzweig can claim that "Jewish life becomes memory" (SE, 442 [E, 397]). Similarly, the future is not only that toward which the present points, the future is actually the *meaning* of the present. Thus, Rosenzweig construes the "not yet" of the future as somehow "already" here. Similarly, Heidegger conceives of the future as that which provides the present with its meaning, its sense of purpose, its very identity. The future for Heidegger is thus what he calls the "towards-oneself" (SZ, 329). In a similar vein, Rosenzweig argues that the redemptive end must be "anticipated at every moment," indeed, within every moment. "Only thus," concludes Rosenzweig, "does the future become the time of eternity" (SE, 252 [E, 226]).

For both Rosenzweig and Heidegger, the present gains its final meaning only and always because it is charged with future meaning.[7] Because of its forward-looking projection, the present thus becomes a vessel of the future. Heidegger argues a similar point when he explains that for Dasein *"the pri-*

---

Stephen L. Weinstein and Robert Israel, ed. Paul Mendes-Flohr (The Hague: Martinus Nijoff, 1979), 11.

7. As Rosenzweig explains, "just as the *tempora* in general are mutually distinguished by their relation to the present, so too the present moment obtains the gift of eternity only here." SE, 252 (E, 226).

*mary phenomenon of original [ursprüngliches] and authentic temporality is the future."* Moreover, in its "having-been futurally [*zukünftig gewesen*]," it is the future itself *"which first of all awakens the Present"* (SZ, 329; my emphasis). For Rosenzweig, it is this projective or "ecstatic" stance that marks the present as capable of redemption. As Rosenzweig explains, *"Every moment can be the last. That is what makes it eternal and that, precisely, makes it the origin of the future, every member of which is anticipated by the first"* (SE, 252 [E, 226]).

## The Ontological Priority of Community

According to Rosenzweig, the holistic structure of a community is uniquely equipped to absorb future meaning into the present. Rosenzweig admits that this does not necessarily ensure the community itself any absolute permanence, yet in a community's form permanence is at least made possible.[8] The reason communities achieve greater if not absolute permanence is that they exhibit a specific "form," and are not shapeless and merely existent things. What is living thus breaks out of the historicist model of time to experience past, present, and future as meaningfully fused within any given moment. To say that communities (and not individuals, states, classes, and so on) are in their very being the unique sites of redemption is to grant them ontological priority. Thus life in community is for Rosenzweig a basic condition of redemption.

Communities for Rosenzweig are unique in that they can experience time with the sense of ecstatic unity essential for redemption. A common sense of purpose toward God, as uttered in the phrase "God is good," helps to forge the orientation by which the present gains eternal meaning. Rosenzweig is quite emphatic that the form of such an utterance must be communal. *"This time grammar emerges, not as a narrative striving to proceed from the narrator to the matter, nor as a dialogue oscillating between two partners, but as a chant which is enhanced with every stanza, and as an archetypal chant, which is always the chant of several parties. It is not a solo"* (SE, 258 [E, 231]; my emphasis). Significantly, Rosenzweig takes care to point out that the bond felt in community must not be confused with that of dialogue, in which one individual encounters another as an inassimilable other: "Originally, . . . the chant is one of many voices which are identical in pitch and breath, and over all content of the song stands the form of this commonalty [*die Form*

8. "That the kingdom is 'among you' [*mitten unter euch*], that it is coming 'today' is a notion of the future which eternalizes the moment." SE, 253 (E, 226). "It cannot be said with certainty that a people or epoch, or an event, a person, a work or an institution really attains immortality; nobody knows this. But the inherent form, even though it submerge again at the end, implies an increase in vitality, even if not eternal life." SE, 251 (E, 225).

*dieser Gemeinsamkeit*]" (SE, 258 [E, 231]). Moreover, the community is not only the form of permanence, it is also its content; simply by being communal, one has already adopted the shape necessary for endurance.[9] Thus *"the content [of community] itself is nothing more than the rationalization of this its form"* (SE, 258 [E, 231]; my emphasis).

At the heart of this idea is the claim that community can never be simply a partnership of individuals nor can it be a collectivity of distinct beings united through dialogue. This is one reason why interpreters of Rosenzweig are mistaken when they read him as a partisan of dialogical philosophy such as Martin Buber. It is also an illustration of how strongly Rosenzweig's philosophy contrasts with any postmodern celebration of disunity and with an ethical philosophy that acknowledges the basic alterity of those around us. The theme of community in Rosenzweig's thought thus contrasts starkly with the philosophy of Emmanuel Levinas, who values difference over communal holism. Indeed, Rosenzweig's affirmation of the community as the specific and irreducible unit of redemptive meaning is so powerful that he refuses to see it as a manifold at all. "'We' is no plural," he argues; rather, "We" is a "mighty unison" (SE, 263–64 [E, 236]). As already noted in the previous chapter, the community thus became for Rosenzweig a kind of collective singularity with all the attributes Hegel had originally ascribed to the individual. In chanting with a single voice in praise of God, the community becomes the basic site of redemption, a precondition for what Rosenzweig called "the new totality." Moreover, he places great emphasis on the inner *uniformity* of such a community. The "We" must decisively reject all of those who do not dwell in the redemptive unity of being-toward-God and *"must eject [them] from its bright, melodious circle into the cold dread of the nothing"* (SE, 264 [E, 237]; my emphasis).

The argument for group uniformity by means of a founding act of exclusion becomes most explicit in a section called "The Decision" ("Die Entscheidung"). In Rosenzweig's account, such a decision is inevitably exclusionary: the "We" must say "You" (the German second-person collective, or "Ihr"). Further, he explains, the exclusion of this "You" is "dreadful" *(grauenhaft)*. To be sure, any such decision is a risk, since it invites God to examine the community so as to determine if its decision was in any way false (SE, 265 [E, 238]). Yet the community "cannot avoid this sitting in judgment, for only with this judgment does it give a definite content to the totality of its We. . . . Thus the We must say You, and the more its own volume increases, the louder the You resounds out of its mouth as well."

9. "[T]he content of the chant must be preceded by the founding of the community, as an exhortation, that is, to communal singing, thanking, acknowledging 'that He is good.' . . . [T]he exhortation itself must stand under the sign of the community." SE, 258 (E, 231–32).

Rosenzweig seems to accept the brutality of this decision. His sole qualification is that God alone ultimately determines who shall belong in the circle of the redeemed. But the community must anticipate God's decision, and must regard "his enemies" as "the enemies of God" as well (SE, 265 [E, 237–38]).[10]

Such exclusion, however, is temporary. What distinguishes Rosenzweig's idea of community from the invidious idea that redemption is only and always for a chosen few is the notion that all humanity belongs in the end within the horizon of a totalized "We." This is why his notion of ethics is altogether different from any ethical theory that finds our primary responsibility in the encounter with the other as truly other.[11] For Rosenzweig, the injunction to love one's neighbor means precisely that—to love the *neighbor (der Nächste),* someone who is most close to oneself. Indeed, while Rosenzweig makes it clear that we are to love the neighbor "as one's self" *(Wie sich selbst),* the object of this commandment is not expected to assume an infinite responsibility for the other that surpasses his own being. As Rosenzweig explains, "Man is not to deny himself. Precisely here in the commandment to love one's neighbor, his self is definitely confirmed in its place." Nor are we called upon to love everyone: "The world is not thrown in his face as an endless melee, nor is he told, while a finger points to the whole melee: that is you." Instead, only one "nearest thing" "is placed before his soul, and concerning this one and nearly [*zu-nächst*] this one only, he is told: *he is like you*" (SE, 267 [E, 239]; my emphasis). Rosenzweig's doctrine of love is thus quite distinct from Levinas's notion that one's relation to the "face of the other" signals a move "beyond" all ontological horizons. Unlike Levinas, Rosenzweig saw love as a phenomenon of "worldliness," since the bond between self and other appears within a single and unified holistic sphere, the life illumined by divine redemption. Indeed, for Rosenzweig, the "face of the other" is wholly in-the-world, so the Levinasian attempt at breaking from holism appears tantamount to idealist unworldliness, or, even worse, it expresses a longing for death. As he wrote Gritli:

> [I]t becomes now more clear to me, what I meant when I said to you that *love does not overstep the bounds of life* [*daß die Liebe die Grenzen des Lebens nicht übersteige*]. In life I love the neighbor, into whose eyes I look, who looks in my eyes, and love him perhaps "sitting within the shadow of God," love him "in" God. Indeed, I love him more than I love or can love God. For it must be so. God's

10. For a more charitable reading of Rosenzweig's intentions in this passage, see Richard A. Cohen, *Elevations: The Height of the Good in Rosenzweig and Levinas* (Chicago: University of Chicago Press, 1994).

11. Cf. an ethical theory such as that proposed by Levinas. For a more extensive treatment of the Rosenzweig-Levinas comparison, see my comments in the Introduction.

face "can no man see and remain living [*bleibt leben*]." (GB [13.4.1918], 72; my emphasis)

Ethics for Rosenzweig is forged from structures of familiarity rather than alterity. Here Rosenzweig's ideas concerning the priority of holistic, communal bonds sets him dramatically at odds with new developments in contemporary Jewish ethics, especially those of Levinas. Indeed, it seems misleading to call Rosenzweig's ideas "ethical" in the customary sense.[12] While he devotes significant (though relatively brief) discussion to the love between individuals—whose encounter takes the form of an "I" who meets a "Thou"—what is perhaps most striking about *The Star* is how rarely it touches upon such moral themes. Those who go looking in it for ethical insights must struggle laboriously to bring out claims about responsibility that, if present at all, remain largely implicit throughout. This is a noteworthy consequence of his fundamentally holistic understanding of group identity. For Rosenzweig, the community is a unified and organic structure, not a collective of discrete individuals. Beginning with religiously dissociated selves cut off from the social and historical world, *The Star* develops a holistic theory of human groups but for this same reason prohibits any sustained understanding of truly "public" life.

Whatever its costs for political thought, Rosenzweig's argument for the ontological priority of community belongs to a rich and respectable tradition most recently developed by communitarians. As Lawrence Vogel suggests, there is an important communitarian strain in Heidegger's philosophy as well, which is most evident in the account of "being-with," as developed in *Being and Time.* For Heidegger, any sense of recognition and mutuality can only first emerge on the basis of a rich and already founded sense of "who" one is in a world of shared meaning. One can recognize another's selfhood only on the basis of one's already sharing a world. This sense of "always already" sharing a world is what Heidegger calls "being-with" or *Mit-Dasein* (SZ, esp. §26, 117–25). Now while it is often taken as a notorious failing that Heidegger did not develop the positive ramifications of this idea before brusquely turning to its risks for our "inauthenticity," it is obvious in

---

12. Else-Rahel Freund observed as early as 1933 that for Rosenzweig even "eternity" becomes not a "time of endless duration," but instead the "simultaneousness of the three qualitatively different times," which as a whole "forms *the basic concept for being-in-community*" (my emphasis, hyphenation in the original). *Rosenzweig's Philosophy of Existence,* 11. Also see Leora Batnitzky, *Idolatry and Representation: The Philosophy of Franz Rosenzweig Reconsidered* (Princeton: Princeton University Press, 2000), who argues that while one must acknowledge the "violence" in monotheistic community-formation, one should also acknowledge that (at least in Rosenzweig's philosophical reconstruction of Judaism) the violence is temporary and may serve a higher universalist purpose. I present a different view at the end of this chapter.

Division Two of *Being and Time* that being-with is something that is necessarily constitutive of Dasein in its authenticity as well. Heidegger affirms that authentic resolve "modifies" but by no means "dissolves" the relation between Dasein and its "concernful co-being with others" (SZ, §60, esp. 298). To live in an intelligible world at all requires that we live within hermeneutic horizons, those shared forms of life that comprise the fundamentally social phenomena of language, history, and people.[13]

In what follows, I shall touch upon the more explicitly political ramifications of this theory. Here it suffices to note that Heidegger and Rosenzweig are basically in agreement that the community is ontologically prior. Rosenzweig's theory of community, of the primal "We" as a nonpluralistic unity, presumes that social being is a transcendental given: it is created *ex nihilo* in a "terrible" act of decision that precedes (and would make possible) anything like rational and public accord. In essence, it is a theory about the holistic grounds of meaning—people, language, ritual, and so on—that first establish the "hermeneutical" horizons of experience.[14] This theory of community is buttressed by a robust commitment to holism, as I will explain in the following section.

## A Theory of Temporal Holism

For Rosenzweig, there is an ultimate moment to redemption that surpasses human capacities altogether. In this moment, the structures of exclusion and familiarity that necessarily shape our lives as human beings are ultimately dissolved through an act of God, who "vanquishes all separation [*tilgt die Scheidung*]" (SE 265 [E, 238]). In redemption, "the We and the You [*Ihr*] sink back into one single blinding light." Here Rosenzweig's argument is exceedingly subtle. Although redemption is "prepared" and "anticipated" by humanity, there is in it a final aspect that remains unaccounted for in hu-

---

13. For helpful commentaries on the theme of "Mitsein" in Heidegger, see inter alia, Lawrence Vogel, *The Fragile "We": Ethical Implications of Heidegger's "Being and Time"* (Evanston, Ill.: Northwestern University Press, 1994) and Frederick Olafson, *Heidegger and the Ground of Ethics: A Study of "Mitsein"* (Cambridge: Cambridge University Press, 1998). Also see the ongoing discussion among Olafson, Taylor Carman, and Hubert Dreyfus: Olafson, "Heidegger à la Wittgenstein, or 'Coping' with Professor Dreyfus," *Inquiry* 37: 45–64; Carman, "On Being Social: A Reply to Olafson," *Inquiry* 37: 203–23; Olafson, "Individualism, Subjectivity, and Presence: A Response to Taylor Carman," *Inquiry* 37: 331–37; and Dreyfus, "Interpreting Heidegger on *Das Man*," *Inquiry* 38: 423–30.

14. From a political perspective, there is nothing intrinsically distasteful about this theory, unless (taking one's cue from Derrida's criticism of Heidegger) one objects to holism on principle. On the evasive and "metaphysical" implications of assigning intrinsic superiority to any specific "Volk" and language, see the suggestive remarks in Jacques Derrida, *De l'esprit: Heidegger et la question* (Paris: Galilée, 1987).

man experience. For this reason, ethical action can never be more than the preparatory ground for redemption—it is not redemption itself.[15]

*The Star* therefore lacks any robust theory welding ethics to redemption; it construes a final act of redemption as beyond human activity. This argument may seem surprising, especially given the prominence of ethics in some interpretations of Rosenzweig's thought. But ultimately Rosenzweig is being consistent, since if ethics were sufficient, this would require collapsing the ontological strata of God and World into the stratum of the merely human—a reduction forbidden by Rosenzweig's exposition of the threefold ontological difference. Redemption must remain a kind of cooperative event—the mutual opening of Man and World, their cooperative readiness toward God, then, finally, the unanticipated intrusion of God into the World. "[R]edemption," concludes Rosenzweig, "originates with God, and man knows neither the day nor the hour" (SE, 269 [E, 2420).

The final achieved state of redemption creates what Rosenzweig calls a "new totality" *(neue Allheit)* (SE, 283 [E, 254]). By this he means that the primal elements—God, Man, and World—are brought together in a stable and enduring temporal relationship. But this new totality is altogether unlike the timeless totality of philosophical idealism. Whereas idealism identifies thought and being, Rosenzweig's new totality distinguishes between the primal elements as distinctive yet brought into a "relation" *(Beziehung)* within the three correlates of religious experience: creation, revelation, and redemption.[16] Notice, however, that this new totality never cancels out the worldly and temporal qualities of man and world. While redemption brings man and world into a relationship with God, they are not fused with God such that they lose their distinctive characteristics. As Rosenzweig explains, man builds "the house of his eternal life *within* [and not beyond] the temporal crosscurrents [*im zeitlichen Hin- und Widerstrom*]" of love and community (SE, 289 [E, 259]; my emphasis).

*The Star of Redemption* thus articulates a metaphysical perspective that I would suggest we call "temporal holism." It recovers the "All" of idealism, which is now regarded as a lived, temporal, and relational structure, not as a seamless and rational totality.[17] Rosenzweig is so aggressively holistic in his

15. Love remains on the level of factical action, and Rosenzweig explains that "*it is not up to love which member it thus seizes with its power and delivers out of the context of life into its eternity.*" SE, 269 (E, 241); my emphasis.

16. The fact that Rosenzweig is willing to employ terms such as "totality" and "unity" makes it difficult to see how *The Star* might anticipate postmodernism. He is too much a holist to subscribe to any theory that would embrace disruption as necessary and constitutive of human experience. Compare Robert Gibbs, *Correlations in Rosenzweig and Levinas* (Princeton: Princeton University Press, 1992), 10 and *passim*.

17. I disagree here with the highly sensitive reading by Reiner Wiehl, "Experience in Rosenzweig's New Thinking," in PFR, 42–68, esp. 62: "The stamp of the *and* form enables man

thinking that in his theory of redemption he seems to move beyond the claim (in Part I) that each primal element enjoys its very own stable identity when it is considered apart from the whole. Redemption solidifies the relationship between the primal elements, especially those that unite man to the world, and so helps "realize" what man and world actually are. Man as he first appears does not wholly belong to world, and only the bonds he forges in love and community can bring him closer to the world—a requirement Rosenzweig calls "soul." Thus man "does not belong to the world until it becomes animated with its own soul, in redemption" (SE, 266 [E, 239]). The new totality that Rosenzweig proposes actually infuses temporality with eternity, yet without truly effacing the finitude of life. Even God's embrace of humanity itself as a community writ large does not annul the fact that human beings still remain within the sphere of life.[18] For the human being, redemption reaches into time to appear as the "eternity in the moment" *(Ewigkeit im Augenblick)*. When all humanity is united in gratitude toward God, eternity is brought into the world. The result is a new "totality" that, unlike the totality of idealism, cannot surpass or "complete" time but actually depends upon a temporal and proleptic relationship to the future. It is only as a temporal "bridge" that the present becomes the theater of eternity. As Rosenzweig explains, "[T]he chorus swells to an immense vision of that We of all the voices which cohortatively drags all future eternity into the present Now of the moment" (SE, 281 [E, 253]).

Even for God, redemption ultimately requires the recognition and embrace of temporality. According to Rosenzweig, God requires redemption just as man and the world do. "[H]e is Redeemer in a much graver sense than he is Creator or Revealer. For he is not only the one who redeems, but also the one who is redeemed. In the redemption of the world by man, of man by means of the world, God redeems himself." God requires redemption so as to "perfect" himself through a process of becoming. Rosenzweig argues this point most explicitly in the "recapitulation" that concludes the second volume of *The Star* ("Schwelle," or "Threshold"). These are exceedingly difficult passages: we read that the new unity of the primal elements is "only a becoming toward unity" *(nur Werden zur Einheit)* and that such a to-

---

to know his own fragmentary being in each of his experiences. His self-understanding always reveals to him only a fragment of his possible wholeness."

18. See the emphasis on time as a holistic context in ND: "Not in time occurs that which occurs, but rather time itself occurs. . . . Just as every single event has its present, its past, and its future, without which it cannot be known . . . , so too *reality as a whole*" (ND, 150; my emphasis). And note that Rosenzweig actually specifies that our communitywide praise of God does not include the dead. SE, 281 (E, 253). But "the kingdom of God prevails in the world [*setzt sich durch in der Welt*] by being prevalent in the world [*indem es die Welt durchsetzt*]." SE, 266 (E, 239).

tality "is only insofar as it becomes" *(sie ist nur indem sie wird)*. But only God "becomes" the unity that brings all to completion (SE, 266 [E, 238]).

This explanation has at least two noteworthy features that bear comparison to Heidegger. First, Rosenzweig's theory of redemption risks transforming divine being into a temporalized phenomenon. God's being, writes Rosenzweig is "the Simultaneity" of his "ever-becoming, all-time, and eternal Being" *(Immerwährend-, Allzeit- und Ewigseins)*, which taken together must be called "a Becoming" *(ein Werden)*. In other words, God is not subject to temporality, but his existence nonetheless exhibits a temporal structure.[19] Second, God's temporal structure is necessarily at one with God's being. The constraints of language almost prohibit Rosenzweig from clarifying this point. He is not saying, for example, that God undergoes a "process" of revelation and then returns to eternity. (Such a concept would simply naturalize God according to the model of evolutionary growth.) Instead, a temporal structure is eternally constitutive of God: "God is from the beginning," but this means that "he is at every moment" and also that "he is always coming" *(immer im Kommen)* (SE, 287–88 [E, 258]). This could not lend God a separate identity for each temporal index—past, present, and future—as this would require that we ascribe to God the very same historicist model of time Rosenzweig denies to human beings. Rather, the temporal indices are only possible because God's being is itself "a becoming." In redemption, Rosenzweig observes, eternity itself becomes "like time" (SE, 324 [E, 292]).

Both of these claims would suggest that Rosenzweig was verging upon a theory of God's thoroughgoing temporality. Clearly, this notion made him uneasy, since it seemed to break too vigorously with the traditional metaphysical idea of the Eternal. But it seems that he had taken a decisive step toward supplanting the standard metaphysical notion of an atemporal God with a post-Nietzschean God, who is in time but eternally so, since he is "always becoming." Perhaps the best proof of this is the section title "The Eternal God," in the conclusion of Part II. The phrase reads like a parody of scholasticism, as it is followed by a variety of qualifications and reversals, culminating in the suggestion that "eternity" now means something quite novel: "eternalization" *(Ver-ewigung)* (SE, 288 [E, 258]). This implies that eternity is a process and so necessarily temporal.[20]

19. Redemption is supposed to somehow guarantee that this temporal structure will return in the end to join with God's primal being, and it "provides this assurance of eternity despite the temporality of self-revelation." SE, 288 (E, 259).

20. Here one may discern a connection between Rosenzweig's idea of God's temporality and Heidegger's famous suggestion that Being's horizon is itself time. On this, see John Macquarrie's explanation for Heidegger's famous phrase, "Only a God can save us": it would be "naïve to assume that by the word 'God' [Heidegger] understands what most Christian theologians would understand by 'God.' . . . When Heidegger does use the word 'God,' he often

## On Judaism and Christianity

It is human experience that is the primary concern in Rosenzweig's account of redemption. The closing passages of the redemption chapter (volume 2, book 3) sketch out a brief picture of how human beings experience redemption in the most abstract sense. Rosenzweig writes of that "immense vision of that We of all the voices which cohortatively drags all future eternity into the present Now of the moment." With this "hymn of praise," we are told, life itself "becomes immortal." But this is not because the discrete individual somehow escapes personal death. Rather, it is the "We" that finds itself enduring through time, and it is only in this sense that Rosenzweig can write that "death plunges into the Nothing in the face of this triumphal shout of eternity" (SE, 281 [E, 253]).[21]

Rosenzweig offers his portrait of redemption as an event within concrete life in the third volume of *The Star of Redemption*. Here he describes two distinctive ways of living out the meaning of redemption, as embodied in Judaism and Christianity. Many interpreters of Rosenzweig's philosophical system have here discerned a kind of mutuality or even partnership between Judaism and Christianity: Rosenzweig devotes one chapter to each, and he assigns them distinctive roles in the process by which the world comes to the final "truth" of redemption. The role of Christianity is that of the "eternal way," while the role of Judaism is that of "eternal life" (SE, 378 [E, 341]). For Rosenzweig, these are different but (apparently) equally valid ways of realizing eternity within time—as different, he explains, as the infinity of a line and the infinity of a point (SE, 379–80 [E, 341]).

On the one hand, Christianity experiences the history of the world as a line that must be traveled. For the Christian, history is "all between," and the believer finds himself "always in the middle of happenings, always in the event and in the course of things" (SE, 378 [E, 340]). Indeed, the very pur-

---

does so in a hypothetical manner, so that, for instance, when he speaks of God as temporal, the sentence should be interpreted, 'if there is a God, then he is temporal', or perhaps, 'The idea of God in Christian or Jewish faith is that of a God who is temporal.'" *Heidegger and Christianity* (New York: Continuum Books, 1999), 95.

21. Here one might conceive of two modes of "eternity," one contemplative and one lived in the world. The contemplative account is first alluded to in the closing lines of the redemption chapter, and it is here that we are given an anticipation of Rosenzweig's closing discussion (volume 3, chapter 3) of the human encounter with God as an actual meeting with the divine countenance. For the time being, Rosenzweig does little more than allude to this redemptive moment: "[T]he pious sit, with crowns on their heads, and behold the radiance of the manifest deity [und shauen in der Lichtglanz der offenbarwordenen Gottheit]." SE, 282 (E, 253). Significantly, this characterization of redemption is inactive, a silent encounter with God's overwhelming truth. But for Rosenzweig it is insufficient precisely because it does not allow for the everyday and concrete ways that communities—various groups that name themselves as "We"—live out their "being by God" *(bei Gott sein)*.

pose of Christianity is to broaden the We within the world—its essence is "diffusion throughout all that is outside" (SE, 385 [E, 347]). On the other hand, Judaism is characterized by "rootedness in the profoundest self." The We of the Jews experiences world history as mere accident such that for them politics are generally speaking a matter of indifference.

Interpreters who are interested in conciliatory relations between the two faiths have tried to see the relationship between Judaism and Christianity in Rosenzweig's argument as basically cooperative. Where Judaism maintains a pure and self-absorbed relationship with eternity such that its successive generations seem to persist as if outside of history, Christianity brings the message of redemption into the peoples of the world so as to prepare time, as it were, for the irruption of eternity. Admittedly, the factual relationship between Jews and Christians is not always a friendly one. According to Rosenzweig, the Jewish community testifies in its very existence to the fact that Christianity has not yet attained its goal and remains still "on the way."[22] On the other hand, Judaism too suffers a certain one-sidedness due to its special dissociation from history. As Rosenzweig explains, Judaism purchases the possession of truth "with the loss of the unredeemed world" (SE, 459–60 [E, 413–14]). Both faiths are therefore necessary and complementary in the narrative of redemption, despite the very real enmity between them. One might even say that each provides a remedy for the sins of its rival— the presumption of universality on the one hand, the arrogance of particularism on the other. But this complementarity between the two faiths is considerably qualified by Rosenzweig's idea that the Jews alone are now redeemed, as I shall explain below.

### The Ontological Priority of the Jews

For Rosenzweig, Judaism enjoys a special priority in the experience of redemption. The entire discussion of community in volume II of *The Star* has suggested that there is a distinctive We that *already* lives "with God," even in the midst of an otherwise unredeemed world. In the third volume, it becomes apparent that this separate and collective We is the children of Israel alone. The reason they enjoy priority is that they alone are capable of acting as the temporal "dwelling" for eternity. Outside of this We, Rosenzweig explains, past and future are experienced as divorced, and only in Judaism can they "grow into one" (SE, 331 [E, 298]). As a consequence, the Jewish people live within time but in the peculiar condition of future-orientation

22. This, on Rosenzweig's view, may help to explain why the Jewish community is often the object of enmity and resentment—a topic Rosenzweig developed at length in his 1916 correspondence with Eugen Rosenstock on the relationship between Judaism and Christianity. See *Briefe,* Franz Rosenzweig and Eugen Rosenstock, "Judentum und Christentum," 673–720.

that provides a privileged experience of eternity in the world. Other nations cling too passionately to the present, to states and territories, and so fail to provide the proper communal setting for the experience of redemption. Even in Christianity, according to Rosenzweig, redemption is not so much a present experience as it is a condition to be awaited. Rosenzweig thus describes Christianity as a "between" condition that does not yet experience eternity since it remains "on the way" in history (SE, 411 [E, 379]). Thus no matter how conciliatory Rosenzweig may be in his various remarks on Judaism and Christianity, nothing should obscure the fact that in the final analysis his book assigns the Jews a unique status as the redeemed community.

The philosophical grounds for Rosenzweig's claim that the Jews alone are uniquely equipped to live within the experience of redemption are found mostly in the first chapter of volume III, entitled "The Fire, or the Eternal Life." Here Rosenzweig makes it clear that if a community is to serve as the We that brings eternity into time, it must itself somehow achieve the status of eternity in time. Rosenzweig calls this special status an "earthly eternity" *(irdische Ewigkeit),* a phrase that seems consciously to turn Schiller's "fear of the earthly" *(Angst des Irdischen)* on its anti-metaphysical head. It is clear that for Rosenzweig, such an earthly eternity can only be achieved within the bounds of collective experience.[23] But not only human collectivity will do. Most communities express their will to eternity in the world by clinging to the soil *(am Boden),* but the soil ends by betraying their longing insofar as political struggle constantly robs peoples of their territory. Political communities are also hopelessly transient, in that political history shows us a series of states rising and falling in what Rosenzweig terms a "bellicose temporality" *(kriegerischen Zeitlichkeit)* (SE, 368 [E, 332]). The only kind of community that will suffice is one that clings neither to land nor to politics yet somehow manages to create a sense of eternity within the world.

Here one can see that Rosenzweig has been driven by the very premises of his philosophy to devise a curiously "temporal" grounding for eternity. Because he wishes to overcome the metaphysical idea of redemption, he tries instead to fold our human yearning for ultimacy back within the temporal horizon. Yet this has some rather surprising consequences. As we have seen, it compels Rosenzweig to adopt unconventional turns of phrase where eternity becomes something "within" temporality—a phrase that is difficult to square with more conventional philosophical language. And because only a community can achieve the kind of eternity that is required, Rosen-

---

23. "In the service of the earth, constantly repeated day in day out and year in year out, man senses his earthly eternity within the human community. In the community—and not as individual, for as individual he senses it rather in the changes of age and in the circuit of conception and birth." SE, 323 (E, 291).

zweig suggests that we must look to a community that lives in time but can create its own eternity within itself. On the one hand, Rosenzweig is quite clear about the fact that there really is no escape from time—this community too must have "its temporality" *(seine Zeitlichkeit)* (SE, 364 [E, 328]). On the other hand, he is equally clear on the idea that there must be some way of experiencing time where it does not overwhelm the community and render it impermanent. For such a community, profane time "has no power over it and must roll past." For this to be the case of a temporal community, it must *"produce its own time"* and thereby *"provide the warrant of its eternity" (die Gewähr ihrer Ewigkeit)* (SE, 331–32 [E, 299]; my emphasis). What is needed is a kind of "self-grounding," wherein the condition for permanence arises from the very community it supports.[24]

For Rosenzweig the only community that meets these conditions are the Jews. While almost all other nations of the world live in states, the Jews alone are permanently stateless. And while states make a promise of eternity, this promise is hollow, since what appears eternal is really nothing more than a "dam upon the stream of life" marking the "small pools" or "epochs" of worldly history (SE, 371 [E, 332–34]). Eschewing the state, Jews live instead within a quasi-soldierly collective—Rosenzweig calls it "comradeship" *(Kameradschaft)*—whose members feel absolute obedience to their sovereign Lord. Rosenzweig also likens this collective to a mobile army, whose "comradely greeting" mimics the political rites of state. And like a troop of soldiers parading before its commander-in-chief, this community owes its absolute allegiance to the whole of the community alone rather than any particular individual within it. "For the soldier," notes Rosenzweig, "feels that the flag and dynasty are older than anything living and will survive it" (SE, 357–59 [E, 321–23]).

Rosenzweig's martial images are peculiar, especially given his postwar reputation as a primarily ethical thinker who was indifferent to power politics. But in fact the comparison to soldierly solidarity is quite in keeping with the dominant themes of his mature thought. The idea that the collective survives while the soldier may perish confirms Rosenzweig's belief in the radical priority of the community to the individual, even to the point of denying that the We is plural. This belief arguably resembles recent communitarian theory; but the military subtext marks a noticeable departure from the spirit of cordiality that characterizes most communitarian thought. Rosenzweig's crucial move here is to reject politics even while pre-

24. The term *Gewähr* is illuminating, since it means a guarantee or a grant of security. It is therefore related to Kant's notion of a *quid juris* or *Rechtsgrund*—the legal title that authorizes our use of the pure concept of understanding within the bounds of all possible experience (KdrV, §13). Like a transcendental ground, Rosenzweig's "warrant" secures a community objective validity across history and time.

serving the ideal of sovereignty that political theorists more typically reserve for states, since only states wield the power necessary to enforce their claims. Rosenzweig thus wanted to build up a non-statist notion of solidarity as strong as—indeed stronger than—the kind backed by state power. So while Jews are dissociated from political life, they are said to exist with a feeling of collective purpose surpassing that of other nations.

The Jews' dissociation from actual power politics makes them what Rosenzweig calls a "community of fate" *(Schicksalsgemeinschaft)*, an artifact of his study of Hegel's political theory (SE, 358 ff. [E, 322 ff.]). Specifically, the Jewish condition of statelessness is the theoretical answer in Rosenzweig's thought to the isolated and "fateful" status of the early Christian community in Hegel's theological writings. Rosenzweig seems to have salvaged Hegel's vision of a people whose indifference to Caesar is a counterpoint to their spiritual solidarity amongst themselves. But where Hegel condemned the Christians for this apolitical comradeship, Rosenzweig makes the Jews' isolation the very desideratum of their survival.

### *"The Dark Sources of the Blood"*

The idea of the blood-community is perhaps one of the most troubling aspects of Rosenzweig's philosophy and so deserves clarification. As explained above, Rosenzweig asserts that the Jewish community has "its time" but they are also uniquely capable of experiencing eternity. This can only be true if they collectively satisfy a special condition, such that "eternity is . . . shifted into time" (SE, 361 [E, 325]). This condition is consanguinity, the generational continuity realized through the Jewish bloodline. Rosenzweig addresses this claim most directly in the section of *The Star* entitled "The Eternal People: Jewish Fate" ("Das Ewige Volk: Jüdische Schicksal"). According to Rosenzweig, the Jews can only enjoy their unique status as an eternal people if they are also a people apart. They must be community of fate in so radical a fashion that even their experience in time may be considered distinctively their own. The Jews enjoy their own special kind of temporality only insofar as they are a "community of blood" *(Gemeinschaft des Bluts)*. (See, e.g., SE, 332 [E, 299], and *passim.*)

In one of the earliest reviews of *The Star of Redemption*, Otto Gründler took strong exception to this idea, which he called a "Jewish naturalism of blood" *(Naturalismus des Bluts)*.[25] He objected to the book's "absolutizing of

---

25. Gründler, "Eine jüdisch-theistische Offenbarungsphilosophie," *Hochland* 19, 5 (February 1922): 621–32, at 631. One could argue that Gründler was predisposed as a Christian to reject any idea of Jewish election. But his negative impression should not be dismissed outright, given that in the remainder of his review he proved himself a fair-minded and

race" and could not accept Rosenzweig's view that Christianity was intrinsically prejudiced against Judaism only because Christians jealously sensed their "on the way" status and recognized that the Jews dwelt "already" by God. For Gründler this argument was itself an expression of Rosenzweig's faulty notion that identity is rooted in blood, since it implied that Jewish and Christian identities are fixed. Whatever one makes of such criticism (and there are good reasons to reject it as unpersuasive), Rosenzweig's language of blood-community clearly invites negative comment. So the question remains whether *The Star* endorses a quasi-naturalistic criterion for Jewish identity.

The question becomes especially pressing when one considers how later interpreters of Rosenzweig's philosophy have grappled with the theme of blood. Stéphane Mosès, for example, has suggested that "the term 'blood community' must be understood to mean what we would now call an ethnic community." (As evidence, Mosès refers to Rosenzweig's apparent claim that there are *many* communities that define themselves by common blood.) [26] A rather different interpretation is offered by Leora Batnitzky, who suggests that the notion of the blood-community is a "philosophical construct" and is "not meant literally or racially." It is a "limit concept for modern philosophy" that dramatizes the radical exteriority of Judaism to the Western idealist tradition. (As evidence, Batnitzky cites a letter addressed to Eugen Rosenstock-Huessy in 1916 in which Rosenzweig argued

---

insightful reader. See Rosenzweig's brief comment, *Briefe*, N.340, An Gertrud Oppenheim (Frankfurt, 14.3.1922), 423.

26. Mosès, *Système et Révélation: La Philosophie de Franz Rosenzweig* (Paris: Éditions du Seuil, 1982), 183–84, referring to SE, 332 (E, 298–99). In *The Star* (in the English translation) Rosenzweig observes, "What holds generally for peoples as groups united through blood relationship over against communities of the spirit, holds for our people in particular." SE, 332 (E, 299). But in the German original, one reads that blood-relationship *"gilt nun in ganz besonderer Weise von dem unsern,"* that is, it "holds for our [people] in a *wholly particular way*" (my emphasis). The original phrase is ambiguous, but the published English translation is misleading. Rosenzweig appears to mean that while there may be a common understanding of blood-community that applies to many different populations, the notion of blood-community as it applies to the Jews is meant in an *entirely special fashion*. In a passage immediately following the one just cited, Rosenzweig elaborates on this point, that "among the peoples of the earth, the Jewish people is, as they call themselves . . . : the one people [*das eine Volk*]. The peoples of the world cannot content themselves with the community of blood." SE, 332 (E, 299). But if the Jews are *"the* one people" and are such *"in a wholly particular way,"* it is difficult to see how the concept of blood-community could apply to them "in the usual sense." Similarly, in a letter to Gritli Rosenzweig calls the Jews "the people" (*das Volk*) as distinguished from "people as such" (*Völker überhaupt*), implying that the Jews are indeed people but in way incommensurable with generic uses of the term. See GB (29.12.1918), 207. The suggestion that one could update Rosenzweig's arguments as talk about ethnicity thus seems improbable.

that since Judaism accepts the notion of conversion, the notion of "blood-connection" [*Blutszusammenhang*] can only have a "symbolic meaning.")[27]

Given its historical associations, scholarly reluctance to find any literal meaning in Rosenzweig's concept of blood-community is understandable. The Nazis famously deployed the category of *Blutsgemeinschaft* to argue that the German people's "superiority" was rooted in putatively distinctive racial characteristics. Hitler claimed in *Mein Kampf* that the world is composed of different peoples distinguished by blood, and so he rejected the liberal view that the Jews were Germans and only different insofar as they belonged to separate "community of religion" *(Religionsgemeinschaft)*. "The religious teaching of the Jews," he added, "is first and foremost a directive toward the maintenance of the Jews' blood-purity."[28] Obviously such argumentation was little more than a crude parody of scientific reasoning. But as a practical ideology its consequences were devastating. Here it is perhaps important to recall that Rosenzweig himself, had he not succumbed to an early but natural illness, would very likely have died as a victim of Nazi racism. So while there may be little commonality between Nazi racism and Rosenzweig's language of blood, it is easy to see why interpreters would find even the most superficial resemblance intolerable.

I disagree with Mosès that Rosenzweig's arguments are really about "ethnicity." And I agree with Batnitzky that they are meant in a symbolic way. But it is more than a "limit concept for modern philosophy"; it also has symbolic *content*. What, exactly, is it supposed to symbolize? Here I shall offer another, quite different sort of interpretation, which seems in my view to best capture Rosenzweig's philosophical intentions. Throughout his excursus on the Jewish role in redemption, there is significant linkage between the concept of blood and a specifically "Jewish" sort of temporality. The temporal qualities of blood makes it especially well suited for Rosenzweig's argument that it grounds Jewish identity. As a fluid rather than static medium, blood captures the idea that philosophy must move within the temporal flow of life. As Rosenzweig explains, the Jewish notion of generational continuity guarantees "that the flow of blood may not cease during the long night of time" ("daß der Fluß des Bluts unversiegend hin durch die lange Nacht der Zeiten dem einstigen Morgen zurolle") (SE, 354 [E, 319]).

Accordingly, blood might be regarded as a name for the Jews' special temporality as against the normal temporality of the world. The Jewish com-

27. Thus the blood-community is "a philosophical construct that is meant to undo the priority of philosophical constructs," and this in turn suggests that "the Jewish people and their revelation are neither irrational nor anti-rational, but they are beyond reason." Batnitzky, *Idolatry and Representation*, 74–76. The letter quoted is in *Briefe*, 693.

28. Adolf Hitler, *Mein Kampf* (München: Zentralverlag der NSDAP, 1939), 335–36; orig. pub. 1925 (vol. I) and 1927 (vol. II).

munity, as Rosenzweig explains, has "its temporality" *(seine Zeitlichkeit)*, a mode of time distinct from and deeper than the merely progressive temporality of the world (SE, 364 [E, 328]). And the circulation of the blood also corresponds to what Rosenzweig calls the "earthly repetition" *(irdische Wiederholung)* in Jewish ritual and may also apply to the mobility of Jewish life in exile.[29] This cyclical and ritually repeated structure of Jewish "temporality" is therefore the deeper meaning behind the arguments about blood. As Rosenzweig explains, "the [Jewish] people is people only through the people" ("das Volk ist Volk nur durch das Volk").[30] In sum, "blood" provides the Jews with a temporality and generative permanence that is deeper than the merely "successive" temporality that governs the world. Just as Jewish law and scripture are "eternally present," so too the Jewish community *"draws its own eternity from the dark sources of the blood"* (SE, 338 [E, 304], my emphasis; note that the English translation omits the word "dark" in this phrase, obscuring its romantic gravity).

As one can see, Rosenzweig's idea of blood-community is not meant in a racial (or even "ethnic") sense. One might call it ontological, since it speaks to the basic temporal conditions that allow for the Jews to be who they are. The Jewish people are for Rosenzweig a blood-community that lives "in its own redemption" because of a self-grounded temporality that it wields independent of its surroundings and as part of its "ownmost" constitution. Because the Jewish people is constituted in its essence by blood alone, Jewish identity is temporally self-sufficient. It is grounded in redemption because it is grounded in itself. "The full force of its will to people," writes Rosenzweig, "is gathered in one point—which for the peoples of the world is only one point among others—the authentic and pure life-point, the blood-community; the will to people *shall not cling to any dead instruments [kein totes Mittel];* it shall realize itself through the people alone" (SE, 333 [E, 300], my emphasis). The crucial idea is that the Jewish people does not look to the world to provide the anchors for its understanding of authentic being. Unlike identity that is rooted in land, Jewish identity displays "rootedness in one's own self" *(Verwurzelung im eigenen selbst)* (SE, 339 [E, 305]). The Jewish community is thereby assured of a permanence unknown to all other peoples. Gaining their grounding through the blood-community alone, the Jews exhibit a temporality that is wholly without roots in the customary sense of territoriality; their condition is one of rooted unrootedness. Rosen-

29. On "earthly repetition," see SE, 323 (E, 291); on Jewish exile, see esp. SE, 332–33 (E, 299–300), and SE, part III, chapter 1, "The Fire," *passim.*

30. Such phrases give expression to Rosenzweig's idea that only through blood can a community "will itself" into a mode of redemption that is nothing less than a mode of life. In a curiously Nietzschean formulation, he calls this the "will to people" *(Wille zum Volk).* SE, 333 (E, 300).

zweig himself calls this condition that of never being "entirely at home" *(in keinem andern Land mehr ganz heimisch)* (SE, 333 [E, 300]); elsewhere he would characterize it as "uncanny" *(unheimlich)*.[31]

The charge that Rosenzweig's portrait of the Jewish community is based upon a "naturalistic" notion of race would thus be inaccurate, for at least two reasons. First, if the concept of race implies that identity is determined by the body, then Rosenzweig's notion of Jewish identity cannot be racist, since his notion of blood at once determines and registers identity—otherwise conversion would be impossible. (That is, blood, or Jewish temporality, is constituted in and through those distinctive ways of being that make one a Jew, so one may feasibly "acquire" Jewish blood.) Second, if naturalism here means that identity is part of the natural world, then Rosenzweig's concept of the Jewish people cannot be naturalistic, since his entire argument about Jewish identity is meant to dissociate it from its surroundings. And surely a naturalistic conception of Jewish existence would not allow for the claim that the Jewish people creates its very own temporality.[32]

## Community and Decision

Quite apart from the charge of naturalism, however, an additional worry about Rosenzweig's definition of the Jews as a blood-community is that it appears to justify an extreme sort of Jewish chauvinism. This worry is perhaps more accurate than some previous interpreters have cared to admit. As noted above, Rosenzweig argues that to be Jewish is to be ontologically unlike all other peoples of the world. Even if there are other "ethnicities" in the world, on his view the Jewish blood-community is constituted "in a

31. Rosenzweig wrote to Gritli: "There is something uncanny about blood. [Es ist etwas Unheimliches um das Blut]." GB (12.2.1919), 236–37. On "unheimlich," see Leora Batnitzky, "Rosenzweig's Aesthetic Theory and Jewish *Unheimlichkeit*," *New German Critique* 77 (spring–summer1999): 87–112. Also see Susan Shapiro, "The Uncanny Jew: A Brief History of an Image," *Judaism* 46, 1 (1997): 63–78.

32. Rosenzweig seems to have strongly associated blood with rootedness in a tradition. In a letter to Gritli, for example, he linked having "no ground and earth beneath one's feet" *(keinen Grund und Boden unter sich)* and being "without tradition," *(traditionlos)* with being "bloodless" *(blutleer)*. See GB (24.12.1918), 203–4. The idea of blood-community may also bear intellectual debts to Martin Buber's famous "Bar Kochba" lectures of 1909: Buber called the Jews a "community of blood" and claimed blood as "the deepest, most potent stratum of our being." See "Judaism and the Jews," in Buber, *On Judaism*, ed. Nahum Glatzer (New York: Schocken: 1967), 11–21, quote at 17. For comments on these lines see Steven Aschheim, "1912: The publication of Moritz Goldstein's 'The German-Jewish Parnassus' sparks a debate over assimilation, German culture, and the 'Jewish spirit,'" in *The Yale Companion to Jewish Writing and Thought in German Culture, 1096-1996*, ed. Sander L. Gilman and Jack Zipes (New Haven: Yale University Press, 1997), 299–305, esp. 303.

wholly particular fashion." This is an unmistakable argument in favor of Jewish uniqueness. The deeper question, however, is whether such an argument for uniqueness is made in a way that is at all defensible, philosophically and morally.

To probe this concern it is helpful to recall Rosenzweig's claim that a religious community first appears upon the basis of an unprecedented "decision" *(Entscheidung),* which first singles out the We from the You, (those "enemies of God"). Rosenzweig admits that such a decision is "dreadful" *(grauenhaft),* since the We expels the You "from its bright, melodious circle into the cold dread of the nothing" (SE, 264 [E, 237]). But he also assures the reader of its necessity, especially for a community that creates its boundaries without the benefit of statehood or land. It would be specious to attach any explicitly political meaning to this idea of decision, since Rosenzweig's fundamental premise is that Jewish life remains ontologically dissociated from its political surroundings. But especially when considered together with his use of military analogy, it is nonetheless a discomfiting theory of community formation.

The writings of Carl Schmitt provide a useful if troubling contemporary comparison. In the essay "The Concept of the Political" (published 1927, expanded 1932), Schmitt argued that the essence of politics lies in the capacity to distinguish between friend and enemy, and that this distinction, like divine creation, is quite literally ex nihilo—a decision *(Entscheidung)* of the sovereign that establishes the fundamental enmity of politics on the basis of "nothing." The notorious appeal of Schmitt's definition had much to do with its simplicity and its contempt for the prevarication of contract-theory, natural-law, and universalist-Kantian ethics. In their place Schmitt argued for a brutal, pre-ethical decisionism, which expanded the definition of politics, since "[e]very religious, moral, economic, ethical, or other antithesis transforms itself into a political one if it is sufficiently strong to group human beings effectively according to friend and enemy."[33]

As Karl Löwith once suggested, there is a barely suppressed theological tenor to Schmitt's political theory.[34] The very notion of a "decision in nothingness" *(Entscheidung im Nichts)* is thinkable only in the space evacuated by God. To assert with Rosenzweig that the founding decision of communi-

33. Schmitt, *The Concept of the Political,* trans. George Schwab (Chicago: University of Chicago Press, 1996), 26ff. and 45; 37. On Schmitt and expressionism, see Ellen Kennedy, "Politischer Expressionismus: Die Kulturkritischen und Metaphyscischen Ursprünge des Begriffes des Politischen bei Carl Schmitt," in *Complexio Oppositorum: Über Carl Schmitt,* ed. Helmut Quaritsch (Berlin: Duncker und Humblot, 1988), 233–51.

34. Löwith, "Der Okkasionale Dezisionismus von C. Schmitt," in his *Gesammelte Abhandlungen: Zur Kritik der geschichtlichen Existenz* (Stuttgart: W. Kohlhammer Verlag, 1960).

ties is both "necessary" and "terrible" means that it establishes the basic horizons of experience. Since they are the conditions for intelligibility, beyond them lies quite literally a "nothingness," the correlate of which would be the God whose will the community can only anticipate with apparent fear. Divine decision and the sovereign's decision from nothingness are thus two sides of the same coin, and Rosenzweig provides no good reason to suppose that there are independently founded (much less, rational) criteria by which to assess the decision. Like Schmitt, he assumes an "origin" to community formation, an origin that is itself prior to (and therefore escapes) moral scrutiny.

One might object that Rosenzweig's philosophy yields no true theory of politics because he rejects the state. But as noted above, Schmitt expanded the concept to embrace any model of group life forged from the decisionistic rupture between friend and enemy. Rosenzweig's concept of a decision between the We and the "enemies of God" thus seems to fall well within Schmitt's patently illiberal definition of political life. Now, as we have seen, Rosenzweig rejects political attachment as promising a bogus metaphysical security. So to characterize his arguments as political at all seems counterintuitive. But if liberal political theory arises from a prior commitment to atomism—that is, the vision of human beings as fungible and individualist by nature—then it is obvious that Rosenzweig does not share the founding premise of political liberalism. And where liberalism sees the social world as constituted through rational deliberation, Rosenzweig saw the deeper bonds of community as arising from a prerational and "terrible" decision, created from a nothingness prior to any imagined state of nature. For Rosenzweig, human beings are organized into distinctive communities even before consideration of their political status, whatever that may turn out to be. Politics presupposes community. His appeal to a patently irrational "decision," then, was perhaps his way of foreclosing any possible thought that a community's claim upon its members derives from precommunal (but rationally intelligible) norms. This is what I have called the "ontological priority" of community.

Communitarian arguments are not necessarily incompatible with liberal commitments. More intriguing, perhaps, Rosenzweig's portrait of the Jewish experience in history seems to reflect a canny recognition of the corrosive effects of liberal ideology upon the Jewish people's ability to maintain group cohesion in the modern world. Dissenting from Hermann Cohen and the Jewish progressive tradition of the nineteenth century, Rosenzweig came to suspect that the liberal-atomistic notion of citizenship and the belief in community were incompatible. For whereas liberalism demands an inward and individualized mode of religiosity—religion as "faith"—Judaism may presuppose communal structures of identification and practice that cannot easily survive if they are expelled from the public sphere into a life of privacy.[35] Unlike his universalist predecessors, Rosenzweig seems to have discerned an abiding tension between liberalism and Judaism. Admittedly, in *The Star* this rueful assessment of liberal political possibilities remains largely implicit. But it may cast light on the book's curious theory that true "redemption" lies elsewhere than politics, in a sphere beyond history and merely "successive" temporality.

As Steven Aschheim has observed, a striking number of Rosenzweig's Jewish contemporaries shared in the atmosphere of growing disenchantment with liberal-universalist politics.[36] But here a distinction is needed. Many other Weimar-Jewish intellectuals, though disenchanted with liberalism, came to believe that it was the European assimilationist model of liberalism that was most at fault, not universalism as such. Such thinkers predicted that when the last traces of antisemitism had vanished, the emancipationist dictum that Jews be embraced only as individuals would spell the end of the Jews as a distinctive group altogether. This was a commonplace argument among Zionists, whose dream of nationalist awakening was therefore compatible with a kind of political universalism, insofar as they demanded for the Jews the very same right of statehood granted in principle to other nations.

Rosenzweig's remarkable diffidence toward Zionism was due partly to the fact that he did not share its quasi-Hegelian faith in politics as the highest theater of human fulfillment. Many of his later critics have faulted Rosenzweig on this score (perhaps because they insist on the notion that Zionism is the only legitimate expression of Jewish modernity). But ironically, Rosenzweig's non-Zionism expresses the very same disillusionment with liberal-assimilationist ideals that had propelled so many of his contemporaries into the nationalist movement. In this respect Rosenzweig was most emphatically not a liberal political thinker. Moreover, unlike the Zionist ideal of the Jews as a nation like all other nations, he eschewed this universalistic kind of nationalism for a theologically based theory of Jewish difference.[37] Re-

35. See, e.g., Rosenzweig's remarks on G. E. Lessing's drama of tolerance, *Nathan the Wise,* that Nathan lacks any real children at the play's end; *Briefe,* N.281, An Gertrud Oppenheim (3.10.19), 372–73.

36. Aschheim, "German Jews beyond Bildung and Liberalism: The Radical Jewish Revival in the Weimar Republic," in his *Culture and Catastrophe: German and Jewish Confrontations with National Socialism and Other Crises* (New York: New York University Press, 1996), 31–44.

37. The exclusivist ramifications of the notion of blood-community worked in curious tension with the notion that the Jews should serve as a "light unto the nations." Indeed, present exclusivity was to presage messianic universality. Thus the extensive remarks to Gritli: "Whether only the Jew knows what blood-community is? *Yes, since to really know means: to know in God. No, because the Jew has absolutely nothing for himself which is not had by everyone in the end.* . . . And between Jewry and other peoples there is no true division of labor as amongst the other

sisting political universalism of any sort, Rosenzweig's disillusionment with liberalism thus drove him away from politics, and away from any general theory of self-determination. Whereas the Zionists asserted the right to state sovereignty upon ancestral lands, Rosenzweig became a philosophical proponent of life in exile.

*Exile as an Ontological Condition*

In his famous study *Jewish Self-Hatred* (Berlin, 1930), Theodor Lessing announced that "the whole life-question of the Jewish people seems to me this: can it overcome the darkness of spirit?" ("Kann es den Dünkel des Geistes überwinden?") This was a question of mortal importance, not only a topic for philosophical speculation. In Lessing's view the Jew suffered primarily as a creature "cut off from the elements of life [*vom Lebenselemente abgeschnittenen Kreatur*]." Of course, claims such as these were common for many Jewish thinkers of the late nineteenth and early twentieth century— especially for those of a Zionist orientation. In their view, to be cut off from "life" often meant to persist in the deracinated condition of exile. It meant to live as an excessively "intellectual" people without territory and state, lacking that sort of groundedness in the world that one often imagines can only come from dwelling and working in a land of one's own. A Zionist such as Aaron David Gordon (1856–1922), for example, would argue that the Jew in exile "did not know life." If Zionism sought a "spiritual renaissance" this was not to be confused with "some shadowy or abstract spirit, which can express itself only within the recesses of heart and mind." The goal was a "vital culture" that, "far from being detached from life, embraces it in all its aspects."[38]

It is striking how much such language seems also at work in *The Star of Redemption*. Its polemic against transcendence anticipates Lessing's complaint about the "darkness of spirit." And its fatal consequence, that the Jew is "a creature cut off from the elements of life" finds an obvious parallel in Rosenzweig's constant refrain that we return from the illusions of transcendence to fully embrace our "life" (see, e.g., SE, 463 [E, 416]: "We cling to our creatureliness"). Unlike the Zionists, however, Rosenzweig did not draw the expected conclusion that the Jews required a state to be fully indepen-

---

peoples, rather Jewry is the mere predecessor [*Vorläufer*] of humanity. When we say Israel, all Israel, we mean the future of all. We will in the end all know in God, that we children of humanity are blood-relations [*dass wir Menschenkinder blutsverwandt sind*]. '*Menschenkind*' is, in all languages in which it is spoken, a Hebraism." GB (25.4.1918), 82–83; my emphasis.

38. T. Lessing, *Der Jüdische Selbsthass* (Berlin: Jüdischer Verlag, 1930), 214, 35. Gordon's comments are from his "The Logic of the Future" (1910) and "People and Labor" (1911), in Arthur Hertzberg, ed., *The Zionist Idea* (New York: Atheneum, 1982), 369–73.

dent. Indeed, for Rosenzweig exile is a prerequisite if the Jews are to be fully who they are. The claim for the priority of the Jewish community found in his philosophy it is not at heart an argument about politics. Rather, it speaks to the practices, the rituals, and rules of kinship affiliation by which the community perpetuates its identity wholly apart from—indeed, indifferent to—the state life and the public sphere. For Rosenzweig, it is clear that such practices comprise an ontological condition, that is, they comprise the necessary and sufficient conditions or grounds for the possibility of Jewish existence. They are necessary conditions insofar as without ritual, without blood-continuity, without sacred events, the Jews cannot persist in being themselves. And they are sufficient conditions insofar as nothing else is required. A state, for example, founded upon sovereign territory, is in Rosenzweig's opinion wholly unnecessary. In fact, it is counterproductive, since Jewish redemption requires that Jews withdraw from ordinary and "merely" historical affairs.

Rosenzweig was therefore a theorist of Jewish exile. In two letters to Rudolf Hallo (1921 and 1922), Rosenzweig calls this condition "Jewish-being" *(das Judesein)*. "To be a Jew [*Jude sein*]," he explains, "*means* to be in 'Golus' [exile]. Jewish *life* is the form through which we make Jewish-being tolerable." [39] It is not just that Rosenzweig celebrated the specificity of the Jewish condition in exile; rather, he believed that exile was intrinsic to the Jewish condition. The wish to "remain" in the world is realized philosophically in idea that the Jews are always a "remnant" *(Rest)* amidst the nations:

> The whole constriction [*Engigkeit*] of direct, naive Jewish consciousness consists in . . . [an] ability to forget that there is anything else in this world, indeed that there is any world outside of the Jewish world and the Jews. . . . In defiance of all secular history, Jewish history is the history of this remnant [*dieses Rests*]; the word of the prophet, that it "will remain," [*daß er "bleiben wird"*] ever applies to it. (SE, 449–50 [E, 404])

The notion of "constriction" provides a helpful summary of Rosenzweig's vision of Jewish life. Being in exile and sustaining themselves with their very own cultural resources, the Jews live in an altogether exclusive fashion unlike all nations in the world. Here one should notice that the very shape of *The Star* forbids Rosenzweig from assigning the Jews any share in normal life

---

39. *Briefe*, N.306, An Rudolf Hallo (Frankfurt am Main, 15.3.21), 398: "Jude sein *heißt* im 'Golus' sein. Das jüdische *Leben* ist die Form, wie wir uns das Jude*sein* erträglich machen können"; Rosenzweig's emphasis. Of the Jewish law he writes that "Judaism *is not* law. It creates law. But it *is not* law. It *is* Jewish-*being*. Thus have I presented the matter in *The Star,* and I know that it is correct." ("Das Judentum *ist nicht* Gesetz. Er schafft Gesetz. Aber es *ist* es nicht. Es *ist* Jude*sein.* so habe ich es im Stern dargestellt und weiß, das es richtig ist.") *Briefe,* N.342, An Rudolf Hallo (Frankfurt a. M., 27.3.1922), 424–45; Rosenzweig's emphasis.

(and from assigning any other group a comparable role alongside the Jews). The Jews alone constitute the "fire"—or point—at the center of the star, and it is difficult to see how the centrality of any other community would be geometrically conceivable. It is precisely because of the Jewish community's altogether unique mode of being in the world that it "lives in its own redemption" ("Es lebt in seiner eignen Erlösung") (SE, 364 [E, 328]).

Life within the boundaries of the Jewish people thus provides the necessary structures and practices by which "eternity is freed from all otherworldly distance [ist die Ewigkeit von aller jenseitigen Ferne befreit]." In Jewish redemption, eternity "is now really there [*wirklich da*]" (SE, 360 [E, 324]). Since the Jewish people in their very constitution provide the distinctive ontological conditions for this convergence, Rosenzweig can then assign the Jews a unique and irreplaceable role in the coming redemption of the world at large. The Jewish experience of redemption is redemption in the name of all humanity : "Israel represents mankind."[40] But so long as there is history, this representative status cannot be other than symbolic.

Exile thus became for Rosenzweig a constitutive feature of Jewish identity, since it helped them to experience their "constriction"—their dissociation from normal history and temporality.[41] Here the concept of fateful separation that Rosenzweig had exposed in Hegel's theological writings came again to the fore in a striking new incarnation. Jewish exile now became the temporal "eternity" of the persecuted remnant. "For the people of God," concludes Rosenzweig, "the eternal is already there, even in the midst of time [Im Gottesvolk ist das Ewige schon da, mitten in der Zeit]" (SE, 368 [E, 332]). Here Rosenzweig's philosophical defense of exile represents a dramatic departure from the Jewish tradition. Redemption no longer signified the overcoming of exile. On the contrary, redemption was only possible *within* exile, which Rosenzweig now regarded as constitutive of Jewish life.[42]

### ROSENZWEIG'S *STAR* IN THE SHADOW OF HEIDEGGER

#### *From Redemption to Authenticity*

At first glance, any attempt to compare Rosenzweig and Heidegger seems destined to eventually founder, since not only does Heidegger lack concept of redemption, he also appears to lack a notion of eternity. If redemption is defined as the entry of the eternal into time, it seems unimagin-

40. On the messianic and mission-theory element in Rosenzweig, see Batnitzky, *Idolatry and Representation*, esp. 11.

41. On "constriction," see the excellent discussion in R. Cohen, *Elevations*, 21–22.

42. See the useful remarks by Amos Funkenstein, *Perceptions of Jewish History* (Berkeley: University of California Press, 1993), 291–95.

able that one could discover any parallel in a lexicon such as Heidegger's, in which eternity falls under a powerful conceptual prohibition. Indeed, as Karl Löwith once suggested, it is just this radical absence of eternity in Heidegger's thought that forces us to conclude that, whatever their superficial similarities, Heidegger and Rosenzweig were at heart metaphysical opponents (TE, esp. 75–77). This is a powerful objection and deserves serious consideration.

In 1924, Heidegger delivered an address to the Marburg Theological Society entitled "The Concept of Time." At first glance, the opening pages of this lecture suggest a striking contrast to Rosenzweig's speculations. Heidegger began boldly, asking "What is time?" Traditional speculation by theologians has taken it for granted that "time finds its meaning in eternity." Theology is concerned with the "temporal Being of such existence in its relation to eternity." For the theologian, eternity is thus presupposed. But this cannot be the argumentative path for philosophy: for theology is concerned "with human existence [*Dasein*] as Being before God [*Sein vor Gott*]." Philosophy, however—and here Heidegger means his own philosophy— would remain "in a state of perplexity so long as it knows nothing of God and fails to understand the inquiry concerning him." So for a philosopher simple appeals to "faith" will not do. (The philosopher, claimed Heidegger, "does not believe.") Philosophy "will never have eternity." Rather, it must understand "time in terms of time" alone ("die Zeit aus der Zeit zu verstehen").[43]

This objection to the concept of eternity may seem somewhat exaggerated. Obviously there are many philosophies that invoke the notion of eternity, such as those of Plato, Spinoza, and Hegel. But we must remember that for Heidegger, as for Rosenzweig, the philosophical narrative of the West had followed a necessary course, culminating in Nietzsche's denial of God. After Nietzsche, the concept of eternity could only appear as its own horizontal shadow upon the temporal plane; eternity became the "eternal return" *(ewige Wiederkehr)*. However, it is also important to recognize that Heidegger's vision of a metaphysical collapse did not necessarily rule out any and all theological speculation. It simply made theology far more "difficult" to conceive as a rigorously philosophical project: "In a theological sense— and you are at liberty to understand it in this way—*a consideration of time can only mean making the question concerning eternity more difficult.*"[44]

This portrait of the "difficulties" of modern theology perfectly captures the basic dilemma of Rosenzweig's philosophy. As we have seen, its chief

---

43. "[D]ann wird die Philosophie die Ewigkeit nie haben." Heidegger, *The Concept of Time,* trans. William McNeill, English-German edition (Oxford: Blackwell, 1992), 2.

44. Heidegger, *The Concept of Time,* 2; my emphasis.

aim was to thematize the theological concept of redemption. But this purpose came up against Rosenzweig's own requirement that any true philosophy must be one that remains within time and the world. The conclusion of *The Star of Redemption* illustrates this dilemma: On the one hand, it describes the human encounter with the "eternal truth," which is manifest as God's face. But on the other hand it warns us that the human being "remains always within the boundaries of created existence" (SE, 463 [E, 416]). Although ultimately the tension between these two claims was not so much fatal as productive, it illustrated the deeper, structural quarrel between the theological and philosophical aspects of Rosenzweig's thought. As Heidegger recognized, any modern theology that genuinely recognized the collapse of metaphysics would be faced with extraordinary difficulty. While Heidegger himself was content to pursue philosophy solely within the temporal horizon, Rosenzweig was more obstinate in his commitment to eternity, even while he embraced the desideratum that philosophy should "take time seriously." Thus, as we have seen, the very distinction between time and eternity became problematic. As Rosenzweig explained, "eternity, by finding acceptance in time, itself becomes—like time" (SE, 324 [E, 292]).[45]

## Heidegger on Authenticity

The question remains whether anything like the category of redemption could possibly appear in Heidegger's more "successfully" temporalized philosophy. My argument here is that there is a close resemblance between Rosenzweig's concept of redemption and Heidegger's notion of authenticity. To understand this suggestion, one must recall that Rosenzweig characterizes redemption as that condition where one lives in what is one's "ownmost" *(das Eigenste)*. To exist in such a fashion is really to exhibit a certain separate and self-sufficient constitution; it is to live according to one's own being rather than according to the meanings of the world. In Heidegger's philosophy a quite similar idea is expressed as "understanding one's *ownmost*

---

45. Rosenzweig thus verged on a wholly temporalized and immanent theory without room for the alterity customarily afforded a monotheistic God. A 1928 review by S. Stern affirmed that Rosenzweig was inspired by the "monistic tendencies" of German Idealism. Indeed, Stern criticized Rosenzweig for theorizing redemption according to a "one-sided Immanentism [*einseitigen Immanentismus*]." The reviewer judged this "monistic" and "immanent" theory in error, precisely because it meant Rosenzweig ignored the "insuperable gap" (*unüberwundene Kluft*) between divine action and human life. "Rosenzweig, Franz. Dr. phil. *Der Stern der Erlösung.* Frankfurt a.M., J. Kauffmann, 1921. 532 S." (review), *Kantstudien* 33 (1928): 326–28; at 327. If, as Stern claimed, Rosenzweig's theory of redemption collapses religious categories into worldly immanence without a remaining "gap," then the Levinasian reading of Rosenzweig as a theorist of alterity needs serious revision.

and uttermost potentiality-for-Being [*eigensten äußersten Seinkönnens*]." This is what Heidegger means by *authenticity (Eigentlichkeit)*, a concept I will now sketch in greater detail (SZ, 263).

Recall that for Heidegger, authenticity describes an exceptional condition of human being, or *Dasein*. As such, authenticity is a modification of Dasein, which usually lives its life in the condition of inauthenticity. The distinction can be summarized as follows. In our normal way of coping with the world, we tend not to acknowledge how our interpretations of the world are simply interpretations. Because the meanings of the world are just those meanings that one finds already in play even before one begins to think for one's self, Heidegger uses the term *das Man*, or "the One," as a name for one aspect of Dasein's integrated existential structure. The One is simply part of being human, and for this reason it would be wrong to read it as an expression of Heidegger's disdain for some other social "group" that one might simply choose to reject. Dasein itself is normally "the One" in the sense that it finds it natural to rely upon the meanings that are readily available to us and indeed pervade us insofar as we always resort to social norms. In this sense, each one of us thinks what "the One" thinks, each of us does what "one does," and so on.

But for Heidegger, the danger is that we are too easily tempted to believe that these interpretations are metaphysically grounded. Because social norms have an appearance of permanency, we anchor our self-understandings in them as if they provided a refuge from impermanence. Anchoring ourselves "outside" of ourselves in this fashion is what Heidegger calls *falling*. What we fall from is our own awareness of groundlessness. We avoid facing up to our own finitude because it is natural to consider our interpreted world wholly secure in its meanings. To acknowledge our finitude would be to acknowledge the ungroundedness of meanings we rely upon in our everyday existence. Dasein therefore finds it most natural to remain in a mode of social "fleeing" (*Flucht*), for which Heidegger employs obviously pejorative terms, such as "busyness," "idle talk," and "superficiality." Though differentiated, all of these are basically terms that characterize Dasein's flight into the public realm and its flight away from "an authentic potentiality-for-Being-its-self (SZ, §40, 184; BT, 229)." Heidegger concludes that typically Dasein remains caught in the condition of inauthenticity.

How then could authenticity ever arise? According to Heidegger, it is only the most extraordinary occurrence that brings us back from our fallenness and reveals to us who we are. Anxiety, or *Angst*, first discloses our finitude and casts us into a privileged understanding of ourselves as finite — as who we truly are in our ownmost being. It returns us, in other words, from our self-abandonment to the various groundings that are offered up by the world as apparent sites of refuge from our finitude. It is important to note here that Heidegger uses the term *authenticity* in order to designate that special mode wherein Dasein understands its "ownmost potentiality for Being" (SZ, 263; BT, 307). Authenticity emerges only if one comes into this special mode in which the quotidian sense of things no longer provides groundedness for meaning. The "world" as such fails us, Heidegger explains, and our being in the world is therefore felt as "uncanny" *(unheimlich)*, or "not-at-home." Only on the basis of this "ungroundedness" disclosed by Dasein's anxiety for its ownmost being can Dasein discover it has "wrenched itself away from the 'One' already" (SZ, 263; BT, 307, translation amended). And only then can Dasein resolve upon possibilities and take up meanings in an authentic fashion. It does so with a kind of temporality that is not borrowed from the world but is part of Dasein's "primordial" constitution. It is this "authentic" temporality that is grounded in Dasein's finitude and first disclosed as finite only in authenticity (SZ, 329; BT, 377–79).

Now there are three special features of authentic temporality that Heidegger singles out as especially important. First, when we are authentically cast back upon our own resources, we cease our conformity to worldly time and instead come to recognize the *unity* of time within ourselves. As noted above, authentic temporality thus has what Heidegger calls three "ecstases"—the character of having-been, the present, and the future—and these are grounded in Dasein's own "temporalizing." Second, because Dasein is a being primarily concerned for what *will* be, the meaningfulness of existence depends upon the sense that it comes to completion: In other words, *"The primary phenomenon of primordial and authentic temporality is the future"* (SZ, 329; BT, 378; emphasis in original).[46] And third, when we take up the meanings of our life in the modified condition of authenticity, we find that those meanings that are available for us just are by definition those that are part of Dasein's world—they comprise its "heritage" *(Erbe)* (SZ, 383; BT, 435). Heidegger calls our authentic exploitation of such a heritage Dasein's "fateful repetition" *(schicksalhaften Wiederholung)* (SZ, 395; BT, 447).[47] These special features of authenticity are brought together in Heidegger's notion of *resolve*. For if we now cast ourselves into time with full acknowledgment that our finitude is who we are, we live out of a heritage and into the future with a special sense of purposeful direction. We live in history, but we do not have the sense that we have abandoned ourselves to it. In *Being and Time*

---

46. That Jewish life in "primordial" time depends upon Jews' unique future-orientation may accord with Heidegger's claim that primordial time "temporalizes"—*"Zeit zeitigt,"* a German phrase that can mean time *unfolds* or *ripens* (thus emphasizing its future-directedness). On the meaning of "temporalization," see Daniel Dahlstrom, *Heidegger's Concept of Truth* (Cambridge: Cambridge University Press, 2001), 225, n. 4.

47. The argument is developed at length in SZ, §76, 392–397.

Heidegger unites all of these concepts in the claim that "once one has grasped the finitude of one's existence, it snatches one back from the endless multiplicity of possibilities which offer themselves . . . —and brings existence into the simplicity of its fate [*Schicksal*]" (SZ, 384; BT, 435).

### Terrestrial Repetition and Constriction

Given the above summary, one can now discern the resemblance between Rosenzweig and Heidegger. Redemption and authenticity arc both exceptional modes of being human. Both are ways of living out the true finitude of existence that is first disclosed in anxiety. Rosenzweig calls this the "fear of earthly things" *(Angst des Irdischen)*; Heidegger calls it simply "Angst." Both authenticity and redemption describe a condition of homelessness, which both philosophers describe as "uncanny," or *unheimlich*. Each further argues that authentic life unfolds for us out of our own self-sustaining temporality, and then allows us to adopt a special mode of future-directedness in which we have gathered up the meanings of our heritage and have projected these meanings forward as an oriented-present state of existing within what is most one's own *(das Eigenste)*. This is one's authenticity *(Eigentlichkeit)*.

Notice, then, the same three crucial features of authenticity apply to Rosenzweig's notion of Jewish redemption as well. First, the category of "blood" in Rosenzweig's philosophy thus fulfills the very same function as "primordial temporality" in Heidegger. Both terms point to a self-grounding and transcendental condition of "internal temporalizing" that arises out of the human being alone and not out of "its world."[48] Second, for Rosenzweig as for Heidegger, the future-oriented character of the exceptional or authentic human being is one that has resolved upon one's heritage and has then projected that as just what one has resolved to be. ("For [the Jewish people] alone," Rosenzweig says, "*the future is not something alien but something of its own* [*ein Eigenes*]" [SE 332 (E, 299); my emphasis].)[49] As an exceptional condition, this future becomes what Heidegger and Rosenzweig both call fate

48. The distinction between understanding Dasein "in terms of itself" rather than "in terms of its world" lies at the heart of Heidegger's definition of authenticity in Division I. See esp. the remarks on "falling" in SZ, I, chaps. 4 and 5. For lucid remarks on Heidegger's notion of primordial time as opposed to public and clock time, see Dahlstrom, *Heidegger's Concept of Truth,* 327–84.

49. Note that Rosenzweig's German text suggests a post-metaphysical notion of transcendence, by substituting temporal directness for the standard theological sense of a "beyond" (*Jenseitiges)*: "Was andern Gemeinschaften Zukunft und also ein der Gegenwart jedenfalls noch Jenseitiges ist,—ihr allein ist es schon Gegenwart; ihr allein ist das Zukünftige nicht Fremdes, sondern ein Eigenes, etwas was sie in ihrem Schoße trägt, und jeden Tag kann sie es gebären."

*(Schicksal).* As Rosenzweig confirms, an individual's fate is what is *most one's own* (*"das eigenste des Menschen ist eben sein Schicksal"*) (SE, 314 [E, 282]).[50] And third, this can be true if and only if we step back from the inauthenticity of our reliance upon the meanings of the world. Heidegger thus calls our authentic taking-up of our heritage "fateful repetition" *(schicksalhaften Wiederholung)*. Similarly, Rosenzweig suggests that the reenactment of Jewish rituals gathers together past, present, and future meanings in a fashion deeper than worldly history and thus exhibits what he calls "terrestrial repetition" *(irdische Wiederholung)* (SE, 323 [E, 290–91]).

The unifying theme in this comparison lies in the powerfully normative distinction between authentic and inauthentic ways of being human. Each philosopher suggests that human existence can either abandon itself to the various meanings of the world—what Heidegger calls "fleeing"—or it can instead choose to acknowledge the ungroundedness of those meanings and strike its roots instead solely and authentically in the self.[51] In a formula that reverses Schiller's exhortation to throw off one's earthly fears, Heidegger calls this *"taking over the thrownness of the Self [Übernahme der Geworfenheit des Selbst]"* (SZ, §74, 383; BT, 434; my emphasis). Rosenzweig calls it "rootedness in one's self [*Verwurzelung im eigenen Selbst*]" (SE, 339 [E, 305]). Both concepts are best characterized as a steadfast refusal to ground one's self in the meanings of the world; both require the very same gesture of recoil upon the "primordial" resources of one's ownmost being.

There is one important characteristic of this recoil that is apt to be misconstrued. Neither Rosenzweig nor Heidegger subscribes to the idea that it somehow lifts the authentic human being beyond the sphere of life. The popular existentialist model of freedom as a complete dissociation from the world and from others—a model most often associated with Sartre—is not found in either Heidegger and Rosenzweig. Rather, both argue that there is an authentic way of being-in-the-world that "modifies" our temporal constitution without retreating from it. As Lawrence Vogel explains,

> Conscience does not call one to retreat from the world or to renounce it, but to be in it without being of it: to open oneself to things and others without understanding oneself primarily in terms of the way the world has been inter-

50. This phrase occurs in the context of a discussion of individual mortality; the "fate" Rosenzweig names is the indissociability of body and soul marking each person as a worldly and mortal being. But fate thus indicates our nontranscendent finitude; much like Heidegger's "mineness"(*Jemeinigkeit*), it disrupts universal talk about death in the abstract. Rosenzweig developed the concept of fate as dissociation and non-relationality out of his book on Hegel (as discussed in chapter 2). For Heidegger's term "mineness," see SZ, §9, 42; and for Heidegger on death as the "non-relational" (*unbezüglich*) see my comments in chapter 3.

51. For Heidegger's remarks on the relation between "fleeing" and *Unheimlichkeit*, see SZ, 287.

preted publicly. The point is not to be out of this world but to be involved in it without being lost to "the others." That existence is mine, that life is first-personal, that ultimately I am responsible for what I make of my circumstance, by no means precludes my desire for love, friendship, and community.[52]

A similar definition would apply to Rosenzweig's notion of Jewish redemption. But unlike Heidegger, Rosenzweig's theism requires that for him conscience manifests itself as a call from God and not as a call from the finitude of the self. Despite this important difference, Rosenzweig shares with Heidegger the view that redemption is a state of transfiguration within temporal life. By owning up to the ungrounded nature of human being, one opts for self-groundedness as the only recourse available within the sphere of finitude.[53]

It is this fundamental insight into the "uncanny" (again, *unheimlich,* or, "not at home") quality of the human condition that perhaps most unites the philosophies of Rosenzweig and Heidegger. In sum, both *The Star of Redemption* and *Being and Time* are in part meditations upon the ungroundedness of human meaning. Rosenzweig interprets this ungroundedness as the truth of Jewish exile; Heidegger speaks of all human being as grounded in the "un-ground" of nothingness.[54] Both argue that for the most part we do not live in such a way as to live up to the ungrounded truth of our being. We would rather cling to land or to the sphere of facile public meaning so as to secure for ourselves an impression of rootedness. But as Rilke noted in the first "Duino Elegy," we human beings "are not fully at home in our interpreted world" ("daß wir nicht sehr verläßlich zu Haus sind in der gedeuteten Welt").

Despite this affinity, Rosenzweig and Heidegger part company on several apparently decisive points. While Rosenzweig argues that only the Jews are equipped to live in the truth of ungroundedness (since only the Jews are rooted uniquely in themselves), Heidegger argues that the capacity to heed the call of conscience and recognize the truth of human "uncanniness" is

---

52. Vogel, *The Fragile "We,"* 47.

53. As Michael Zimmerman has convincingly argued, Heidegger's mature concept of authenticity emerged out of his early theological work: "For Paul, the man of faith has a totally new self-understanding because he experiences the presence of God here and now. *Only for that reason can he let go of the desire for security which at one time concealed God from him.*" Thus "Heidegger formalized ontologically the temporal understanding of human existence presupposed by Paul's conception of faithful existence." *Eclipse of the Self: The Development of Heidegger's Concept of Authenticity,* rev. ed. (Athens: Ohio University Press, 1986; orig. pub. 1981), 14; my emphasis.

54. Significantly, Heidegger also discerns in Parmenides a connection between the uncanny and the ontological difference, for "through the event of homelessness [*Unheimlichkeit*] the whole of the being is disclosed." EM, 127.

something shared by all peoples (even if the call occurs with great infre-
quency and only for the briefest moment, in what Heidegger calls a blink of
an eye, or *Augenblick*). Rosenzweig picks out a constitutive difference between groups; Heidegger distinguishes between modes of individual being.
But this obvious dissimilarity—between a collectivist as opposed to an individualist norm—is not as decisive as may first appear. First of all, both
norms demand a recoil from the social sphere. In this sense, Rosenzweig's
attitude toward the other peoples of the world is very much like Heidegger's
attitude toward the public at large. For Rosenzweig, redemption manifests
itself as a special kind of Jewish withdrawal from the non-Jewish world, from
other nations, and from any deep investment in their historical and political life. (In Rosenzweig's language, the Jew must "constrict himself to Jewish
feeling"; SE, 450 [E, 404]).⁵⁵ Similarly, Heidegger makes authenticity available to any individual for whom the awareness of finitude "snatches one
back" from any investment in the social sphere and its various kinds of fleeing, superficiality, received wisdom, and political busyness. (In Heidegger's
language, the authentic self is called out of the public and is thrown upon
its ownmost resources.)

However, as noted, Rosenzweig and Heidegger disagree upon whether
the recoil from publicity takes a collectivist or individualist form. For Rosenzweig one recoils from social and political life because one finds truth only
within the enchanted sphere of the Jewish people; for Heidegger one recoils from publicity so as to achieve a selfhood deeper than any and all group
identification. One is left with the impression that for Rosenzweig, redemption is radically exclusive, since it is an experience denied to all other peoples in the world, while for Heidegger authenticity is in principle inclusive,
since it is a latent possibility for each and every individual.

Readers may find this difference ironic, since it is Heidegger's philosophy that is often accused of national chauvinism. Yet Rosenzweig's argument, not Heidegger's, risks devolving into a set of observations about how
different peoples are constituted. Indeed, Rosenzweig concludes that there
is one people *alone* that is uniquely able to live in a state of permanent redemption. Heidegger, however (at least where he is philosophically consistent), cannot assign such an ability to only one individual or group. For Heidegger, "being authentic" is always a potential within each and every
individual. Authenticity is thus necessarily a universal modality of the self,
even if this potential is almost always forgotten in the public "business" and
leveling noise of "the One" *(das Man)*. The Heidegger who wrote *Being and*

55. For a somewhat different reading of this same line, see the helpful remarks in R. Cohen, *Elevations*, 22.

*Time* could not restrict the luminous experience of authenticity to any particular nation.[56]

One possible objection to this interpretation is that it misses Rosenzweig's universalist allegiance to the ideal of "ethical monotheism," according to which the Jews are chosen precisely to serve as a "light unto the nations." Leora Batnitzky and Richard A. Cohen have argued (though in different ways) that Rosenzweig's particularistic claim that the Jews alone are chosen must be understood as antecedent to the universalistic claim that all humankind will be one day redeemed. But to call this argument universalist misses the paradox at the heart of the idea of Jewish election.[57] Consider Rosenzweig's idea that universalist redemption is a future possibility, not a lived experience: Given this idea, universalism is thus built into his concept of redemption in *only a proleptic sense*. Rosenzweig goes so far as to argue that for the present, Jewish election actually intensifies the broader awareness that redemption does *not* yet include all nations. (Incidentally, this argument was crucial to his analysis of antisemitism, which he saw as almost unavoidable, given that the very presence of the Jewish people serves as a constant and unwanted reminder to the rest of humanity that it does not yet know the redeemed life reserved for the Jews.) More impor-

---

56. Heidegger's curious talk of "German Dasein" (in the notorious 1933 rectoral address) and his claim that the Germans are the "most metaphysical" of peoples represent a philosophical departure from the general account of authenticity as a universal possibility. It lapses into a far more "theological" and hence "onto-theological" register. See Jacques Derrida, "*Ousia and Grammé:* Note on a Note from *Being and Time,*" in his *Margins of Philosophy,* trans. Alan Bass (Chicago: University of Chicago Press, 1982), 29–67; see esp. 63. In his later work Heidegger repeatedly insinuates that the Germans enjoy a special potential for authenticity (they live in greater "danger," their poetry is especially attuned to Being, they are the inheritors of Greek thought, and so on). But even if he were right in this (though he obviously is not), his argument might still be construed as one factual realization of the formalist point that authenticity is a mode of human being which is in principle available to everyone. For Rosenzweig, on the other hand, the redemption of the Jews seems to be constitutive of their being. While it is of course possible in Rosenzweig's scheme to convert to Judaism, the consequence would be to become *a member of* the redeemed nation; the argument that this nation alone is redeemed remains unchallenged. The idea that only one people enjoys by its nature a privileged experience of truth therefore appears to be a more essential feature of Rosenzweig's philosophy, while the claim to privileged experience seems to be a contingent element in Heidegger's thought where it appears at all.

57. The claim that Rosenzweig was a partisan of universalistic "mission theory" and thus an "ethical monotheist" in the tradition of Mendelssohn and Hermann Cohen is the central thesis of Batnitzky's suggestive book *Idolatry and Representation.* (However, Batnitzky does recognize the paradox and insists that Rosenzweig incorporates the acknowledgement of exclusivity into a new and more subtle kind of universalism. I thank her for clarifying this point in a private conversation, July 17, 2000). And see R. Cohen's chapter on "Jewish Election in the Thought of Rosenzweig," in *Elevations,* esp. 16–23.

tantly, Rosenzweig did not make it clear just how the living experience of Jewish redemption offers any actual encouragement toward the realization of universal redemption in the future. As Cohen has noted, Rosenzweig seems to make concrete "missionary" work toward the redemption of all peoples a specifically Christian task, while Jews are to remain in a condition of "self-absorption."[58]

It seems, then, that rather than helping toward realizing universal redemption or inviting others to participate in any cooperative effort, Jewish election for Rosenzweig becomes, precisely through *nonparticipation,* a living symbol for how all humans will one day exist in God's intimate embrace. Jewish redemption itself thus embodies a paradox, in that its dissociation becomes a universal example. To be sure, this paradox may be symptomatic of both Christian and Jewish forms of "ethical monotheism," since both religions claim present truth for a select group, even while in principle they yearn for a time when it will be generally recognized. But Rosenzweig's argument is even stronger, since he conceives of Jewish separation as an intrinsic, noncontingent stage in the redemptive process. On the one hand, it is preparatory, temporary, anticipating the moment of generalized, redemptive "Truth." But on the other hand, for the time being the Jews alone are uniquely qualified, and there is no indication that their experience could grow gradually more inclusive. Indeed, as I have already noted, Rosenzweig's understanding of the future makes it an eternal orientation, an eternal future that is *always* "not-yet"—and thus structurally, permanently proleptic. To call this doctrine universalist seems misleading, since it downplays the paradox that universalist hope can only function on the basis of present exclusion.

### CONCLUDING REMARKS

In the previous chapter and this one, I have argued that Rosenzweig's philosophy of redemption displays a startling and rich resemblance to Heidegger's philosophy of Being. *The Star of Redemption* deploys a phenomenological method, at once revolutionary and restorative, so as to overturn in a modernist fashion what Rosenzweig took to be a moribund tradition of ide-

---

58. As early as 1913, Rosenzweig argued that Judaism, unlike Christianity, remains apart from social events and therefore embodies the quiescence that will come to all nations at history's end: "The synagogue, immortal, but with a broken staff and a blindfold upon the eyes, must renounce all worldly effort and devote all of its powers to maintaining itself in life and purely from life. . . . Here it gazes fixedly into the future." *Briefe*, N.59, An Rudolf Ehrenberg (1.11.1913), 73–76, quote at 75. For further comments on this theme, see the fine discussion in R. Cohen, *Elevations*, 21.

alism in Western thought—a tradition that first took flight with Parmenides and reached its most powerful expression with Hegel, finally collapsing with Nietzsche and his atheistic defense of human freedom. Against the older idealism and its deceitful promise of salvation, *The Star* develops an alternative model of redemption as remaining in the world, a model that is constrained by mortality and, in refusing transcendence, so helps to sustain the ontological differentiation among human beings, God, and the world. With life as its inescapable horizon, *The Star* develops a hermeneutic of religious experience as it is existentially grounded in community, language, and ritual practice. I have called this Rosenzweig's temporal holism. And it is this method that informs his theory of redemption. According to Rosenzweig, it is the Jews alone who are truly redeemed. They alone enjoy the particular resources and endure the special fate that make it uniquely possible to resist the public world of superficial meaning, to root their existence in the blood-community, and to live out their redemption *in* the world, even while remaining indifferent to those contingent facts of politics and history that are merely *of* the world and thus can have no bearing on the eternity-in-time of an ever-arriving future.

Despite significant dissimilarities, Heidegger agreed with Rosenzweig on a great number of points, both methodological and topical. Like Rosenzweig, Heidegger deploys a phenomenological method to salvage original meaning from a moribund tradition of cognitivist metaphysics. The error of this tradition is the very same error Rosenzweig called "idealism," the dogmatic belief that being can be seized conceptually as wholly present. Heidegger argues that this error, first spawned in the Platonist-Idealist misprision of pre-Socratic wisdom, persisted through modern idealism to reach an uncertain conclusion in Nietzsche's "metaphysical" denial of God, an atheism in defense of freedom. Against this older cognitivist metaphysics (specifically, against Husserl's egological self as transcendent to the world), Heidegger develops a picture of human being-in-the-world as finite and constrained by mortality. Like Rosenzweig, Heidegger construes being-toward-death as deeper than cognitivist transcendence; indeed, it is a potentiality that exposes the "nothingness" between mind and world. The "irrational" objects of philosophy, disclosed through nothingness, are made available for a new discipline of metaphysics. Heidegger then develops a hermeneutic of human life as an always-prior horizon of familiarity, deeper than transcendence and existentially grounded in community, language, and pragmatic concern. But to this existential analytic Heidegger supplements a peculiar suggestion, that one always exists in the world in either an "authentic" or an "inauthentic" fashion. As I have suggested, here one may discern an instructive resemblance between the norm of authenticity and Rosenzweig's ideal of Jewish redemption.

Admittedly, this comparison is surprising, especially so since one does not usually regard the two philosophers as belonging to a shared intellectual canon. However, one might consider how the very idea of a separate canon first arose. Perhaps the chief message of Rosenzweig's philosophy is that the Jews do not share in the wider historical life of the nations. It is not surprising, then, that this idea of Jewish separation has also become the guiding principle for reading his work. And if one also takes into consideration Heidegger's frequent reference to the uniquely "metaphysical" status of the German people, one can understand how any comparison between Rosenzweig and Heidegger would appear as a violation of canonical as well as national boundaries.

Still, the parallels suggested above are not exact. Indeed, there is one particularly powerful objection that demands attention. While Rosenzweig's concept of redemption is robustly theological, Heidegger's concept of authenticity is just as vigorously atheistic. For Rosenzweig, it is nonsensical to conceive of redemption without God, who provides a common point of orientation toward which man and world unite in hope for eternity-in-time. For Heidegger, however, the concept of authenticity can make no appeal to a third element beyond man and world, since authentic "resolve" only characterizes the individual who has properly sensed the "nothingness" beneath worldly experience. Resolve is only possible in a world from which the gods have fled. So while in Rosenzweig's system theism remains the normative light, what remains of normativity in Heidegger's thought can only make its appearance once that theism is fully extinguished. Any comparison between them seems bound to failure.

But this objection misses the point. Clearly, Rosenzweig and Heidegger saw themselves as engaged in quite different projects, and any comparison that did not take cognizance of their disagreement concerning theism and atheism would be neglecting a crucial topic. The issue, however, is to understand what kind of disagreement it really is. In these concluding remarks, I want to suggest that the comparison between authenticity and redemption is instructive precisely because it brings to light a deeper resemblance between Heidegger's atheism and Rosenzweig's theism.

Any reader of Heidegger's work knows that the concept of authenticity is one of its chief sites of interpretative disturbance. The problem with authenticity is that it is conceptually indeterminate. Throughout *Being and Time,* despite the note of moral urgency that occasionally intrudes upon the discussion, Heidegger categorically denies that there is any normative purpose guiding his sketch of the basic structures of being human. The "existential analytic" purports to describe constitutive features of our being; it investigates only *how* we are, not how we *should* be. Indeed, Heidegger vigilantly warns the reader more than once that the authenticity-inauthenticity split is not meant in a moral sense at all.[59] These denials are troublesome, however, because so much of the language Heidegger uses to describe our existence—language such as "falling" and "fleeing"—seems unabashedly normative. Consequently, the language of authenticity in Heidegger's work is conceptually indeterminate—neutral yet nonneutral, descriptive yet portentous, condemning and praising by turns. A convincing explanation for this indeterminacy is that it should be read as a theistic residue. Indeed, it would remain enigmatic were it not for Heidegger's religious origins.[60] Authenticity might thus be understood as an afterthought of redemption within a nonreligious philosophy. For paradoxically, the "nothingness" that should signal Heidegger's decisive departure from theism is itself a locus of value—it yields the lesson of complete nihilism that becomes the only true basis of authentic resolve. Heidegger's atheistic cosmos therefore depends upon the theism it rejects. God is expelled, but his very expulsion becomes the grounds for a new, post-theological normativity.[61]

Rosenzweig sensed this paradox. According to the argument in his 1929 essay "Exchanged Fronts" ("Vertauschte Fronten"), one can trace a line of intellectual influence extending across ten years—from Heidegger's atheistic thought back to Hermann Cohen's late philosophy of religion. Whether this specific claim about Cohen is truly accurate can be left for later. What is noteworthy is that Rosenzweig sensed the religious urgency in Heidegger's thought. So if Heidegger was an unacknowledged heir to, and the ironic culmination of, a historical crisis in the philosophy of religion (despite his open denial of any such affiliation), then the difference between Rosenzweig's unabashedly theological philosophy and Heidegger's seemingly atheistic ontology may be far less pronounced than may at first appear.[62] The concept of authenticity, I would argue, is itself the best indication that Rosenzweig was correct. As a locus of normativity in an otherwise

---

59. See esp. SZ, §9, 42–43, and §38, 179, where Heidegger warns the reader off from thinking that the phenomenon of "falling" (*Verfallen*) has any connection to "ontic" talk about the sinfulness and corruption of human nature.

60. Michael Zimmerman proposes a comparison with Rudolf Bultmann's concept of sinfulness in *Eclipse of the Self,* 43–44 and *passim.*

61. Hence Löwith's description of Heidegger as "a theologian by tradition, and an atheist as a scholar," as well as a "displaced preacher." *My Life in Germany Before and After 1933: A Report,* trans. Elizabeth King (Urbana and Chicago: University of Illinois Press, 1994), 47, 30.

62. Heidegger himself made it plain that "the thinking that points toward the truth of being as what is to be thought *has in no way decided in favor of theism. It can be theistic as little as atheistic.*" This twofold denial makes any categorization of Heidegger as an atheist facile and misleading. See Heidegger, "Letter on Humanism," in *Pathmarks,* ed. William McNeill (Cambridge: Cambridge University Press, 1998), 267, my emphasis.

descriptive work, it drew its luminous power from a light whose presence it couldn't acknowledge, even while it seemed always to cast an unmistakably theological shadow. The concept of authenticity in Heidegger's philosophy was a religious residue, a gesture of redemption making its belated appearance in the light of a never-completed disenchantment.[63]

Of Rosenzweig's philosophy, one may argue the reciprocal point. Just as there is a suppressed memory of theology in Heideggerian authenticity, so too there is an anticipation of secularism in Rosenzweigian redemption. I have repeatedly stressed that Rosenzweig must be understood as a specifically modern philosopher, that is, one whose work registers the broader ramifications of the death of God. But the enduring tension in Rosenzweig's philosophy is that he wished to be modern yet simultaneously dedicated himself to retrieving the "primary" experiences of religion from its later, degraded manifestations. As I have shown above, perhaps the most perplexing quality of *The Star* is exactly that it seems to construe redemption as a *lived condition* rather than a specific event surpassing the horizon of experience. One peculiarity of this idea was that it stood in uncomfortable proximity to the atheism it denied. Ironically, in construing redemption as a lived experience, Rosenzweig risked sacralizing the Jewish people in a fashion that closely resembled the "atheistic theology" he attacked in a famous essay by that name.[64] Like authenticity for Heidegger, redemption for Rosenzweig is a modification within the world, not a transcendence of it.[65] It is therefore what I have called (borrowing a term from Heidegger), "redemption-in-the-world." While this phrase may seem an unduly provocative, in my view it captures the precise compromise between theology and modernity in Rosenzweig's thought. For as I have suggested above, *The Star*'s

63. Heidegger's inability to completely escape the metaphysical traces in his own thought has been much discussed in critical literature. His later rejection of *Being and Time* as "too Kierkegaardian" suggests that he at least came to recognize the fundamentally theological grounding of the category of authenticity. For a related argument, see Derrida, *Margins of Philosophy*, 29–67. Elsewhere Derrida argues that "Heideggerian thinking often consists, notably in *Being and Time*, in repeating on an ontological level Christian themes and texts that have been 'de-Christianized.'" *The Gift of Death*, trans. David Wills (Chicago: University of Chicago Press, 1995), 23.

64. Rosenzweig tried to account for the union of modernism and original religious experience with his idea of "translation"—e.g., in "The New Thinking," where he argued that the new post-metaphysical philosophy of the Weimar era would "translate" theological concepts into the human and human problems into the theological. ND, 153. But see his "Atheistische Theologie," KS, 278–90. A similar argument is made by Steven Schwarzschild, "Franz Rosenzweig and Martin Heidegger: The Turn to Ethnicism in Modern Jewish Thought," ed. Maimon Schwarzschild and Almust Schulamith Bruckstein (MS, 1999).

65. On the centrality of the "world" for Rosenzweig, see also the letter to Gritli characterizing the Kaddish (the Jewish commemorative prayer) *not* as a prayer for the dead but a prayer "for the world." GB (25.4.1918), 82–85, esp. 84.

challenge to transcendence makes a distinctively modern point about the collapse of metaphysics. But unlike Heidegger (whose theology remained surreptitious) Rosenzweig had the intellectual probity to register this metaphysical collapse on an explicitly religious plane.[66]

If, as Margarete Susman observed, *The Star of Redemption* was a work "*beyond the zenith of atheism,*" one may conclude that the gap between Rosenzweig's theism and Heidegger's atheism was not truly so wide as one might at first suspect.[67] Of course, religious and ontological speculation are distinct; it would be facile to translate between "God" and "Being."[68] But it is worth noting that, while distinct and untranslatable, for each of them temporality became an ultimate horizon of meaning: Rosenzweig defined redemption as that condition where the Eternal itself has become "like Time" (SE, 292 [E, 324]). And in *Being and Time* Heidegger suggested that what "reveals itself as the horizon of Being [is] time" (SZ, 437; BT, 488). For both, since the dream of detemporalizing metaphysics was done, the claim that something "is" amounts to the claim that it is temporal. Naturally this lesson must then apply a fortiori for those objects that philosophers once considered the grounds of metaphysics, whether such grounds are "God," "Being," or "The Eternal." But what remains that might distinguish theology from ontology if both are identical with time? This question haunts Rosenzweig's *Star of Redemption* and was never satisfactorily resolved. On the one hand, as a modernist philosophical work in the shadow of Nietzsche, it contrived bravely to "take time seriously." On the other hand, as a restorative theological work in the shadow of the older metaphysics, it could not fully relinquish the idea of God's atemporal being. Not surprisingly, *The Star* negotiates but fails to reconcile these two quarrelsome spirits. In this sense

66. Funkenstein notes that *The Star* "conceives Judaism, at one and the same time, as a radically historical and as a radically ahistorical phenomenon . . . [since] Rosenzweig needed a structure that is temporal while defying temporality; historical, while defying historicistic relativism." *Perceptions of Jewish History,* 301. And Leo Strauss observed: "What is true of Nietzsche is no less true of the author of *Sein und Zeit.* Heidegger wishes to expel from philosophy the last relics of Christian theology like the notions of 'eternal truths' and 'the idealized absolute subject.' But the understanding of man which he opposes to the Greek understanding of man as the rational animal is . . . the Biblical understanding of man as created in the image of God. . . . The efforts of the new thinking to escape from the evidence of the Biblical understanding, . . . i.e., from Biblical morality, have failed. . . . Considerations of this kind seemed to decide the issue in favor of Rosenzweig's understanding of the new thinking, or in favor of the unqualified return to Biblical revelation." *Spinoza's Critique of Religion* (New York: Schocken Books, 1965; orig. pub. in German, 1930), esp. 12–13.

67. Susman, "The Exodus from Philosophy," *Frankfurter Zeitung,* June 17, 1921, 1 Morgenblatt, N. 441; my emphasis (reprinted in *Franz Rosenzweig's "The New Thinking,"* ed. and trans. Alan Udoff and Barbara Galli (Syracuse: Syracuse University Press, 1999).

68. I disagree here with George Steiner, *Martin Heidegger* (Chicago: University of Chicago Press, 1989; orig. pub. 1979), 155–56.

Heidegger was correct that the collapse of metaphysics made any partner-ship between philosophy and theology exceedingly difficult.

But not impossible: Rosenzweig's ultimate solution to this difficulty carried him beyond philosophy. If *The Star* was a "system" of philosophy, upon its completion its author seems to have anticipated Heidegger's conclusion that "the time of systems is over." After publishing *The Star*, Rosenzweig would attempt to cope with the collapse of traditional philosophy in a new and perhaps more productive way, since it now seemed that only in a poetic and narrative form could one truly address the strange post-metaphysical insight that God is "like time." The fruit of Rosenzweig's effort was a new German translation of the Bible—the topic of the following chapter.

# Chapter 5

# "Facing the Wooded Ridge"

*The Hebrew Bible in the German Horizon*

*Es sagen's allerorten*
*Alle Herzen unter dem himmlischen Tage,*
*Jedes in seiner Sprache;*
*Warum nicht ich in der meinen?*
　　—GOETHE, *Faust I, Marthens Garten, 3462−65*

*Every God creates a new language.*
　　—FRIEDRICH GUNDOLF, *George, 1920*

In 1924, Franz Rosenzweig began the monumental task of translating the Hebrew Bible into German. A cooperative project between Rosenzweig and Martin Buber, the Bible translation is now widely recognized as one of the most unusual works of German literature. It is also an object lesson in the philosophical invention of Jewish identity. For translating the Bible meant re-inventing Jewish origins from the ground up. Every Hebrew patriarch and prophet acquired a new and unfamiliar name; the landscape, once green with vegetation from the Middle East, was now crowded with Germany's native fauna, and even the historical sections now flashed with the "luster of fables" (*fabelhaft Glanz*). One might argue that the Buber-Rosenzweig Bible thereby aimed to provide readers with a specifically German-Jewish literary past. In this sense, it was an act of literary assimilation, from Hebrew to German. Yet it was simultaneously an act of bold differentiation, a means to dramatize the apparent chasm between contemporary German culture and those ancient Hebrew "origins" that Jews claimed as their own.[1]

Epigraphs: Johann Wolfgang Goethe, *Gedenkausgabe der Werke, Briefe und Gespräche*, vol. V, *Die Faustdichtungen*, ed. Ernst Beutler (Zürich: Artemis Verlag, 1950), 251: "It is said in every place, / All hearts under heaven's days, / Each in his own language; / Why not I in mine?" (My translation.) Friedrich Gundolf, *George* (Berlin: Georg Bondi, 1920), 9.

1. "Luster of fables" from *Die Kreatur* 2, 3 (fall 1928), quoting Paul Schubring in *Die Hilfe* (Wochenschrift, Berlin) 34 (1928). As one recent critic has observed, the purpose of the Buber-Rosenzweig Bible was "to construct a memory." Klaus Reichert, "'It Is Time': The

Because the Buber-Rosenzweig Bible is a translation and not an "original" text, it is often assessed on philological grounds alone. But this approach is misleading. As I shall explain, the Buber-Rosenzweig Bible was a creative work of philosophy in its own right. Moreover, it is an unmistakably modernist document that displays some surprising commonalities with other works in Weimar literature and thought. In this chapter, I shall explore this wider meaning of the translation in three interlocking steps. First, I shall briefly look at how the new translation was received as a literary artifact in its time. Second, I will explore the philosophical and cultural assumptions of the translation theory. Third, I will show how these factors might help us to understand the translators' belief that they had revived a forgotten sense of revelation. Bringing these three strands of argument together, I will conclude with a comparison to key elements of Heidegger's philosophy.

### ARCHAISM AS MODERNISM

In his book *The Philosophy of Modern Music* (1948) Theodor Adorno attacked Igor Stravinsky for promoting the "chimerical rebellion of culture against its own essence." Whether it was the bassoon's mournful lines in its upper register, in evocation of some prehistoric mammal (in *Le Sacre du Printemps*), or the carnivalesque mimicry of hand organs (in *Petrouchka*), Adorno heard the sham intimations of a "mythically monumental past." In *Le Sacre,* the dream of a "non-alienated state" was captured onstage as prehistory. The costumes betrayed "an uncanny resemblance to Wagner's ancient Germanic figures." As Stravinsky's subtitle made plain—it was called "Scenes from Pagan Russia"—the ballet enacted modernism's self-destruction as a battle between "the archaic and the modern."[2]

Whatever the merits of such criticism, Adorno's unease regarding Stravinky's "archaic" tendencies may serve as a useful point of departure for evaluating the early reception of the Buber-Rosenzweig Bible.[3] Both works

---

Buber-Rosenzweig Bible Translation in Context," in *The Translatability of Cultures: Figurations of the Space Between,* ed. and trans. Sanford Budick and Wolfgang Iser (Stanford, Calif.: Stanford University Press, 1996), 169–85, esp. 176.

2. Adorno, *The Philosophy of Modern Music,* trans. Anne G. Mitchell and Wesley V. Blomster (New York: Seabury, 1973; orig. pub. in German, 1948), esp. "Stravinsky and Restoration," 135–217. Adorno went on to compare Stravinsky's accomplishments in music with Husserlian phenomenology. Both long to disclose "a realm of 'authentic' Being," and both are consumed by "distrust of the unoriginal." And both, according to Adorno, succumb to the paradox of false transcendence by denying their own historicity.

3. On the politics of the reception of the Buber-Rosenzweig Bible, see Martin Jay, "Politics of Translation: Siegfried Kracauer and Walter Benjamin on the Buber-Rosenzweig Bible,"

arguably belonged to a specific stream of the interwar avant-garde, an aesthetic of modernist archaism that shocked spectators by framing scenes anterior to civilization. With a nod toward the quasi-anthropological speculations of his day, Stravinsky attempted to bring music back to its embodied partnership with dance, while Buber and Rosenzweig wished to retrieve the Bible from its fallen status as a "mere" text and return it to the rhythm and breath of the human voice. *Le Sacre* challenged its bourgeois audiences to witness onstage a violent re-enactment of sacrifice, while Buber and Rosenzweig cast aside Luther's demure vocabulary in order to recall a forgotten theology of fear and trembling. (Thus in their version Abraham nearly sacrifices Isaac upon a " slaughter site," or *Schlachtstatt;* Luther had only asked that Isaac lay himself upon an "altar," in German, *Altar.*) And while Nijinskii's dancers were dressed in the costumes of pagan Russia, the biblical heroes of the Buber-Rosenzweig translation seemed to some reviewers a curious spawn of Hebrew and Teutonic myth.

Such comparisons were naturally controversial. But almost all of the early reviewers agreed the translation was an unusual mixture of old and new. The cultural critic Siegfried Kracauer claimed that the new Bible was "stranded on a form of speech that is surely not of today." Its style, he suggested, resembled the Hellenistic mock religiosity of the George Kreis, which "pretends to be sacred and esoteric" by employing a mode of expression that seemed "to a great extent archaizing." Yet Kracauer's criticism, while it has recently attracted much scholarly attention, was not in fact representative of the contemporary reception. More typical was the favorable review by Albrecht Schaeffer, the German classicist and translator of Greek literature. Taking exception to Kracauer, Schaeffer argued that although the style of the Bible translation was "not of today," this was all for the better, as poetic speech must be radically unlike common speech. The translation displayed all kinds of "un-German transformations," which could only be called German "in a higher sense." This unfamiliar language, however, served a nobler purpose. The use of words foreign to German offered readers the "deepest sense of the mysterious goings-on of strange people and a foreign time." Though the result was a Bible of startling unfamiliarity, it was the right of the poet to employ a lexicon of past, present, and future—to call upon the "entire range of language lying before him, a Hades field of unborn souls."[4]

---

LBIY, 1976, 3–24; Lawrence Rosenwald, "On the Reception of the Buber-Rosenzweig Bible," *Prooftexts* 14 (1994): 141–65; and Reichert, "'It Is Time.'"

4. Kracauer, "Die Bibel auf Deutsch: Zur Übersetzung von Martin Buber und Franz Rosenzweig," Part 1, *Frankfurter Zeitung* 70, 308 (April 27, 1926): Feuilleton, 1–2; Part 2, *Frankfurter Zeitung* 70, 311 (April 28, 1926): Feuilleton, 1; reprinted in Kracauer, *Schriften* V, *Aufsätze*

If critics such as Schaeffer hesitated in assigning a temporal index to the language of the new Bible, this was perhaps due to the fact that the translation contained a bewildering mixture of archaisms and neologisms. The "Hades field" was strewn with words long departed from common parlance, as well as words never before uttered in German. Naturally, the translators brought forth a wealth of theoretical justifications for their idiosyncratic language. For Luther's familiar phrases, Buber and Rosenzweig substituted unfamiliar terms that in many cases were intended to mimic in German the root-meanings of the Hebrew.[5] Whatever the intentions, the result in German was an unusual compromise between novelty and archaism that many readers found difficult to accept.

Archaism thus became the focal point in the debate between critics and defenders of the new translation. For Kracauer, its supposedly "ancient" qualities amounted to "völkisch" and "antiquarianizing romanticism."[6] The translation also used "restorative expressions," such as "cultmaiden" *(Wiehbuhle)*, and the biblical heroes said "ohnemaß" (beyond measure) and "fürwahr" (forsooth), or "by your leave, my lord!" ("Mit Verlaub, mein Herr!"). The consequence of such "stained-glass expressions," Kracauer complained, was an affected "ur-German" that was only a few decades old and a Hebrew variation upon the familiar style of Teutonic kitsch.

For Schaeffer, such criticism was intolerable. A good rendering of an ancient text would understandably produce a "forwards and backwards effect, perfecting itself in grasping once again what is primordially old." Such a translation was "only apparently unveiled to us in its old form" while in actual fact it was "alienated from its original appearance." But this "renewal of the old" was not to be mistaken for archaism, which would have implied that the translators had produced the anachronistic effects of their new work by design. Buber and Rosenzweig, however, wished only for an authentic "return to origins." And this, in Schaeffer's opinion, was the sole means of achieving renewal in an age now "emptied of gods."[7]

---

(Frankfurt am Main: Suhrkamp, 1971), part II, 355–56; in English in Kracauer, *The Mass Ornament*, trans. Thomas Y. Levin (Cambridge, Mass.: Harvard University Press, 1995). Albrecht Schaeffer, "Bibel-Uebersetzung, Erstes Stück (Aus Anlaß der neuen von Martin Buber und Franz Rosenzweig)," *Preußischer Jahrbücher* (Berlin: Georg Stilke, 1926) 205: 58–82, and "Bibel-Uebersetzung, Zweites Stück (Aus Anlaß der lutherischen)," *Preußischer Jahrbücher* 206 (1926): 47–62.

5. For a helpful summary of the Buber-Rosenzweig root-meaning theory, see Reichert, "'It Is Time,'" and Rosenwald, "Reception of the Buber-Rosenzweig Bible."

6. A shining example was the translators' *Erdvolk* (e.g., Genesis 10:25), which to Kracauer smacked of earth-mysticism, whereas Luther had rendered the Hebrew *aretz* as *Welt*.

7. Schaeffer insisted that archaism arose when poor translators attempted only "to give the old from the old." "Archaizing is what we must call acquiescing in the use of old-fashioned words for the sake of sound ... or ... for the sake of its archaic charm." "Bibel-Uebersetzung, Erstes Stück," 75.

The debate between Schaeffer and Kracauer is intriguing chiefly because their roles were in a certain sense reversed. The establishment critic favored an aesthetic of alienation, while the socialist critic objected to any tampering with tradition. Kracauer argued that because the social struggle had emerged from its theological clothing, the "truth" once embodied in religion "must remain in Luther's translation, or else it no longer exists." It was therefore the "anachronistic quality" of the new translation that lent it a reactionary meaning. It belonged to a climate of mystified spirituality that trumpeted a so-called "transformation in Being [*Wandel des Seins*]." Kracauer's conclusion was decisive: "If reality can be reached only by means of a path that leads through the 'unreality' of the profane, *then today Scripture can no longer be translated.*" Schaeffer disagreed: a new translation promised the younger generation a reinvigorated sense of scripture now that Luther's text had lost its force. He thus ridiculed Kracauer for playing the traditionalist's role: "We the living trust in ourselves too little," he observed. "When someone amongst us undertakes a work that seems to us to lie outside our customary lines of order or seems to break through what . . . seems to us inborn, we can only bring ourselves to shudder, 'What daring! What audacity!'" Such conservatism was in his view all too common: "Half the world," he jested, "is Kracauered [*verkrakauert*]."[8]

The dispute over the alleged "archaism" of the Buber-Rosenzweig translation attracted the attention of many readers. Walter Benjamin, for example, agreed with Kracauer that Rosenzweig poorly understood the historical meaning of translating the Bible anew.[9] But the reception appears to

8. The debate was regarded by some as a contest between modernists and antimodernists. See, e.g., Karl Wilker, "Bücher Besprechung: Albrecht Schaeffer, Wilhelm Michel, Martin Buber, und Die Kreatur," *Das Werdene Zeitalter: Eine Zeitschrift für Erneuerung der Erziehung,* ed. Elisabeth Rotten und Karl Wilker, 5, 4 (1926). Kracauer, "Die Bibel auf Deutsch," *Schriften,* 367; my emphasis; Kracauer himself italicized "no longer." Schaeffer, "Bibel-Uebersetzung, Erstes Stück," 78. For Schaeffer, Kracauer was a mere "publicist, ungifted and wholly foolish," whose judgments revealed an "inborn envy of whatever is meaningful and distinctive" ("Erstes Stück," 72). The contemporary world had grown "disenchanted," thanks to the this "Jewish" sort of skepticism, while Buber and Rosenzweig were paragons of Jewish authenticity: only "our Jewish fellow-citizens could have dared to create a synthesis out of two so mutually foreign languages," since they alone preserved a "secret relation" to each ("Zweites Stück," 61).

9. In a letter to Kracauer, Benjamin seemed particularly critical of Martin Buber, whose philosophy exemplified the mystical irrationalism of the "southwest-German Religious" circle (i.e., Buber's group in Heidelberg), a group that was "almost as whispering and sanctimoniously school-building as the southwest-German 'Philosophers'" (i.e., the George Kreis in Darmstadt ). Benjamin regarded Rosenzweig's reputation as "forever damaged" through his association with Buber, and he complained that Rosenzweig "seems not to consider the sole question that everything amounts to: the translating of the Bible *now* and into *German.*" *Briefe an Siegfried Kracauer,* ed. Theodor Adorno (Marbach am Neckar: Deutsche Schillergesellschaft, 1987), 16n. On Benjamin's hostility to Buber, see Momme Brodersen, *Walter Benjamin: A Biography,* trans. Malcolm R. Green and Ingrida Ligers (London: Verso, 1996); and

have been more or less evenly divided between those who attacked archaism as an anachronistic effect and those who considered it a legitimate poetic device. In this sense the dispute expressed broader issues concerning the relation between modernism, religion, and antiquity: Does modernism require the outright rejection of the past, or is there a mode of seizing upon the past that is itself modernist in sensibility? Can there be a forward-looking method of translating an ancient text, and can a translation that is itself modern also call modernity into question by underscoring the differences between past and present? Could a German language unfamiliar to contemporary readers be used to evoke a non-German difference, a distance of geography, history, and worldview? To what extent was neologism a warranted device in the translation of an ancient text? If one were to reject all neologisms, should one abandon modern parlance entirely in order to capture a truly "antiquated" time?

Such questions plagued early discussion of the Buber-Rosenzweig Bible. Defenders as well as critics noted the peculiar tension between novelty and archaism. And while some readers found the innovations imaginative, others condemned any tampering with Luther's canonical language. There is little doubt that such objections were largely a defense of the familiar; Luther's word choices, though no less arbitrary, had over the years acquired the patina of inevitability. For example, Luther had translated the Hebrew word *nabi* as *Prophet*. Buber-Rosenzweig instead chose *Künder* (harbingers, or bringers of intelligence). Some readers found this revision cloying and intrusive; Kracauer even suggested that the translators had borrowed it from Stefan George's poem "The Star of the Covenant." Similarly, Luther's "burnt offering," *(Brandopfer)* described the same action as the Hebrew term, *olah*. But according to Buber and Rosenzweig, this did not capture the literal sense in the Hebrew root "'a-l," which implies raising upward, or height. Accordingly, the translators preferred a near-literal German equivalent, *Hochgabe*. Luther's *Brandopferaltar* (the altar for burnt offerings) was thus razed to the ground and in its place the translators erected the far less ecclesiastical *Statt der Hochgabe*.[10] They defended this neologism as a closer approximation of the Hebrew. But in German the effect could be jarring. For while *Gabe* was a familiar term for a gift or offering, *Hochgabe* was a hybrid; it harmonized with other words such as *Hingabe* (devotion or surren-

---

Gershom Scholem, *Walter Benjamin: The Story of a Friendship,* trans. Harry Zohn (New York: Schocken Books, 1981), esp. circa July 1916, 19–51.

10. In Buber's emended postwar edition of the text, *Hochgabe* was replaced by *Darhöhung*, which is also a neologism, reflecting in fact an even more literal equivalent for the Hebrew: *Dar* suggests little more than a direction "to-there" and "höhen" meaning to raise. Klaus Reichert has suggested that Buber wished to enforce a parallelism between this *dar* of sacrifice unto God and God's highest name, "Ich bin da."

der) and its meaning echoed *hochheben* (to raise up). For German ears more accustomed to Luther's language, the new selections seemed bold, and sometimes unacceptable.

But even defenders of the Buber-Rosenzweig Bible found its language highly unusual. Many critics imagined that the translators' style reflected a "distant," even "Eastern" world. One critic found in the new Bible "the sublimity of the wide, pure heavens of the Orient." Another compared it to the recent translation by Karl Eugen Neumann of the speeches of Buddha. While some critics attacked this as archaism, the expressionist poet Oscar Loerke found that the new Bible brought "a heretofore undisclosed breath from the East, from the early age of man, whose essence cannot by any means be captured by such terms as archaic or barbaric." Its phrases revealed a "terse, reposeful mode of thought striving for intuition in a far greater ruggedness, strangeness, even wildness, but also greater immediacy."[11]

To demonstrate this supposed difference between East and West, many reviews cited lines from Luther's version and compared them with the corresponding passages from the newer translation. Thus the following passage from Genesis 2:6:

> Aber ein Nebel ging auf von der Erde und feuchtete alles Land.
>
> (But a fog went out upon the Earth and watered all the land.)[12]

The contrast between this passage and the version by Buber and Rosenzweig was dramatic:

> Gewog stieg da aus der Erde und tränkte alle Fläche des Ackers.
>
> (Surging stepped there out of the earth and soaked all the flat places of the soil.)

The new version, as one critic observed, was "darker," somehow "unmusical"—it recalled a past of greater simplicity. Another critic agreed that "this new, strictly factual and orientalizing translation is to be welcomed."[13] For most critics, this "oriental" quality was synonymous with a matter-of-fact, even plain aesthetic, one that lacked all decoration and sophistication. The problem with Luther's translation is that it contained many melliflu-

11. "'Eastern' world" and reference to Neumann from Felix Braun, "Neue Deutsche Uebersetzungskunst," *Das Tagebuch* 32 (1926): 1158–60. "Sublimity" and other comments from Oskar Loerke, review in *Neue Rundschau* 38 (1927), cited in *Die Kreatur* 2, 2, (1927).

12. Note that all English translations of Luther and the Buber-Rosenzweig Bible are my own. These translations are provided merely to give some sense of the differences between German versions; they are, of course, imprecise.

13. Felix Braun, "Neue Deutsche Uebersetzungskunst," *Das Tagebuch* 32 (1926): 1158–61, at 1159. Paul Schubring, review, *Die Hilfe,* 34 (1928), cited in *Die Kreatur,* 2, 3 (fall 1928).

ous turns of phrase, effectively forcing the Bible into a Western narrative style. When at last the text was liberated from these constraints, the language was revealed to be something flatter, less storylike than rhythmic. In Luther's version, for example, Adam was born with the following words (Genesis 2:7):

> Und also ward der Mensch eine lebendige Seele.
>
> (And thus became the man a living soul.)

while in the new translation, one read:

> und der Mensch ward zum lebenden Wesen.
>
> (and the man became living being.)

In a comparison of these two phrases, Felix Braun described Luther's edition as "personal, European," and the Buber-Rosenzweig edition as "impersonal, Asiatic."[14]

Nowhere, perhaps, was the difference more dramatically felt than in the beginning passages of Genesis. Luther's German version retained the connectives ("und"), creating the continuity of an everyday sentence:

> und die Erde war wüst und leer, und es war finster auf der Tiefe;
>
> (and the Earth was deserted and empty, and there was shadow upon the deep)

The new translation, by contrast, omitted the connectives, resulting in phrasing that was far more condensed, an effect some readers associated with "oriental" minimalism.[15] Other critics, citing the same passage, remarked upon the fact that the translators had managed to approximate the internal rhymes of the Hebrew. The alliterative Hebrew phrase *tohu v'vohu* ("without form and void") was lost in Luther's "wüst und leer." But in the new version one read:

> Und die Erde war Wirrnis und Wüste.
> Finsternis allüber Abgrund.
>
> (And the Earth was Wild and Waste,
> Darkness upon the Abyss.)

Perhaps the most striking difference in this passage was the substitution of *Abgrund* (abyss) for Luther's *Tiefe* (depths). As in English, the German *Tiefe* also connotes richness or profundity. Whereas "depths" seems environmental and poetic, "abyss" (implying an absence of ground, *Ab-grund*) is

---

14. Braun, "Neue Deutsche Uebersetzungskunst," 1158–60.

15. Writing in the *Deutsche Literaturzeitung*, Paul Volz described this as "the most pregnant brevity." Cited in *Die Kreatur* 1, 4, (spring 1927).

haunting and dangerous. As Margarete Susman noted, such choices lent the new translation a markedly "existential-religious" quality.[16]

In general, readers discovered in the new Bible a new (or ancient) style of simplicity. The rhythmic compression of the phasing and the immediacy of many of the metaphors seemed to return the Bible to a forgotten and premodern facticity. In a prominent review, Roland Schacht praised the translation for its "clarity" and "corporeality." And he was careful to note (against Kracauer) that Buber and Rosenzweig had reproduced the *actual* "archaisms" of ancient biblical form without the slightest hint of artifice.[17]

To be sure, some readers detected a measure of willful exoticism, especially in the translators' effort to retain the Hebraic sounds of proper names. In Luther's text, for example, the first woman was called by her naturalized German name, "Eva," while Buber and Rosenzweig had chosen instead to transliterate the original sounds of the Hebrew, thus their name, "Chawa." (Similarly, Luther's "Mose" (Moses) became "Mosche" in the new translation, and so on.) Critics disagreed as to the success of such stylistic choices. Predictably, Kracauer objected to these irruptions of Hebrew in the midst of the German as a "völkisch" affectation. But many felt the new names captured the feeling of the original text, especially as the odd spelling seemed somehow inelegant and premodern. Generally speaking, "archaism" meant candor, not the elaborate mannerism of arabesque. "All the oriental color has been retained," Schacht noted. And yet "the style has the great naturalness and the blank facticity of a Damascus blade." Seconding this comparison, the novelist Arnold Zweig suggested that the translators had created a Bible with the "tone, the elevations, and the bowed tension of an heroic epic from Mediterranean antiquity." Here was a "pathetic style of speech," which recalled the "authentic [*echtes*] epics of ancient Greece" but also revealed "a new world."[18]

Some reviewers found the translators' rhythmic effects artificial. The literary critic Emmanuel bin Gorion doubted that rhythmic fidelity to the original really yielded any new or deeper insight. The description of Eden's

16. Susmann, "Was kann uns die Bibel heute noch bedeuten?" *Der Morgen* 2, 3 (August 1926): 299–310, at 310. "All words," she said, including the ancient words of the Bible, are "thrown into the abyss of our present age."

17. Roland Schacht, "Soll man die Bibel neu übersetzen?" (review of *Das Buch Im Anfang*), *Die Literarische Welt* 2, 21/22 (February, 1926).

18. The "Erdvolk," quipped Kracauer, were "given their land rights" in these mock-Hebraic names. Kracauer, "Die Bibel auf Deutsch," 367. Schacht, "Die Bibel neu übersetzen?" Zweig, *Jüdische Rundschau*, cited in *Die Kreatur* 1, 4 (spring 1927). Similarly, Walther Petry compared the new Bible to Hölderlin's translations of Sophocles and George's translations of Dante. He praised Buber and Rosenzweig for having brought the Bible "into a circle of speech that is at once pathetic and simple, antiquated and quite modern [*altertümlich und sehr modern*]." Cited in *Die Kreatur* 2, 1 (1927).

forbidden fruit, for example, seemed more cloying than authentic: "Köst-
lich war der Baum zur Speise," complained bin Gorion, bore a regrettable
similarity to the childish rhyme "trauernd tief saß Don Diego."[19] Other reviewers voiced a similar complaint concerning the translators' attempt to
reproduce in German the Hebrew device of paronomasia, the doubling of
words or word roots in neighboring words, as in "to sing songs." Kracauer
considered such gimmicks more Teutonic than Hebrew. He complained
that "They take the Luther text, 'and the Lord smelled the lovely scent
[Und der Herr roch den lieblichen Geruch]' and elevate it to the lofty German formulation, 'Thus HE scented the scent of assentment [Da roch ER
den Ruch der Befriedung].'" In Kracauer's opinion, "the stench of these al-
literations stems not from the Bible but from runes of a Wagnerian sort."[20]

Schaeffer granted there was some resemblance between Buber's "bardic"
mysticism and the language of Wagnerian bards such as Felix Dahn.[21] But
he found Kracauer's criticism misplaced. While Schaeffer admitted his ig-
norance of Hebrew, as an important translator of Greek epics (his rendering of Homer's *Iliad* had recently appeared), he was confident that Buber
and Rosenzweig "did not seek the alliteration, but rather discovered it." For
in Greek as well as in every "original" language, one found the device of
"connection by means of repetition." Moreover, the repetitive structure was
a sign of a profound cultural difference: "Tautologies of this kind, between
verb and object," reflected the "naïveté and primordial simplicity" of the
ancient world. Many critics agreed with this assessment. The great advantage of the new translation was that it captured the "naive" spirit of the Hebrew Bible as against sophistication of modern life. It could therefore act as
a force of rejuvenation. For just as Luther's translation seemed "hopelessly
old and obsolete," the German language overall showed signs of age and
wear. Hermann Hesse thus welcomed the new Bible's appearance as a rare
event in what he called "our brutalized and mechanized language."[22]

19. For bin Gorion, the translators erred in that their ostensibly "faithful" rendering
yielded a German blind to its own historical setting. "[T]he naive man of antiquity" was "devoted to the primordial message of his time [*der Urkunde hingegebene Mensch*]," and so enjoyed
a certain right to his ancient cadences. But "a modern cannot artificially draw forth such ar-
maments once they are discarded." *Ceterum Recenseo: Kritische Aufsätze und Reden* (Tübingen:
Alexander Fischer Verlag, 1929); see esp. the essay, "Kritik und Besprechung: Eine neue Verdeutschung der Bibel," 21–38.

20. As Lawrence Rosenwald has observed, Kracauer seemed ignorant of the fact that Hebrew too tends naturally toward this kind of alliteration. See the excellent discussion of this
problem in Rosenwald, "Reception of the Buber-Rosenzweig Bible," 157.

21. They are, Schaeffer punned, "both *bearded* [*bärdig*] as well." Schaeffer, "Bibel-Uebersetzung, Erstes Stück," 76.

22. Schacht, "Die Bibel neu übersetzen?" Hesse, *Berliner Tageblatt* (issue unidentified), cited
in *Die Kreatur* 1, 3 (1926).

There is of course a difference between an "original" text *(Urtext)* and "original news" *(Urkunde).* But the two concepts are easily linked, perhaps especially in a Protestant context that idealized the return to textual sources as the desideratum of correct faith. Thus the Buber-Rosenzweig Bible in Germany was widely regarded as the "first attempt" to reproduce "the rhythmic structure of the Urtext," and this idea of philological fidelity was often associated with the *message* of the translation itself.[23] In one periodical after another one finds this same claim, that only by means of the "peculiarities" of the language, only in this "wholly new" and "uncustomary speech" *(ungewöhnliche Sprache),* could one also return to the Ur-wisdom of the Hebrew. As Kurt Münzer observed, the translation was so effective that "when Moses speaks, when God pronounces, it is almost as if one heard it for the first time."[24]

From this survey of the contemporary reception, there emerges a common sense of paradox; the Bible seemed at once modernized and restored. Its simplicity and its rhythms evoked the childhood of humankind, a world anterior to civilization. Yet these effects were only achieved by means of a language that radically reversed the traditional German turns of phrase. Some readers objected to this assault upon tradition. In a provocative review, Richard Koch characterized the new translation as a "stylized myth."[25] But others welcomed the "alienated" experience of a once-familiar work,

23. Hence the unidentified reviewer of the first volume noted that, thanks to the translators' formal understanding of the "prehistoric speaking song" *(vorzeitlichen Sprechgesang)* the "primordial news" *(Urkunde)* at last rang clear. Review of "Die Schoepfung," *Jüdische Rundschau* 100–101, "Literatur-Blatt," 30, 23 (December 1925): 831.

24. Paul Rießler, in an unidentified issue of the *Theologischen Quartalschrift,* cited in *Die Kreatur* 1, 4 (spring 1927). Another critic similarly linked the theory of translation with the promise of wisdom when he wrote that "in word choice the translators turn as tightly as possible toward the Hebrew text, answering root for root in German, repeating repetitions, giving unfamiliarities for unfamiliarities and the customary with the customary," all in the belief that "the primordial word [*das Uralte Wort*] is capable of revelation [*offenbarungsträchtig*] today as always." Paul Alverdes, in *Der Kunstwart,* cited in *Die Kreatur* 2, 3 (fall 1928). Münzer, review of *Die Schrift, Zweites Buch, Das Buch Namen,* in *Die Literatur* 29, 2 (November 1929), 113–14.

25. Koch, "Bemerkungen zur neuen Verdeutschung der Heiligen Schrift" (review of Martin Buber and Franz Rosenzweig, *Die Schrift: Die fünf Bücher der Weisung, Erstes Buch* [Berlin: Verlag Lambert Schneider]), *Der Morgen* 1, 6 (February 1926): 714–16. In response, Buber and Rosenzweig admitted that "our book is a German book." See Buber and Rosenzweig, "Zu einer Uebersetzung und einer Rezension," *Der Morgen* 2, 1 (April 1926): 111–13. They went on to argue that familiarity with the language of origin was an absolute prerequisite for any judicious assessment of a translation. To this Koch objected strenuously that no matter how carefully one goes about translating, "no two translations end up the same" and without reference to the original one could judge a translation "on its own particular quality [*Eigenart*]." This, Koch concluded, "is recognizable for me and for others in the *style* . . . just like an artwork." "Schlußbemerkung" [rejoinder directly following Buber and Rosenzweig], *Der Morgen* 2, 1 (April 1926), 113–14.

and they praised the new translation for its "otherness." As has been shown, however, this otherness had a dual meaning: it indicated an orientation against Luther's translation (a difference from tradition) as well as a foreignness that seemed to resist the present (a difference from modernity). The aesthetic effect of this dual orientation was a highly unusual language poised between archaism and neologism—a return to the past that seemed simultaneously to have wrested itself free from history entirely.[26] A brief examination of the theoretical assumptions behind the translation will help to explain how these two seemingly incompatible tendencies could fruitfully coexist.

## A THEORY OF TRANSLATION

In a note to his 1778 translation of the *Iliad*, the poet Friedrich Leopold von Stolberg lamented, "Oh, dear Reader, learn Greek, and throw my translation in the fire!" More than a century and a half later, von Stolberg's words appeared as the leading epigraph to Franz Rosenzweig's volume of translations from the Hebrew verse of the medieval Jewish poet Jehuda Halevi. Rosenzweig borrowed the phrase because he shared von Stolberg's ambivalence about translation. Rosenzweig did not wish his readers literally to burn his volume of poetry; but he did wish for its symbolic disappearance. He denied his translations any semblance of autonomy; the German in which they were written was to serve as a kind of theater for the performance of the poems' Hebrew origins. In the preface to the Halevi volume, he wrote: "[T]hese translations want to be nothing but translations. Not for a moment do they want to make the reader forget that he is reading poems not by me, but by Jehuda Halevi, and that Jehuda Halevi is neither a German poet nor a contemporary."[27]

But this disavowal cuts two ways. On the one hand, it makes the translation more clearly an independent thing. ("These translations want to be nothing but translations.") On the other hand, it displaces the reader's investments from the German to the original. (The reader is to feel that the poems are by someone who is "neither a German poet nor a contemporary.") Taken at once, the implicit theory of translation hidden in this disavowal produces a sense of being beholden to what is elsewhere—the

26. On "otherness," see Schaeffer, "Bibel-Uebersetzung, Erstes Stück," 59. And see, e.g., Schaeffer's own translations of Greek heroic saga, which are staged in just such an "Urzeit," where the gods move "in a realm of light, beyond Okeanos, without strife or want, blissfully alone in their existence without end." Schaeffer, *Griechische Helden-Sagen, neu-erzählt nach den alten Quellen* (Leipzig: Insel Verlag, 1929).

27. Rosenzweig, *Sechzig Hymnen und Gedichte des Jehuda Halevi. Deutsch. Mit einem Nachwort und mit Anmerkungen.* Orig. pub. 1924; reprinted in FR, IV, 1: 1.

translation calls attention to itself only to confess its derivative status. Acknowledging that it has fallen away from its origins, it wishes to turn back, to restore the original even if it must endure the exile of being in another language. As I shall explain, this unusual combination of modernist estrangement and antimodernist longing is the central feature of Buber and Rosenzweig's translation theory.

Buber and Rosenzweig published several of their theoretical essays separately in the 1920s; the Schocken Verlag then published them in a 1936 collection under the title *Die Schrift und ihre Verdeutschung*. Even the title presents some difficulty: the first volume of the new Bible, containing Buber and Rosenzweig's translation of Genesis (*Das Buch Im Anfang*, or "The Book In the Beginning")—was identified has having been "translated" or, more literally, "Germanized" *(verdeutscht)*. But several of the Bible's critics remarked on the strangeness of the word. The idea of *Verdeutschung* is indeed unusual; the more customary term for translation is *Übersetzung*, or (more rarely) *Übertragung*. Both of these latter terms imply a carrying-over of something from one space to another, a task that may seem as easy as picking up luggage and traveling somewhere new. The locale changes, the person does not. To "Germanize," however, implies a deeper transformation: it means not only adopting a new language; it means changing one's self. Ironically, however, Buber and Rosenzweig seemed to have as their dramatic goal to emphasize the "*un*-German" qualities of their work. Their *Verdeutschung* was meant to render the Bible less German, not more so.[28]

To understand this riddle, it is important to consider that the Buber-Rosenzweig Bible appeared as a reaction to Luther's translation. In the essay, "Letter from the Translator," Luther had announced that he wished to create biblical language "like [that of] the mother in her home, and . . . the common man." For Luther, "speaking German well" meant this everyday register.[29] Now while Luther's text has been revised, its basic contours have remained in place down to the twentieth century. And like most translations that become canonical, it is hardly ever experienced as if it were merely an approximation of a foreign original. Its language seems simply the most

28. The difference between *Übersetzung* and *Verdeutschung* thus has an analogue in the social distinction between emigration and assimilation. Max Dienemann, in a contemporary review, made this analogy explicit when he wondered whether some of the neologisms of the new translation could truly enjoy their "civil rights" in the German tongue. Review of *Die Schrift, Das Buch, Er rief. Das Buch, In der Wüste, Der Morgen* 3, 3 (August 1927), 343–44. It is worth noting that the Yiddish analogue, "fertaschten," means "to translate" in the generic sense; so in principle one can even "translate" *out of* German.

29. For comments on the comparison between the Buber-Rosenzweig version and Luther's Bible, see Bertha Badt-Strauß, "Die deutsche Bibel," *Jüdische Rundschau* 31, 11 (Berlin, February 9, 1926). Luther cited from "Sendbrief vom Dolmetschen," in *An den christlichen Adel deutschen Nation, und andere Schriften* (Stuttgart: Reclam, 1960), 166–90.

natural, even inevitable vehicle of biblical meaning. To be sure, this "naturalness" was itself a creation. In substituting Christian stories for pagan Teutonic legends, Luther not only created a new Bible, he created a new past: As Albrecht Schaeffer observed, Luther "re-created the Book of the Jewish People as a Book of the Germans." "What was originally Jewish [*ursprünglich Jüdische*] was thus Germanized [*eingedeutscht*]."

Luther's translation thus obeyed a principle of identity. It transformed what had once seemed foreign into something "customary" and familiar. Through style and word selection, Luther "collected into living odes the entire life and essence of the Germans, not only words and phrases, sentence structure and rhythm, but also demeanor and gestures, the poetry and costume, and brought [these] . . . into the popular stratum of speech." In Luther's translation, then, Jews became proto-Germans, and the German past was remade in the image of Scripture, such that everything that had been lost in the *Germanic* past was given back "*as if inborn*" *(wie angeboren)* in a language that was "idiomatic [*mundgerecht*] to the German mouth."[30] In Schaeffer's phrase, "Where the Oak fell, there now stood the Cloister."[31]

By contrast, Buber and Rosenzweig's new translation obeyed what might be called a principle of difference.[32] This is the basic message of Rosenzweig's 1926 essay, "The Scripture and Luther." As he described it, translation is torn—it means "serving two masters." Citing Friedrich Schleiermacher, Rosenzweig explained that there are two kinds of translation, those that "leave the writer in peace and move the reader in his direction" and those that "leave the reader in peace and move the writer."[33] In the first case, the original demands satisfaction, and it forces the target language to accommodate the meanings and cadences of the original text. But in the

30. Schaeffer, "Bibel-Uebersetzung, Zweites Stück," 50–51; my emphasis. Indeed, the Jewish people were actually, in Schaeffer's assessment, "*identified with* the German people" (52; my emphasis).

31. Schaeffer, "Bibel-Uebersetzung, Erstes Stück," 50–52. Just as Adam was "the tribal father [*Stammvater*] of the human race," so the personalities of Luther's Bible were, for German readers, not Jews, but "only men" like themselves, which is to say, *German* men.

32. On the theme of "difference," see the recent volume of translation theory inspired by the work of Jacques Derrida, *Difference in Translation,* ed. Joseph F. Graham (Ithaca: Cornell University Press, 1985).

33. Rosenzweig, *Die Schrift und Luther* (Berlin: Lambert Schneider, 1926), 23. Rosenzweig admits that the antithesis is somewhat artificial—it is "dazzling and nothing more." But "taken sensibly," he writes, Schleiermacher's distinction "can help to clarify the two dominant tendencies of translation." See also Rosenzweig's short review of the new edition of Zadoc Kahn's French translation of the Hebrew Bible, where he confirms the Goethe-Schleiermacher distinction between these two poles of translation. Rosenzweig, "Rezension: La Bible. Traduite de text original par les Membres du Rabbinat français sous la direction due Grand Rabbin Zadoc Kahn," *Der Morgen* 5, 1 (April 1929): 95.

second case, the target language itself demands recognition as an active partner in the creation of meaning, and it may sometimes impose a new sense and cadence quite at odds with the original. To Rosenzweig, it seemed obvious that Luther's German Bible had obeyed the second principle. For while Luther was occasionally willing to "give the Hebrew some room" and could even "put up with such words" as might better reflect the Hebrew, to him this meant tolerating what he regarded as merely unavoidable lapses within an otherwise idiomatic German.

Rosenzweig readily conceded that the identity principle was perhaps more natural. ("[A]fter all," he wrote, "translation is into the language of the reader and not into the language of the original.") But a translation that demanded "moving the reader," was nonetheless "*more instructive and interesting.*" Only a translation that preserved the sense of unfamiliarity could ensure the longevity and force of the original, even where this required a creative violation of German linguistic convention. Since Luther had erased this unfamiliarity, his Bible translation had lost its status as living revelation:

> The voice of the bible is not to be enclosed in any space—not in the inner sanctum of a church, not in the linguistic sanctum of a people, not in the circle of the heavenly images moving above a nation's sky. Rather this voice seeks again and again *to resound from outside* [*von draußen schallen*]—from outside this church, this people, this heaven. It does not keep its sound from echoing in this or that restricted space, but it wants itself to remain free. *If somewhere it has become a familiar, customary possession* [*vertraut, gewohnt, Besitz*] *it must again and anew, as a foreign and unfamiliar sound from outside* [*von draußen*] *disturb the complacent satedness of its alleged possessor.*[34]

Buber and Rosenzweig regarded their new translation as "different" in this sense. Against the Lutheran model of translation that aimed toward a naturalness of meaning, syntax, and cadence, the new Bible would confront the reader with an almost aggressive unfamiliarity as if its language were coming "from outside." The emphasis was to be placed squarely on the representation of *otherness*, both historical and cultural.

The Buber-Rosenzweig difference theory of translation embraced several more specific methods, all of which aimed to recreate the rhythms and repetitions of roots of the original. Most of all, they believed that the Bible was primarily a text designed to be spoken aloud, and they saw writing as little more than a decayed trace of the voice. Accordingly, since speaking happens in units of breath, the new Bible was to be divided into to *Atemkolen,* or breathing units. As Rosenzweig explained, the cumulative effect was "to restore" *(zurückgeben)* to the Bible "the free, oral breathing of the

34. Rosenzweig, *Die Schrift und Luther,* 23; my emphasis.

word," where this had been formerly "ensnared . . . in the writtenness of Scripture."[35]

In addition, Buber and Rosenzweig aimed to reproduce in the German text the repetition of roots found in the Hebrew original. Against an "aerial view" of the verbal "landscape" (which might miss recurring patterns that sometimes lie far from one another in the text), Rosenzweig proposed a more "geological" method that would burrow to the "roots of words" in search of the "roots of meaning." Like a miner, the translator was supposed to seek out the "glimmer glowing from the veins of the text itself," to discover *(entdecken)* in the affinities of roots and repeated phrasings a "conceptual circle" that could then be re-created in the other language.[36]

The unifying principle of these methods is that the new Bible should exhibit insofar as possible what Rosenzweig called "fidelity to the scriptural word" *(Treue zum Wort der Schrift)*.[37] Like many translators, Buber and Rosenzweig were concerned to represent themselves as responsible philologists, whose primary obligation was to respect the form and content of the original text. Significantly, Rosenzweig resorted to archaeological metaphors, reinforcing their view that the new translation was an act of rediscovery, not creative interpretation. It is important to recognize, however, that the translators were nonetheless aware that "restoration" in a new language was not the same as simply returning to the original. The context of the target language inevitably lent the text a novel character. But for fidelity's sake, the translators were willing to violate customs of the German language. This was permissible even if it meant transgressing the "boundaries of linguistic possibility." It was wrong, they argued, to "render remote [*entlegene*] Hebrew with familiar [*geläufige*] German." The new version in German was to sound like the original Hebrew even where the original sounded obscure, such that the very strangeness of the new text would signal its distant origin.

The theoretical underpinnings of the Buber-Rosenzweig Bible therefore represent an unusual compromise between the ideals of estrangement and restoration. The chief aim was to create a translation that, while written in German, read as if it were a restoration of the Hebrew original. Accordingly, the German language became a kind of theater for the staging of Hebrew difference. But by invoking the ideal of philological fidelity, the translators could claim that the otherness of their work had nothing to do with artifice, since it was simply the consequence of their attempt to restore the Bible

---

35. Rosenzweig, *Die Schrift und Luther,* 43.

36. To illustrate this method, Rosenzweig provided the example of "service" *(Dienst),* which in the Hebrew *(avodah)* is a word that describes both Egyptian slavery and service to God *(avo-dath elohim)*. *Die Schrift und Luther,* 49; the example, however, was well known (e.g., Cohen, RV, 58–61).

37. Rosenzweig, *Die Schrift und Luther,* 49.

to its "original" character. The ideal of restoration thus served as justification for the radical unfamiliarity of the new text. And readers expecting a Bible in idiomatic German would find themselves confronted with what Schleiermacher had called the "foreignness of the foreign" *(die Fremdheit des Fremden)*.

The methods of differential translation were not peculiar to the 1920s. (Similar ideas can be found, for example, in the writings of the German Romantics.) [38] But the rise of literary and artistic modernism infused new life into the notion that translation could itself serve as a vehicle for the overcoming of tradition. In the 1923 essay "The Task of the Translator," Walter Benjamin argued,

> Unlike a work of literature, translation does not find itself in the center of the language forest but on the outside facing the wooded ridge; it calls into it without entering, aiming at that single spot where the echo is able to give, in its own language, the reverberation of the work in the alien one.

For Benjamin, a good translation exists as if "at the edge" of the one language; it listens and strives to reproduce the sounds and sense of the other, and in mediating between languages "intends language as a whole." Benjamin concluded that the traditional idea of translation aiming at familiarity should be abandoned. For a "real translation" is "transparent." It does not "cover the original" or "block its light." Rather, it "allows the pure language, as though reinforced by its own medium, to shine upon the original all the more fully." [39]

Many theorists, poets, and critics of the Weimar era promoted the modernist ideal of translation as simultaneously restoration and estrangement. The classicist Wolfgang Schadewaldt argued that the age of similarity was over and advocated translations that exhibited "the otherness [*Andersartigkeit*] of other nations and times." [40] Similarly, Rudolf Pannwitz complained

38. Its most classic formulation can be found in Goethe's comments upon the death of Christoph Martin Wieland, the famous Shakespeare translator: "There are two maxims in translation. One requires that the author of a foreign nation be brought across to us in such a way that we can look on him as ours; the other requires that we should go across to him as foreign and adapt ourselves to his conditions, its use of language, its peculiarities." "Zu brüderlichen Andenken Wielands, 1813," in *Werke,* vol. XII, *Biographische Einzelschriften* (Zürich: Artemis Verlag, 1947), 693–716; quote at 705.

39. Benjamin, "The Task of the Translator," in *Illuminations,* trans. Harry Zohn (New York, Schocken Books: 1974), 79.

40. Schadewaldt, "Das Problem des Übersetzens," *Die Antike: Zeitschrift für Kunst und Kultur des klassischen Altertums,* ed. Werner Jaeger, 3, 4 (1927): 293–94. For Schadewaldt the aim in translating a work from another era is "to grasp the Historical in sensual fashion." Citing Schleiermacher's 1813 lecture, "Über die verschiedenen Methoden des Übersetzens," he argued that a good translation involved "surrender to the original" as well as the "renunciation of one's own linguistic capacities and proficiencies" so as to "sound like something distinctly

that "our translations, even the best ones, proceed from a wrong premise." They want "to turn Hindi, Greek, English into German instead of turning German into Hindi, Greek, English," and seek to preserve "the state in which [their] own language happens to be instead of allowing [it] . . . to be powerfully affected by the foreign tongue."[41] And Schaeffer claimed to prefer translations that reshaped the German language rather than risking any "misrepresentation" of the original. His translation of *The Odyssey,* first published in 1927, received much abuse for its "bad German." But Schaeffer argued,

> What [my] translation strives toward is, within the humble limits of the possible, the form of the original [*die Gestalt des Originals*]. This translation [*Verdeutschung*] does not want, therefore, to "bring near," that is, it does not want to multiply what is customary to us by means of what appears once again as customary; rather, it wishes to show the foreign and far [*Fremde und Ferne*] in all their extremity and uniqueness.[42]

The frequency of such arguments may appear to signal the emergence of a distinctively modernist aesthetic, loosely associated with the terms defamiliarization, estrangement, and difference.[43] As a principle of translation, however, the modernist assault on tradition can also turn nostalgic. For what may appear as a rebellion against the "customary" can serve simultaneously to express longing for the "original." (Here, in fact, we are quite close to Benjamin's belief that all translation recalls the Edenic immediacy of "language as such.") Indeed, it may be that the very activity of translation encourages such a dual-orientation, since the modernist aesthetic here stakes

---

other [*nach etwas betimmten Anderen klingen*]," thus helping readers toward "a deeper penetration and more comprehensive regard for the foreign nationality, epoch and generation."

41. Pannwitz, *Die Krisis der europäischen Kultur* (Nurenberg: H. Karl, 1917), quoted in Benjamin, "The Task of the Translator," 81. "Our translators," Pannwitz complained, "have a far greater reverence for the usage of their own language than for the spirit of the foreign works . . . Particularly when translating from a language very remote from his own [a translator] must go back to the primal elements of language itself and penetrate to the point where work, image, and tone converge. He must expand and deepen his language by means of the foreign language." Benjamin ranked Pannwitz's remarks alongside Goethe's *Notes to the West-östlicher Divan* as "the best comment on the theory of translation that has been published in Germany."

42. Schaeffer, "Poetischer Sprachverfall," *Preußischer Jahrbücher* 208, 3 (January–March 1927): 312–18.

43. Hence Adorno's remark that foreign words that have been imported into a national vocabulary are "the Jews of language." *Notes to Literature,* ed. Rolf Teidemann, trans. Shierry Weber Nicholson (New York: Columbia University Press, 1991). For a discussion of "difference" in the theory and practice of translation, see the fascinating collection of essays Joseph F. Graham, ed., *Difference in Translation.* (Ithaca: Cornell University Press, 1985).

its validity upon an appeal to original meaning. Rosenzweig's polemic against Luther, for example, articulates a modernist defense of the unfamiliar in the face of tradition. But as many commentators noted, a theory of translation is praised for its defense of the "unfamiliar" chiefly because it claims to more accurately reflect the "Urtext."[44] Although allied with Weimar modernism, when applied to the Bible the differential theory of translation acquired a paradoxically antimodernist character.

The nostalgic aspect of the Buber-Rosenzweig translation theory is perhaps most evident its attempt to mobilize the notion that Jews enjoy a special "understanding" of Biblical meaning. For this reason, some regarded Buber and Rosenzweig as uniquely capable of translating the Old Testament. Others regarded Jews in general as especially gifted translators, for as one critic suggested, Jews are by history and habit negotiators of cultural difference. Of course, such arguments were often used in an antisemitic fashion. But one of the characteristics of the new spirit of Jewish self-assertion in the 1920s was that it valued precisely those qualities for which Jews had long stood condemned. One could therefore speak of a distinctively Jewish "talent for mediation." Jews, some claimed, possessed a heightened sensitivity for the otherness of the original text, since the experience of exile demanded a "transposition" of their heritage in ever-new settings.[45] For other commentators, however, the Buber-Rosenzweig translation was a powerful expression of Jewish cultural nationalism. Else-Rahel Freund, for example, noted that the Bible translation made an important contribution to the "great debate of Assimilation versus Dissimilation," which ran "like a red thread through all our history."[46] For the Jew translation was therefore

---

44. See *Die Kreatur* 1, 3 (1926), citing an unidentified issue of *Neue Wege* (Zürich).

45. On the question of Jewish identity and cultural mediation, see Jacques Le Rider, *Modernity and the Crises of Identity: Culture and Society in Fin-de-Siècle Vienna* (New York: Continuum, 1993). But note Richard Wagner's remark, "The Jew speaks the language of the nation within which he lives generation after generation, but he speaks it always as a foreigner." *Judaism and Music*, trans. Edwin Evans (New York: Charles Scribner's Sons, 1910), 20–21. On the Jewish "talent for mediation," see Lutz Weltmann, "Juden als Übersetzer," *Der Morgen* 11, 10 (January 1936): 458–61. But as I have already noted, this type of argument was not unique to translators of Jewish descent. See, e.g., Schaeffer's defense of his own "Hellenistic" modernism in "Poetischer Sprachverfall."

46. Freund, "Das Prinzip der Buber-Rosenzweigschen Bibelübersetzung," *Jüdische Rundschau*, 98 (December 7, 1934), 3. Kurt Münzer, in a review of Rosenzweig's Halevi translations made the analogy of cultural nationalism clear: "[C]lever men . . . believe in the end of Jewry, in its gradual disappearance into the mass of Europeans: But men such as the centuries-old Halevi and the young Rosenzweig are witnesses to a power that is immortal. . . . [T]he song lived and lives, is resurrected in Rosenzweig's words." Thus "Jew after Jew may fall, but Judaism survives its generations, and no century will lack for a Rosenzweig to renew it." *Die Literatur, Monatsschrift für Literaturfremde* 26, 10 (July 1924): 626–27, quote at 617.

an existential necessity, since "in language itself he [looks] for a homeland [*Heimat*]."[47]

A perceptive critic noted that Rosenzweig's Halevi translations read "as if he had been compelled to translate into a German that was not yet there." One may doubt whether this is actually possible, but it aptly summarizes Rosenzweig's predicament. Again, like Count von Stolberg, Rosenzweig did not literally wish for readers to cast his translation into the fire. He wished to create a German text that through various "Hebraicized" turns of phrase might pay homage to the original beyond its borders. It is this nostalgic element of the translation theory itself which makes the Buber-Rosenzweig Bible so difficult to categorize. Clearly, it was a modernist translation, aiming to disrupt the customary (Lutheran) expectations of the German readership. But it was also an antimodernist translation, breaking habits of language in the name of a "primordial" revelation. The result, as one critic noted, appeared to suggest that Rosenzweig meant "to speak Hebrew in German."[48]

As I have shown, the peculiar theoretical posture of the Buber-Rosenzweig Bible translation reinforced a nostalgic identification with the Hebrew past—call this "Hebraism." Now while this posture as applied to Jewish texts was new, the theory itself was not. As Rosenzweig's quotation from von Stolberg suggests, Weimar-era Hebraism was itself modeled after the older, Germanic habit of identification with ancient Greece. More than one critic remarked upon the analogy (and, of course, Rosenzweig himself suggested the link when he compared the Halevi translations to von Stolberg's renderings from the Greek). Arnold Zweig compared the new Bible to "a heroic epic from Mediterranean antiquity." And Bertha Badt-Strauß, in a 1926 review for the *Jüdische Rundschau*, suggested that Buber and Rosenzweig's translation of "the book of books" offered German Jewry a "path homeward." It revealed a world of miracles and heroism, in which one could find "that noble simplicity and quiet grandeur [*edlen Einfalt und stillen Größe*]" that in a past age had stirred Winkelmann towards love of Greece."[49] In both cases, however, love for the ancient past was distinct from mere nostalgia. As we have seen, the belief that a past civilization, Athens or Jerusalem, might hold out a more authentic mode of existence than the present was accompanied by a strong affirmation that no true return was possible. (After all, if one could simply reanimate the foreign texts and their

47. Weltmann, "Juden als Übersetzer."

48. Oskar Loerke, review of *Jehuda Halevi, 92 Hymnen und Gedichte: Der 60 Hymnen und Gedichte zweite Auflage, Neue Rundschau;* cited in an advertisement from *Die Kreatur* (1925).

49. Zweig, *Jüdische Rundschau;* cited in an advertisement from *Die Kreatur* 1, 4 (spring 1927). Badt-Strauß, "Die deutsche Bibel."

worlds, translation would be superfluous.) The aesthetic tension between archaism and modernism was thus resolved in a theoretical posture that affirmed exile as a necessary and irremediable condition.

## TRANSLATION AS ONTOLOGICAL RETRIEVAL

Of all the tasks confronting Rosenzweig and Buber as they began translating the second book of Moses, perhaps none demanded so much philosophical acuity as the selection of the proper German forms for God's name. If carried out with sufficient sensitivity, translation was no longer a merely philological or aesthetic task; it promised nothing less than restoring to the Bible its "original" role as a carrier of metaphysical insight. The problem was particularly acute in the third chapter of *Namen* (the translators' title for the second book of the Pentateuch, reflecting the Hebrew *Schemoth,* or "Names.") Here a divine voice emanates from the burning bush and commands Moses to convey its message to the Israelites. Moses then asks what he shall say if the Israelites inquire who has sent him, and God replies with the Hebrew phrase, "eheye asher eheye," customarily rendered into English as "I am that I am."

It is not surprising that this phrase has provoked interminable speculation. In whatever language one writes it, it is at once palindrome and tautology. Yet it seems full of portent. It is arguably the most dramatic theophany of the entire Bible, God's first and most consequential revelation to man. Indeed, there is a long tradition of philosophical speculation as to the exact meaning of the words. Translating the phrase into German was bound to be difficult.

Understandably, Buber and Rosenzweig regarded Luther's translation as their most powerful antecedent, and they were determined to render the phrase in such a way as to make their differences with Luther palpable.[50] Luther's German text (3: 14) reads as follows:

50. The Hebrew *(ma-sh'mo)* seems literally to mean "What is his name?" For this Luther chose the more elegant and idiomatic "Wie heißt sein Name?"—difficult to paraphrase in English, but generally rendered as "What is he called?" or, more crudely, perhaps, "What is-called his name?" The difference is significant. If the question concerns *what God's name is,* God's response would seem to be the answer to this question. That is, God reveals his name. But if the question concerns *what Moses should tell the Israelites* when they ask after God's name, the response need not be construed as a name at all. Rather, it might be taken as a clarification as to *what this name means.* This distinction proved to be of great importance for Buber and Rosenzweig. They objected strenuously to Luther's interpretation precisely because they believed he had failed correctly to understand the sense of this exchange. Moses, they insisted, asked not for a *what,* but after a *meaning.* One could therefore interpret God's response as a clarification of his true ontological status.

Gott sprach zu Mose: Ich werde sein, der ich sein werde. Und sprach: Also sollst du zu den Kindern Israel sagen: Ich werde sein hat mich zu euch gesandt.

(God spoke to Moses: I will be, that which I will be. And said: Thus shall you say to the children of Israel: I will be has sent me to you.)

Rosenzweig and Buber translated the same passage thus:

Gott aber sprach zu Mosche:
Ich werde dasein, als der ich dasein werde.
Und sprach:
So sollst du zu den Söhnen Jissraels sprechen:
ICH BIN DA schickt mich zu euch.

But God spoke to Moses:
I will be-there, as that which I will be-there.
And said:
So shall you say to the Sons of Israel:
I AM THERE sends me to you.

Vast as the differences may be, the crucial distinction can be isolated by paying attention to the tetragrammaton, traditionally understood as a gloss on the Hebrew phrase "eheye asher eheye." In Luther's version, God responds: "Ich werde sein, der ich sein werde." In the Buber-Rosenzweig version, God says: "Ich werde dasein, als der ich dasein werde." The heart of the matter, philosophically as well as philologically, lay in their rejection of Luther's *sein* (to be) and their substitution of the more rarified German verb *dasein* (to exist). In the Buber-Rosenzweig translation, God elaborates upon his answer by decomposing the word "existence" into its particles, "being" and "there" *(da* and *sein),* and for greater emphasis the entire phrase is placed in upper-case: "ICH BIN DA schickt mich zu euch."[51]

It is important to note that the proper choice could not be made on philological grounds alone, since the original phrase is grammatically idiosyncratic even according to the conventions of ancient Hebrew grammar.

51. The choice of *Dasein* as opposed to *Sein* is also to be found at other moments in the biblical narrative: At Namen (Exodus) 4:15, Luther rendered the phrase thus: "Du sollst zu ihm reden und die Worte in seinen Mund legen. Und ich will mit deinem und seinem Munde sein und euch lehren, was ihr tun sollt." Rosenzweig suggests instead: "Dann rede zu ihm, lege die Worte in seinen Mund! Ich werde dasein bei deinem Mund und bei seinem Mund, und euch weisen, was ihr tun sollt." The crucial difference here is once again "dasein" as against "sein." Significantly, the substitution was apparently a matter of course at this point; the initial decision had been made the theophany at the burning bush. In his working papers for the translation, Rosenzweig's commentary on Namen 4:15 does not even address the transformation of "sein" into "dasein," suggesting that he and Buber had resolved the philosophical intricacies of the problem already at 3:13–14. See *Arbeitspapiere,* FR, IV, 2: 98.

Thus Luther settled for a future-tense—"Ich werde sein"—while Buber and Rosenzweig decided upon the present—"Ich bin da"—though neither response captures the full dimension of the Hebrew.[52] It would thus be naive to suppose that Buber and Rosenzweig had merely selected the most accurate of terms. Like all translators, they were committing an act of interpretation, and because selection of the proper German term was hardly obvious, their choice of words displayed a specific preference within the horizon of German-language meanings. The significance of their choice is especially noteworthy since they rejected the claim that the Hebrew phrase is simply a proper name: had they considered God's utterance as a name, one might have expected them to have translated God's response much as they translated other "names" in the Hebrew Bible, that is, by means of mimetic transliteration.[53]

In distinguishing between name and meaning, Rosenzweig and Buber relied upon a pathbreaking article by the biblical philologist Benno Jacob, "Moses at the Burning Bush," first published in 1922.[54] According to Jacob, the Hebrew verbal particle *eheye* "is not a mere copula" but in itself expresses "power and meaning." God's response was best understood as a condensed explanation of the ontological status of the divine. But on Jacob's interpretation the response held two distinct meanings. On the one hand, it revealed God as an existent being who is fully "there" in the sense of "being-there" ("*Da-Sein*," as hyphenated in Jacob's text). But on the other hand, it

52. In Hebrew, *eheye* is future in its form (or imperfect in "aspect"), but uncertain in its modality. Notice also that the Hebrew *asher* that connects the two verbs itself suffers a critical ambiguity of meaning: It can mean both "that" and "where." See, e.g., Ruth 1:16, where Ruth says to Naomi, "for wherever [*asher*] thou goest, I will go." Buber and Rosenzweig's "da" in the verb "dasein" may have been an attempt to capture this more rare locative sense, though none of their papers confirms this possibility. I would like to thank Ruti Adler at the University of California at Berkeley for a helpful discussion of the grammatical issues.

53. The mimetic alternative was in fact quite important for their translation. In reproducing the names of virtually all of the human characters in the biblical story, Rosenzweig and Buber settled upon transliterating as closely as possible the *sounds* of the Hebrew. This method resulted in names that looked quite foreign to the German reader who felt accustomed to the Lutheran spellings: Where Luther had written "Isaak," they wrote "Jizchak," for "Josua" they wrote "Jehoschua." But when it came to rendering God's response, mimesis was not an option. To write the sound of God's response would only make sense if had they considered it a proper name or an acoustic event to be recorded as closely as possible in the textures of a foreign alphabet.

54. Jacob, "Mose am Dornbusch," *Monatsschrift für Geschichte und Wissenschaft des Judentums,* 1922, 11–33 and 116–200. As Jacob explained, "If a substantive follows after *ma* [what], this is never a question as to the name of the substantive which one does not know—for how could one then have pronounced it already?" Rather, it asks after the "*sense and meaning* [*Sinn und Bedeutung*]" of the name (32; emphasis in original). It was a question of interpretation, not naming as such.

also indicated God as the unique Being *(Seiende)*, the very ground and origin of the world.[55] Since Jacob provided philological evidence for both interpretations, it is intriguing that Buber and Rosenzweig chose only the first—*dasein* as against *sein*. As indicated above, Luther had preferred the latter, in accordance with his desire to create a Bible using the more natural language of his time. The difference has important consequences for both style and content. Stylistically, *sein* belongs to everyday German, while *dasein* is, like the English "exist," somewhat more elevated in register, and richer in specifically philosophical and literary overtones. Moreover, the German language Buber and Rosenzweig employed necessarily brought their text into the horizon of contemporary German meanings. To understand the contemporary resonance of their choice thus requires some comment on the status of the term in its original linguistic terrain.

The scholastic term *existentia* first entered into native German discourse via the early eighteenth-century writings of Christian Wolff, for whom it became by turns *Dasein, Existenz,* or *Wirklichkeit* (existence or reality). Down to Crusius and Mendelssohn, *Dasein* was used to indicate "the real existence of a thing" as against its simple possibility as "the mere Being [*Sein*] in thought." Its customary application was to be found in philosophical speculation concerning the existence of God. But with Kant, it suffered a terrible demotion in status. In the first critique, in the section entitled "On the impossibility of an ontological proof of the existence of God [*Dasein Gottes*]," Kant demonstrated that one cannot prove God's existence, as being is not really a predicate. Rather, *dasein* in its logical use is "solely the copula of a judgment." It is therefore illegitimate to speak of some necessary mark or predicate called "existence" that may supposedly be found alongside God's various other qualities. That God exists, Kant concluded, is "of the nature of an assumption which we can never be in a position to justify" (KdrV, 500–507).

It is not surprising that Mendelssohn considered Kant the "all-destroyer."[56] Indeed, most of German philosophy ever since has been marked in some fashion by the violence of his achievement. Of Kant's

---

55. To clarify this point Jacob partitioned the word as *Da-Sein,* to stress God's existence after the Latin sense of *existere,* which itself can be broken into German, as *Ek-sistenz* (standing-out, or being-there). The Hebrew *haya,* he explained, "is essentially the 'being-there [*Da-Sein*]' of that which is connected to nothing before it." It is therefore the true word for the first act of Creation: "God said, Let there be light! [*Licht sei!*] and light was there! [*Licht war da!*]." The Hebrew verb *to be* thus indicated that "every happening is a miracle, an unmediated springing forth of Being from Not-Being [ein unvermittelter Sprung aus dem Nicht-Sein ins Sein]." "Mose am Dornbusch," 132.

56. On Mendelssohn's relation to Kant, see Amos Funkenstein, *Perceptions of Jewish History* (Berkeley: University of California Press, 1993), 222–29.

immediate contemporaries, many were consumed with the hope that his logic could be dismantled. While some denied the supremacy of reason altogether, arguing in favor of "life" ( Jacobi, Herder, Hamann) or "faith" (Schleiermacher), others chose a more artful subterfuge, dialectically healing Kant's rift between reason and the world (Hegel). But when *Dasein* at last won a new and more modest place in philosophical language, it was precisely with the new meaning of human limitation. Its referent had fallen from the sphere of ontological proofs and, as if drawing the necessary consequences from Kant's "Copernican Revolution," now lodged itself in the language of self-reflexive anthropology. The fact that the ontological argument had failed was henceforth incorporated into the newer philosophies of human existence as a sign of what is most distinctive of humanity; *Dasein* came to be burdened with the intelligence that we cannot know and are therefore wholly dissimilar to God, that we are finite as opposed to infinite, temporal as opposed to eternal, and, most importantly, that our being is in-the-world rather than its transcendental ground.

It is this more humble and quintessentially human meaning that predominates in most post-Kantian thought. Schelling spoke of *Dasein* as the "determinate, limited lawful Being" of a thing, as opposed to *Sein,* the "pure" and "absolute" being of a thing. Fichte distinguished between "finite *Dasein*" and "unconditioned Being [*Sein*]," and Feuerbach understood by *Dasein* "Existence, in the sense of an immediate being-here [*Hierseins*]" with the "metaphysical meaning" of "the true ontological proof of the *Dasein* of an object outside of our heads." Kierkegaard protested against Hegel's philosophy for its attempt to make man what he can never be: the medium for Absolute Spirit. For the finite mind, even human existence now became opaque. "There is something," wrote Kierkegaard, "that does not allow of being thought: the existent [*das Existieren*]." And while Schopenhauer confessed that "the Problem of *Dasein* is so great as to overshadow all other problems and goals," he despaired that "our *Dasein* has no other ground and foundation upon which to rest than the ever-dwindling present." Of course, no single definition for this term can be determined in all of German philosophical literature. But even in the twentieth century *Dasein* retained nonetheless some of the meaning it had first borrowed from the Latin. It is still the customary way to indicate the "standing out" of a thing in reality as against its merely dwelling in the mind. And as being-in-the-world, it still signals human finitude as against the unknown and unworldly being of God.[57]

---

57. See, inter alia, Max Apel, *Philosophisches Wörterbuch* (Berlin: Walter de Gruyter Verlag, 1930); Paul Thormeyer, *Philosophisches Wörterbuch* (Leipzig and Berlin: B. G. Teubner, 1930); Heinrich Schmidt, *Philosophisches Wörterbuch* (Leipzig: A. Kröner, 1934).

It is precisely this meaning that Heidegger was to employ in his philosophy. He, too, seized upon the word for the purpose of capturing what is most distinctively and exclusively human; *Dasein,* as he interprets it in *Being and Time,* is "this entity which each of us is himself and which includes inquiring as one of the possibilities of its Being" (SZ, 7). But *Dasein* "stands out" in the midst of beings. If it is to be at all, it cannot be other than as thrown into the world. "*Dasein* always understands itself in terms of its existence—in terms of a possibility of itself: to be itself or not itself" (SZ, 12). The peculiarity of this terminology was later noted by Hannah Arendt, who remarked that "Heidegger . . . [is] making of man what God was in earlier ontology." Yet in refusing any traditional metaphysics, Heidegger had also accepted man's fallenness from God, whose existence belonged to his essence. Perhaps one of the most central lessons of Heidegger's thought was that only God may claim to be a wholly self-sufficient subject: "[N]ever before," Arendt commented, "has a philosophy shown as clearly as his that this goal is presumably the one thing that man can never achieve."[58]

Although the translators' work on God's encounter with Moses antedates the publication of *Being and Time* by some two years, the language of their translation belonged to the very same linguistic horizon. Their rejection of Luther's more robustly metaphysical language can therefore be understood as part of the general turning from idealism to existential ontology in German thought following the First World War. Whereas the idealist model construed thought as prior to existence, the newer philosophies insisted on the primacy of worldly being. Accordingly, Rosenzweig spoke of Luther's translation as "hopelessly Platonized."[59] And even before the Bible translation, Rosenzweig had argued for the priority of existence to Being. As I have already noted in my discussion of *The Star of Redemption,* Rosenzweig blamed the Parmenidean "idealist" tradition for having reversed the true order of things: "[I]f derivation is at issue here, it were better the derivation of Being from Existence [*Dasein*], than the ever-again attempted derivation, as in the ontological proof, of Existence from Being" (SE, 19–20 [E, 17]).

Elsewhere, in his translations of poetry from Jehuda Halevi, Rosenzweig complained that the idealist use of Being makes of it "the most abstract word imaginable." It is, he wrote derisively, "the typical word of philosophers." Moreover, he regarded it as an interloper upon Jewish terrain. In his commentary upon the Halevi poem, "ha-Shem" (The name), Rosenzweig noted that modern readers had mistaken as otherworldly abstraction what was really just an effect of poor translation. Western scholasticism commonly

---

58.  Hannah Arendt, "What Is Existential Philosophy?," in *Essays in Understanding, 1930–1954,* ed. Jerome Kohn (New York: Harcourt Brace and Company, 1994), 163–91, at 178.

59.  Rosenzweig applied this criticism to all "post-Platonic languages," medieval Hebrew not excepted. See, e.g., *Arbeitspapiere,* FR IV, 2: 93–96.

speaks of God as "a being who exists [*Existieren*]," while "taken in its strict sense [it] *should have been translated as Dasein*" (my emphasis). In Rosenzweig's view, Judaism discloses God's being in a fashion that undercuts the ontological distinctions of scholasticism (reiterated in Luther's translation) between this-worldly and other-worldly being. "The most abstract God of Philosophy," Rosenzweig remarked, lies not in the beyond but within "the innermost corner of human existence."[60]

Perhaps the most striking example of Rosenzweig's rejection of idealist ontological language is to be found in one of his last essays, "The Eternal: Mendelssohn and the Name of God" ("Der Ewige: Mendelssohn und der Gottesname" [July 1929], in KS, 182–98). An extensive commentary upon Mendelssohn's 1780 Bible translation, the essay takes special exception to Mendelssohn's German rendering of God's name (printed, however, in Hebrew characters) as "I am the essence that is eternal" ("Ich bin das Wesen, welches ewig ist").[61] For Rosenzweig, this interpretation of the divine name as "The Eternal," or, alternately, as "the eternal essence" was "austere, sublime," and "genuinely 'numinous.'" But its origins were Hellenistic, not Jewish. As Rosenzweig explained, in the Greek translation of the Apocryphal "Letter of Baruch," God was first misidentified as *ho Aionios* (the Eternal). This interpretation had then traveled from medieval Aristotelianism to French Calvinism (which translated it as *L'Éternel*) and from the Huguenots into the salons of the Berlin Aufklärung. Thus Mendelssohn had been misled by Hellenistic and German-Enlightenment speculation into choosing an "abstract" and "philosophical" term that construed God as nothing other than a Being possessing "existential necessity." Eschewing a genuinely Jewish revelation, Mendelssohn's God had dwindled away into the indifferent "God of Aristotle" ("Der Ewige," 183–84, 192).[62]

According to Rosenzweig, this fundamentally "Hellenistic" interpretation missed Judaism's richly personalist and this-worldly understanding of God. Indeed, Rosenzweig regarded Mendelssohn's translation as a sign of

60. Rosenzweig, "Der Name," in *Jehuda Halevi: Fünfundneunzig Hymnen und Gedichte, Deutsch und Hebräisch, mit einem Vorwort und mit Anmerkungen.* FR, IV, 1: 72–73.

61. The full text of Mendelssohn's "broad paraphrase" is as follows: "Gott sprach zu Mosche: Ich bin das Wesen, welches ewig ist. Er sprach nämlich: So sollst du zu den Kindern Jisraels sprechen: 'Das ewige Wesen, welches sich nennt: ich bin ewig, hat mich zu euch gesendet.'" ("God spoke to Moses: I am the Essence that is eternal. He said in fact: Thus should you say to the children of Israel: 'The eternal Essence, which calls itself, "I am eternal" has sent me to you'"; my translation).

62. Rosenzweig further writes: "In Mendelssohn's case the spirit of the age made alliance with the Aristotelian spirit of Maimonides, whom Mendelssohn had honored all his life, against the sure instinct of Jewish tradition." On Rosenzweig's quarrel with medieval Jewish rationalism, see my essay "The Erotics of Negative Theology: Maimonides on Apprehension," *Jewish Studies Quarterly* 2, 1 (1995): 1–38.

"attenuated belief." For to interpret God as an "essence" misses the priority of God's presence-in-the-world, a presence that provides the only consolation for human life: "What meaning for the despairing and wretched Israelites would be offered by a lecture on God's existential necessity [*notwendig Existenz*]?" ("Der Ewige," 188). Like Moses, the children of Israel require not the abstractions of religious rationalism but instead an "assurance of God's Being-with-them [*Bei-ihnen-Seins*]," and they seek this assurance precisely by asking, through the mediation of Moses, after the meaning of God's "old, dark name." In Rosenzweig's words, the Israelites required "not the eternal Being" *(Ewigsein)* but rather God as "For-You- and By-You-Existence and becoming-Existence" *(Für-euch- und Bei-euch-dasein und dasein-werden).* For God's response is a more than a name, it reveals God "not as the one who persists in his Being [*Sein*] and Essence [*Wesen*]" but rather as "he who inclines downward in Ex-istence [*da-Sein*]" ("Der Ewige, 197).

Whatever the claims to philological fidelity, Rosenzweig's complaints against the Mendelssohn translation are clearly indicative of his deeper philosophical commitments.[63] (Note, for example, that when Rosenzweig "corrects" Mendelssohn's word-choice, he somewhat disingenuously compares it to his own translation as if it were simply the Hebrew original.)[64] Indeed, so far as philosophy was concerned, Rosenzweig saw little difference between the Mendelssohnian and Lutheran translations. Both cast God as an indifferent specter, residing somewhere amongst the Platonic Ideas. To bring God into the world required the vocabulary of this-worldly existence, and this was precisely the modern meaning the translators had inherited from the post-Kantian German philosophical tradition.[65] Generally speak-

63. In Rosenzweig's working papers for the Bible translation, we find other evidence of this reasoning. For Rosenzweig, Luther's "Ich werde sein" is "hopelessly Platonized." And the last thing Rosenzweig wanted to do was to reproduce the "abominations" of the Septuagint. Since the Hebrew is "in fact not a name but, like all explanations, a really spoken phrase," Rosenzweig calls it a "self-unveiling" and an "illumination" of the "unpronounceable Name." FR, IV, 1: 93–96.

64. The comparison betrays an amazing self-assurance. Rosenzweig writes (in German, of course) that Exodus 3:14 "in the Original reads somewhat as follows." He then quotes the text in German as if it were in fact the original Hebrew: "Gott aber sprach zu Mosche . . ." By presenting his own translation as the "original," he thus assumes what he set out to prove.

65. In a fascinating letter to Martin Goldner (June 23, 1927), Rosenzweig explained his word choice thus: "All those who find Being [*Sein*] or the Being [*den Seienden*], or the Eternal [*den Ewigen*] are platonizing." The "immediate sense is different, more pointed and direct": "God calls himself not the Being [*Den Seienden*] but rather the Existing [*den Daseienden*]" and "the existing-to-you [*den dir Daseidenden*]." He continues: "The Hebrew term *haya* [Hebrew in text] is not a copula, as in the case of the Indo-Germanic 'sein,' that is to say, it is not static. Rather, it is a word of becoming, of stepping forth, of happening. . . . [God is] set free from my need and my moment, but indeed, [he is] only to be set free because every future moment could stand in the place of my very own now. This eternity is visible only in one, in my Now, this

THE HEBREW BIBLE IN THE GERMAN HORIZON

ing, then, one may regard the Buber-Rosenzweig Bible as the poetic realization of an "existential" ontology.[66]

If the scene at the burning bush is the most obvious example, few other
translation choices were as fraught with metaphysical implications as the
passage from Genesis 1:2, "v'ruach elohim m'rachefet 'al p'nei ha-maim"
("and the Spirit of God hovered on the face of the waters"). Luther rendered *ruach* as *Geist* (spirit): " und der Geist Gottes schwebte auf dem Wasser." It would be difficult to overestimate the importance of this phrasing,
since *Geist* is without question one of the most resonant philosophical terms
in the German language.[67] Accordingly, Buber and Rosenzweig made much
of their decision to reject Luther's word choice. Their 1925 edition reads:
"Braus Gottes brütend allüber den Wassern."[68] In his essay, "On Word
Choice in a Translation of the Scripture," Buber explained that in Hebrew
*ruach* originally meant both "wind" *and* "spirit," an ambiguity also found
in the Greek *pneuma* and in the Latin *spiritus*. And before Luther, wrote
Buber, even the German term *Geist* retained both the physical and the

---

'absolute Being' [*absolute Sein*] only to my present *Dasein*, this 'Pure' only to the most impure
[*Unreinsten*]." *Briefe*, N.502, An Martin Goldner (23.6.27), 599–603, at 601–2.

66. In sum, the hallmark of this "existentialism" is the doctrine that the proper horizon
of human religion is time, not eternity: "In the presence of time's vitality, the human longing
for eternity learns to be silent [Vor der lebendiggewordenen Zeit lernt das Verlangen des
Menchen nach Ewigkeit schweigen]" ("Der Ewige," 197). While there was naturally disagreement between Buber and Rosenzweig on how to best translate certain passages, in their antagonism toward "idealist" or "platonizing" renderings they were largely in accord. In some
cases Buber's later amendments of the translation only intensified this basic philosophical
message. In Luther's translation, for example, when God calls to Moses, Moses responds, "Hier
bin ich" ("I am here"). In the first edition of the Buber-Rosenzweig translation (published during Rosenzweig's lifetime), Moses' response followed Luther, "Hier bin ich." But in Buber's
postwar amendment of the text (first published in 1954), he changed Moses' response to "Da
bin ich" ("there I am"). At first glance this may seem a rather idiosyncratic choice. But Buber's
aim was less literalism than philosophy: By construing Moses' initial encounter with God with
the words "da bin ich," the phrase was brought into an intimate association with God's reply
(Exodus 3:14) "Ich bin da." (The phrases are mirror images of one another.) Buber thus provided a vivid illustration of Cohen's principle of correlation, while also reinforcing the Biblical
precept that God created man "in his image and likeness."

67. The Jerusalem Bible reads "wind," while the 1935 Berlin Torah translation reads
"Windhauch," and Kautsch's scholarly edition of 1922 (4th ed.) has "Geist." Hegel's *Phenome-
nolgie des Geistes* is arguably written in the shadow of Luther's translation. And Heidegger's polemic in *Being and Time* against the "anthropology of Christian theology" (which interprets
man as *Geist* rather than *Existenz*) derives its full meaning only if one recalls that "Spirit" in German has an irrevocably Biblical meaning. See, e.g., SZ, esp. 48, and 117. On the persistence of
"spirit" in Heidegger, see Jacques Derrida, *De L'ésprit: Heidegger et la question* (Paris: Galilée,
1987).

68. Buber amended the 1930 edition to "Braus Gottes spreitend," and in the 1954 edition
changed this again, to "Braus Gottes schwingend über dem Antlitz der Wasser." But the crucial
choice—*Braus* as against *Geist*—remained unchanged.

metaphysical meanings of wind and spirit (as in the writings of the German mystic Meister Eckart). But with Luther's language, *Geist* had abandoned its bodily and climatic associations to become a purely supersensible phenomenon.

According to Buber, however, *ruach* meant not only both, but both *at once*. It was God's "breath" that first infused life into the beginning cadences of the Bible, as into Adam's mouth. The word itself, Buber implied, belonged to a prelapsarian moment, before the modern fissure of nature from spirit: *ruach* expressed a "primordial unity of the meant reality [*die Ureinheit der damit gemeinten Wirklichkeit*]." "We must not take a word such as this, that bears two meanings, a 'natural' and a 'spiritual' as something to split unbridgeably in two [*in zwei zerspalten*] as has commonly been the case," Buber wrote. "Rather we must consider that the spiritual meaning would itself be immediately falsified should it lose its bond to sensation." Furthermore, the dualism of spirit and matter was grounded in a modern understanding of time, the distinction between eternal Being and worldly impermanence: the German substantive *Geist* retained little of the sense of a temporal *happening* found in the Hebrew. Buber therefore suggested transfiguring *Geist* as a gerund, *Geisten*, that is, "spirit-ing". But this would still leave intact the irresistible *cultural* associations of *Geist* with Church dogma.[69] No solution better suited Buber and Rosenzweig's philosophical purposes than the term *Braus* (often found in the poetic pairing "Saus und Braus," as in the "rush and roar" of the wind or ocean). This captured what Buber termed "the primordial surging of creation's beginning" (*jenes Urwehen des Schöpfungsbeginns*), whose "roaring" Buber still thought he could hear in Hölderlin's poetry.[70]

All of these translation choices rehearse a similar philosophical polemic. They assert the superiority of a worldly ontology while criticizing the attempt to seize upon a permanent realm of ideas beyond time and the world. Translation was therefore an attempt to overcome the idealist heritage in language—in Heidegger's phrase, a "destruction of tradition." Buber and Rosenzweig saw their chief task as the restoration of biblical revelation to

69. Buber, "On Word Choice in a Translation of the Scripture," in *Werke*, II: 1128. In his working papers, Rosenzweig complains that *Geist* is burdened too heavily with "Christian and Trinitarian" meaning—an allusion, naturally, to the "heilige Geist" or Holy Spirit. *Arbeitspapiere*, FR, IV, 2: 3.

70. "When Hölderlin calls: 'O sister of the spirit that lives and rules within us, holy air!' he is recalling the affinity of the two meanings from *ruach*, but recalls the primordial unity itself when, returning to the third chapter of John the Evangelist, he points to the secret of the 'spiritual surging.'" This reference to Hölderlin is found only in Buber's emended version of the essay "On Word Choice," printed as a supplement in "Zu einer neuen Verdeutschung der Schrift: Beilage zum ersten Band," in Buber and Rosenzweig, *Die fünf Bücher der Weisung*, vol. I (Berlin: Lambert Schneider, 1956).

its proper moorings within the world. By disclosing an ostensibly "ancient" phrase that had been lost over the centuries, translation became for them an act of ontological retrieval, whose purpose was to wrest forgotten meaning from a text disfigured by the various "idealisms" of history. Against both the "eternal essence" of Mendelssohn's Pentateuch and the "Spirit" of Luther's Bible, the translators claimed—on philological grounds alone—to have recovered the true nature of God's being. It is astonishing, however, that for this purpose they selected the term *dasein,* as this meant going *against* the grain of contemporary philosophical discourse, in which the language of existence was customarily reserved for *human being alone.* However, this merely underscores the radicalism of their achievement. The translators employed a term of contemporary philosophical ramifications such that the new text functioned as a seismograph of post-Nietzschean thought. Yet the new Bible simultaneously denied its modernism, displaying its treasures as if they had been mined from an ancient source. The result was a dramatic paradox: a return to religion that registered the lessons of metaphysical calamity.

### HEIDEGGER AND ROSENZWEIG ON TRANSLATION

In the preceding sections, I have suggested that the Bible translation cannot be understood merely as an exercise in philology. It must rather be regarded as the poetic realization of a basic philosophical attitude: its key insight is that language is not a neutral vehicle of meaning but is rather a horizon of intelligibility, the context in which the world is first revealed. On this view, modern translation always presents a potential risk, since it may either enable or obscure a basic ontological understanding of the way things are. For Rosenzweig and Buber, the modern Lutheran Bible has largely obscured such an understanding. To restore it, however, cannot mean simply turning back to the original Hebrew text. For the world we inhabit has itself fallen away from those ancient beginnings. We are moderns and no longer ancients, and so translation is for us unavoidable. A proper translation, then, will be one that successfully conveys this sense of dislocation, so as to commemorate its exile from the original truth—in Benjamin's image, it will be directed, not toward the heart of the forest, but toward "the wooded ridge." As I have shown, the Buber-Rosenzweig Bible translation was in this sense both modernist and archaic. Although written in German, it thereby reinforced a belief in Hebrew as the "Adamic" language, the site of an original but nearly forgotten revelation.[71]

71. A similar faith sustained members of the George Kreis, as Friedrich Gundolf explained in his hagiographic essay: "Language is the innermost bulwark of the Spirit in a world of things;

This philosophical account of translation is quite close to that of Heidegger. For Heidegger as well, translation is a force that may either destroy or recuperate ontological insight. And Heidegger, too, believed that for the most part the history of Western understanding is one of linguistic deformation and forgetting. In *An Introduction to Metaphysics* (*Einführing in die Metaphysik,* 1935), he argued that the translation of key philosophical terms from Greek to Latin was not "accidental and harmless." It marked "the first stage in the process by which we cut ourselves off and alienated ourselves from the original essence of Greek philosophy" (EM, 10–11). But mistranslation for Heidegger is not only a fatal turning point in meaning. The divergence of a translation from its original sense is both a linguistic and a metaphysical event: it not only represents a failure in understanding, but it also warps the very texture of Being. Buber and Rosenzweig argued along much the same lines: the mistranslation of the Bible must encourage an impoverishment of religious belief; it weakens the bond between man and God. As discussed above, Buber argued that the *ruach Elohim* is best understood as "Braus Gottes" because this indicates the "primordial unity of . . . reality." Only a Cartesian sensibility would divide this unity into its "natural" and "spiritual" components. The modernist and metaphysical account of religion is thus born of mistranslation and only accelerates the process of ontological forgetting. Correct translation, for Heidegger as well as for Buber and Rosenzweig, is a metaphysical retrieval—an act of anamnesis.

Broadly put, one might say that Heidegger regarded language not simply as a tool of expression but as the horizon in which the world is revealed.[72] It is instructive in this regard to note the kinship between the biblical concept of revelation (*Offenbarung*) and the Greek notion of *Aletheia* (truth as unconcealment), terms that Heidegger used almost interchangeably. In the 1929 essay "Vom Wesen des Grundes," for example, he played upon close association between "revealing" (*Offenbarmachung*) and "disclosure" (*Entdeckung*).[73] The misunderstanding of *Aletheia* itself is partly a problem of translation:

---

when there is no longer a Church steeped in soulfulness, no longer an open sphere of magic, no longer mystery, it is the last refuge of God in man." *George,* 1.

72. Heidegger thus wrote: "But now let us skip over this whole process of deformation and decay and attempt to regain the unimpaired strength of language and words; for words and language are not wrappings in which things are packed for the commerce of those who write and speak. It is in words and language that things first come into being and are." EM, English, 13.

73. Here one may notice that "revelation," or *Offenbarung,* is a linguistic sibling. See Heidegger, "Vom Wesen des Grundes," in his *Wegmarken* (Frankfurt am Main: Klostermann, 1967), 123–76; in English, "On the Essence of Ground," in *Pathmarks,* ed. William McNeill (Cambridge: Cambridge University Press, 1998), 97–135.

[T]o the *Logos* [original in Greek] belongs unhiddenness. . . . To translate this word as "truth," and, above all, to define this expression conceptually in theoretical ways, is to cover up the meaning of what the Greeks made "self-evidently" basic for the terminological use of *Aletheia* as a pre-philosophical way of understanding. (SZ, 219)

Although it would be wrong to equate the Greek notion of disclosure with the biblical concept of revelation, it is striking how closely Heidegger follows Buber and Rosenzweig in his argument that there was an "original" sense to the phenomenon called "unhiddenness" that was subsequently "covered up" in the course of the intervening millennia. Both *Offenbarung* and *Offenbarmachung* are primal kinds of "unhiddenness" (*Unverborgenheit*)—although one derives from the Bible and the other from a fragment of Heraclitus, which Heidegger described as "the oldest of philosophical treatises" (SZ, 219).

For Heidegger, however, the problem of "disclosure" is not simply one example of mistaken translation among others. Disclosure is both a mode of understanding that must be rescued from the philosophical tradition gone astray and the method of translation necessary for this retrieval. As Jan Aler has argued, Heidegger's use of language is animated by a single purpose: "to unveil original meanings, to bring the past to life again, and to free once more the forces that have produced the past."[74] Heidegger insists that his reliance on the original sense of words stays clear of "uninhibited word mysticism"; nonetheless, "the ultimate business of philosophy is to preserve the *force of the most elemental words* in which Dasein expresses itself" (SZ, 220). These "most elemental words" belong to a "primordial" understanding—in the sense of being prior to the present, but also in the sense of being prior to "deformation and decay." Thus the "unimpaired strength of language and words" is disclosed by means of translations that necessarily do violence to our customary understanding. Just as Buber and Rosenzweig presented their biblical account of revelation as an "overcoming" of Luther's translation, so too Heidegger believed that returning to Greek origins—a project that always remains incomplete—demands an overcoming of the past. This explains Heidegger's paradoxical requirement that one may discover the forgotten sources only by means of a "destruction of tradition."[75]

Gaining some sense of the complex relationship among estrangement, restoration, and destruction in Heidegger's philosophy may also help in

74. Aler, "Heidegger's Conception of Language," in *On Heidegger and Language,* ed. Joseph Kockelmans (Evanston, Ill.: Northwestern University Press, 1972), 33–64.

75. On "destruction," see esp. SZ, §6, "Die Aufgabe einer Destruktion der Geschichte der Ontologie," 19–27. Also see Werner Marx, *Heidegger and the Tradition,* trans. Theodore Kisiel and Murray Greene (Evanston, Ill.: Northwestern University Press, 1971), and my comparative remarks on Rosenzweig's "destruction" of idealism in *The Star of Redemption,* in chap. 3.

characterizing his distinctive literary style. Even the most naive reader will be struck by "a peculiar tension" in his choice of words. The effect, perhaps most pronounced in Heidegger's early works, is due to a misalliance of technical and everyday vocabulary. On the one hand, Heidegger employs terms of classical and scholastic origin, erecting an apparatus with an unmistakably modern feel. On the other hand, he borrows words one might have thought were better suited to "lyric poetry or . . . edifying prose."[76] No doubt this is partially due to the conflict between Husserl's scientific methods and Heidegger's own darker tendencies. (For Heidegger's debt to Husserl, see, for example, SZ, 38, n. 1.) But independent of his specific aims, Heidegger's style exhibits a fusion of archaism and modernism quite common to the literature, poetry, and even music of the period.[77] Heidegger strains in his language against current usage, or abandons it entirely; and sometimes he fashions a neologism by breaking a common word into its component parts, as in *"Da-Sein"* or *"Zeug."*[78] His use of paronomasia is notorious, as I have discussed above: in *Was ist Metaphysik?* (1929), "Das Nicht selbst nichtet" ("The nothing itself nihilates"); in *Vom Wesen des Grundes* (1929), "World abides insofar as it worlds"; or in *Being and Time* (1927), "Zeitlichkeit zeitigt" ("temporality temporalizes"). Such language is reminiscent of the Hebraic doublings that fascinated Buber and Rosenzweig, as in the opening lines of Genesis: "God's brewing brews" ("Braus Gottes brütend."). Heidegger's use of paronomasia may well have originated in his study of ancient Greek, where, as in ancient Hebrew, it is a poetic convention. But its reflexive quality, whether oracular or biblical, also describes the reigning figure of his philosophy, the hermeneutic circle.[79] It demonstrates that the static appearance of the subject is an illusion—Being is in itself an event. Thus this seemingly insignificant feature of Heidegger's style in fact points toward his deepest philosophical concern—the question of Being, or *Seinsfrage.*

As I have suggested above, Buber and Rosenzweig regarded God's self-revelation to Moses as a philosophical lesson: Moses received not God's *name* but rather this name's ontological *meaning.* Rosenzweig summarized the meaning of this name as "Ich werde dasein" (or "I shall exist") and,

76. Aler, "Heidegger's Conception of Language," 34.

77. Jeffrey Herf addresses the marriage of technology and illiberalism in his study *Reactionary Modernism: Technology, Culture, and Politics in Weimar and the Third Reich* (Cambridge: Cambridge University Press, 1984). One could add that even in language, Heidegger joins modernist techniques with archaizing impulses.

78. On "Zeug" see Aler, "Heidegger's Conception of Language," 38. The breakdown of "da-sein" into its two constituent terms is so pronounced in literature from the Weimar period one could almost call it a fashion.

79. See Erasmus Schöfer, "Heidegger's Language," in *On Heidegger and Language,* ed. Kockelmans, 291.

in the longer essay on Mendelssohn, as "Für-euch- und Bei-euch-dasein und dasein-werden" (that is, "for-you- and by-you-existence and becoming-existence"). For Rosenzweig, then, the relation between God and man is one of ontological co-determination: God becomes fully what he is only in relation to man, and vice versa. This idea, inspired by Cohen's principle of correlation, also informs the theory of love in *The Star of Redemption*.[80]

The Buber-Rosenzweig Bible thus provided an illustration of the intimate and reflexive bond between human existence and its ontological ground. Something of this same relation persists in Heidegger's philosophy: in *What Is Called Thinking?* he observed that "every . . . thinking doctrine of the essence of man is *in itself already* a doctrine of the Being of beings [*Sein des Seienden*]." And conversely, "every doctrine of Being is *in itself already* a doctrine of the essence of man." To be sure, one cannot say that Heidegger's interpretation of Being is the very same as Rosenzweig's interpretation of God. The point is only that in relation to the human sphere, Being and God exhibit a similar correlation with human existence. Heidegger writes:

> We ask what the relation is between man's nature and the Being of beings. But, as soon as I thoughtfully say, "man's nature," I have already said relatedness to Being. Likewise, as soon as I say thoughtfully: Being of beings, the relatedness to man's nature has been named. Each of the two members of the relation between man's nature and Being already implies the relation itself.[81]

For Rosenzweig as for Heidegger, a proper understanding of this relation poses the single greatest burden for thinking. And this is also why the correct translation of God's name seemed to Rosenzweig a matter of such overwhelming importance. God's Being had to be conceived in such a way as to enable his correlation with man. In a certain respect, it is the "question" itself that first forges the relation. God calls to Moses, and Moses asks after God's name, and it is in the circle of questions between them that they both become what they are. Heidegger, too, saw that the bond between Dasein and Being is first implied in the fact that Dasein is by nature "the being that questions" (SZ, §4, 11 ff).

To be sure, for Heidegger there is no *personal* dimension to the bond between Dasein and Being. So the analogy with Rosenzweig's idea of the bond between human being and God is only partial. Nor could one say that

80. In the Buber-Rosenzweig Bible, even the first exchange of greetings between man and God suggests a correlation: when God calls Moses, he responds, "Da bin ich" (or, in the earlier translation, "hier bin ich"), and when Moses asks after God's name, he responds, "Ich bin da." As I have noted above, Buber's postwar changes reinforced the mirroring effect in this greeting.

81. Heidegger, *Was Heißt Denken?* (Tübingen: Max Niemeyer Verlag, 1954), 73–74. In English, *What Is Called Thinking?*, trans. J. Glenn Gray (San Francisco: Harper and Row, 1968), 79.

Heidegger's work builds in any profound way upon the divine-human relationship described in the Bible. Heidegger had to reject the Bible as a contributing factor in the misshapen genesis of Western metaphysics. What else could Heidegger make of the phrase—"the Spirit [Geist] of God hovered over the waters"—but an inaugural moment in the "forgetting" of Being?[82] As we have seen, Rosenzweig too was fond of this claim. But he could not believe the blame lay with the Bible itself. The holy writ was the original document of existential ontology; all it required was the proper translator.

At first glance, it may seem odd to treat a literary artifact such as the Buber-Rosenzweig Bible translation as if it were a philosophical document. But one must remember that, for the translators as well as for Heidegger, an intimate bond obtains between poetry and thought. Just as Heidegger devoted considerable attention to the philosophical sense embedded in poems by Hölderlin and Trakl, so, too, Buber and Rosenzweig did not consider their translation in isolation from the philosophical matters that absorbed them elsewhere. Rosenzweig was perhaps especially sensitive to the relationship between poetry and thinking, given his earlier study of *The Oldest System Program of German Idealism,* attributed to Schelling, which asserts, "The philosopher must possess as much aesthetic force as the poet" and that "in the end, [poetry] will again become what she was in the beginning—the instructress of humanity."[83] Schelling claimed that poetry was *originally* united with speculative thought, and therefore regarded their cleavage as an invidious consequence of idealist reason. Heidegger, too, urges us to move freely across the boundaries that separate poetry from speculative prose. Hence his remark about Parmenides from *An Introduction to Metaphysics* (1935) that "we must remind ourselves of the essential and initial connection between poetic and philosophical discourse." This is especially the case for ancient Greece, since the origin (*Ursprung*) of philosophy is to be discovered in myth.[84] Both poetry (*Dichtung*) and "thinking" (*Denken*) "first awakened and established the historical being-there (*Dasein*) of a people" (EM, 165).

From these ideas of translation and poetic origin, Rosenzweig and Heidegger developed two distinctive cultural fantasies, Hebraism and Hellenism. As I noted in my earlier discussion of *The Star of Redemption,* Rosenzweig

82. See Heidegger's handout for the Davoser Arbeitsgemeinschaft, reproduced as an appendix to KPM.

83. Cited in ASP; also, see David Farrell Krell, "The Oldest Program Towards a System of German Idealism," *The Owl of Minerva* 17, 1 (fall 1985): 5–19.

84. See especially Heidegger's remarks on myth in his review of Cassirer's *Philosophie der symbolischen Formen, II Band,* included in the appendix to KPM.

and Heidegger disagreed upon Parmenides' share of culpability in the establishment of idealist metaphysics. Rosenzweig spurned Parmenides as the first idealist and thus renounced Greek thought entirely for the ontological "alternative" found in ancient Judaism, while Heidegger interpreted Parmenides' didactic poem as anti-idealist, and thus regarded Greek thought as the still viable (if largely forgotten) "other beginning" for ontology. Accordingly, the general quarrel between Hebraism (Rosenzweig) and Hellenism (Heidegger) reflected a specifically philosophical disagreement about the merits of Biblical as opposed to Greek poetry.

Neither Rosenzweig nor Heidegger could separate their theories of poetry and language from their deeper philosophical commitments. As Rosenzweig had asserted on many occasions—most famously in the essay "The New Thinking"—language was nothing less than the horizon of human being. It is especially interesting that Rosenzweig and Heidegger each claimed that translation itself is somehow implicit in human understanding. Translation, they argued, need not occur *between* languages, as all speech is *already* translation. Thus in his Parmenides seminar, Heidegger claimed:

> Speaking and saying are in themselves a translation whose essential unfolding is by no means exhausted by the fact that translated words and the words to be translated belong to different languages. . . . We forget . . . that we always already translate our own speech. . . . An originary translation [*ürsprungliches übersetzen*] prevails in every dialogue [*Gespräch*] and monologue [*Selbstgespräch*].[85]

In "The Scripture and Luther," Rosenzweig wrote:

> Whoever speaks, translates from his own meaning into that of the other from whom he expects understanding. . . . Everyone has his very own language. Or rather, everyone would have his very own language if there were in fact a monological language . . . if all speaking were not already dialogical speaking.[86]

The arguments are remarkably similar. Both Rosenzweig and Heidegger regard human meaning as lacking any transcendental ground: all language is already translation, and translation between languages simply dramatizes the inner opacity of language as such.

However, both Rosenzweig and Heidegger compromised this theory of "originary translation" in sustaining the fantasy that there exists an original "untranslated" language, whether Hebrew or Greek. Accordingly, if translation identifies the original as the site of original truth, it must also evacuate

---

85. Heidegger, *Parmenides*, Freiburger Vorlesung, Wintersemester, 1942–43, in GA, 54: 17 ff.

86. Rosenzweig, *Die Schrift und Luther*, 5.

the new language of its independent power. This is one of the most striking aspects of the Buber-Rosenzweig Bible. It seems to have capitalized on what might be considered an intrinsic feature of any translation—the subordination of the target language to the original. For Heidegger, the writings of the pre-Socratics enjoyed quasi-revelatory status, such that to translate away from Greek meant inevitable loss. For Buber and Rosenzweig, to translate the Bible was to aggravate this imbalance to the point of devotion. Translation, then, became at once renewal and nostalgia. It granted the truth of revelation a passage into exile, but also recast modernity as an exile from truth.

# Chapter 6

# "An Irony in the History of Spirit"

*Rosenzweig, Heidegger, and the Davos Disputation*

By the spring of 1929, the progressive paralysis that would ultimately take Rosenzweig's life was already well advanced—he would die the following winter. Immobilized and confined to his home, he was nonetheless acutely aware of the affairs of the world. He kept himself informed through newspapers and extensive correspondence, and while devoting the greater share of his energies to the Bible translation with Martin Buber, he still found time to reflect on matters of contemporary interest in the wider field of philosophy. Sometime in May 1929, he wrote an intriguing essay entitled "Exchanged Fronts" ("Vertauschte Fronten"), a document that was to be published just months after his death.[1]

One might call it a gesture of farewell. Scarcely two and a half pages in length, it begins as a commentary on the recently published second edition of Hermann Cohen's *Religion of Reason*. Halfway through, however, Rosenzweig seems to shift topics abruptly. He now addresses the famous encounter between Ernst Cassirer and Martin Heidegger that had taken place in Davos, Switzerland, earlier that spring (March 17–April 6, 1929). Rosenzweig's argument is curious and seemingly improbable: he hints at a subterranean line of influence spanning the entire decade—from the later Cohen's philosophy of religion to the young Heidegger, from neo-Kantianism to existentialism, from the rationalist methods of the Marburg School to the religious phenomenology now fashionable among the younger generation. Astonishingly, Rosenzweig suggests that Heidegger, though an antagonist of

1. Rosenzweig, "Vertauschte Fronten"[VF], *Der Morgen* 6, 6 (April 1930), 85–87; reprinted in FR, III: 323–26 and in KS; all citations are to the original publication.

Marburg idealism, is nonetheless an intellectual descendent of the later Cohen. Further, Rosenzweig claims that because he, too, is a disciple of Cohen's religious thought, Rosenzweig and Heidegger are in fact philosophical brothers. Although Heidegger speaks the language of phenomenology and Rosenzweig forges his philosophy from Jewish sources, they are united in sensibility and intent. Both advocate the "leap into existence." Rejecting idealism in every form, each resists the traditional promise of philosophical transcendence and turns instead toward the simple facticity of human being in time and in the world. Heidegger too, Rosenzweig concludes, is a partisan of the "new thinking."

There is no reason to doubt the sincerity of Rosenzweig's claim to intellectual kinship with Heidegger. As one of the last documents he wrote, the essay represents the author's attempt to situate himself for posterity among the most influential thinkers of the age. The attempt was partly strategic; by inscribing Jewish thought into the German canon, it performed the characteristic gesture of assimilation. But it also reversed this gesture; against the customary chauvinism that Jews were incapable of true creativity, Rosenzweig cast Heidegger from the seat of master thinker and made of him a humble disciple, while Cohen assumed his place as the more "original" philosopher. But beyond questions of Jewish identity, the essay also holds a more general interest; it addresses one of the most dramatic moments of transformation in Continental thought—the waning of idealist epistemology and the ascent of existential ontology between the two world wars. It thereby asserts the inseparability of two streams of thought, Jewish and German. Without relinquishing his bond to Judaism, Rosenzweig places himself squarely within the dominant trend, exposing a hidden network of affinities between German and Jewish philosophy, forging from out of a seemingly disparate field of concerns the sense of a shared tradition— a common project as well as a common canon. In short, the essay represents Rosenzweig's last attempt to position himself at the crossing of these two streams, as both summary and guarantee of his place in the history of ideas. It is, in covert form, Rosenzweig's intellectual epitaph.

In this chapter, I take up the suggestion that the Davos dispute provides evidence of Rosenzweig's intellectual kinship with Heidegger. Of course, the dispute itself yields insufficient proof. What interests me here is why Rosenzweig would have regarded it as a culminating moment in Weimar thought. His provocative idea that Hermann Cohen's religious thought exerted a hidden influence upon Heidegger is provocative. Understood literally, it must be rejected as implausible. But it nonetheless gets at an important truth about Weimar philosophy in the 1920s, as I shall explain.

## PHILOSOPHY ON THE MAGIC MOUNTAIN

The Davos Hochschulkurs was an international and interdisciplinary conference of more than two hundred students and scholars who had traveled there from universities across Europe. The second annual Davos conference held its opening session in the Hotel Belvedere on Sunday, March 17, 1929. The central event of the three-week gathering, a public disputation between Heidegger and Cassirer, is justifiably famous in the history of twentieth-century thought. Following upon three individual lectures, their discussion was broad-ranging and informal, in accordance with the then-popular ideal of an *Arbeitsgemeinschaft,* or workshop. But reports and memoirs recall it as a turning point in the development of modern philosophy. Emmanuel Levinas, at that time Husserl's disciple, was in attendance and would later claim that the philosophical discussion seemed to involve more than the usual academic stakes. "[A] young student," he remembers, "could have had the impression that he was witness to the creation and the end of the world."[2]

2. Cited in François Poirié, *Emmanuel Levinas: Qui êtes-vous?* (Lyon: La Manufacture, 1987), 78. In this chapter, I rely upon numerous contemporary reports, most importantly an anonymous report from a special issue of the *Davoser Revue* (published by Jules Ferdmann and generally a review of expressionist literature and painting), "Bericht über die II. Davoser Hochschulkurse, 17. März bis 6. April," *Davoser Revue,* 4, 7 (April 15, 1929), hereafter cited as DR. See also the student essay by E.H., "Betrachtungen zu den Davoser Hochschulkursen," NZZ, Morgenausgabe (Wednesday, April 10, 1929) 150, 677. The workshop itself is described in Ernst Cassirer and Martin Heidegger, *Débat sur le Kantisme et la Philosophie (Davos, mars 1929), et autres textes de 1929–1931,* ed. Pierre Aubenque., trans. P. Aubenque, J.-M. Fataud, P. Quillet (Paris: Editions Beauchesne, 1972). Most useful is the transcription by Heidegger's students Otto Friedrich Bollnow and Joachim Ritter, "Davoser Disputation zwischen Ernst Cassirer und Martin Heidegger," in KPM, Appendix IV, 274–96; in English as "Davos Disputation Between Ernst Cassirer and Martin Heidegger," in KPM, English, 171–85. In this chapter I cite this version of the debates, hereafter abbreviated as DVS, followed by the appropriate pagination from the German edition of KPM or, where necessary, the pagination for both the German (G) and the English (E) versions. Also see Ludwig Englert, "Als Student bei den Zweiten Davoser Hochschulkursen, März, 1929," in *Die II. Davoser Hochschulkurse 17. März bis 6. April.* (Davos: Kommissionsverlag Heintz, Neu und Zahn, 1929), reprinted in *Nachlese zu Heidegger,* ed. Guido Schneeberger (Bern: Buchdruckerei AG Suhr, 1962), 1–6; and Otto Friedrich Bollnow, "Gespräche in Davos," in *Erinnerung an Martin Heidegger,* ed. Günther Neske (Pfullingen: Verlag Günther Neske, 1977), 25–29.

The critical literature on the Davos disputation is extensive. See, e.g., Calvin O. Schrag, "Heidegger and Cassirer on Kant," *Kantstudien* 58 (1967): 87–100; Karlfried Gründer, "Cassirer und Heidegger in Davos, 1929," in *Über Ernst Cassirers Philosophie der Symbolischen Formen,* ed. Hans-Jürg Braun, Helmut Holzhey, and Ernst Wolfgang Orth (Frankfurt am Main: Suhrkamp Verlag, 1988); Pierre Aubenque, "Le Débat de 1929 entre Cassirer et Heidegger," in *Ernst Cassirer: De Marbourg à New York, L'intinéraire philosophique,* ed. Jean Seidengart (Paris: Les Éditions du Cerf, 1990), 81–96; Dennis A. Lynch, "Ernst Cassirer and Martin Heidegger: The Davos Debate," *Kantstudien* 81 (1990): 360–70; Wayne Cristaudo, "Heidegger and

The contrast of personalities was indeed dramatic. Heidegger seemed the very embodiment of Naphta, the Jesuit revolutionary from Mann's 1924 novel *The Magic Mountain*. Heidegger, too, had trained in scholasticism. Observers recall him as being somewhat pugnacious and impatient with academic proprieties; he wore a strangely "unmodern" suit and came to at least one of the sessions still dressed in his skiing clothes. In her memoirs, Toni Cassirer recalls her husband's discomfort when he came face to face with "this remarkable nemesis." Cassirer, by contrast, seemed to many the very embodiment of Mann's "humanist," Settembrini. Cassirer was an eminently respected scholar of both the Renaissance and the Enlightenment. While his theory of symbolic forms was in many respects a departure from the neo-Kantian methods of his teacher, Hermann Cohen, Cassirer was nonetheless widely regarded as the last great representative of the spirit of Marburg. An assimilated Jew as well as a dedicated liberal, he had also played a small role in promoting the constitution for the fledging Weimar Republic. Even in appearance Cassirer seemed more dignified and older than his opponent; though only 44, his hair had gone completely white.[3]

Whatever its more personal symbolism, most participants regarded

Cassirer: Being, Knowing, and Politics," *Kantstudien* 82 (1991): 469–83; John Michael Krois, "Aufklärung und Metaphysik: Zur Philosophie Cassirers und der Davoser Debatte mit Heidegger," *Internationale Zeitschrift für Philosophie* 2 (Stuttgart: J. B. Metzler) (1992): 273–89; Frank Schalow, "Thinking at Cross-Purposes with Kant: Reason, Finitude, and Truth in the Cassirer-Heidegger Debate," *Kantstudien* 87 (1996) 198–217. Also see Pierre Aubenque et al. (roundtable), "Philosophie und Politik: Die Davoser Disputation zwischen Ernst Cassirer und Martin Heidegger in der Retrospektive," *Internationale Zeitschrift für Philosophie*, 2 (1992): 290–312.

3. An attending reporter for the *Neue Zürcher Zeitung* actually remarked on parallels with Mann's novel; see Hans Barth, "Davoser Hochschulkurse 1929," NZZ (Saturday, March 30, 1929) 150, 609: 1. Toni Cassirer, *Aus meinem Leben mit Ernst Cassirer* (Hildesheim: Gerstenberg Verlag, 1981; written in New York in 1950). For a touching portrait of Cassirer, see Charles Hendel, "Ernst Cassirer, Man and Teacher," *Philosophy and Phenomenological Research* 1, 6 (September 1945): 156–59. See also David R. Lipton, *Ernst Cassirer: The Dilemma of the Liberal Intellectual in Germany, 1914–1933* (Toronto: University of Toronto Press, 1978); and Hendrik J. Pos, "Recollections of Ernst Cassirer," *The Philosophy of Ernst Cassirer*, vol. VI, ed. Paul Arthur Schlipp (Evanston, Ill.: Library of the Living Philosophers, 1949), 61–72. The theatricality of this opposition proved irresistible. At a nighttime celebration following the official events, a group of students hit upon the idea of reenacting the debate. Among the players was a young Emmanuel Levinas, who prepared himself for the role of Cassirer by disguising his black hair with white powder. The taller, more somber young Otto Friedrich Bollnow, himself Heidegger's student, played the part of his teacher. Levinas dreamed up fitting phrases for the play, such as the parodistic "[T]o interpret means to set something upside down." There are several records of this play: Levinas remembers it (with a few points of imprecision) in his interview with Francois Poirié in *Qui êtes-vous?* A reference to the play is also in the second half of Herrmann Herrigel's report of the conference, "Denken dieser Zeit, Fakultäten und Nationen treffen sich in Davos, II. (Einblicke in die übrige Arbeit der Davoserkurse," *Frankfurter Zeitung*, Abendblatt (Friday, May 10,1929) 73, 345: 4.

the Heidegger-Cassirer encounter as an event of immense historical and philosophical significance. And it was generally agreed that Heidegger was the decisive victor. He embodied the "new time" and the "new pathos of thought." Even Cassirer's students conceded their teacher's defeat, but rather than praising Heidegger, they regarded him a prophet of the "mood philosophy" now bewitching the academic scene. Beside him, the once grand figure of Cassirer seemed bathed in twilight: Levinas saw in him "the end of a particular kind of humanism." Whatever their perspective, participants saw the dispute as "the encounter between representatives of two ages."[4] But it was also an encounter between two fundamentally opposed conceptions of philosophy.

## KANT, FINITUDE, AND TEMPORALITY

The Arbeitsgemeinschaft between Heidegger and Cassirer took up an entire Tuesday morning during the third week of the conference. The philosophers were supposed to address the themes each had raised in their three respective lectures of the preceding weeks. Heidegger had lectured on "Kant's *Critique of Pure Reason* and the Task of a Groundlaying of Metaphysics." Cassirer had lectured on "The Fundamental Problems of Philosophical Anthropology," as well as a special lecture on "Spirit and Life

4. "New time," Bollnow, "Gespräche in Davos," 27–28. "New pathos . . ." (in French, "nouveau pathétique de la pensée"), Levinas, in Poirie, *Qui êtes-vous?* 78. "Mood philosophy" and Cassirer's "defeat," Pos, "Recollections of Ernst Cassirer," 61–72. "End . . . of humanism," Levinas, in Poirie, *Qui êtes-vous?* 77. "Encounter between . . . two ages," H.H. [Hermann Herrigel], "Denken dieser Zeit: Fakultäten und Nationen treffen sich gegenüber in Davos, I," *Frankfurter Zeitung,* Abendblatt (Monday, April 22, 1929) 297: 4; hereafter cited as Herrigel, "Denken dieser Zeit, I." Thus Bollnow's remark that one had "the sublime feeling, to have lived as witnesses to an historical moment, precisely like that of which Goethe had spoken in his 'Campagne in Frankreich': 'From here and now a new epoch of world-history begins'—in this case, of philosophical history—'and you will be able to say, that you were there.'" "Gespräche in Davos," 28.
    Other events at Davos strengthened the impression that Heidegger best represented contemporary intellectual fashion. The Munich professor and priest Erich Przywara spoke on "the metaphysical and religious problem of existence" and called for philosophy to abandon its idealist methods so as to recognize man as a creature finitude and humility. The Parmenides scholar Karl Joël offered a philosophical-historical interpretation of the nineteenth century as a series of generational shifts. Kurt Riezler, anticipating the dispute between Heidegger and Cassirer, spoke of a new "groundlaying of metaphysics" (*Grundlegung der Metaphysik*) and argued that humanity required not "redemption from" (*Erlösung von*) but rather the "struggle with" (*Ringen mit*) its constitutive fatality. For a summary of Davos events, see DR, 199–201; and Hans Barth, "Davoser Hochschulkurs, 1929," NZZ, Morgenausgabe (March 27, 1929) 150, 588: 1–2. For a summary of other lectures, see DR, 202–5; DR, "Bei den Studenten," 205–7; and E.H., "Betrachtungen zu den Davoser Hochschulkursen," 1.

in Scheler's Philosophy."⁵ In some respects, these topics anticipate their deeper disagreement. As is well known, Heidegger was always careful to distinguish his views from philosophical anthropology; but this was precisely the discipline that Cassirer saw as Heidegger's natural domain. Similarly, Heidegger's aim was to demonstrate once and for all that the neo-Kantian interpretation of the *Critique of Pure Reason* was in error. The first critique, he said, was not primarily "a theory of mathematical-natural-scientific knowledge," as the neo-Kantians suggested; rather, it represented Kant's tentative steps toward a "groundlaying of metaphysics."⁶

Various claims in Cassirer's lectures seem directed against Heidegger. Scheler's interpretation of spirit *(Geist)* as "powerless" and life as powerful rehearsed what Cassirer called a crisis in metaphysics. Philosophy for Scheler was therefore a struggle between "Being" and "Not-being," with roots traceable as far back as Parmenides. He thus exemplified the "passionate complaint against Spirit" that dominated so much of the recent philosophical literature. The difficulties of this enterprise were for Cassirer the common "fate of metaphysics" in modernity.⁷

Similarly, Heidegger takes aim at the neo-Kantian interpretation of the first critique as an epistemological grounding of scientific method. Heidegger's own interpretation exploited Kant's famous remark (in the schematism chapter) that the origin of our capacity for a priori knowledge must be found in a "third thing," which is born from a "common root" (transcendental imagination) beneath both understanding and sensibility. For Kant,

---

5. See Gründer, "Cassirer und Heidegger in Davos," 293. The German title for Heidegger's lectures is "Kants *Kritik der reinen Vernunft* und die Aufgabe einer Grundlegung der Metaphysik." See Heidegger, "Vorwort zur ersten Auflage," KPM, xvi. Cassirer's lectures anticipate the essay "Geist und Leben in der Philosophie der Gegenwart," *Die neue Rundschau* (Leipzig: Fischer Verlag) 41, 1 (1930): 244–64. Cassirer's criticism of Heidegger was first developed in an unpublished manuscript under a similar title, "Geist und Leben: Heidegger," which seems to have formed the basis for Cassirer's published review of KPM in *Kantstudien*. See John Michael Krois, "Cassirer's Unpublished Critique of Heidegger," *Philosophy and Rhetoric* 16, 3 (1983).

6. Heidegger quoted in DR, 194. Cassirer considered Nicolai Hartmann (not Heidegger) the best contemporary representative of new "ontological" trends; see his "Erkenntnistheorie nebst den Grenzfragen der Logik und Denkpsychologie," *Jahrbücher der Philosophie* (Berlin: E. S. Mittler und Sohn, 1927), 3: 31–92; reprinted in Cassirer, *Erkenntnis, Begriff, Kultur,* ed. Rainer A. Bast (Hamburg: Felix Meiner Verlag, 1993), 77–154. See KPM, Appendix III, which is listed under the original mimeographed title of the lectures as "Kants *Kritik der reinen Vernunft . . .*" and anticipates the general interpretation of Kant that Heidegger had been developing at least since the winter semester of 1927–28. The same themes appear in the body of KPM. In revising proofs for the fourth edition of KPM in 1973, Heidegger told his publishers that he had written the book immediately upon leaving Davos, the bulk of it without pause in three weeks' time.

7. Cassirer, "Erkenntnistheorie," 54, 50.

the purpose of the schematism was to ensure that the pure concepts of understanding may relate to the transcendental condition of time. But as he admitted, the nature of the schematism remains "an art hidden in the depths of the human soul" ("eine verborgene Kunst in den tiefen der menschlichen Seele"; KdrV, 185, B181). Inspired no doubt by this uncharacteristically cryptic phrase, Heidegger concluded that if imagination and temporality lay at the root of human thought, then the sovereignty of reason is far less secure than it may seem. In fact, reason's claim to priority is an illusion, since it is immersed in the "primordial" temporality of Dasein.

Heidegger concluded that Kant's very radicalism "had brought him to a position, before which he must draw back in fear" ("vor der er zurückschrecken mußte"). But Heidegger was bold enough to embrace the position Kant found unacceptable. Kant's deeper insight into the finitude of reason now needed to be retrieved for thought. Heidegger thus called a new inquiry into the possibility of metaphysics as "the natural tendency of man" a "metaphysic of Dasein" directed at "the possibility of metaphysics as such." But the ramifications of Kant's original insight were far more dramatic than even Kant had imagined; they implied nothing less than the "destruction of all previous foundations of Western metaphysics," and an end to the erstwhile rule of "Spirit [*Geist*], Logos, and Reason."[8]

The quarrel between Heidegger and Cassirer over how to read Kant's philosophy was by no means superficial. It hinted at a deeper disagreement over the relation between time and mental activity. If the neo-Kantians were correct, then one could regard the mind as the transcendental condition for time and the origin for temporal experience. (This was the doctrine expressed in Cohen's principle of origins). But if Heidegger was correct, then the mind's much-vaunted capacity for transcendental grounding was actually an illusion. (And this was a truth, said Heidegger, that even Kant had known). For Heidegger, the insight that the human being dwells within a "primordial temporality" dislodges reason from its seemingly sovereign position. Finitude goes deeper than reason.

The dispute at Davos was so acute that Cassirer and Heidegger could hardly agree upon the language to recognize its terms. (Cassirer even objected to Heidegger's portrait of neo-Kantianism, which, he complained, had become the "scapegoat of the newer philosophy.")[9] Heidegger ob-

8. KPM, Appendix III ("Kants *Kritik der reinen Vernunft*"). Heidegger's Kant interpretation illustrates what might have been in the never-written second part of *Being and Time,* which was to be a "destruction" of the history of metaphysics. On the continuity between *Sein und Zeit* and KPM, see the preface to the first edition of KPM, xvi.

9. This was a provocative remark, given that Heidegger's hostility toward Cohen has been interpreted as antisemitism. The German phrase, lost in the published translation, is "der

jected to neo-Kantianism insofar as it rehearsed the traditional effort to encompass Being in thought—in the language of *The Star of Redemption,* "Knowledge of the All" (SE, 3 [E, 3]) and passim; e.g., "the All of philosophy," 10). In Heidegger's view, neo-Kantianism had sought to master the question of "the whole of knowledge" *(im Ganzen der Erkenntnis).* But since the human and the natural sciences had "taken possession of "the totality of what is knowable" *(die Allheit des Erkennbaren),* the question arose, "What still remains to philosophy, when the totality of beings has been divided up under the sciences?" To this question, the neo-Kantians had left philosophy "only the knowledge of science, not of beings."[10]

### THE CREATION OF REASON

Cassirer objected to this characterization, since it neglected the deeper neo-Kantian commitment to freedom. In ethics, he argued, any sense of human restriction to a determinate sphere must fall away. Ethics thus "leads beyond the world of appearances" and beyond the realm of objective, scientific knowledge. Heidegger's protests notwithstanding, ethics was for Kant "the decisive moment of metaphysics" in which philosophy achieved an actual "breakthrough" *(Durchbruch)* from the realm of appearance to the "intelligible world" *(mundus intelligibilis).* "[I]n the ethical," Cassirer concluded, "a point is achieved that is no longer relative to the finitude [*Endlichkeit*] of the knowing being" (DVS, E, 174; G, 278).

But to Heidegger it seemed obvious that even in the ethical sphere man never truly breaks free from finitude. If the heart of ethics is the categorical imperative, it by definition must refer to a subject who is thrown under the stringency of law.[11] The sphere of ethics, therefore, never transcends fini-

---

Sündenbock der neueren Philosophie" (the English version of KPM has "whipping-boy"). Pierre Bourdieu has argued that Heidegger's philosophical antipathy to neo-Kantianism was encrypted antisemitism, and that the critical spirit of neo-Kantianism that animated Cohen's philosophy (and therefore Cassirer's too) came to represent in Heidegger's imagination the modernizing, antimetaphysical forces of liberal Judaism. *L'Ontologie politique de Martin Heidegger* (Paris: Editions de Minuit, 1988).

10. Even phenomenology, lamented Heidegger, was not immune from these tendencies; between 1900 and 1910 Husserl too had "fallen into the arms" of neo-Kantianism." DVS, E, 174; G, 278.

11. In the second critique, Kant himself explained that practical reason is applicable only to finite subjects, since the concepts of interest, incentive, and maxim can be applied "only to finite beings [*nur auf endliche Wesen*]. For without exception they presuppose a limitation of the nature of the being, . . . they presuppose that the being must be impelled in some manner to action. . . . They cannot, therefore, be applied to the divine will [*auf den göttlichen Wesen*]." *Kritik der praktischen Vernunft,* 9th ed., ed. Karl Vorländer (Leipzig: Felix Meiner, 1929), 93; in English, *Critique of Practical Reason,* trans. Lewis White Beck (New York: Macmillan, 1956), 82.

tude. "[T]his going-beyond to something higher is always just a going-beyond to the finite creature, to one which is created," that is to say, *"an angel."*[12] (I return to this example below). Here Heidegger could not agree with Cassirer that ethics overcomes temporal limitation: "This transcendence too still remains within the realm of creatureliness [*Geschöpflichkeit*]" (DVS, E, 174–75; G, 278–79).

Against Cassirer, Heidegger regarded the human being as "created," not creative. And against the neo-Kantian view of reason as generating Being, Heidegger objected that the human being is "never infinite and absolute in the creation of Being itself." Since human beings are "bound essentially to ontic experience," the infinitude that "breaks out" in the power of imagination is the "strongest argument" for our limitation: "Ontology," observed Heidegger, "requires only a finite creature." In other words, the understanding that first allows ontological inquiry requires that we first discover ourselves in the midst of beings. The ontological question is one that only a being who is thrown into the world would feel compelled to ask; it is an exclusively human question. As Heidegger noted, "God does not have it." Thus ontology is the very "index of finitude" (DVS, E, 175; G, 279).

In dramatizing the contrast between what is created and what is creative, Heidegger (borrowing from Kant) exploited what may seem at first glance a rather surprising example—angels. But there is warrant for this. Angels only seem to be transcendent, while in fact they are themselves created and limited beings. So Heidegger's last remark—that God does not "have" an ontology—was another way of illustrating his objection to granting the human mind any capacities like that of the *intuitus originarius,* or creative intuition. Recalling his interpretation of Kant's schematism, Heidegger contrasted God's "creative" understanding with the "created" (human and angelic) understanding which must remain "bound to ontic experience."

The various disagreements between Cassirer and Heidegger reveal two rival characterizations of philosophy, hinging upon the meaning of infinity and freedom. And it seems obvious that here Rosenzweig was right to discern his own basic resemblance to Heidegger. For as noted above, the apparent difference between theism (Rosenzweig) and atheism (Heidegger) was not as dramatic as one might suppose. Heidegger, despite his apparent hostility toward traditional theology, nonetheless had the peculiar habit of invoking concepts with a distinctively theological heritage (for example, in his references to God and to angels). But he would then call into question

---

12. DVS, E 174; G, 279; my emphasis. The meaning of the word "angel" is obscure in the original: "Auch dieses Hinausgehen zu einem Höheren ist immer nur ein Hinausgehen zu endlichen Wesen, zu Geschaffenem (Engel)." On the meaning of "angels" in philosophical expressionism, see my comments in the introduction.

the relevance of this concept for human existence, thus evacuating its original sense. Heidegger proceeded by first naming, then canceling, a theological value that has been deposited in the lexicon of philosophy across centuries of religious speculation. Heidegger's thought might thus be regarded as the fruit of a theological sensibility that had collapsed back into the human sphere—a realization of Rosenzweig's principle that the new thinking "translates" from theological to human values.

### ETERNITY AND ANXIETY

The question of translation between theology and philosophy became most pronounced at Davos as Heidegger and Cassirer moved on from specific questions of interpreting Kant to the larger, more basic disagreements concerning the task of philosophy. Here the dispute turned upon the meaning of eternity, which Heidegger introduced in reference to "Cassirer's question concerning universally valid eternal truths." Heidegger claimed that one could not regard the "peculiar" validity that we call truth as something "permanent" and "eternal." ("What does eternal actually mean here?" he asked. "From where, then, do we know of this eternity?") For Heidegger the alternative was clear. We construe eternity only as it is constituted out of the time structures of Dasein itself, our pastness in recollection, our presence and futurity. The question of truth must always collapse back onto the question of the temporality of Dasein, as the horizon in which truth first becomes possible. Heidegger thus asked Cassirer: "What path does man have to infinitude? And what is the manner in which man can participate in infinity?"(DVS, E, 176–77; G, 280–81).

To this question Cassirer responded that the human being has a path to infinity "by no other means than through the medium of form." (This was of course a reference to Cassirer's own theory of symbolic forms, which treats the a priori projective patterns of mind that govern the various spheres of culture.) Cassirer's larger point was that the mind is not wholly limited to the receptive role of sensibility. It is also a faculty of spontaneity, projecting upon the world the very order it will then encounter.[13] But Cassirer insisted that spontaneity was not to be confused with any real breakthrough in a metaphysical sense. Kantian forms do not actually grasp the infinite so much as create a transcendent realm still *within* the human sphere. Cassirer called this "immanent infinitude." Man "can and must have . . . the metabasis which leads him from the immediacy of his existence

---

13. See John Michael Krois, *Cassirer: Symbolic Forms and History* (New Haven: Yale University Press, 1987). For a discussion of the theme of spontaneity in Cassirer's response to Heidegger, see Schrag, "Heidegger and Cassirer on Kant."

[*Existenz*] into a region of pure form. And he possesses his infinity solely in this form." Transcendence is therefore a projective act of the mind and not an adventure in metaphysics: "The spiritual realm is not a metaphysical spiritual realm; the true spiritual realm is just the spiritual world created from himself." If man has a "path to infinity," it is to be found solely in the projective capacities of the understanding. Form, Cassirer concluded, is the very "seal of his infinity" (DVS, E, 179; G, 283).

One can understand that Cassirer would have been reluctant to commit himself to the existence of a robustly metaphysical realm. Nor did he wish to consign infinity to the dreamworld of logical invention.[14] He was therefore compelled to resort to seemingly paradoxical language. Infinity, he insisted, was a far "stranger sphere." Because the mind's capacity for transcendence remains within the realm of "immanence," infinity is just the "fulfillment" of finitude. Here Cassirer meant that the human world exhibits a plenitude of meaning in the forms that are projected outward from human being itself. Quoting Goethe, Cassirer explained, "If you wish to step into the infinite, you have only to go out into finitude in all directions." The concept of infinity was not, then, "an opposition to finitude" but was, in a certain sense, "the totality" as such *(die Totalität).*

One can now see how the disagreement between Heidegger and Cassirer was rooted in a fundamental difference concerning the possibility of redemption. Cassirer wished to conceive of the infinite as a transcendental, primarily cognitive condition by which the mind conceives of the whole of what there is. Heidegger objected to this characterization as trespassing upon the finitude underlying the mind itself. He further objected to the basic animating principle of Cassirer's philosophy of culture, that redemption could be found in cultural expression. For Heidegger this seemed to depend illicitly upon the older metaphysical idea (popular at least since Plato) that thought brings release from the world of appearance. In contrast, Heidegger called for what he called the "setting free" of existence:

> In order to get into this dimension of philosophizing, which is *not a matter for a learned discussion* but is rather a matter about which the individual philosopher knows nothing, and which is a task to which the philosopher has submitted himself—*this setting-free of the Dasein* in man must be the sole and central task which philosophy as philosophizing can perform. (DVS, E, 178; G, 281–82; my emphasis)

14. That is, Heidegger's objection that the neo-Kantian notion of an "eternal task" merely exploited the peculiarity of German, superadding a privative *(Un)* to the concept of finitude *(Endlichkeit)* in order to then propose without warrant that infinity *(Unendlichkeit)* was a concept of independent and prior standing. Hence Heidegger's question to Cassirer, "Is infinitude to be attained as [a] privative determination of finitude, or is infinitude a region in its own right?" DVS, E, 179; G, 281–82.

To explain his opposition to Cassirer's model of "setting-free," Heidegger used his own more idiosyncratic terminology, invoking the notion of "anxiety" *(Angst)*, which he had already introduced in *Being and Time:*

> To what extent does philosophy have as its task to be allowed to become free from anxiety? Or does it not have as its task to surrender man, even radically, to anxiety? (DVS, E, 180; G, 286)

Cassirer responded that philosophy does indeed hold out the promise of liberation from the "anxiety of mere disposition" *(Angst der bloßer Befindlichkeit)*. But this kind of freedom occurs in a spontaneous mental act and not as a decisive step into the metaphysical sphere. Freedom, said Cassirer, is to be found only along "the path of progressive freeing" and must therefore be characterized along neo-Kantian lines as "an infinite process" *(ein unendlicher Prozeß)* and not a finite accomplishment (DVS, E, 180; G, 286–87).

This response contained a direct criticism of Heidegger's technical notion of *Befindlichkeit* as a "mood" *(Stimmung)* and "fear" *(Angst)* as perhaps the most fundamental of such moods (SZ, esp. §29–30). For Cassirer, however, philosophy could hardly occupy itself with such matters as "mere" mood or disposition. In fact, philosophical inquiry according to Cassirer "takes no notice [of] the subjectivity of the individual" ("nicht mehr Rücksicht nimmt auf die Subjektivität des Einzelnen"). But given Heidegger's insistence upon such themes, Cassirer felt himself compelled to confess his own worldview. It was clear, he said, that philosophy must be made to serve a loftier purpose than merely to "surrender" human existence to its fears. Its primary objective must be human freedom. Cassirer summarized this idea with a quotation whose source he did not name: "Cast off your fear of earthly things!" ("Werft die Angst des Irdischen von euch!"). This, he concluded, "is the position of idealism which I have always confessed [*bekannt*] as my own."

For the reader familiar with Rosenzweig's philosophy, Cassirer's response to Heidegger is of remarkable interest. The key phrase—"cast off your fear of earthly things!"—is from Schiller. And, as we have seen, it is this phrase that provides Rosenzweig an ironic portrait of idealism in the overture to *The Star of Redemption.* But Cassirer presents it without irony as characterizing the true task of philosophy.[15] The coincidence is striking but of course

---

15. Cassirer later provided a more elaborate treatment and cited the full stanza of Schiller's poem (the same as parodied by Rosenzweig) in a 1931 review of KPM. "Kant und das Problem der Metaphysik—Bemerkungen zu Martin Heideggers Kant-Interpretation," *Kantstudien,* 36, 1 (1931). As Cassirer there explained, Heidegger's interpretation of the first critique had gravely misunderstood the "intellectual atmosphere" infusing all of Kant's thought. In Cassirer's view, Kant was "in the most sublime and beautiful sense of this word a thinker of the Enlightenment: he strives toward air and light, even where he senses the deepest and most

mere accident; taken alone it would hardly suffice to prove Rosenzweig correct in his claim that Cassirer represented the "old" philosophy as against the "new thinking" of both Rosenzweig and Heidegger. But it is significant that Schiller's image of redemption remained in circulation as a symbol of idealist values. And as we have seen, Rosenzweig's opposition to such imagery was only one indication of his deeper antipathy to the philosophical assumptions it expressed. As I have already suggested, the basic disagreement between the older model of philosophy as endorsed by Cassirer and the newer model proposed by both Heidegger and Rosenzweig is that the newer view construes the idealist perspective as promising a bogus metaphysical release. What Cassirer characterized as liberation from worldly anxiety seemed for Rosenzweig as well as Heidegger a metaphysical impossibility.

Against Cassirer, Heidegger argued that freedom should be considered as "becoming free for the finitude of Dasein." Cassirer's faith in the humanities was unfounded, for they were themselves entangled in the metaphysical understanding of redemption Heidegger wished to surmount. Only with great exertion, he argued, could one "break through" *(durchbrechen)* these disciplines and wrest oneself free from the prejudiced understanding of man as spirit, in order to grasp man more properly as Dasein, and move from Dasein to the question of Being. The chief question of the conference, "What is man?," could not be construed in "some isolated ethical sense." Rather, "the question concerning the essence of human beings only makes sense . . . insofar as it derives its motivation from philosophy's central problematic itself, which leads man back beyond himself and into the whole of beings in order to reveal to him there, despite all his freedom, the nothingness of his Dasein [bei all seiner Freiheit die Nichtigkeit seines Daseins offenbar zu machen.]" But for Heidegger, this "nothingness" should not prompt "pessimism and melancholy." Rather, it should awaken a new vision of life as "opposition" and authentic existence: for "authentic activity takes place only where there is opposition [*Widerstand*] and philosophy has the task [of retrieval] from the lazy aspect of a man who merely uses the work of the spirit [*die Werke des Geistes*] and of throwing man back . . . into the hardness of his fate [*die Härte seines Schicksals*]" (DVS, E, 182; G, 290).[16]

---

hidden 'grounds' of being." Kant's model of philosophy thus accorded with the Enlightenment understood as a self-liberation of mind. On this point, also see Frank Schalow, "Thinking at Cross-Purposes with Kant," 199; and for more on the general disagreement, see Krois, "Cassirer's Unpublished Critique of Heidegger."

16. In his commentary on the Davos debate, Rosenzweig misquotes Heidegger (and Herrigel) on this line, reading "to call back" *(zurückzurufen)* for the original "to throw back" *(zurückzuwerfen)*.

With this rejoinder the true locus of disagreement between Cassirer and Heidegger was clearly in view. In essence, what Heidegger was proposing was a dramatically new kind of philosophy in which "freedom" was now construed as a struggle within and for finitude. Against Cassirer's metaphors of redemption as cognitive transcendence, Heidegger offered a new but still powerfully normative substitute in terms of this-worldly "opposition" and "authentic existence." As I have suggested, the contraposition of Cassirer's idealist portrait of freedom with Heidegger's revision of this transport within finitude seems to imply that the new thinking is best understood as supplanting both traditional theology and metaphysics. Rosenzweig's "redemption" and Heidegger's "authentic existence" carry forward a poignant longing for ultimacy as their theological inheritance. (Heidegger, as noted above, felt it necessary to exploit a theological notion of eternity even if only to serve him as contrast.) But both Rosenzweig and Heidegger had moved a long way toward abandoning the metaphysical framework in which this longing had once made sense. Theology and post-metaphysical thinking now came together in the image of freedom as a this-worldly recoil from inauthenticity and as an "opposition" that provided them both with the best definition of "fate."[17]

There is more to be written of the Davos encounter. Clearly, Heidegger and Cassirer were divided upon quite fundamental issues touching upon some of the deepest and perennial concerns of philosophy. And, I have suggested, their disagreement may have rested in part upon deeper, barely acknowledged theological and metaphysical commitments. The question remains whether there was actually a philosophical conversation between the participants. For true dialogue may only be possible if speakers inhabit the same universe of meaning.

Here even the final moment of the encounter holds an ambiguous symbolism. There is a discrepancy in the reports as to whether the opponents actually shook hands. One account is Heidegger's own testimony. During a postwar interview conducted at Heidegger's Freiburg home by Maurice de Gandillac (later published in *Les Temps Modernes*), the interviewer relates how some of Heidegger's "good humor" seemed to emerge as he recalled how, "after long discussions about Kant, he had not hesitated publicly to shake the hand of the Jew Cassirer." In the atmosphere of recrimination following the war, such facts had become (in Gandillac's words) "certificates of an upstanding life." But conflicting testimony (admittedly partial to Cassirer) comes from Hendrik Pos, who recalls that in the uneasy moment at

---

17. For the relationship between authenticity and redemption, see esp. the concluding sections of chap. 4.

the very end of the debate, Cassirer extended his hand, and Heidegger refused to grasp it.[18]

We do not know which of these contradictory testimonies is correct. But the story of Heidegger's refusal is at least plausible, as it corresponds with widespread impressions that there was a disparity between the participants in their concern for academic etiquette. Cassirer kept speaking of a common language that formed a "bridge" between himself and his opponent, while Heidegger, with seeming aggression, kept insisting on the chasm that divided them. Many of the witnesses to the debate felt that the participants could not achieve anything beyond mutual comprehension of the most basic sort. A reporter for the *Neue Zürcher Zeitung* observed wryly that "instead of seeing two worlds rebounding off of one another, one enjoyed at most a play, in which a very nice man and a very violent man, who also exerted a terrifying effort to be nice, engaged in monologues." And Levinas saw no irony in borrowing a Kantian term to describe the encounter as "*une antinomie indépassable.*" It seemed clear that the meeting ended in a radical failure of communication.[19]

## ROSENZWEIG'S KNOWLEDGE OF HEIDEGGER

Rosenzweig's interpretation of the Davos encounter accords with prevailing contemporary opinion. But his knowledge was secondhand; he seems to have relied exclusively on newspaper reports, chiefly those published by Hermann Herrigel in the *Frankfurter Zeitung*.[20] There is no evidence of other sources. Some scholars may conclude that this disqualifies Rosenzweig as a commentator. But this charge is unimpressive beside the more serious possibility that Rosenzweig may have lacked any other, more direct acquaintanceship with Heidegger's philosophy. By the spring of 1929, only *Being and Time* was available, but Rosenzweig left no indication in his let-

18. It was well known that Heidegger needed evidence of an "upstanding life," and he seems to have kept it ready at hand: "Without a moment's difficulty, he opened a drawer and produced a photograph of 'those innocent times.'" But Gandillac adds the sour afterthought: "[I] doubt that, in that recent period of the past when the fear of the Gestapo reigned everywhere, he could have found this item of testimony quite so easily." Gandillac's interview, "Entretien avec Martin Heidegger," was published together with a brief essay by Alfred de Towarniski, "Visite à Martin Heidegger," as "Deux Documents sur Heidegger," *Les Temps Modernes,* January 1946, 713–24. Pos, "Recollections of Ernst Cassirer," 69.

19. O. F. Bollnow recalled that Heidegger would at times answer, "with a sharpness bordering on impoliteness," that one must first of all recognize the clear differences between his own position and that of Cassirer. "Gespräche in Davos," 28. Levinas's quote in Poirie, *Qui êtes-vous?* 77.

20. See esp. Herrigel, "Denken dieser Zeit, I."

ters or in his published work that he had read it.[21] Whether he did or not, the philosophical comparison between Rosenzweig and Heidegger would stand, independent of Rosenzweig's individual perceptions. But one might still object that his knowledge through Herrigel was too meager for any judicious assessment of the Davos encounter. Before we can turn to Rosenzweig's commentary itself, this objection merits discussion.

Hermann Herrigel was a rather peripheral figure in the popularization of the new thinking. He participated with Martin Buber, Viktor von Weizäcker, and Josef Wittig in writing for the short-lived journal *Die Kreatur* (1927 to 1930). During the years 1916–39, he served as journalist and editor of the education page of the left-liberal *Frankfurter Zeitung*, to which he contributed reports on the Davos conferences from their inauguration in 1928 to the final year, 1931. He was more widely known in intellectual circles for his dozens of essays on theology, philosophy, and methods of education, as well as his (ultimately unsuccessful) efforts between 1933 and 1939 to create a forum for Protestant-Catholic dialogue. And inspired by Rosenzweig's essay on the new thinking, he published his own book under the same title, *Das neue Denken*.[22]

Herrigel was mainly a popularizer of current philosophy. His *New Thinking* traces the philosophical and cultural transformation in Germany since the end of the First World War. He writes of the bankruptcy of the older idealism—he chiefly targets Cohen's Marburg colleague, Paul Natorp—as a "merely reflective" theory of knowledge. In phrases reminiscent of Rosenzweig, he proposes a new thinking that will abandon the search for transcendent essences and would instead "throw down bridges between" objects. Most characteristic of this new philosophy will be its unflagging attention to the temporality of experience. It will be an "absolute empiricism," avoiding all "concepts of tradition" so as to "draw near to the things of reality." It will thus dissolve the traditional boundaries of the disciplines, particularly the boundary between philosophy and theology. Most of all, however, Herrigel criticizes the neo-Kantian chauvinism of "the pure, formal, and contentless Idea" that "lies in the infinite," whereas the human being should in fact be wholly absorbed with "the problem of finitude."[23]

21. Heidegger's smaller essays "Vom Wesen des Grundes" and "Was ist Metaphysik," as well as *Kant und das Problem der Metaphysik* were all published later in 1929. *Being and Time* had appeared in a special volume (8) of the *Jahrbuch für Philosophie und phänomenologische Forschung* in 1927.

22. See Ursula Schulz, *Hermann Herrigel: Der Denken und die deutschen Erwachsenenbildung. Eine Bibliographie seiner Schriften zum 80. Geburtstag* (Bremen: Bremer Volkshochschule, 1969); Herrigel, *Das neue Denken* (Berlin: Lambert Schneider, 1928); and Herrigel, *Zwischen Frage und Antwort* (Berlin, Lambert Schneider, 1930).

23. Herrigel, *Das neue Denken*, 55. See, as an example of popularizing, his "Was ist heute Philosophie?" *Der Morgen* 6, 1 (April 1930): 88–93 (the same issue as Rosenzweig's VF).

Rosenzweig did not associate closely with Herrigel and seems to have regarded him with some mistrust.[24] On the other hand, Herrigel's very lack of originality may lend his reports greater factual credibility, and clearly Rosenzweig relied upon the newspaper's perspective. In fact, his view of the Davos debate as a "representative encounter between the old philosophy and the new thinking" seems directly in line with Herrigel's interpretation.[25] But in the final analysis Rosenzweig's own commentary is both deeper and more broad-ranging; it bespeaks greater confidence concerning the philosophical stakes of the debate. While it is true that Rosenzweig learned of the Davos encounter chiefly through the newspapers, it appears likely that he knew much more about both Cassirer and Heidegger than his brief comments might at first suggest.

## "EXCHANGED FRONTS"

Rosenzweig's essay begins with a seemingly unrelated comment: "Ten years after Hermann Cohen's death," he writes, the great philosopher's influence was apparently at an end, and the original edition of his final work of religious philosophy, *Religion of Reason,* was now out of print. The first edition of the *opus postumum* stood under an "unlucky star" *(Unstern).* As noted in chapter 1, it had been printed with innumerable mistakes throughout the manuscript (especially common where there were quotations from Hebrew) and under a misleading title, as *Die Religion der Vernunft aus den Quellen des Judentums.* Its actual title, Rosenzweig recalls, lacked the first article—it was supposed to be simply *Religion der Vernunft aus den Quellen des Judentums.* The difference, Rosenzweig tells us, is significant, since the definite article renders its name "aggressive and intolerant." But neither would an "indeterminate" article suffice, for this would have rendered the religious origins of the book indeterminate as well. What Cohen had intended was neither "arrogant exclusivity" nor a more comfortable mood where "everything is permitted." He meant the reader to understand that Judaism has its share in the "one and general religion of reason." But sources are "originary sources" *(Urquellen),* Rosenzweig reminds us, since "humanity drank from them."

---

24. Even before the publication of Herrigel's book, Rosenzweig expressed his doubts: "Whether the 'new thinking' has had more benefit than damage, I still don't really know." Rosenzweig complained that "[Herrigel] is resting on my shoulders," adding that his work emerged from what was surely "not the very best or most critical of minds." The fact that Herrigel had recently purchased a copy of Rosenzweig's *Star of Redemption* made a "great impression" on its author, but perhaps not a wholly positive one. *Briefe,* N.452, An Gertrud Oppenheim (30.11.25), 548.

25. Herrigel, "Denken dieser Zeit, I."

For Rosenzweig, the Jewish specificity of Cohen's book did not imply exclusivity, but exemplarity: Judaism provided material for philosophical reflection but was not to be conceived as a closed and complete system. Accordingly, Rosenzweig believed that the true meaning of Cohen's work lay beyond its specific contributions to the philosophy of Judaism. Upon its first publication in 1919, this broader meaning may have been difficult to discern. But in the intervening period of ten years, the philosophical environment had grown far more hospitable. In 1929, Cohen's *opus postumum* was reprinted in a revised, second edition by the J. Kauffmann Verlag, now with the correct title, without the "intolerance" of a determinate article. In his essay, Rosenzweig comments on this new edition, insisting that the "Jewish side" of the book had never been its most significant feature. Rosenzweig admits, somewhat grudgingly, that Cohen's task of laying down a "Jewish ethics and philosophy of religion" could be ranged among "the classical solutions." (In Rosenzweig's lexicon, this is hardly a gesture of praise. To become a classic for him implies obsolescence.) But for what Rosenzweig calls "the present moment" and for "the philosophical situation," this classical meaning is of lesser significance. By contrast, the "actual meaning" of the work only became visible with Cohen's death, and, indeed, this meaning may have been "beyond Cohen's own intent and insight." In this sense, Rosenzweig concludes, Cohen suffered "a strange fate for a thinker."

Again we are confronted by Rosenzweig's persistent habit of reading Cohen despite and even against the master's purposes. The essay commits an unintended pun regarding the fate of Cohen's book in the suggestion that the 1919 edition stood under an "unlucky star," as if the true nature of Cohen's philosophy would only be revealed from some future vantage point and in the light of Rosenzweig's own work. Cohen suffered a "strange fate" because he was foreign to his own age; his earlier works, those of the "master time" *(Meisterzeit),* were "barely noticed outside the narrower school." This narrative of Cohen's fate is curiously reminiscent of Rosenzweig's larger vision of Jewish existence:

> [T]hus the great comprehensive system, for which the time ostensibly asked, entered, not into the time, but rather alongside it, the off-center work of a spirit very moved by the age, yet foreign to it. (VF, 86)

The analogy is not coincidental, because for Rosenzweig Judaism must always stand outside history; thus it was Cohen's final expression of Judaism in the *Religion of Reason* that was to suffer the harshest fate. Since Cohen was accepted only as an exponent of critical philosophy, it was almost inevitable that the deeper meaning of his last work would remain "excluded." But for Rosenzweig, times had changed. In the *Religion of Reason* Cohen had at last stepped forth, "not into his own time, but over and out from it, into our own."

And here the essay shifts to the Davos encounter, in which Rosenzweig discerns the signs of Cohen's arrival:

> In Davos recently there took place before a European forum that conversation between Cohen's most distinguished pupil, Cassirer, and the current custodian of Cohen's Marburg chair, Heidegger, [which Herrigel interpreted] as a representative encounter between the old and the new thinking. And here Heidegger, the student of Husserl, the Aristotelian scholastic, whose tenure in Cohen's chair can only be felt as an irony in the history of spirit by every "old Marburgian," represented against Cassirer a philosophical position, just that position of our, the new thinking, that lies wholly in the line descending from that "last Cohen." (VF, 86)

For Rosenzweig the Davos encounter thus marked the conclusion of a philosophical transformation originating in Cohen's posthumous writings. It was a moment of clarification for the interpretative quandaries of the previous ten years, crystallizing the various issues that divided the traditional, idealist philosophy from the new thinking. For Rosenzweig, the Davos encounter therefore possesses an emblematic status in the history of ideas; it is a culmination that joins Rosenzweig to Heidegger and declares their common victory.

But the closure it performs for that history is indeed ironic. Heidegger's animosity toward the neo-Kantians, and toward Cohen above all, was well known. Even at Davos he seemed intent upon wresting Kant from their control. (As Cassirer observed, neo-Kantianism had by then become "the scapegoat of the newer philosophy.") Yet on Rosenzweig's view, Heidegger's revolt against the neo-Kantians ended by repeating Cohen's apostasy. So although Cassirer represented the most original fruits of Cohen's neo-Kantian orthodoxy, Heidegger's own work, while critical of that orthodoxy, bore a striking resemblance to the philosophical innovations of Cohen's final years. This surprising outcome is what Rosenzweig calls an "exchange of fronts." The struggle is institutional, but also Hegelian; it is an episode in the cunning of historical reason:

> Those who have survived the "school"—not Cassirer!—would be pleased to make the dead master into a schoolmaster. The living, progressing history of spirit extracts him from such schoolboyish activities; it cares not for such claims and, when the dead Cid now rides forth anew, exchanges fronts [*verwechselt die Fronten*]. (VF, 86)

For clarity the argument may be broken down into two distinct points, one historical, the other contemporary. The first argument opens a path in the history of ideas: Heidegger, not Cassirer, is the true heir of Cohen's last and most innovative philosophical efforts. The second argument stakes a claim to intellectual affinity: Heidegger's success represents the victory of Rosenzweig's new thinking. The historical and the contemporary arguments may be analytically distinct, but for Rosenzweig they are indissociable. This is because Rosenzweig sees Cohen's late philosophy of religion as his very own inheritance. In naming features of Heidegger's thought that seem to betray the subterranean influence of Cohen's "last" writings, Rosenzweig deepens the suggestion that there is a fundamental affinity between Heidegger and himself. They are, as it were, the twin disciples of a dead master (VF, 87).

### FROM COHEN TO HEIDEGGER

Rosenzweig's comparative remarks on the supposed resemblance between Heidegger and the later Cohen is one of the most provocative specimens of German and Jewish intellectual history written in the twentieth century. It is also among the most contentious. Given Rosenzweig's limited information concerning the Davos encounter, there is good reason to doubt his odd suggestion that Cassirer and Heidegger were the embodiment of two successive phases in Cohen's spiritual journey. And given his controversial interpretation of Cohen's philosophy (which exploits Cohen's private letter to August Stadler and a single chapter from the *Religion of Reason* on reason as a created faculty), there is also reason to doubt whether Cohen's spiritual journey was really what Rosenzweig believed it to be. The comparison, it seems, is built of rather meager stuff.

But worries about evidence should not distract us from considering the possible merits of Rosenzweig's argument. First, we should note that for Rosenzweig a central concern of the new thinking is that it finally addresses the finitude of the individual. As I have noted in chapter 1, Cohen's letter to Stadler was of special philosophical importance for Rosenzweig in that it captured Cohen's deeper doubts regarding the capacity of neo-idealism to recognize this finitude. For Rosenzweig this failing ultimately meant that neo-idealism merely "thinks" individuals as examples, without recognizing their inner subjectivity beyond the magic circle of concepts. Death itself (the theme of Cohen's letter to Stadler) first exposes the gap between intelligible entities and their finite ground, a gap Heidegger called the ontological difference. (Indeed, for Rosenzweig the entire philosophical tradition is brought to a crisis when it distinguishes the mortal philosopher from the pretensions of his philosophy.) [26]

This theme of isolation pervades Rosenzweig's work. As early as the "Urzelle" of 1917 (the "germ-cell," so called because this text contains the

---

26. See, e.g., Rosenzweig's remarks on Nietzsche in SE, 10 [E, 10].

primitive arguments for *The Star*), Rosenzweig had written to Rudolf Ehrenberg that one of the great scandals of philosophy is that it misses the individual. When philosophical reason "has taken the all into itself, and has proclaimed its self-sufficient existence [*Alleinexistenz*], suddenly the human being discovers that he, who had for so long ingested matters philosophically, is still there [*noch da ist*]." The individual remains behind, like Jonah without the protection of the palm leaves:

> Not as a human being with his palm-branches—who the whale had once swallowed and who can now while away the time singing psalms in the whale's belly—but rather as "I, who am mere dust and ashes." I, the wholly common private subject, I, first and last name, I dust and ashes, I am still there [*Ich bin noch da*]. ("Urzelle," in KS, 359)

While philosophy strives to comprehend the whole as a system of eternal necessity, it abandons what is most unique in the individual. Rosenzweig called this "Ich-bin-noch-da"; Heidegger, with greater economy, called it "Da-sein." Both name the finite, temporal existence that constitutes the specifically human way of being-in-the-world.

In Rosenzweig's view, Cohen's fate as a thinker demonstrated just this tension between system and person. The Marburg school had carried on in Cohen's absence as if the philosopher himself and his personal concerns had not mattered. For this reason, Rosenzweig was especially fond of the letter to Stadler, which seemed to offer a glimpse of Cohen's private self. What Rosenzweig found most striking there was Cohen's apparent disdain for the promises of ethical idealism. Cohen ridiculed the idea that the "authentic value" of human life is to be achieved by means of an "intellectual flight into the eternity of culture," since this idea passed over the lonely individual who remained behind *quand même* (that is, nonetheless). Here, Rosenzweig believed, were the seeds of a radically new insight that would only later appear in philosophical guise with the publication of Cohen's study *The Concept of Religion in the System of Philosophy* in 1913–15 and his *Religion of Reason* in 1919. In his introduction to Cohen's *Jewish Writings*, Rosenzweig says:

> The human being before God—this is no longer that self of ethics which was capable of giving itself only eternal tasks. It is, rather, the real [*wirklich*] human being, who, in the passion and suffering of his sin-ridden moment, cannot be helped with the consolations of eternity. The "Individual quand-même" of that letter, who, in his sins and his remorse cannot fix his sights on the generality of humanity, but must consider himself as unique as—God, is here discovered for philosophy.[27]

27. Rosenzweig, Einleitung to Hermann Cohen, *Jüdische Schriften*, 1924); reprinted in FR, III: 117–224, 206.

The Stadler letter thus occupied (or so Rosenzweig imagined) a place in Cohen's intellectual development much like that which Rosenzweig assigned his own "Urzelle" of 1917 in the evolution of his own philosophy. In the "Urzelle," Rosenzweig would describe the lonely individual who is "still there," a theme clearly akin to Cohen's "individual quand même."

But the image of Cohen and his thought that preoccupied Rosenzweig throughout his intellectual career was partly Rosenzweig's invention. Indeed, his fixation on Cohen as an "individual" allowed him to be rather more creative with Cohen's philosophical corpus than was otherwise justified. In Rosenzweig's eyes, Cohen himself was a "remnant" left behind by his system. Accordingly, Cohen's rich contributions to critical philosophy could be dismissed as an intellectual flight into "the eternity of culture," while the private letter to Stadler came to assume an importance disproportionate with its length and content.

Rosenzweig's deep attachments to Cohen as both a philosopher and a person should be kept in mind as we begin to evaluate the surprising notion that there is an affinity between the late Cohen and Heidegger. The argument is indeed provocative. But what kind of argument is it? It is obvious that Rosenzweig did not mean to say that Heidegger was an actual *disciple* of Cohen; we know this was not the case.[28] There is also the question of an institutional inheritance: Rosenzweig finds irony in the fact that Heidegger was at that time the holder of the prestigious Marburg Lehrstuhl in philosophy, the post Cohen himself had once occupied.[29] But this relationship is wholly accidental and is not meant to suggest a personal or intellectual bond. Rosenzweig suggests only that Heidegger's views "represented . . . a philosophical position . . . that lies wholly in the line descending from that 'last Cohen.'" In other words, he is making a case for the similarity of their perspectives, and he is not suggesting that Heidegger somehow borrowed his insights from Cohen. The argument is meant to expose an affinity, not a real origin.

In his Davos commentary, Rosenzweig discerns several points of similar-

28. Heidegger was, of course, trained in the shadow of neo-Kantianism—his teacher at Freiburg was Heinrich Rickert, whose views were, however, quite dissimilar from those of Cohen. In fact, Rickert seems to have viewed Cohen with some disdain, once remarking to a Jewish student that Cohen's work contained "more race than philosophy." See Steven Schwarzschild, "Franz Rosenzweig's Anecdotes about Hermann Cohen," in *Gegenwart im Rückblick: Festgabe für die Jüdische Gemeinde zu Berlin 25 Jahre nach dem Neubeginn* (Heidelberg: Lothar Stiehm Verlag, 1970), 209–18, at 215. Schwarzschild cites Nahum Goldmann, who relates Rickert's negative comments on Cohen in Goldmann, *The Autobiography of Nahum Goldmann* (New York: Holt, Rinehart and Winston, 1969), 69.

29. On the history of the Marburg Lehrstuhl, see Heidegger's essay, "Die Geschichte des Marburger Lehrstuhls," reprinted in Appendix VI, KPM, 304–11.

ity between the "last Cohen" and the early Heidegger. Both seemed to believe that philosophy must disclose, not transcend, man as a "specifically finite being." The late Cohen grew increasingly dissatisfied with formalist ethics and came to realize that the unique interior of the individual resists the logic of exemplarity. His philosophy of man as "creature"—the self as dust and ashes—was the fruit of this dissatisfaction. The helplessness of the individual before God is the true starting point for Cohen's so-called principle of correlation. One finds a similar sentiment in Heidegger, who inherited from scholasticism the burden of original sin, set free from its theological trappings: man is in essence "nothingness, in spite of his freedom." Where idealism speaks of reason as a productive force, Heidegger and Cohen both seemed to recognize that human reason is a derivative faculty, dependent on its being in the world: reason is created, not creative.[30] Furthermore, at Davos Heidegger remarked that *Dasein* (surely among the most cherished of terms in his lexicon) does not admit of translation. Naturally, this remark indicated far more than Heidegger's refusal to engage in dialogue with Cassirer. It reflected his larger, more systematic belief that the Western philosophical tradition as a whole rests on a misunderstanding of Being, a misunderstanding that the language of the tradition could only aggravate. Heidegger's rejection of the customary philosophical language is arguably reminiscent of the later Cohen, who abandoned the language of idealism and retrieved from out of the sources of religion a handful of new concepts, uniquely capable, he thought, of revealing human existence in its facticity. As discussed already in chapter 1, it was unclear just how the new language of religion was supposed to be compatible with the older language of ethics and whether translation between them was possible at all.

But if we follow the comparison between Heidegger and Cohen too far, it begins to founder. One area of disagreement between the two has to do with their divergent interpretations of man's social being. Cohen learned to distrust ethics, but his later philosophy of religion was probably not intended as a dismissal of his earlier ethical system; he perceived the inadequacy of ethics, not its obsolescence. In Heidegger, the impulse toward reflection on issues of an ethical nature was severely atrophied, a matter of frank, even notorious, indifference. But the contrasting evaluation of social life is only one illustration of a far deeper disagreement. Cohen and Heidegger part company over their most fundamental understandings of the philosophical task, its *terminus ad quem*. Cohen's later writings may begin with the problem of guilt, but ultimately his work is sustained with the promise of forgiveness by a loving God. Finitude is therefore the beginning-

30. Compare, for example, with RV, esp. chap. 5.

place of his philosophy, not its end.[31] There is no such God in Heidegger, so man's redemption from his fallen condition is a task assigned to man alone: his authenticity must be wrenched from out of his very own existence, Münchausen-like, in a moment of courage and decision. In Heidegger's thought it would be difficult to discover any moment of redemption in the traditional sense. Where idealism must finally seek a path out from finitude, Heidegger circles jealously around it, refusing to surrender his prize.

The lack of any sustainable comparison between Cohen and Heidegger should come as no surprise. For given what we have learned about Rosenzweig's habits of interpretation, it seems clear that he was far less interested in the comparison than it may at first appear. What actually piqued his curiosity was his own relationship to Heidegger. If we understand this as the true purpose of the essay, we can recognize that Cohen's texts served as little more than a medium, providing Rosenzweig with a background upon which to make sense of the commonality between Heidegger's work and his own.

The Davos encounter thus provided Rosenzweig with an allegory for describing the emergence of two radically distinct philosophical tendencies in Cohen's wake. While it had been possible for those two tendencies to coexist, as inhabitants of the very same system, the indeterminacy of meaning in Cohen's magnum opus allowed for the emergence of two contrasting interpretations of the work among philosophers of the period. According to one school, Cohen's last work was more or less compatible with his earlier philosophy, while according to the other school it represented a radical departure, a repudiation of the critical system and its methods.[32] Rosenzweig, of course, was among the most vocal advocates for the latter interpretation. But even in 1924, there was little justification for presenting his perspective as anything more than a "private opinion." The Davos debates seemed to provide a public vindication of his views. The different tendencies in Cohen's work, more divergent than ever, were at last visible for all to see. Rosenzweig's understanding of the Davos debates therefore rested on a

31. See RV, 463, for Cohen's quintessential statement on the idea of the human being freed from his finitude and "soaring upwards" into the arms of divine infinity. This presents the most dramatic of contrasts to Heidegger's manner of thinking about finitude. Rosenzweig does not quite countenance this aspect of Cohen, seeing only the individual who is *yet* to be saved (the finite self, i.e., Dasein) but not the self that has been saved already.

32. Cassirer was to argue with stubborn consistency that Cohen had never abandoned his Kantian faith in the primacy of practical reason. In June 1935, Cassirer presented a paper entitled "Cohen's Philosophy of Religion" before the Oxford Jewish Society. Here, he makes it clear that the identity of God in Cohen's late work was bound up with his vision of humanity; that is, it was "not a metaphysical, but an ethical identity." He further argued that "in his philosophy there is no room left for the fundamental problem that is at the root of medieval theological and religious thought. Cohen does no longer discuss the problem of the existence of God." This essay was first published in the *Internationale Zeitschrift für Philosophie* 1 (1996): 89–104; quotes at 100, 99.

more fundamental interpretation of the 1920s as a period of increased philosophical polarization. The new thinking had been born from a latent ambiguity within the older school, and what had been a mere fissure in the edifice of idealism was now a tremendous gulf. The suggestion of a bond between Cohen and Heidegger was not meant to indicate that they were fundamentally alike. If Heidegger departed from Cohen's example in various ways, this was because he represented an intensification of Cohen's most radical, indeed uncharacteristic themes.

The genealogical aspect of Rosenzweig's essay may ultimately prove to have been a failure, containing more invention than insight. But it may offer a useful corrective to the idea that Rosenzweig wholly rejected the academic methods in which he was originally trained. In his attempt to identify Cohen as the "hidden" influence upon the Davos encounter, one might detect the enduring influence of Rosenzweig's schooling in the history of ideas. It is widely believed that Rosenzweig abandoned these methods after writing *Hegel and the State.* But perhaps his rebellion was not as thorough as generally supposed. Rosenzweig's genealogical interpretation of Davos looks suspiciously like the older sort of genetic reasoning that was characteristic of Meinecke's historicism, in which perceiving any resemblance of ideas may encourage a false inference as to their effective continuity. This was precisely the error in Rosenzweig's belief that Heidegger's vague resemblance to Cohen was truly meaningful.

There is a more prosaic reason to doubt Rosenzweig's interpretation. Sometime in the 1960s, Heidegger received from Karlfried Gründer a copy of Rosenzweig's essay on the Davos encounter. Expressing thanks, Heidegger's only remark was that Rosenzweig had erred about some of the details concerning Heidegger's appointment to the Marburg Lehrstuhl, and that Gründer should be certain to correct these in his documentation of the debates.[33] That is all we know of Heidegger's response. But even this somewhat dismissive remark may strengthen our suspicion that Heidegger's "affiliation" with Cohen was less important than Rosenzweig believed. Heidegger himself was apparently of the opinion that his only real link to Cohen was a mere accident of institutional inheritance. Concerning the suggestion of a deeper intellectual bond Heidegger offered no comment.

As to Heidegger's true opinion of Rosenzweig's essay, one may hazard a few speculative remarks. The proposed affiliation with Cohen may have seemed offensive, if only because Heidegger had expended such great energy throughout his career attempting to distinguish his philosophical efforts from the "narrow" accomplishments of the neo-Kantians. Heidegger may also have resented the implication that his work represented but one

33. Gründer, "Cassirer und Heidegger in Davos, 1929," 301.

variation on a general philosophical theme, as such an implication surely diminished his stature as an original thinker. And given what is now known of Heidegger's occasional expressions of anti-Jewish feeling, the suggestion that his philosophy owed an unconscious debt to a Jewish thinker may well have struck him as disagreeable.[34] To be sure, Heidegger readily acknowledged his intellectual debts to various philosophers of Jewish descent (most famously Edmund Husserl, but also Max Scheler and Henri Bergson). But these were thinkers who did not claim for their work any true grounding in the Jewish tradition. Unlike such philosophers, Hermann Cohen claimed his late philosophy had emerged as if from "the sources of Judaism" (albeit through the mediation of reason). For Heidegger to accept Rosenzweig's assessment therefore required that he admit an unmistakably Jewish provenance at the core of his work. That Heidegger would have welcomed this suggestion seems rather unlikely.

FROM JUDAISM TO PAGANISM: LOSS AND REVELATION

While Rosenzweig may have been wrong to regard Heidegger as Cohen's unwitting disciple, his own claim to philosophical kinship with Heidegger was largely correct. As shown above, one of the basic themes of the Davos disputation was the relation between temporality and mental reflection. Whereas Cassirer insisted upon the idealist principle that in cognition the human mind gains access to a realm of atemporal Being, Heidegger insisted that our reason is itself grounded in temporality; he thus regarded the history of philosophy as a perennial "flight" from this recognition. Here Kant assumed a paradigmatic status as a thinker struggling to suppress his own insights into reason's finitude.

On this point Heidegger and Rosenzweig agreed. As I have shown, the cardinal principle of Rosenzweig's new thinking was that it "take time seriously." But this meant that reason could no longer conceive itself as the origin of experience. Rather, philosophy found itself compelled to recognize the "irrational" facet of things prior to all cognition. Thought is no longer

---

34. For a recent confirmation of Heidegger's antisemitic tendencies, see Ulrich Sieg, "Die Verjudung des deutschen Geist," *Die Zeit* 52, 22 (December 1989), 19. Already by 1929, Heidegger despaired of a "growing Jewish influence" and the need to counter it "through a renewed infusion of genuine, native teachers and educators" for the sake of "German intellectual life." And in 1933 he complained of "the neo-Kantian school" as a "philosophy . . . tailor-made for liberalism, [in which] the essence of man . . . is thinned down to a general, logical world-reason." Thus "on an apparently rigorous scientific basis, [one] turns away from man in his historical rootedness and his national . . . origins in earth and blood," encouraging a loss of "all metaphysical questioning." Such claims may confirm Bourdieu's view that Heidegger's anti-cognitivism was antisemitism in code. See Bourdieu, *L'Ontologie politique de Martin Heidegger.*

the origin of temporality but is itself awash in the temporality that makes thought possible. The new thinking thus supplants reason with a "narrative philosophy" that brings reason before the finitude it would prefer to conceal. As I have shown, Rosenzweig regards this recognition as a difficult, even fearful event. For Rosenzweig as for Heidegger, the history of metaphysics is a history of suppressed insight. Kant, Nietzsche, and even Cohen sustain the illusion of reason's sovereignty, even while on a deeper level they recognize its power as an illusion.

Rosenzweig and Heidegger's shared belief in the "temporality" of reflection was grounded in the more basic insight that all human experience is marked by finitude. As we have seen, Heidegger especially objected to Cassirer's suggestion that ethics somehow "breaks free" of this finitude into a realm of objective value. Cassirer had argued that the *form* of a categorical imperative implies a transcendence of all factical limits. But Heidegger insisted that the very sense of an imperative underscores the fact that it requires a finite being. (The ethical "going-beyond," he claimed, remains a "going-beyond" within the sphere of finitude, or *Endlichkeit*.) On this point, Heidegger echoed Rosenzweig's insight into the nature of law as "commandment." Against the neo-idealist belief that form is the route to transcendence, Rosenzweig insisted that form is itself a hermeneutic horizon, which merely underscores the bounded quality of all action, ethics included. So in his commentary on Davos, Rosenzweig cites Heidegger's talk of human "nothingness, despite all freedom [*bei aller Freiheit Nichtigkeit*]" (VF, 87).

Most of all, Heidegger and Rosenzweig shared the insight that reason is "created," not creative. As noted above, Heidegger disagreed with Cassirer upon the question of whether ontological understanding demands access to something eternal. Cassirer insisted upon the idealist account of transcendence as a mental grasp of eternal form. Against this view, Heidegger regarded such transcendence as an illusion, and he insisted that ontological understanding requires only a "finite being." Here the dispute contrasted the neo-Kantian principle of origins—which regarded reason as "creative" (*erzeugende*)—and the new philosophical view of reason as created. Heidegger argued that even in what Cassirer called transcendence, the human being remains within the sphere of creatureliness [*Geschöpflichkeit*]." "[T]his going-beyond to something higher," he insisted, "is always just a going-beyond to the finite creature, to one which is created [*zu Geschaffenem*]" (DVS, E, 174–75; G, 278–79).

At first glance it may seem peculiar that Heidegger invoked the language of traditional theology. But as I have already suggested, the Heidegger-Cassirer dispute was in many respects the secular counterpart to an originally religious discussion concerning the validity of eternity. Heidegger, like Nietzsche before him, denies "eternity" in the metaphysical sense any legitimate role in modern thought. But in his sketch of human limitation Heidegger nonetheless stakes a covert appeal to what he openly denies. As cited above, he asserts, against Cassirer, that "God does not have" an ontology. Human transcendence, he says, is therefore less divine than angelic: it cannot surpass the realm of "creatureliness." Naturally, an argument for the essential finitude of the human being does not require a theological background. But as I have shown, Heidegger's account of finitude is marked by a sense of loss. For only if "God is dead," can "nothingness" hold normative potential. It is not so much nothingness *itself* that yields a moral lesson. Rather, it is our shock at finding ourselves without shelter *as if for the first time;* since only through this shock are we awakened to an anxiety that prompts the move to authentic resolve.

Here I believe Rosenzweig was correct to discern a suppressed theological element in Heidegger's thought. Of course, the contrast between reason as creative (the neo-Kantian view) and reason as created (the theological view, also the later Cohen's) was meant chiefly as an epistemological distinction.[35] But if, with Heidegger, one reads "creative" reason as God's domain, its removal finds "created" reason suddenly exposed: it is this theme that Rosenzweig calls Heidegger's "leap into existence" *(Einsprung in das Dasein)* (VF, 87) and that he likens to Jonah without the palm branches. In *The Star of Redemption,* this same quarrel—between creative and created reason—informs the opening polemic against Schiller's exhortation to "cast off the fear of earthly things." For Heidegger as for Rosenzweig, the human being is a "being that questions" only insofar as it first discovers its existence within horizons it had no share in creating.[36]

If Rosenzweig was right in discerning philosophical kinship with Heidegger, there remains the puzzling fact that Heidegger suppressed the theology Rosenzweig openly endorsed. Could Rosenzweig be correct even if Heidegger wished to deny theology its due? To answer this question, one should recall Rosenzweig's ecumenical portrait of the new thinking:

> I have received the new thinking in these old [i.e., Jewish] words, and thus I have rendered it and passed it on. I know that to a Christian, instead of mine, the words of the New Testament would have come to his lips; to a pagan, so I think, although not words of his holy books—for their ascent leads away from the original language [*Ursprache*] of mankind, not toward it like the earthly path of revelation [*Erdenweg der Offenbarung*]—but perhaps in words entirely his own. (ND, 155)

35. "Not in vain is there to be found the ingenious chapter in the work of old age, which leaves all of 'Marburg' far behind, replacing the 'creative' [*erzeugende*] reason of Idealism with the God-created, reason as creature [*Kreatur*]." VF, 87.

36. Rosenzweig writes that "Heidegger, against Cassirer, gives to philosophy the task to reveal to man 'the specifically finite being [*spezifisch endlichen Wesen*].'" VF, 87.

Löwith's claims against Heidegger's paganism notwithstanding, Rosenzweig readily admits paganism's legitimacy alongside Judaism and Christianity. Significantly, Rosenzweig objects to the Greek metaphysical tradition, whose "holy books" he considered responsible for diverting us from revelation's "earthly path." Heidegger's predominantly Hellenistic but decidedly non-metaphysical perspective thus provides no warrant for denying his share in the new thinking. In fact, Rosenzweig embraces Heidegger's "paganism," but only on the condition that it is genuinely *antimetaphysical*—the ecumenism of the new thinking stops where metaphysics begins.

Interpretation is a deeply interested activity, guided by personal and political concerns. Rosenzweig's interpretation of Heidegger as a philosophical ally was quite possibly an expression of Rosenzweig's own longing for greater prominence. But a fair measure of a philosopher's success is the degree to which his ideas retain their prestige in later and unfamiliar settings. So it is difficult to imagine that Rosenzweig would not have taken some satisfaction at the thought that a rising star in German academic philosophy was speaking his language.

Whatever his motives, the essay has left an important clue as to how one might now situate his work in the history of ideas. As he neared death, Rosenzweig surely found consolation in the belief that he was leaving behind such a guide for the perplexed thinkers of the younger generation, German and Jewish alike. It was a hopeful gesture, an expression of faith that he would not pass into obscurity. But it was hopeful too in choosing to ignore the signs that indicated a parting of ways between German and Jewish intellectual life. Those signs may have been easy to ignore in the spring of 1929. Within a few short years, however, Rosenzweig's intellectual epitaph would begin to seem less hopeful than blind. As the common atmosphere that held together German and Jewish thought began slowly to dissipate, it was no longer easy to perceive the similarities between them. One perceived the differences instead. The longing for inclusion, surely a factor in Rosenzweig's essay, began to sound plaintive, even naive. The comparison itself, though once accepted without controversy, came to be seen as an offense. Even the broader commonalties that joined Rosenzweig to his age began to feel improbable, as if to confirm his belief in the isolation of Jewish existence from history.

This was Rosenzweig's strange fate as a philosopher. In retrospect, he appears peripatetic, a foreigner to the world he inhabited. Heidegger's deep engagement with National Socialism, beginning in 1933, forever transformed the way philosophers would examine his work. In 1929, however, one could still read Heidegger's philosophy without being drawn into a controversy concerning its relationship to National Socialism, antisemitism, and the like. The German philosophical world as a whole still cloaked itself in a mantle of relative innocence. Rosenzweig belonged to this world, and if he knew anything at all of Heidegger's political tendencies, he left us no trace of his concern. But for this very reason, his remarks on the encounter at Davos may seem eerily lacking in reality, and it is difficult to suppress the thought that he must have intended the whole idea of an "exchange of fronts" as merely a provocation. Rosenzweig described it as a moment of irony in the history of spirit. But he could not have foreseen how the irony might someday strike readers as intolerable. Few nowadays wish to entertain the suggestion that Rosenzweig and Heidegger were philosophically akin. But if the suggestion has suffered in plausibility, this may be because it appeals to historical conditions long since defunct. Rosenzweig's interpretation of Heidegger can therefore serve as a fitting epitaph to those conditions—a bitter, if unintended, commentary on the end of a tradition.

# Conclusion

# Germans, Jews, and
# the Politics of Interpretation

I have argued in this book that Rosenzweig's philosophical achievement is most properly understood when restored to the horizon of interwar Weimar thought. By insisting on this point, I do not mean to invoke some putatively historicist concern for origins. The point should be to understand primarily the movement of concepts, not merely the conditions of their development. But Rosenzweig is an enormously challenging philosopher. Amidst the occasional indulgence of his imagery and his elaborate digressions toward seemingly distant concerns, the precise concepts in his writing are not always easy to discern. So it is perhaps unsurprising that some of the most forceful works of secondary literature in the now-burgeoning field of Rosenzweig studies are those interpretations that set Rosenzweig alongside other, more familiar or, at least, more *systematic* bodies of thought, such as those of Levinas, Schelling, Gadamerian hermeneutics, and Freudian psychoanalysis. Each of these powerful instruments has helped us to explore certain dimensions of Rosenzweig's work, most especially the arguments that run through his notoriously difficult text, *The Star of Redemption*. Each interpretation has cast a helpful light on what might otherwise have remained dark in Rosenzweig's vast conceptual universe.

Surely no interpretation can fully and definitively illuminate another body of thought—the very finitude of interpretation forbids it. It is surprising, however, that no interpretation until now has taken its cue from Rosenzweig himself, who bequeathed us specific guidelines of how his philosophy might best be construed. My chief aim in this book has been to follow Rosenzweig's own cues in this regard, as presented in his late commentary on the Heidegger-Cassirer debate, "Exchanged Fronts," which, I have proposed, might well be regarded as Rosenzweig's intellectual epitaph: it describes the trajectory of German interwar thought—from neo-idealism to existential ontology—and it traces out the development of the so-called new thinking, from its apparent origins in Cohen's posthumous writings on religion to its culmination in the works of both Rosenzweig and Heidegger. Accordingly, I have attempted here to simply take Rosenzweig at his word, regardless of where this might lead.

There are good reasons why the comparison between Rosenzweig and Heidegger has long suffered neglect. Given what we know of Heidegger's political record, even to propose that there might be bonds of a conceptual nature between them has seemed to many readers a nearly intolerable offense. The characterization of Heidegger's work, especially in those circuits of modern Jewish thought most wounded by Nazism, has been understandably negative: Heidegger, we are told, was a pagan, an antisemite, an obscurantist, an intellectual tyrant. It is not surprising—and perhaps it is even justifiable—that in modern Jewish thought truly favorable comparisons to Heidegger have little currency. How, after all, could such comparisons survive within a climate of abiding and all-too-human resentment? Philosophy recoils where memory still holds sway.

By contrast, since the dark years of the Third Reich Rosenzweig has only gained in moral stature. Although he died in 1929 and therefore remained ignorant of both Heidegger's incubating politics and Nazism's true potential, the impulses of commemoration and martyrdom have attached themselves retroactively to his name: Rosenzweig, we are told, was a pious Jew, a teacher, a model of interfaith dialogue, an ethicist, a poet. But here one might ask concerning Rosenzweig a question that mirrors the one posed above: How can interpretation survive if it must toil beneath these blazing lamps of hagiography? The fact is, it cannot. That Rosenzweig and Heidegger were in many respects intellectually *dissimilar* is a point that deserves emphasis, but to consider such dissimiliarity as the sole point of comparison is mere ideology. Yet that has been the habit of previous scholarship.

The historical irony is marked. A wealth of interpretative literature has continued to accumulate surrounding Rosenzweig's philosophical legacy, and an even more voluminous interpretative work continues to discover new and unfamiliar facets of Heidegger's intellectual achievement. Yet one finds, at the juncture between them, a tradition of non-interpretation. Scholars touch on the comparison, to be sure, but it is a very small literature indeed, and it is tinged with bitterness and misunderstanding. But this is to say that we have missed just what Rosenzweig most wished us to see: we have remained quiet concerning just that moment in Rosenzweig's life when he most boldly proclaimed his intellectual bond with perhaps the most prominent philosopher of his own day. Heidegger is no doubt a difficult and politically troubling figure. But we have it on the authority of Rosenzweig himself that, by wielding instruments borrowed from his contemporary, we might forge a new (though perhaps also the original) opening onto

Rosenzweig's own intellectual universe. And, passing through it, we might arrive at a deepened appreciation of its meanings and ramifications. To neglect this route would be to sacrifice a richer sense of Rosenzweig's philosophy—both for us and for what he himself believed his philosophy to be.

## ROSENZWEIG'S "ONTO-THEOLOGICAL" LEGACY

First and foremost, Rosenzweig believed himself to be the architect of a truly modernist philosophy; he regarded *The Star of Redemption* as merely one contribution to the ecumenical movement of Weimar's post-metaphysical constellation of the new thinking. It is therefore somewhat deceptive, and surely imprecise, to range Rosenzweig's thought within the category of "Jewish" thought. He famously insisted that his philosophy was only incidentally Jewish. The language of Judaism, he claimed, was merely the *medium* in which he felt he could express his thoughts most fully, with greatest consonance to his own biography and thus without poetic artifice. But he admitted that other thinkers might find Christianity and paganism more serviceable, since those traditions, too, harbored resources for exploring what he called the "earthly path of revelation" (ND, 155). It is this concession—that Judaism, Christianity, and paganism belong together in the field of Weimar thought—that permits a fruitful comparison between Rosenzweig and Heidegger. For Heidegger was by origin a Christian philosopher but a pagan by development. Heidegger's own "path of thinking" thus took him down an earthly course running closely parallel to Rosenzweig's own.

Here it might be wise to remind the reader of one of chief attractions of Rosenzweig's work, its brave attempt to negotiate between philosophical modernity and religious commitment. Clearly, Rosenzweig was serious about his dedication to Judaism, but he was equally serious about his dedication to modern philosophy, and integrity forbade him from violating the imperatives of either commitment for the sake of the other. The challenge, however, was considerable: for Rosenzweig, "modern" philosophy meant philosophy in Nietzsche's turbulent wake. He wished somehow to incorporate Nietzsche's dictum that "God is dead"—which, taken philosophically, spelled the end of the metaphysical tradition. His assignment, then, was to lay out a plausible description of religious experience fully consonant with the modernist sense that metaphysics had reached a point of collapse.

It is at this point that the comparison with Heidegger becomes most helpful. In many respects, Heidegger, too, was a thinker caught between a powerful longing for the religious past and an equally powerful desire to break free of the philosophical tradition. Rosenzweig and Heidegger shared the belief that modern culture and modern thought have gone astray from some original truth. This is why Rosenzweig was so intent upon the idea that Judaism and Christianity were not "originally" religions at all.

And it is also why Heidegger expressed such great interest in the "real" contents of pre-Socratic thought prior to its mistranslation. For both philosophers, however, nostalgia for what modernity had lost was combined with a strong belief that modernity is inevitable. It is this twofold orientation that explains the peculiar aesthetic of archaic modernism in their work. It further explains their shared interest in "translating" between religious concepts and modern philosophy. Their writing, in consequence, is marked by an experience of uncanniness and loss that cannot be undone. Both Rosenzweig and Heidegger were, in this sense, philosophers of metaphysical exile.

At his best, Rosenzweig confirmed exile as irremediable. But he also considered it the mark of Jewish redemption. The idea of redemption, I suspect, is not something for which many philosophers would express much sympathy today. Still, it is perhaps a sign of Rosenzweig's integrity that he considered exile and redemption as indissociably linked. Yet there is, in my opinion, something dishonest in the claim that one has privileged access to the inner truth of a heritage. It is altogether natural that those wishing to claim for themselves an authentic identity (whether national, cultural, or religious) would attempt to ground such an identity in the past. But to claim that they know what this past truly consists of and to further claim that it offers a singular solution to the present is to commit a scandalous hermeneutic error, since there is no access to the past that is not mediated by the present, and, therefore, no authenticity that is not plagued by historical change.

In some of his writing, Rosenzweig expresses the view that exile is an irremediable condition of language. But many of his remarks in *The Star of Redemption* betray a contrary thought, that the difference between our contemporary moment and past origins may be fully overcome. This idea, that the Jews might live "authentically" (that is, true to their ownmost identity) and beyond the reach of history, seems to me mistaken. However, I do not find this idea objectionable, as some of Rosenzweig's critics may, because it denies the importance of state politics or fails to appreciate the necessities of power. (On the contrary, I find that idea salutary, especially in an age that seems bent on celebrating power as an end in itself.) It is mistaken in a different way because it presumes that there is such a thing as living in full consonance with oneself. In my reconstruction of *The Star of Redemption,* I have tried to suggest that this notion of a consonant life rests upon a deep faith that there is in principle some holistic structure to things, some way that experience can be rendered fully harmonious. For Rosenzweig redemption just is this holistic structure. But, on Rosenzweig's view, such redemption was only an *anticipation,* and it is by virtue of this future possibility that the Jews alone can live, despite the surrounding world's obvious incoherence, an internally coherent life.

I have suggested that Heidegger's strange attachment to the notion of authenticity (which he thankfully abandoned in his later work) was a vestige of this same holistic belief. Accordingly, I have argued in agreement with such critics as Karl Löwith and Jacques Derrida that the concept of authenticity was a theological—or, as Heidegger himself called it, an "onto-theological"—residue. Even in Heidegger's later writing, perhaps, frequent allusions to the pre-Socratics and to the German poets betrayed a stubborn belief in the possibility of immediacy. Now it is this dimension of Heidegger's work that strikes many readers as least compelling; indeed, some of his most perspicacious interpreters have preferred to banish this theme from their accounts.

It is instructive, I think, that the very idea one regards as suspect in modern philosophy is afforded a qualified legitimacy in religion. This is why the most sophisticated Heidegger scholars suppress his latent theological impulses, while attempting to banish theology from interpretations of Rosenzweig would end in absurdity. I have suggested that Heidegger wished us to glimpse the atheistic nothingness beneath his holism, but it is not clear that his holism could be sustained without reference to its religious origins. Rosenzweig, too, shared with Nietzsche and Weber a nihilistic vision of the modern world as lacking orientation. (Those who do not believe in redemption, Rosenzweig suggested, were to be cast into the "cold dread" of the nothing.) But, unlike Heidegger, Rosenzweig retrieved theism as the organizing principle of his thought. For, unlike Heidegger, Rosenzweig could argue that there is a way of living wherein we might plausibly claim to draw upon a future sense of "the truth." Heidegger believed that we gain this truth only by becoming aware that there is no such metaphysical grounding. But it is unclear just why being aware of this condition should grant us truth, unless "being aware" of groundlessness itself functions as a new dispensation. That sense of post-metaphysical revelation is what makes the latter half of *Being and Time* so endlessly perplexing. Thus, one of the chief differences between Rosenzweig and Heidegger was that only Rosenzweig made his theological commitments fully legible. Heidegger effaced those commitments as much as he feasibly could. But, like a divine breath endowing clay with life, they nonetheless continued to animate the body of his thought.

Rosenzweig's most lasting philosophical accomplishment was his attempt to create a brave and unlikely fusion—between a guileless philosophical modernism on the one hand, and a genuine theological commitment on the other. As Rosenzweig saw it, his task was that of mutual "translation," wherein theological problems are transfigured as human, and human problems as theological. The risks of this fusion are manifold, since it can quite easily veer off toward either of its two poles, toward a cynical instrumentalization of one's faith or claustrophobic solemnity—toward mere citation or kitsch. I have tried to alert the reader to those moments in Rosenzweig's philosophy where the fusion may have failed. But it was not inevitably a failure. Indeed, if one wishes to remain in touch with the theological ground of things, yet also alive to the fullest potentials of modernity, one could do worse than to follow Rosenzweig's example. I have also tried to refrain from taking any final stand as to whether one should judge his global efforts a success. For many readers, myself among them, Rosenzweig's thought will continue to exemplify both the possibilities *and* the limits of this combination.

## THE POLITICS OF THE APOLITICAL

Some readers will no doubt feel troubled by the neglect of explicit political themes in this study. One reason it has seemed wise to avoid such matters is that to address them might only encourage the notion that they are somehow fundamental, the "inner" sense to the intellectual transformations described here. The history of ideas, however, need not be understood as grounded finally and fully in political reality. As I have taken care to note, the philosophical comparison between Rosenzweig and Heidegger is admittedly provocative, in that it raises all sorts of discomfiting political concerns. But one of my broader aims in this book has been to recall a moment in German intellectual life when the philosophical bond between Germans and Jews appeared altogether natural and relatively untroubled by political events. We now know that politics was soon to intrude violently upon the discussion. But that is no reason to now dismiss it as unreal. Of his apolitical nature, Rosenzweig wrote in a letter to Gritli that "I am so far removed from politics [*heraus aus der Politik*], that now I no longer know whether it is true" (GB, [28.4.1918], 86).

Still, the political dimension of the comparison deserves brief mention. Paradoxically, one of the deeper "political" similarities between Rosenzweig and Heidegger is that they were both profoundly inept at thinking intelligently about politics. Neither one displayed any true dedication when it came to ruminating upon the real problems of public and political life; and neither showed any real aptitude for interpreting the various social issues of the day. Heidegger's crude misunderstanding of National Socialism is a case in point. Rosenzweig's belief that Jewish life happens elsewhere than politics displays a similar inaptitude. But (unlike Heidegger) Rosenzweig remained what Thomas Mann called "an unpolitical German."[1]

---

1. See Mann, *Betrachtungen eines Unpolitischen* (Berlin: S. Fischer, 1918; 2nd ed. 1922; 3rd ed. 1929); in English, *Reflections of a Nonpolitical Man,* trans. Walter D. Morris (New York: The Ungar Publishing Company, 1987). And see Fritz Stern, "The Political Consequences of

Some may fault Rosenzweig even for this, since, especially in times of crisis, political indifference itself can be regarded as either criminal or naive. Here, of course, there is a crucial difference between Rosenzweig and Heidegger. Heidegger's political idiocy had disastrous political consequences; Rosenzweig's insensibility allowed him merely to remain aloof from the political world as such. But as I have noted in this study, there are features in Rosenzweig's thought that may prompt the worry as to just what kind of politics might have developed out of his philosophy had it somehow found a viable means of expression. I do not think the answer to this worry is at all obvious. But one may perhaps be thankful that Rosenzweig clung with such vehemence to the idea that Judaism and state politics must remain metaphysically distinct. This "liberal" commitment to the separation of religion and state, while not actually argued from liberal premises, may have shielded Rosenzweig from some of the possibly illiberal consequences of his own philosophy.

This suggestion may give pause to recent critics who would borrow from Rosenzweig to lay the foundations for a new Jewish ethics, whether progressive or postmodern. Their efforts, in any event, are not nearly so surprising as recent studies that purport to find liberal-democratic themes in Heidegger. Both cases invite skepticism. The point, however, is that one need not agree with a philosophy in all respects to find it worth consideration. Some readers may feel that I have cast Rosenzweig in a rather unfavorable light, but this has not been my intent. Rosenzweig remains a fascinating and in many ways appealing figure, whatever his politics and whatever his somewhat romanticized hopes for cultural restoration. If there is any normative purpose guiding this study, it has been only to resist any of the familiar impulses of self-affirmation and commemoration that continue to constrain the study of modern Jewish thought, especially in the German-intellectual context. Indeed, I venture to hope that this book has served as a further stimulus to the sincere assessment—and appreciation—of Rosenzweig's philosophy.

## HEIDEGGER AND HEBRAISM

By way of conclusion, I would like to offer some impartial reflections upon the possibility of claiming Rosenzweig as a bona fide Jewish philosopher. It seems to be a persistent habit in the study of religious traditions that one believes each new appearance of a theological insight to be continuous with the one preceding it. And this movement, it is supposed, must eventually

---

the Unpolitical German," in his *The Failure of Illiberalism: Essays on the Political Culture of Modern Germany* (New York: Knopf, 1972).

throw one back upon a formula one deems original and from which one believes all later manifestations are derived. Even if this belief is merely methodological, however, it reiterates what is essentially a theological doctrine of revelation: it establishes the origin as a transcendent norm. A more agnostic perspective would be that interpretation through its forward movement is always creating new norms, even if part of the progress of interpretation is to claim the origin as the ultimate authority of its motion.[2]

The broader claim of this book has been that this kind of religious impulse need not guide us in our assessment of Rosenzweig's thought. His philosophy of Judaism was quite far from being a belated expression of Judaism's essence (if there is such a thing as Judaism's essence, which one may rightly doubt), nor was it part of the ongoing process by which Judaism repeatedly intrudes upon new historical contexts; rather, it was something imagined as Jewish, but by an imagination that was itself formed in the matrix of German philosophy.

So what was the identity of Rosenzweig's work? The very question seems either too easily answered or impossible. If interpretation, as it stretches forward in time, creates a sense of continuity with the past, then there is nothing false in suggesting that Rosenzweig's work of interpretation created for itself a very real grounding in Judaism. To interpret one's own thoughts *into the grain* is just what it means to live within an interpretative tradition. Here the distinction between discovery and invention must break down, since even the origins that are thought to authorize future invention are understood interpretatively. And, since we cannot leap out of our history, such past origins are understood only on the basis of one's own interpretative labor in the present.[3]

If this is so, the question of what *identity* one might ascribe to a given body of thought seems to become endlessly self-reflexive. Identity itself, it seems, has no timeless marks of its own. The demand, then, to know definitively whether Rosenzweig's philosophical labors are continuous with one tradition or another, Jewish or German, seems largely beside the point. In the matter of the politics of identity, scholarship should remain agnostic, although this agnosticism indeed cuts violently against Rosenzweig's own self-understanding: As a matter of fact Rosenzweig proudly acknowledged his participation in the broader philosophical conversation of his time. But in

2. For the classic statement on Judaism as a hermeneutic process, see Simon Rawidowicz, "On Interpretation," in *Studies in Jewish Thought,* ed. Nahum Glatzer (Philadelphia: Jewish Publication Society, 1974), 45–80.

3. On open-ended interpretation as a compromised principle of religious authority, see the suggestive comments in Robert Alter, *Canon and Creativity: Modern Writing and the Authority of Scripture* (New Haven: Yale University Press, 2000), esp. chap. 1, "The Double Canonicity of the Hebrew Bible."

his work he argued on the contrary that Judaism enjoys the miraculous capacity of resisting all historical participation. Ironically, he so successfully promoted the idea that Judaism is beyond history that some of his readers have forgotten that his arguments for this idea were not.

But what if Rosenzweig were correct? What if his thoughts are somehow afterthoughts, emerging directly from the womb of the Jewish tradition itself, from what he considered Judaism's original and unreligious "event"? What if, despite the language of German thought, there were in Rosenzweig's new thinking something utterly old? What if it were truly timeless, calling to us across the landscape of modernity from the ancient sources of revelation? I am too much of a skeptic to endorse this possibility. But those who remain wedded to the revelation model of intellectual history might find that this argument brings Judaism into contact with the most unlikely regions of recent thought. For if Rosenzweig's work drinks from ancient springs, then the strong resemblance between Rosenzweig and Heidegger that I have examined in this book would prompt us to consider the startling possibility that Heidegger's philosophy itself might somehow derive from Judaism.

This is an unsettling thought, but it is not unfamiliar.[4] After all, what is Heidegger's Being if it is not a Being that will not permit us to regard it as being, that refuses to become available, as essence and as presence, that forbids us to dream that human agency is sovereign, and that would banish those who wish to identify its face with the countenance of man and world? Some critics have discerned in these thoughts a type of Christianity. To be sure, Heidegger was, by origin at least, a Christian theologian. But his thinking would have to be a Christianity without incarnation, a monotheism denying to itself, perhaps out of deeply held chauvinism, the original language by which to bring forth its idea. Christian or Jewish, it seems clear that Heidegger's philosophy is not primarily a celebration of the *vita contemplativa*. For its ultimate message is that we are creatures so saturated with concern and so constituted by our investment in time that human understanding itself must forbid any thinking of Being beyond temporality. Like Rosenzweig, Heidegger would forgo the language of "the Eternal." Instead he would locate even the highest achievement of human existence not in contemplation but in practice, within the temporal and always finite boundaries of being-in-the-world.

4. See, e.g., Leo Strauss, *Spinoza's Critique of Religion* (New York: Schocken Books, 1965), esp. 12–13; and Stanley Rosen, *Hermeneutics as Politics* (New York: Oxford University Press, 1987), esp. 162. For the unusual argument concerning a possible Kabbalistic influence upon Heidegger (via Schelling), see Marlène Zarader, *La Dette impensée: Heidegger et l'héritage hébraïque* (Paris: Editions du Seuil, 1990); and for a general comparison, see Thorleif Boman, *Hebrew Thought Compared with Greek* (Philadelphia: Westminster Press, 1960).

But these are the principles of worldliness, finitude, and sin, and of doing above knowing, that Matthew Arnold identified with *Hebraism,* not Hellenism. Did Heidegger, then, dissent from the Greek dispensation? And is this why his much-discussed passion for the Greeks stops short just before their metaphysics? If we wrest ourselves free of history—which we of course cannot—the comparison between Heidegger and Rosenzweig would look very different indeed: it would no longer be an affinity of philosophers but a convergence in worship. And we might then be forced toward the strange conclusion that Heidegger's struggle to think Being-as-temporality expelled him from the Hellenistic tradition and brought him, however reluctantly, before the altar of a possibly Hebraic God.

# INDEX

Abraham, 62, 94, 95

Absolute, 32, 44, 166, 261. *See also* All; Totality

Abyss, 49, 148, 244

Actuality, 61, 183

Adam, 62, 244, 266

Adorno, Theodor, 254n43; *Jargon of Authenticity,* 23; *Philosophy of Modern Music,* 238

Agnosticism, 312

Aletheia, 268–69

All, 32, 57, 89, 143, 154, 166–68, 176, 181. *See also* Totality

Alterity, 10, 54, 93, 251–53, 258; and Levinas, 11, 201, 222n45. *See also* Existence

Anamnesis, 140, 267–68

Anarchism, 9, 51, 132

Anaximander, 48

Angel: *Angelus Novus* (Benjamin's remarks), 24; of history (Benjamin), 142; as illustration of created being (Heidegger), 283, 302

Anthropology, xxi, 261

Anthropomorphism, 54, 63, 164

Anti-cognitivism, 172, 300n34

Antimetaphysical, 113, 303

Antimodernism, 241n8, 249, 255–56

Antisemitism: assimilationist view of, 217; Cohen's response to, 54n28; and Heidegger, 300n34, 303; Löwith as victim of, 15; Rosenzweig's analysis of, 229

Anxiety, 141, 302; and authenticity, 223–25; and being-towards-death, 170–71, 174;

dread, 199, 209; and eternity, 284; and nothingness, 34; and Schiller's poem, 143–46, 286; and this-worldly being, 148

Apolitical, 27, 310

Aquinas, Thomas, 153

Arendt, Hannah, xxi, 16, 78n92, 262

Aristotle, philosophy of, 49, 153n5; Aristotelianism, 263

Arnold, Matthew, 314. *See also* Hebraism

Art, 126, 281. *See also* Expressionism

Asiatic interests, 243–44

Assimilation, 22, 24, 54n28, 237, 255, 275

Atheism: and Heidegger, 283; and Nietzsche, 159–65, 231–34; and Rosenzweig, 21, 143, 164, 253

Augustine, 180n101

Auschwitz, 10

Authenticity: and Bible-translation, 246; Heidegger's idea of, xxix, 117, 192, 202, 222–29, 231–36, 287–88, 298; and inauthenticity, 201, 231; Jewish authenticity, 22, 241n8, 256; and philosophy, 50, 163, 170; Rosenzweig's idea of, 5, 308–9. *See also* Ownmost being

Autonomy, 248

Avineri, Shlomo, 84n4

Baeck, Leo, 184

Batnitzky, Leora, 8, 124n9, 132n26, 212, 220n40, 229; blood community, 211, 212n27; on Gadamer, 12n29, 182

Beautiful soul, 99. *See also* Hegel

modernist turn to religious origin in, 142–43; Nietzsche, significance in, 159–65; and nothingness, 34, 50; Parmenides, signifcance in, 154–59, 262, 272–73; phenomenology of religious experience in, 138–42; as polemic against crucifixion, 113; practice, hermeneutics of, 182–85; publication of, 82; reception of, 9n21, 133; redemption, meaning in, 113, 192–220; remaining as theme in, 148–50; revolutionary conception of philosophy in, 135–38; and Schiller's poem in, 143–47; strategy of reversal in, 32; style, 122–43; temporal holism, 202–5; temporality in, 194–98

State, xxiii, 80, 84–85, 88, 96, 100–113, 116, 118, 195, 208–10, 215–17, 218–19, 221. *See also* Politics, *or* Political

Steiner, George, 235n68

Stolberg, Friedrich Leopold von, 248, 256

Strauss, Leo, xxiv, 7n16, 78n91, 111, 112n66

Stravinsky, Igor, 23n54; *Le Sacre du Printemps*, 238–39

Stumpf, Carl, 28, 29

Subject, 65, 282; subjectivity, 57, 64, 107n54, 108, 109n59, 110–12, 286

Sublime, 93, 96

Suffering, 8, 57–58, 62, 65, 79, 107, 111, 295

Susman, Margarete, 143, 164, 176, 190, 235n67, 245, 253

Symbol, 40, 65, 278, 284, 287

Temporality, *or* Time: and angel, 24; and being-toward-death, 166; and blood-community, 213–14; continuous versus sequential, 196–97; of created being, 283; directedness, 225n49; duration, 191, 193; and "the earthly" (George), 190; ecstases, 35, 194, 197–98; and eternity, 17–19, 187–89, 220–22, 231, 265n66; futuricity, 65–66, 195, 197–98, 204, 224–25, 230, 284; and God, 60, 265n66; and human existence, or Dasein, 5n11, 87, 261, 290 (Herrigel), 295, 301; and Kant, 42–44, 145 (compared to Schiller), 172, 279–81; and language, 36; and paralysis, 178–79; past, present, future, 177, 186, 196–97, 207, 226, 239; and political history, 208; and practice,

184; and reason, 300; and redemption-in-the-world, 192; and Schiller, 145–48; and science, 33; successive, 217; "taking time seriously," 177, 185, 187; temporal holism, 202–5; timelessness, 185–86; transcendental condition of time, 281

Thales, 48, 136, 155n60

Theism, 227, 232, 283

Theology, xxviii, 18, 134, 151, 221, 239; atheistic theology, 164, 170; and Cohen, 47, 54; and German idealism, 88; and Hegel, 85, 91, 113, 160; and Heidegger, 20, 30, 205n20, 227n53, 283–84, 309; and intergenerational conflict, 26; and the new thinking, 5, 12, 20–21, 36–37, 288, 310–12; theistic residue, 233–34, 309; traditional, 152, 154, 288; and translation into philosophy, 142, 149, 236, 284

Thing-in-itself, 42–46

Thinking, and gratitude, xxii, 138, 204

Thrownness, 117n80, 128, 226, 283

Time. *See* Temporality, *or* Time

Tönnies, Ferdinand, 104, 110

Totality, 57–58, 63, 67–68, 89, 154n59, 157, 166, 175, 282; new totality, 203–4

Trade wind, xix, xxii, xxiv

Tradition, xix, xxii, xxiv, 5, 26; end of, 304; errancy of, 136–37, 154, 179; existential, 28; Gadamer and, 182; Heidegger and, 117; Jewish, 11 (philosophical), 21–22, 24, 300, 312; metaphysical, 62, 79, 143, 147, 149, 150–51, 153, 159, 161–62, 164–65, 188–89, 191, 231, 307; religious, 18, 36, 140–41, 160; theology, 3, 152, 154, 288; and translation, 241, 254–55; Western philosophical, 2, 32, 127, 129, 138–40, 150, 155–57, 167, 173–75, 180–81, 185, 196, 231, 236, 293, 298

Tragedy, 96, 110, 113

Trakl, Georg, 32, 37, 130, 272

Transcendence: and Cassirer, 285, 288, 301; and essence (Herrigel) 290; ethical, 68; and Heidegger, 283; and Judaism, transcendent norm of, 312; the new thinking, rejection of, 26, 32, 34–35, 187, 218, 231, 276; and Schiller, 146–47, 187

Transcendental: as distinguished from empirical, 42–43; ground, 261, 273, 281; logic, 47; phenomenology, 72, 179; reality, 74; and transcendence, distinction, 146n47

WEIMAR AND NOW: GERMAN CULTURAL CRITICISM

*Edward Dimendberg, Martin Jay, and Anton Kaes, General Editors*

|  |  |
|---|---|
| Compositor: | G&S Typesetters, Inc. |
| Text: | 10/12 Baskerville |
| Display: | Baskerville |
| Printing and binding: | Friesens Corporation |